TANTRIC BUDDHISM IN EAST ASIA

Tantric Buddhism in East Asia

EDITED BY RICHARD K. PAYNE

WISDOM PUBLICATIONS • BOSTON

Wisdom Publications, Inc.
199 Elm Street
Somerville MA 02144 USA
www.wisdompubs.org

Library of Congress Cataloging-in-Publication Data
Tantric Buddhism in East Asia / edited by Richard K. Payne.
    p. cm.
  Includes bibliographical references and index.
  ISBN 0-86171-487-3 (pbk. : alk. paper)
    I. Tantric Buddhism—East Asia.   I. Payne, Richard Karl.
  BQ8912.9.E18T36 2005
  294.3'925'095—dc22

                                        2005025140

ISBN 0-86171-487-3
First Printing.
10 09 08 07 06
 5   4   3   2   1

Cover design by Rick Snizik.
Interior design by Gopa & Ted2, Inc. Set in DGaramond 11/14 pt.
Cover line drawing: © Daishin Bijutsu Co., Ltd. Kiyotaka Kobayashi. Used with
permission.

Dedicated to the memory of my teacher,

Rev. Chisei Aratano
d. 26 September 2002

who persevered in the face of progressive kidney failure
to complete his year as Hōin-daikajō-i
for Kongōbuji, Kōyasan

Contents

Preface

THE IMPORTANCE of tantric Buddhism in the spread and formation of East Asian Buddhism has only recently become a matter of scholarly acknowledgment. Though usually unrecognized, tantric Buddhism has pervaded East Asian Buddhism, its rituals and ceremonies, its philosophical and psychological speculations, and its popular reception.

Much of the Western-language literature on tantric Buddhism in East Asia—what little there is—has until recently been scattered through obscure journals difficult to locate for many scholars and students. The few essays published in more easily accessed journals stand alone and, being read in isolation, are not fully appreciated.

This collection gathers these scattered stones of scholarship to demonstrate the hitherto unseen contributions of tantric Buddhism to East Asian Buddhism and provide a foundation for further research. With a few exceptions, the essays appear here largely in their original form. While reference notes have been reformatted for consistency, matters such as capitalization, italics, and the use of Wade-Giles transcriptions have not been altered. The major exception is that Chou's essay has been edited for length and with a more general readership in mind.

Two and a half decades ago, the late Michel Strickmann encouraged me to realize my idea of a collection on East Asian tantric Buddhism. Although the work has taken far too long for him to see it, it would not exist without the memory of his encouragement. I express my appreciation to Scott Mitchell, who assisted in the laborious task of copy editing this collection, and to the students in the three classes in which this collection was "beta tested" as a class reader. I also thank the Graduate Theological Union for the Newhall Grant that allowed Scott and myself the opportunity to co-teach the last of those three classes and bring this collection to its conclusion. Additionally, I thank my friend Robert Buswell for generously answering some technical and linguistic questions. All of the contributors also deserve my thanks, as do the editors and staff of Wisdom Publications, who did so much to make this collection better.

Acknowledgments

Earlier versions of the following essays are reprinted by permission.

Chou Yi-Liang, "Tantrism in China," *Harvard Journal of Asiatic Studies* 8, no. 3/4 (1945): 235–332.

Henrik H. Sørensen, "Esoteric Buddhism in Korea," in *The Esoteric Buddhist Tradition*, ed. Henrik H. Sørensen, SBS Monograph, no. 2 (Copenhagen: The Seminar for Buddhist Studies, 1993).

Henrik Sørensen, "On Esoteric Practices in Korean Sŏn Buddhism during the Chosŏn Period," in *Hanguk chonggyo sasang ŭi chae cho'myŏng: Chinsan Han Kidu paksa hwagap kinyon munjip*, 2 vols. (Iri, South Korea: Wong-wang taehakkyo ch'ulp'an kuk, 1993).

Hisao Inagaki, *Kūkai's "Principle of Attaining Buddhahood with the Present Body,"* Ryukoku Translation Pamphlet Series, no. 4 (Ryukoku Translation Center, Ryukoku University, 1975).

Ian Astley, "The Five Mysteries of Vajrasattva: A Buddhist Tantric View of the Passions and Enlightenment," *Temenos* 24 (1988): 7–27.

Dale Todaro, "An Annotated Translation of the *Pañcābhisaṃbodhi* Practice of the *Tattvasaṃgraha*," *Mikkyō Bunka* 159 (1987): 131–146.

Pol Vanden Broucke, "The Twelve-Armed Deity Daishō Kongō and His Scriptural Sources," *Romanian Journal of Japanese Studies* 1 (1999), http://www.opensys.ro/rjjs/nhtml/frameset1.html.

James H. Sanford, "Breath of Life: The Esoteric Nembutsu," in *Esoteric Buddhism in Japan*, ed. Ian Astley, SBS Monograph, no. 1 (Copenhagen: Seminar for Buddhist Studies, 1994).

H. Byron Earhart, "Shugendō, the Traditions of En no Gyōja, and Mikkyō Influence," in *Studies of Esoteric Buddhism and Tantrism* (Kōyasan: Kōyasan University, 1965).

Helen Hardacre, "The Cave and the Womb World," *Japanese Journal of Religious Studies* 10, no. 2/3 (1983): 149–176.

Technical Notes

T IS USED as an abbreviation for what is now perhaps the most widely used edition of the Chinese Buddhist canon, known as the *Taishō Shinshū Daizōkyō*. The scholarly literature employs various ways of identifying texts and citing references within this vast collection. Where a specific citation is being given, this will usually appear as something like: T. 21.404b25. This means that within the Taishō, as it is customarily referred to, this citation appears in the twenty-first volume, on page 404, in the second ("b") of three folios that appear on each page of the printed edition, in (vertical) line 25 counting from right to left. Some authors simply give the volume and page number: T. 21.404. When a particular text is being referred to as a whole, the most common way that this reference appears is something like this: T. vol. 19, no. 1009. As all of the more than three thousand texts are numbered sequentially, some scholars seem to feel that it is unnecessarily redundant to give both the volume and the index number. Another form that is also found gives volume and index numbers followed by the page number. Some of the works in the Taishō are collections with several individual texts, in which case a text number is added in parentheses: T. vol. 51, no. 2089(4). Similarly, some texts appear in different versions, in which case the version is indicated by a lowercase roman letter in parentheses: T. vol. 57, no. 2203(a).

The best index for the collection is the *Répertoire du Canon Bouddhique Sino-Japonais: Édition de Taishō*, compiled by Paul Demiéville, Hubert Durt, and Anna Seidel (Paris: Librairie d'Amérique et d'Orient, Adrien-Maisonneuve; Tokyo: Maison Franco-Japonaise, 1978). This is commonly referred to as the "Hōbōgirin index," as it is an annex volume to the important and on-going *Hōbōgirin: Dictionnaire Encyclopédique du Bouddhism d'après les Sources Chinoises et Japonaises.*

K. Some authors also cite the Korean catalogue number: Lewis R. Lancaster, with Sung-bae Park, *The Korean Buddhist Canon: A Descriptive*

Catalogue (Berkeley: University of California Press, 1979). This catalogue is particularly useful as it also includes citations to other catalogues of the Chinese canon, including the Taishō, as well as locations of any Tibetan translation in the five versions of the Tibetan canon.

P. The most widely available edition of the Tibetan canon is the Peking version, reprinted in reduced photo-mechanical form in Japan. The catalogue numbers for Tibetan works in this edition are introduced by the capital letter P. The catalogue numbers are found in D. T. Suzuki, *Catalogue and Index of the Tibetan Tripitaka, Peking Edition* (Tokyo and Kyoto: Tibetan Tripitaka Research Institute, 1961).

In their translations of texts some contributors have enclosed clarifying or interpolating words or phrases in brackets or parentheses. Some of these brackets and parentheses have been removed in this volume to enhance readability. The volume editor's insertions are enclosed in braces.

Some contributors note that a Sanskrit name, title, or phrase is reconstructed from the Chinese, indicating this with an asterisk at the beginning of that name, title, or phrase. In some cases authors indicate the Sanskrit root of a term with the symbol used in mathematics to indicate a radical.

Introduction

Richard K. Payne

Our subject is tantric, or Vajrayāna, Buddhism in East Asia—its history, practices, and influences on popular religious culture. Western scholars have recognized the importance of the Vajrayāna traditions of Buddhism since about the mid-1960s, when the Tibetan Vajrayāna tradition became much more accessible. Prior to that time—and living on in the spectral world of college textbooks—the common perception among students of Buddhism was that tantra constituted a decadent form of Buddhism in particular, and of Indian religion more generally.[1] (The "decadence" of tantric Buddhism is connected with the tendency to characterize tantra solely in terms of its transgressive quality, discussed below.)

This conception of Vajrayāna as the decadent phase of Buddhism is in large part a consequence of the deep influence that the Hegelian view of history as an organic process has had on the writing of history, historiography.[2] According to this view societies, religions, and social institutions have a life cycle which can be analyzed into a series of stages: birth and growth, maturity and stability, old age and decline, and death and dissolution. Given this assumption, the final stage of Buddhism in India must have been the most decadent form—and, indeed, some have suggested that Vajrayāna was responsible in some way for the disappearance of Buddhism from the Indian subcontinent.

Particularly after the flight of Tibetans from the Chinese conquest, greater attention began to be paid to tantric Buddhism, and it came to be recognized as a valid area of study in its own right. The connection, however, commonly made between tantric Buddhism and Tibet has led to a misunderstanding of both. On the one hand, Tibetan Buddhism is a wide-ranging tradition containing within it the entire spectrum of Buddhist scholasticism. On the other, tantric Buddhism is found not only in Tibet but much more widely throughout the Buddhist tradition. It is this latter issue that this collection of essays hopes to address—at least to the extent of helping to establish Vajrayāna Buddhism in East Asia as a recognized field of study.[3] While this collection focuses on East Asian tantric Buddhism, there is also a historically important tradition of tantric Buddhism in South and Southeast Asia.[4] The study of this tradition is, however, outside the scope of this collection. South and Southeast Asian Vajrayāna, much less developed than the study of East Asian Vajrayāna, offers a rich field for future research.

Categories and Terms

Already here at the very beginning we find ourselves confronted with a terminological issue: What is the proper term for our subject? Or is there one? Although the terms "Vajrayāna" and "tantra" have already been used here, other terms are equally plausible.

CRITICAL REFLECTIONS ON CATEGORIES

Categories such as Mahāyāna and Vajrayāna, sūtra and tantra, are often simply presented as natural and unproblematic, as if the categories simply reflected some reality found out there. Critical reflection on intellectual categories and the schema they form starts with the insight that they are constructed, but much more than this needs to be recognized. José Cabezón has identified five aspects of intellectual categories which assist us to reflect on those categories critically.[5] First, we need to know whether the categories are those that the historical figures being studied themselves employed or are later imaginative reconstructions. Both kinds of categories—emic and etic as they are also known—have their utility. Second, the task is to see what the categories occlude and to elucidate their social utility. Third, category schemata are never universal, but rather diverge from one another, and these divergences reveal as much about those who formulate them as about the things being categorized. We will see this below, for example, in the discussion of two different bibliographic schema—that commonly employed in Tibet and that employed by the Shingon tradition of Japan. Fourth, the history of category schema needs to be seen as twofold: reflecting intellectual concerns—such as doctrine, logic, and belief—and also sociopolitical concerns. Fifth, it is necessary to critically reflect not only on traditional, or emic, categories but also on our own intellectual categories. For example, perhaps the most problematic of our own intellectual categories is the distinction drawn between religion, philosophy, and psychology, which originates largely in nineteenth-century Euro-American institutions of higher learning, but which at best correlates with Buddhist thought only very loosely and at worst systematically distorts Buddhist thought and creates pseudoproblems. In the following several of these issues will be highlighted.

In the study of a religious tradition, terminological considerations are more than simply definitions. The "objects" of our study are not natural entities, not things that can be pointed to, but rather social entities, constructions. This means that we cannot use ostensive definitions, those that simply point out an exemplary instance of a category. We need rather to recognize that the terms and categories employed are in large part our own creation, and avoid reifying them by turning them into objects existing independently of our use. As such, we are responsible for the terms we use and for using them with adequate reflection on the presumptions they bring—often covertly—into the field of study. In particular, the three currently dominant approaches to the study of religion approach the question of terminology and definition in quite different fashions.

These three approaches are the comparative, the phenomenological, and the postmodern. Comparative studies are interested in similarities and continuities between religious traditions, and as a consequence terms are used as a means of identifying general characteristics of religion found in a variety of instances. For example, the term "shaman," which originated in the Siberian cultural zone, has come to be a general category for a wide range of what appear to comparativists to be fundamentally the same religious form. (The use of the term "form" here suggests the Platonic background to this approach.)

Phenomenological studies are informed by two different understandings of the goal of study. One usage, more classical for the study of religion, is basically concerned with typology, that is, creating comprehensive systems of categories according to which the phenomena of religion may be understood.[6] Much of the usual work of Buddhist studies, such as the textual studies included in this collection, can be seen as having been motivated by the traditional understanding of the "history of religions" *(Religionswissenschaft)* as serving to provide "data" for this kind of phenomenology of religions.

The other understanding of phenomenology is specifically informed by Husserlian phenomenology. In this approach the goal is the accurate description of experience so as to be able to characterize the objects of experience. Both understandings of the phenomenology of religion are often either in service of or not distinguished methodologically from the comparative understanding of the study of religion. For example, the term "mysticism" is used both as a category of religious experience (Husserlian phenomenology of religion) and as a religious form having a specific location in relation to other religious forms such as worship and sacrifice (comparative religion).

In contrast to both the comparative and phenomenological approaches, the postmodern approach focuses on the specific instance and its social, historical, and cultural locatedness. This emphasis on the location of the specific arises from a self-reflective awareness of our own involvement in the creation and imposition of categories, often for reasons other than purely intellectual ones.[7] For example, the lingering category of "primitive" religions is inherited from the religious imperialism of the colonial era in which colonialism was often justified by reference to the duty of the colonizers to assist in replacing primitive religions with the higher religion of Christianity.[8] For postmodern studies, terms are in the service of making distinctions, and not with identifying similarities or establishing value-laden hierarchies. The anthropological distinction between emic and etic categories seems at least congruent with, if not having directly informed, the postmodern approach.[9] Emic categories are those used by a specific social group, while etic ones are those used by those outside that group to talk about that group.[10] A postmodern approach, for example, would distinguish between the emic significance of the Japanese term *kami* used in a specific social, cultural, and historical setting such as the Heian era from an etic category such as "nature spirit," and value the former over the latter.

Each of these three approaches has its own validity as a distinct intellectual project, and a fully informed study of religion considers all three as complementary and mutually corrective. This collection seeks to bring together several complementary methodological and theoretical approaches.

For our purposes here, we should note the incredible complexity of the terminological issue. For East Asian Vajrayāna we have a variety of source languages—Sanskrit, Chinese, Korean, and Japanese—each of which implies a different religious culture. As a consequence, even those terms used as translations have different semantic ranges, or as Cabezón puts it, the category schemata diverge from one another. Further, within these different religious cultures there are a variety of specific traditions, lineages, and schools of thought that have employed different terminologies or used the same terms in different ways.[11] In an English-language study, the terms also carry connotations from such sources as the popular understandings of Tibetan Buddhism (e.g., the lama as the fourth jewel), the lingering effects of colonial categories (e.g., tantra as decadent), and New Age religiosity with its own strong neo-Platonic foundations (e.g., etheric energies). Because of this complexity, the following discussion can at best provide some preliminary terminological considerations as a basis for an informed reading of the essays included in this collection. As the field of East Asian Vajrayāna Buddhism develops it can be expected that the terminology and categories will become more refined.

KEY TERMS

Tantra. The term "tantra" originates as a bibliographic one, that is, it identifies a category of texts. According to Herbert Guenther, the first appearance of the term tantra in English in 1799 was with just this meaning.[12] Like the term sūtra, tantra also seems to have been drawn from the imagery of sewing and weaving. Where sūtra is a thread used to string or sew things together, and also the warp on a loom (the lengthwise threads), tantra identifies the weft (also, woof, the crosswise threads) on a loom. As religious texts, sūtras and tantras string together teachings.[13] According to Hugh B. Urban, "the oldest texts bearing the title 'tantras' are Buddhist, beginning with the *Guhyasamāja Tantra*, which is thought by some to have been written possibly as early as the third century CE."[14] Problems arise, however, when a bibliographic term such as "tantra" is employed to identify a religious tradition. As Donald S. Lopez, Jr., has expressed it, "The problems of definition multiply exponentially when the term 'tantra' is excised from its place in the colophon of a Sanskrit manuscript and allowed to float free as an abstract noun."[15] The use of tantra, or tantric, as a category for religious praxis originates in the nineteenth-century European study of Indian religion and culture.[16] Thus, the difficulty of defining tantra as anything other than a bibliographic category results from there being no object to which it refers. This is not to say that it has no existence at all, but rather to point out that it exists solely as a social convention, an intersubjective entity, specifically, as a category within our own academic discourse. Intersubjective entities do have ontological and epistemological status, but exist solely in the realm of society and its discourses.

Urban has described how the category of tantra arose within Orientalist discourse as a means of delineating Indian religions for colonialist purposes.

In this discourse Indian mentality was conceived as "essentially passionate, irrational, effeminate," and set in opposition to the "progressive, rational, masculine, and scientific" mentality of modern Europe. "'Tantrism,' it would seem, was quickly singled out as the darkest, most irrational core of this Indian mind—as the extreme Orient, the most Other."[17]

Despite this, the category seems to have become so well entrenched in the religious studies discourse that it will probably not go away. It appears in several of the essays compiled here. But although in the following discussions "tantra" will be used as largely synonymous with Vajrayāna, we will attempt to indicate its bibliographic origins by not capitalizing it.

Mantranaya. Although not widely used in contemporary scholarly discourse, "Mantranaya" is important as one early means to distinguish this newly developing form of practice. The term is a compound of *mantra*, the evocative verbal formulae that take a central role in the new practices, and *naya*, meaning a principle, system, or method in the sense of both organizing and motivating.[18] The traditional "system of perfections" (Skt. *pāramitānaya*), now considered to define the Mahāyāna, required heroic efforts over many lifetimes before one could attain awakening. In contrast, the new "system of mantra" opened the opportunity for more direct attainment. As David Snellgrove puts it, "there were in general two approaches toward buddhahood, the slower but surer way as taught in the Mahāyāna sūtras, i.e., the way of the Bodhisattva . . . and the risky way as taught in the tantras, which could result in buddhahood in this very life, but which employed methods which only those of strong faculties should dare to use."[19]

Mantrayāna. Like "Mantranaya," the term "Mantrayāna" highlights the central role of mantras in this new praxis, that is, the interaction between practice and doctrine. *Yāna*, usually rendered as "vehicle," fits this new form into the rhetorical structure already established by the appellation "Mahāyāna," and used to distinguish Mahāyāna from what was thereby defined as a lesser vehicle, the "Hīnayāna." In such a usage, Mantrayāna asserts itself as the third, and even higher, vehicle carrying one to awakening. While the division into three *yānas*—Hīnayāna, Mahāyāna, and Vajrayāna—has become commonplace, there are other ways of construing the history of the Buddhist tradition.

The great Tibetan exegete Tsong kha pa considers there to be only two major forms, Hīnayāna and Mahāyana. The latter he divides into the Perfection Vehicle (*pāramitayāna*) and Secret Mantra Vehicle (*guhyamantrayāna*).[20] While at first this might appear to be a distinction that makes no difference, it does serve to place tantric Buddhism firmly within the philosophy and practice of Mahāyāna.

A different kind of distinction is drawn by Luis O. Gómez, who identifies three strands of tantric Buddhism. It is the earliest of these that he calls Vajrayāna. Although perhaps originating as early as the fourth century, he uses the term "to describe the early documented manifestations of Tantric practice, especially in the high tradition of the Ganges River valley after the seventh century." Traditionally attributed to the Kashmiri yogin Lūi-pa (c. 750–800), the earliest documented form of Sahajayāna is from early ninth-century Bengal. Gómez considers the *Kālacakra Tantra* as a third, distinct form of Buddhist tantra.[21] Vesna A. Wallace places the *Kālacakra* in the early eleventh century, and notes that while it may have originated in south India, its "sphere of influence in India was confined to Bengal, Magadha (Bihar), and Kaśmīr, wherefrom it was transmitted to Nepal, Tibet, and eventually to Mongolia."[22]

Herbert Guenther, one of the pioneers in the contemporary study of Vajrayāna Buddhism, preferred the term "Mantrayāna" to "tantra." In his view "the philosophical significance of Mantrayāna has been much obscured by applying to it the name 'Tantrism,' probably one of the haziest notions and misconceptions the Western mind has evolved." He goes on to explicate the negative view of tantra "as a degenerative lapse into a world of superstition and magic," pointing out, however, that "nothing of what is thus fancied about Tantrism is borne out by the original texts."[23] Despite these reservations, he acknowledges that "tantra" is now the commonly accepted term. Common acceptance, however, does not obviate the need for critical reflection on the consequences of a particular set of categories and terms.

Zhenyan and Shingon. The categories of mantranaya and mantrayāna form the background for the Chinese term *zhenyan,* pronounced *"shingon"* in Japanese. The characters for these terms translate literally as "true word," referring to mantra. This rendering of mantra points to the Indian philosophy of language in which mantras are effective because they make the primal creative energies manifest. This idea is expressed in the Mīmāṃsā theory that the eternal text of the Vedas exists as the foundational energy creating the phenomenal universe. Through proper ritual use, this energy can be manifested, making the ritual effective.[24] Although formulated as a distinct philosophy of language in the context of Hindu tantric thought, many of these ideas about extraordinary language were also integrated into

Buddhist conceptions of mantra and were transmitted to East Asia. For example, in his justification of the efficacy of reciting the name of the Buddha Amitābha, Danluan (476–542) distinguishes two kinds of words: those that are meaningful by reference to some object and those, such as the names of buddhas, that are identical with what they identify. In this way the name of Amitābha is understood in a manner entirely congruent with some of the understandings of mantra found in Indian philosophy of language.

Mijiao, Mikkyō, and "Esoteric" Buddhism. Our subject is sometimes referred to in English as "esoteric" Buddhism. This conveys the meaning of the Chinese term *mijiao,* and its cognates in Korean, *milgyo,* and Japanese, *mikkyō.* To the extent that Vajrayāna tradition itself maintains that access to practice properly requires initiation by a properly ordained representative, the term "esoteric" is appropriate. In other words, the practices of the tradition are not openly or publicly available—no weekend workshops—without both an expression of commitment and an acceptance into the tradition. As is discussed more fully below, however, to advertise that something is esoteric or secret is a way of claiming that it is superior, special, and desirable.

However, caution in the use of the term "esoteric" is advisable. This is because in contemporary Western religious culture "esoteric" can carry connotations unwarranted in the East Asian Buddhist context. These take the form of preconceptions regarding a universal category of "the esoteric"—or mystical, or occult, or gnostic—which manifests through the particular forms of different religious traditions. This is the view of Perennialism, which holds that there is a mystical core to all religions, and that that core mystical experience—open only to "true initiates"—is the same in all religions.[25] Differences in the expression of this essence are explained away as simply the unavoidable consequence of expressing an ineffable experience of the higher reality through the contingencies of a particular language and culture. In this book we are concerned not with "Buddhist esotericism," not, that is, with the Buddhist form of the Perennialist conception of the universal category of the esoteric, but with "esoteric Buddhism," the form of Buddhism that presents itself as constrained by concerns for the transmission of its powerful psycho-spiritual technologies only to those capable of using those technologies properly.[26]

Identifying Vajrayāna: Definitions, Characteristics, and Issues

Having introduced some of the key terms, we are now ready to examine the issues involved in attempting to define and characterize Vajrayāna Buddhism. We begin by examining two different strategies for defining Vajrayāna. Then we discuss several issues in the study of Vajrayāna: phonic mysticism, the three sets of vows, proto-tantra, scholastic classifications, and transgression.

STRATEGIES FOR DEFINING VAJRAYĀNA

One approach to defining Vajrayāna is to focus on specific elements of practices, such as mantra, mudrā, maṇḍala, and abhiṣeka. One of the elements that has frequently been taken as the defining characteristic of tantra has been "ritual identification" (Skt. *ahaṃkāra*, rendered into Jpn. as *nyu ga ga nyu*, literally "entering me, me entering"), that is, the ritual act in which the practitioner becomes one with the deity evoked. For example, Michel Strickmann has claimed that identifying ritual practices as tantric is possible "if we accept as a minimal definition of this imprecise but useful term that they center upon the visualization by the officiant of a deity to whom the rite is addressed, with whom the officiant then proceeds to identify himself or otherwise unite."[27]

One problem with an approach that attempts to define tantra in terms of its elements is that each of the elements commonly associated with tantra is found in earlier and in non-tantric religious movements. Robert Brown has said of this approach that while "the pieces of Tantrism (doctrines and practices) can be listed, none is exclusively Tantric, and all are components of other religious systems."[28] Or, conversely, elements may be absent from traditions that are clearly tantric. As noted previously, mantra dates back to the Vedic sacrificial tradition. Similarly, abhiṣeka is drawn from royal consecration rites, and in the form of yantras maṇḍalas were used in Ayurvedic medicine. This kind of problem is reflected in debates in Tibet regarding the status of the Heart Sūtra (the Prajñāpāramita Hṛdaya Sūtra). Does the mantra found at the end of the sūtra, "Gate gate paragate parasamgate bodhi svaha," mean that the text is to be classed in the category of tantra? Or, given that it falls into the category of *Prajñāpāramita* texts, is it to be classified as a sūtra?[29] *Ahaṃkāra* is an instance of the absence of a supposedly definitional element, in that the tantric, but dualist, tradition of Śaiva Siddhanta does not employ ritual identification in its practices.

The same situation is found in East Asian Buddhism. Robert Sharf notes that the problem with characterizing Vajrayāna in terms of "invocation, worship, and meditative communion with deities in elaborately scripted ceremonies" or in terms of "the trope of sacred kingship" is that "the use of *dhāraṇī*, mantra, and the invocation of deities, coupled with a quest for divine grace and thaumaturgical powers, have been a staple of Chinese Buddhist monastic practice since its inception."[30]

More sophisticated than such a listing of elements is the listing of characteristics. In his study of Hindu Śākta tantra, Douglas Renfrew Brooks suggests ten characteristics "shared across sectarian lines [and which] involve both speculative and theoretical elements."[31] Summarizing and paraphrasing these:

1. Tantric texts and traditions are not part of the Vedic tradition, which is often considered the touchstone of orthodoxy in India. Brooks calls this characteristic "extra-Vedic."
2. Special forms of yoga and spiritual disciplines are taught, usually based on esoteric physiologies.
3. In general the tradition is religiously theistic and philosophically non-dual (we should note, however, that there are dualist tantric traditions, for example, Śaiva Siddhanta).
4. The tradition includes elaborate speculations on the nature of sound and the use of extraordinary language, for example, mantra.
5. It employs diagrammatic representations, e.g., yantras and maṇḍalas.
6. It gives particular emphasis to the authority of the teacher (guru).
7. It employs "bipolar symbology," including, for example, imagery of conjugal union.
8. As a path it is secret, that is, limited to initiates judged qualified by teachers of the tradition, and is dangerous and expeditious.
9. It transgresses social standards through the use of conventionally prohibited substances and antinomian acts.
10. Initiation—the key giving access to the practices—does not reflect the usual established criteria of caste and gender.[32]

Stephen Hodge employs this approach in the introduction to his translation of the Vairocanābhisaṃbodhi Sūtra (frequently also referred to as the Mahāvairocana Sūtra), confining himself "to a summary of those features which characterize the spirit of Buddhist tantric thought."[33] As a review of the kinds of characteristics that scholars have thought worth noting in relation to Vajrayāna, and calling attention to the similarities with Hindu tantra as described by Brooks, it is worth citing this list in its entirety:

1. Tantric Buddhism offers an alternative to the standard Mahāyāna path to awakening.
2. Its teachings are particularly intended for lay practitioners, and not for monks and nuns.
3. As a consequence, it validates mundane aims and attainments, and it employs practices that are more magical than spiritual.
4. It teaches unique types of meditation *(sādhana)* as the path to awakening, practices that are understood to transform the individual into an embodiment of the awakened mind of the buddhas quickly, either in this lifetime or shortly thereafter.
5. Such meditative practices make extensive use of maṇḍalas, mudrās, mantras, and dhāraṇīs as concrete expressions of reality.
6. Visualization of various deities, either externally or internally, is central to tantric meditation practice.
7. There is an exuberant proliferation in the number and types of buddhas and other deities.
8. The guru is very important because of the necessity of receiving instruction and appropriate initiations for the *sādhanas* from him.
9. Speculation on the nature and power of language, particularly in relation to the Sanskrit syllabary, is prominent.
10. Various customs and rituals, often of non-Buddhist origin, are incorporated into the tradition and adapted to the Buddhist goal of awakening.
11. A spiritual or esoteric physiology is seen as facilitating the process of awakening.
12. The tradition stresses the importance of the feminine and employs sexual yogas of various kinds.[34]

This kind of approach has antecedents in the Tibetan scholastic tradition as well. Commentaries on the *Guhyagarbha Tantra*, the paradigmatic tantra for Nyingma Mahāyoga, analyze "ten or eleven 'practical principles of tantra' *(rgyud kyi dngo po).*"[35] Mipham, the nineteenth-century Nyingma scholar and *ris med* (eclectic) reformer, employs this system, listing eleven aspects of tantra: "the triad of view, contemplation, and conduct; the triad of maṇḍala, empowerment, and commitment; the triad of actualization, offering, and enlightened activity; and the dyad of seals and mantra."[36]

While such an approach may be useful for a general orientation, it is not without its problems: (1) All of the characteristics are unlikely to be found in every instance of the subject of interest. This is true of both the modern, Western lists and those of the Tibetan scholastic tradition itself. (2) These characteristics do not exist separately from our own use of them as generalizations. In a commentary on the *Kun byed rgal po*, kLong chen rab 'byams pa notes that "these aspects can not be found upon analysis to exist as discrete tangible essences."[37] (3) Some of the characteristics identified are not unique to the subject. As has been noted, the use of mantra originates in Vedic religious praxis. Even more generally, such aspects as the importance of a teacher and of the feminine may be found in a variety of religious traditions around the world. (4) Some of the characteristics may reflect the self-understandings promoted by the religious tradition of the compiler of the list, rather than those of the tantric traditions themselves. (5) Some of the elements may be more speculative than well grounded on historical evidence, as in the assertion that tantra originates as a lay movement. Finally, (6) taken uncritically, such a list cannot reflect, and indeed obscures, the differences in the various bodies of tantric literature that result from historical development. Instead, such a conception implies a monolithic, unchanging, essentialized conception of tantra and the view that any variation from this normative vision constitutes a failing of some sort—deviancy, degeneracy, inadequacy, or inferiority.

For example, contemporary Shingon Buddhism, which certainly considers itself to be an instantiation of Vajrayāna, does not have any emphasis on esoteric physiology, nor on "the feminine," and does not employ any form of sexual yoga. This is not to say that such strains are not found anywhere in East Asian Vajrayāna—for example, the Tachikawa-ryū of medieval Japan appears to have actively used sexual practices[38]—but rather that as a general characterization, these do not apply to all the forms that are of interest.

The category of magic, found in many characterizations of tantra, is problematic. The concern with "mundane aims and attainments," often claimed to distinguish magic with its worldly and profane concerns from (true) religion with its spiritual concerns, is hardly unique to Vajrayāna. Attempts to control weather and disease have been almost universal to religions around the world. Similarly, such practices as rites for the safe construction of buildings are found widely. In the same vein, dhāraṇī practice is now found in Thai Buddhism,[39] and it pervades the Lotus Sūtra—forms of Buddhism that would hardly be considered Vajrayāna.

The notion that there is a clear distinction between religion (other-worldly, spiritual, good) and magic (this-worldly, materialistic, bad) is a Western one, not reflected outside the scope of the three Western monotheisms. The rhetorical use of the term "magic" as a category for religious studies is in large part a modern one, arising in the nineteenth century in the context of discussions about the relation between religion and science.[40] Science was identified as having effective instrumental knowledge, allowing for control of the material world. In contrast religion become identified with spiritual concerns, or with the mistaken notion that intercession in this world could be achieved through petitionary prayer. As the third term of contrast, magic was identified with the mistaken notion that religious practices were directly instrumental, having direct control of the material and spiritual worlds. In keeping with nineteenth-century notions of progress, the three terms were often not simply contrasted but set up as a sequence: the failures of magic as instrumental control were thought to give rise to religious petitionary appeals to spiritual powers, which were then replaced by the true instrumentality of science.

Similarly, the question of the use of "various customs and rituals, often of non-Buddhist origin," implies a problematic preconception of purity and authenticity. It suggests that there are two categories that can be clearly delineated: Buddhist practices and non-Buddhist practices. Does the fact that Śākyamuni Buddha utilized yogic meditation mean that he employed "non-Buddhist" practices? If he did so, might we not consider such use and adaptation to be very Buddhist?

Hodge gives no evidence for the claim that Vajrayāna teachings are particularly "aimed at lay practitioners." One is perhaps justified in thinking that the claim is simply circular and speculative, rather than based on any historical evidence.[41] The circularity would be that, having identified Vajrayāna with magic, it is assumed that monks and nuns would be concerned with "true spirituality" and that therefore such "magical" teachings must have been intended for the laity. That presumption then becomes offered as the cause for such "magical" practices. Once we call into question the presumption that the distinction between spiritual and materialistic is appropriate in this context, the basis for the assertion that Vajrayāna teachings are primarily aimed at the laity begins to look almost purely speculative.[42] More concretely, we do in fact know that many monks were actively involved in the study and practice of Vajrayāna.[43] It would be presumptuous and insulting to suggest, as might be done in order to explain such involvement, that they only did so as a cynical response to the mistaken conceptions of the laity.

Hodge himself is certainly cognizant of the problematics of historical development: "During the proto-tantric and early tantric phase only a few of these elements may occur together in any given text, but as we enter the middle and late phases, we find that an increasing number of them, in one form or another, are incorporated into the texts. This process of synthesis and development extended over several centuries, from the earliest proto-tantric texts down to the elaborate *Kālacakra Tantra*, which was possibly the last tantra to be developed in India."[44] We should note, however, that the historical actualities are much more complex than the single, uniform line of development that might be read from Hodge's description. There are texts with some of the elements, and therefore "proto-tantric" in this use, which are written well after some of the classic texts identified clearly as tantric.

THE IMPORTANCE OF PHONIC MYSTICISM

Tantric traditions all seem to have a concern with the power of speech, and in East Asia the power of writing.[45] André Padoux has described the pervasive presence of phonic mysticism throughout tantric practices: "Such is the case in ritual, every act of which will be accompanied by formulas (mantras), and more specially syllabic formulas (*bīja*: the phonic 'seeds,' which will almost entirely supersede the Vedic-type mantra), sometimes endlessly repeated loudly or softly, or only mentally, and which are used for the worship of the deity, for vivifying its image, for identifying the adept with the deity, for purifying him, and so forth."[46] The use of mantras derives from the Vedic sacrificial tradition in which fragments from the texts of the Vedas are used in ritual to identify a ritual action with an action of the deities. Extraordinary uses of language, that is, uses other than for ordinary communication, are found throughout the Buddhist tradition. The Pāli contains several texts known as *parittas* or *rakṣās*, which are recited for protection, and are often accompanied by ritual.[47] Such extraordinary language use continued in a variety of forms in Mahāyāna and tantric Buddhism.[48]

Three terms for the extraordinary language found in tantric Buddhist ritual texts are "mantra" (Jpn. *shingon*), "dhāraṇī" (Jpn. *darani*), and "vidyā" (Jpn. *myōshu*). Mantra are verbal formulae that are sometimes used as objects of mental concentration. However, in the context of tantric ritual they play an instrumental role, usually in combination with a hand gesture, mudrā. Dhāraṇī originated in Indian Buddhism as a mnemonic device, or as a condensed and therefore powerful version of the teachings found in a sūtra. In later Mahāyāna texts they are treated as the possessions of bodhisattvas evidencing their accomplishments. Found extensively in such non-tantric texts as the *Lotus Sūtra*, the common assumption that dhāraṇī alone constitute evidence of a tantric presence or influence is mistaken.[49] Recently, Jacob Dalton has suggested, however, that manuals for the ritual recitation of dhāraṇīs formed an important phase in the creation of texts identified as "tantras."[50] Despite these qualifications, it is also fair to say that dhāraṇī are in fact often treated as if they are mantra, or even simply as a kind of magical formula. This is particularly understandable in East Asia, where any meaning to be derived from the Sanskrit, even a mnemonic stimulus, would have been lost to the vast majority of practitioners. For them the transliteration would simply be a series of meaningless sounds, much as an English-speaking practitioner unfamiliar with Sanskrit would experience upon encountering the following:

tadyathā ane ane ane mukhe mukhe mukhe samantamukhe dsyotisome satyārāme sauti yugate nerugate nerugate prabhe hili hili kalpe kalpe si sārc sarvati buddhavati hili hili hile hile hile hile mahāhilile hili dunde tsande tsarā tsarāne atsale matsale anante anantegate anantegate arene nirmare nirbhavane nirvartane nirdante dharmadhare nihare nihara vimale viśodhane śīlavoṣhane prakritidhīpane bhavane bhavavi bhavani asaṃge asaṃgavihare dame śame vimale vimalaprabhe saṃgarśane dhire dhidhire mahādhidhire yaśe yaśovate tsal atsale matsale samatsale dedhasandhi susthare asaṃge asaṃghavihare samghanirhare nirharanivimale nirharaviśoṣhani didhi some sthara sthama sthama vati mahāprabhe samantaprabhe vipulaprabhe vipularaśmi sambhave samantamukhe sarvatrānugate anantshedye pratibane dhāraṇīdhāne dharmanidhanitre samantabhadre sarvatathāgata-adhiṣṭhāna-adhiṣṭhite svāhā.[51]

It is commonly noted that dhāraṇī are generally longer than mantra.

While "mantra" and "dhāraṇī" are used almost interchangeably in the East Asian tantric Buddhism, Michel Strickmann has asserted that whereas mantras are found throughout Indian texts, dhāraṇīs are only used in Buddhism.[52] Jan Nattier refines this by pointing out that dhāraṇīs are only found within the realm of Mahāyāna Buddhist discourse.[53] She goes on to point out that while both mantras and dhāraṇīs are formulae used in ritual contexts, "dhāraṇī" has the additional, and probably more original, meaning of "mnemonic device."[54] In the East Asian context, Strickmann identifies this along with two other meanings for the term "dhāraṇī." Referring to the *Dazhidu lun* (attributed to Nāgārjuna and bearing the reconstructed Sanskrit title *Mahāprajñāpāramitāśāstra*), Strickmann identifies three functions of dhāraṇīs: "Memory, perception and protection of the equilibrium of the spirit: these are the three principal functions of dhāraṇī for our author."[55] The *Dazhidu lun*, translated by Étienne Lamotte, expands on the protective uses of dhāraṇīs by identifying two functions, holding together and holding off. Dhāraṇīs are capable of holding together that which is beneficial and holding off that which is not.[56] Dhāraṇīs are repeatedly identified as possessions of a bodhisattva, an idea found repeatedly in such texts as the Lotus Sūtra. Vidyās are a subset of mantras, and yet at the same time refer to "feminine deities that were appropriated by Buddhists,"[57] also known as vidyās. Ritually, vidyās function in the same way as other mantras, being accompanied by mudrā.

THE THREE SETS OF VOWS

One of the ways in which a distinct identity has been created for esoteric Buddhism is through the use of three sets of vows, or what are also called the three great codes of discipline.[58] These are the prātimokṣa vows, the bodhisattva vows, and an additional distinct set of mantrayāna vows. Kūkai, founder of the Japanese Vajrayāna tradition of Shingon, presents the mantrayāna vows (Jpn. *samaya*) as a set of four: not to abandon the correct Dharma or to develop any incorrect behavior, not to give up the aspiration to attain enlightenment, not to be tight-fisted about any of the teachings, and not to go without benefiting all sentient beings.[59]

These three sets of vows are found in both Tibetan tantric and Japanese tantric traditions.[60] (It is unclear, to me at least, as to whether or not the three sets of vows were used in China.) This may serve as a criterion for identifying where an institutionalized form that identifies itself as Vajrayāna Buddhism actually exists, rather than simply the use of those elements identified as typical of the tradition, such as mantra, mudrā, dhāraṇī, and maṇḍala, within a broader Buddhist praxis.

ON "PROTO-TANTRA"

With all of the definitional vagaries outlined in this introduction, it should be apparent that there are no clear dividing lines by which we can delineate what is or is not tantra. For this reason the attempt to identify a category of "proto-tantra" is problematic. As Robert Sharf notes, "Without a coherent notion of 'pure Tantra'—be it a self-conscious tradition, lineage, or school—the anachronistic and teleological category of miscellaneous or proto-Tantra threatens to lose its historical or analytical purchase."[61] Similarly Ronald Davidson comments that the use of the idea of proto-tantra as a bibliographic category "provides us with a misleading sense that somehow these collections understood that they were anticipating the later, mature system, which was certainly not the case."[62] The same issue—assuming that earlier forms only exist as preliminary to later higher developments—is found in the scholastic categorization of tantric texts.

SCHOLASTIC SYSTEMS OF CLASSIFICATION: SHINGON (HETEROPRAX VS. ORTHOPRAX) AND TIBETAN (FOUR TANTRAS)

The history of Buddhist thought has frequently been marked by scholasticism, that is, attempts to organize and systematize the vast textual heritage.[63] Perhaps the best-known East Asian scholastic systematization is that of Tiantai Zhiyi, with his organization of the canon into "five periods and eight teachings"[64]—a system that had broad influence in Japan as well as China. It should be noted at the outset of our discussion, however, that all such systems are constructed with polemic intent.

In contemporary Western scholarship the most frequently presented Vajrayāna scholastic system derives from the Tibetan Buddhist tradition. This is the fourfold system of Action tantras (Skt. *kriyā*, Tib. *bya*), Performance tantras (Skt. *caryā*, Tib. *spyod*), Yoga tantras (Skt. *yoga*, Tib. *rnal 'byor*), and Supreme Yoga tantras (Skt. *anuttara yoga*, Tib. *bla na med pa rnal 'byor*). The Action tantras are characterized as being focused on "a wide range of externally performed ritual activities." In contrast, the Performance tantras focus on "ritual activities in balance with meditative practices." This shift away from ritual practice continues in the Yoga tantras, which "are predominantly oriented towards meditative and yogic practices." Finally, the Highest Yoga tantras consider the mind to be the "chief agent of all human activities" and, therefore, give their attention to its purification and control.[65]

Frequently these are presented as a sequence of increasingly more sophisticated and powerful teachings such that the lower stages can be abandoned at the upper levels. David Snellgrove has noted that "one finds it asserted that these four grades have been taught to suit the capabilities of various beings, whose faculties may be categorized as inferior, mediocre, superior or truly excellent, as though all four grades were available at all times."[66] He goes on to note, however that "those who come latest onto the historical scene tend to grade the various phases that preceded them as descending stages of inferiority, and it is precisely this that occurs with the later categorizing of all the accumulated masses of tantras and the various consecrations that they bestow. Thus in order to make some sense of the various explanations offered by traditional scholars for the existence of such a variety, one needs to keep in mind the all-important factor of historical development."[67]

Rather than employing the fourfold system found in Tibet, the Shingon system works on a distinction between those texts that present "proper practice" ("orthopraxy"), and those which present practices which are both proper and improper, that is mixed ("heteropraxy").[68] The contemporary Shingon terminology for these two categories are "pure" esoterism (Jpn. *seijun mikkyō*, or *junmitsu*) and what is variously translated as "mixed," "miscellaneous," "diffuse," or "impure" esoterism (Jpn. *zōbu mikkyō*, or *zōmitsu*). Orthopraxy is associated with the texts of the Dainichikyō (Skt. Vairocanābhisaṃbodhi Sūtra) and Kongōchōgyō (Skt. Vajraśekhara Sūtra), together with their attendant cycles of rituals and maṇḍalas. It was these two traditions of practice that Kūkai reports he was initiated into during his sojourn in China, and which have provided the organizational structure for Shingon praxis since.

In much of Western-language scholarship on Vajrayāna Buddhism, the fourfold system of the Tibetan scholastic tradition is taken as normative.[69] Thus we find, for example, Reginald Ray noting that Shingon and Tendai Vajrayāna "are based on the practice of Kriya and Charya tantras, understood in Tibet as the 'lower' or more conventional tantras."[70] While strictly accurate as far as it goes, to categorize the Shingon and Tendai tantras according to the Tibetan categories is only valid from the Tibetan perspective. It would be equally valid—from the Shingon or Tendai perspective— to classify the Tibetan tantras according to the Japanese categories. From that perspective the vast majority of tantras in use in Tibet—that is, other than the Vairocanābhisaṃbodhi, Sarvatathāgatatattvasaṃgraha, and Sussidhikara—are heteroprax.[71]

For the critical scholar, however, both systems of classification are simply information about the respective traditions. On the one hand, they are instances of the scholastic efforts of each tradition. On the other, they reflect polemical efforts to establish relations of superiority and inferiority between different textual traditions and schools. The critical scholar can take neither system, not the Tibetan fourfold nor the Shingon twofold, as normative for the entire Vajrayāna tradition, but must, as Snellgrove suggests, attend to the actual textual history.[72]

RUNNING WITH SCISSORS, PLAYING WITH MATCHES: THE ROMANCE OF THE TRANSGRESSIVE

While "tantra" serves as a bibliographic category, "tantrism" as a religious category was formed by Europeans—novelists, colonial administrators, and scholars. Formative in the creation of the idea of tantrism was transgression. All transgressions were seen as tantric, and all tantrism transgressive. Virtually the only image of tantric practice presented in the highly influential *Philosophies of India* by Heinrich Zimmer is one that is transgressive. Zimmer presents the notorious "five m's" ritual as emblematic of the entirety of tantra. This is the practice of sacramental transgression involving five elements, all of which begin with the letter *m:* the consumption of wine *(madya),* meat *(māṁsa),* fish *(matsya),* and parched grain *(mudrā),* prior to sexual intercourse *(maithuna).*[73] Serinity Young notes that "the first four are described as aphrodisiacs and lead up to the fifth, actual or symbolical sexual union."[74]

This is a very problematic issue, however, requiring a great deal of attention to the specific social context. André Padoux expresses serious reservations, for example, in his discussion of the role of sex in tantric practice. Noting that in the Brahmanic tradition sexual activity and its representations are justified by their auspiciousness, he goes on to suggest that such significance "should also be their purpose in the Tantric sphere is far from impossible, much to the contrary. Transgression would thus be confined to cases where impurity is sought as a path toward a sacrality that transcends social norms, and as a means of conquering the supernatural powers that are associated with anomic deities. The transgressing of usual norms of conduct (ritual or otherwise) should however not always be taken as expressive of some kind of 'transgressive sacrality.'"[75]

In his study of tantric ritual in Bhaktapur, Nepal, Robert I. Levy comments on two issues relevant to the question of transgression. First, the idea of there being special tantric powers entails for the uninitiated the projection of a variety of fantasies about the nature of those powers and the practices that produce them. These fantasies are "encouraged by the Tantric strategy of protecting esoteric doctrines through multiple veilings and obfuscations of its doctrinal and symbolic implications."[76] Thus it is that noninitiates "often believe that Tantric *pūjās* are associated with major violations of ordinary moral and religious regulations such as the eating of forbidden foods and overt sexual intercourse—including (according to one informant) even the incestuous intercourse between brothers and sisters."[77] Second, there is the related issue of secrecy. Although tantric practices may be secret, and outsiders are therefore able to project their own denied desires onto them,[78] at the same time the fact that secrets exist has to be known. "The secrecy of a group becomes a *mystery* for those who know there is a secret, but do not know what it is. To turn a secret into a mystery means that there often have to be ways of signaling, of advertising the presence of secrets."[79]

Transgression is indeed a characteristic of tantra as broadly understood. Hugh Urban asks rhetorically, "Do these texts really contain any of the scandalous, sexy, and transgressive materials that we today associate with the category of 'Tantra'?" His short answer is "Yes, of course they do."[80] One of the earliest translations of a Buddhist tantra into English is *The Caṇḍa-mahāroṣaṇa Tantra*, which contains the following instructions to the yogi who is in the "Variegated" position with his consort:

> Optionally he may secrete or not
> secrete, having his mind solely on
> pleasure. If he does, he should
> lick the Lotus, on his knees.
>
> And he should eat with his tongue,
> the white and red of the Lotus. And
> he should inhale it through a pipe
> in the nose, to increase his power.
>
> After washing the Lotus with the
> tongue, he should have Wisdom stand
> up and he should kiss her. And,
> after hugging her, he should eat meat
> and fish.
>
> He should drink milk or wine, in
> order to increase his desire. After

his fatigue has decreased, he should
desire with pleasure, etc.

And, in the foregoing manner, the
couple should begin again with each
other. By this repeated practice,
Great Pleasure is attained, and in
this very lifetime the practitioner
gains the title of Caṇḍamahāroṣaṇa.[81]

While the practice prescribed in the *Caṇḍamahāroṣaṇa* is an individual one, there were also group rites. These tantric feasts, or sacramental circles *(gaṇacakra)*, formed a significant part of Indian tantric Buddhist practice. Davidson points out that there can be "little doubt about the general purpose of its exercise: acquisition of the sorcerer's *(vidyādhara)* powers through the community's sacramental experience of otherwise forbidden items."[82] He also notes the effects of what he calls the "domestication" of these rites, in which the rites are explained simply as actions to be visualized, or are in some other way sanitized (or deodorized, as Urban calls this process). Such sanitizing of the instructions for transgressive rites in the tantras is not at all limited to the representation of tantra for modern Western audiences; it seems to be long-standing. In the case of Newari tantra, David Gellner notes that "while it is likely that most would accept only a symbolic interpretation of the antinomianism implied by Tantric ritual, it also seems certain that some took it literally."[83] While acknowledging the emphatic literalism of the *Kriyāsamuccaya*—"that sacramental circle *(gaṇacakra)* that is without [sex with] a female partner *(prajñā)* is a [mere] meeting of rice scum"—Elizabeth English goes on to assert that the instructions of the *Vajravārāhī Sādhana* are metaphoric and that the tantric feast is to be performed as a visualization.[84]

The tantric Buddhist texts, like their Hindu counterparts, clearly do contain instructions regarding transgressive practices.[85] Beyond this, however, context becomes everything. As suggested by Padoux, the meaning of sex in medieval India may have had a different value than it does for us today. Similarly, different practitioners may look at the same text and interpret it differently, as literal instructions for physical actions or as metaphoric instructions for visualized actions. Indeed, texts do not in fact indicate that the practices prescribed in them were actually engaged in—they could be little more than the pornographic fantasies of their authors. Generalities based on an idealized view of Buddhist tantra, or on a colonialist denigration of tantra as simply decadent, do nothing to assist in untangling the issue of the transgressive in tantra. Rather, attention to specific texts and their specific locations—social, cultural, historical, economic, and political—will probably reveal a wide-ranging diversity of practices, some transgressive, others not, some actualized, some visualized.

Historical Considerations

Having outlined some of the issues involved in characterizing the tantric Buddhist tradition, our next step is to raise a series of historical considerations about our understanding of the tradition. We begin with theories regarding the origin of tantra. Then comes an examination of the two different kinds of Buddhist practitioners who contribute to different forms of Buddhist tantra—monks and siddhas. Lastly, brief attention will be given to problematizing the historiographic narrative of the "three countries," which structures much of our understanding of East Asian Buddhism generally.

THEORIES OF ORIGINS

The two theories regarding the origins of tantra that appear most frequently are the "pre-Aryan/tribal-origin narrative" and the "Vedic-origin narrative."[86] The first argues that tantra is the reemergence of autochthonous, pre-Vedic religious culture into the historical record. This theory also tends to see a continuity between particular aspects of the archeological record of Indus Valley sites and the tribal religions of India—most especially the emphasis on goddesses. It is this latter characteristic, the centrality of the feminine, that has come in the minds of many scholars to be the defining characteristic of tantra. For example, Narendra Nath Bhattacharyya considers the basis of tantra to be "a primitive worship of the reproductive power of the Earth, imagined in female form, which is tied to the powers of sexuality."[87] Similarly, when J. G. de Casparis and others asserted that there was no tantric background to Borobudur—either as symbolism or as organizing principle—it was because of the absence of the feminine, that is, the explicitly sexual.[88] It should be noted that the presence of such elements alone, however, does not itself establish a direct, historical connection between the pre-Vedic and autochthonous religions of India and

Buddhist tantra. The pre-Aryan/tribal-origin narrative is appealing because it would seem to explain why there are tantric traditions within each of the three dominant traditions—Hindu, Buddhist, and Jain.

An example of this first narrative is M. C. Joshi's identification of tantra as a whole with devotion centering on "supreme power," that is, *śākti*. Implicitly, tantra simply is Śākta tantra. With this conception of tantra as focused on the feminine hypostatization of power, Joshi is able to assert that "Śākta Tantrism has its roots in prehistoric concepts of a fertile mother goddess and ancient systems for her worship."[89] He locates the origins in the Upper Paleolithic. In this reading of the origins of tantra, it is indigenous to India and continuous from the earliest times. One of the common characteristics of this theory is a questionable equation of prehistoric Indus Valley religion—about which very little uncontested knowledge exists—with medieval tribal religion. Despite this, it has been a very popular theory, being employed by Mircea Eliade and, more recently, Miranda Shaw and Luis O. Gómez.[90] Eliade says that "the irresistible tantric advance also implies a new victory for the pre-Āryan popular strata."[91] Shaw for her part emphasizes the connection with tribal and lower-caste religion, suggesting that "practices that had great antiquity in India's forests, mountains, and rural areas, among tribal peoples, villagers, and the lower classes, were embraced and redirected to Buddhist ends."[92] Commenting on the symbolic interpretations of the sexual symbolism of the tantras, such as semen being a symbol for *bodhicitta* (the aspiration for awakening), Gómez goes on to say, "Behind the Buddhist interpretation, of course, one discovers the non-Aryan substratum, with its emphasis on fertility and the symbolism of the mother goddess."[93]

In contrast to Joshi's delimitation of tantra to Śākti worship, Thomas McEvilley chooses to focus on esoteric physiology—the flow of energy up or down the spinal channel, together with conceptions of the control of that flow—and finds parallels not only in pre-Indo-European seal motifs from the Indus Valley, but also throughout the ancient world, including Greek, Sumerian, Egyptian, and Chinese instances. His gaze expands to include Australian aboriginal rituals, as well as !Kung Bushmen. Not surprisingly, perhaps, he says that such evidence "seems to direct our gaze into the darkest depths of human prehistory."[94] Like Joshi, McEvilley's reading gives tantra prehistoric origins, but instead of Indic ancestry it is a panhuman phenomenon dispersing from African origins.

Like many others, these two studies depend on the argument by analogy: two things appear to be similar, so there must be some significant connection between them. In logic, the argument by analogy is considered to be one of the very weakest forms of argumentation. Despite this, analogies are perhaps the most prevalent form of argument. As Jonathan Z. Smith has pointed out, the argument by analogy is the core of the comparative method.[95] Similarities alone, however, are meaningless. Their significance emerges only in light of a theory, an idea about how things work. In both of the cases discussed, however, the theory is left implicit—perhaps a strategy to make the arguments appear stronger.

Urban traces the Vedic origins theory back to the apologist for the tantra, Sir John Woodroffe (who also used the pen name Arthur Avalon). This argument has two dimensions: first, that the tantras are continuous with Brahmanical Vedic traditions, and second, "that they are in fact the very essence and inner core of Vedic teachings." Such an approach gives greater emphasis to those aspects of the tantric traditions that are most easily assimilated to elite, Sanskritized Hindu religious culture. This representation is, according to Urban, reflected in much recent scholarship, which downplays the "antinomian, radical, and transgressive aspects" of tantra.[96]

It is quite clear that the ritual technology of Vajrayāna has direct historical links with Vedic ritual practices. The most prominent of these are initiation *(abhiṣeka)* and the fire ritual *(homa)*.[97] Similarly, much of the ideological underpinnings of the practices draw on Vedic speculative philosophy. As indicated above, for example, the philosophy of language evident in Japanese Shingon Buddhism appears to be directly descended from Indian philosophy of language. More generally, in both China and Japan esoteric Buddhism was identified with the court and aristocracy, and with monastic elites. The segments of society that supported Buddhist tantra in East Asia were not attracted to the "antinomian, radical, and transgressive aspects" of tantra.[98]

MONKS AND SIDDHAS

Ronald Davidson has discussed the origins of tantric Buddhism in medieval India, outlining two varieties of Buddhist praxis out of which what we today commonly consider to be Vajrayāna was formed.[99] One of these is the well-known *siddha* tradition, which has become valorized as the "crazy wisdom" tradition. It is this latter idea that has contributed to the equation of tantra exclusively with transgressive behavior, and with low or outcaste peoples. Davidson describes this image, saying:

The siddhas, one may suppose, were unconcerned with allegiance of any variety, preferring the untrammeled existence of a psychic world in which ritual systems, social rules, lineage concerns, scriptural continuity, and the other paraphernalia of institutional Buddhism were simply jettisoned for personal liberation. Going naked along their own paths, devoted solely to their own subjective experiences, the siddhas—in this argument—represented a purity of religious expression devoid of scholastic hairsplitting or legalistic wrangling, which was so much the obsession of the great monasteries of the medieval period.[100]

As appealing to our own romantic conceptions as this imagery may be, Davidson argues that it is created by scholars having depended too much on a single work, the "Lives of the Eighty-four Siddhas" *(Caturaśītisiddha-pravṛtti)*, as an historical source.[101] In contrast to the idealized representation of siddhas as outside the social order, Davidson suggests that "the category of 'siddha' is the logical consequence of a civilization whose medieval expression is a concern for (and sometimes obsession with) status, hierarchy, political power, religious authority, and personal indulgence. Accordingly, the goal of turning into a siddha frequently becomes the aspiration of those excluded from status and hierarchy, either by birth or by accident."[102] Thus, although the association with people of low social status is accurate, the idea that siddhas were in active rejection of social goals is not. The other thread that Davidson identifies is the monastic Buddhist community. It was monk practitioners who, borrowing the imperial metaphor, established new images that became central to Buddhist tantra. These are the maṇḍala, the image of the imperial retinue and domains, and the overlord *(rājādhirāja)* or universal ruler *(cakravartin)*, an individual who assumes kingship and exercises dominion, which is "the central and defining metaphor for mature esoteric Buddhism."[103]

There is a long-standing tendency to locate the origins of new scriptural sources, including the tantras, in the visionary experiences of isolated individuals, the forest recluses or wilderness dwellers *(āraṇyaka)*.[104] Davidson points out, however, that the evidence regarding the composition of esoteric literature—siddha hagiographies—emphasizes the social environment. The institutionalization of tantra, that is, its formation as a major strain within late Indian Buddhism, is the work of monks concerned not only with propagating a religious praxis but also with ensuring the survival of their monasteries. As Davidson says, "The monks who were creating institutional esoterism evidently considered their scriptures central to the longevity of their institutions and needed to articulate the values of authority and duty that could ensure scriptural transmission."[105]

It certainly seems plausible that at least some of the novel elements of tantra as it developed were the result of individual visionary experience,[106] in contrast to other possible sources, such as borrowing from tribal cults. A note of caution is warranted, however, since an emphasis on the isolated individual fits all too well with our own neoromantic view of founders as decontextualized religious virtuosos (itself probably a legacy of the Christian assertion of the unique status of Jesus). It is essential to correct this one-sided view by calling attention to the importance of the ability to communicate a new vision to others. If this visionary experience had been entirely unique and not integrated into the religious culture, we would know nothing about it today.

PROBLEMATIZING THE HISTORIOGRAPHY OF THE "THREE COUNTRIES"

Most of the contemporary Western writing on the history of East Asian Buddhism has employed an implicit way of telling its story, a historiographic narrative. This narrative structure, which comes from Japanese Buddhist historical writings, is that of the "three countries," referring to India, China, and Japan. India is defined as the wondrous land of Buddhism's origin. China, or perhaps more specifically Tang dynasty China, is the great continental transmitter of Buddhism. Japan is the final recipient of this great project of transmitting Buddhism.

During the medieval period in Japan, the three countries narrative interacted with another powerful Buddhist narrative, that of the final age of the dharma *(mappō)*. Mark Blum has shown that as a consequence, two contradictory understandings of Japan are found in Japanese Buddhism histories.[107] In one of these Japan is portrayed as a marginal, barbarian country at the edges of the civilized world, unworthy to play such an important role. In the other, Japan is the center of the world and destined to protect the true Buddhadharma in the age of its decay elsewhere.

To write the history of Buddhism in this way, that is, to present it as a singular line of development from India through China and culminating in Japan, marginalizes many important aspects of Buddhism. For example, the development of Buddhism in China after the Tang dynasty is largely ignored, implying that it is unimportant.[108] This way of constructing the history of Shingon Buddhism was in a sense established by Kūkai himself. In *A Memorial Presenting a List of Newly Imported Sutras and Other Items* Kūkai claims that Huiguo, the seventh patriarch of esoteric Buddhism, made him the eighth patriarch and directed him to carry the teachings to Japan. This version of history, which has been accepted within Shingon sectarian histories,[109] has contributed to a tendency to ignore the broader history of esoteric Buddhism in China both before the time of Śubhākarasiṃha, Vajrabodhi, and Amoghavajra, and after the time of Huiguo.

Overview

In chapter 1, "Tantrism in China," Chou Yi-Liang examines the lives and works of the three "founders" of East Asian tantrism: Śubhākarasiṃha (Shan Wu Wei), Vajrabodhi, and Amoghavajra, as recorded by Tsan-ning in his *Sung kao-sêng chuan.* Tsan-ning lived about two centuries after Śubhākarasiṃha arrived in China, and as a consequence his record presents a fairly accurate picture of the way these three figures were understood at this time. What this record reveals is the highly legendary quality of that understanding. These figures work miracles, including taming destructive Tibetan bandits, bringing rain, and curing illnesses. Beneath this legendary overlay, both ritual and technical skills can be perceived. Mastery of mantras and dhāraṇīs, and knowledge of the proper construction of altars and maṇḍalas for various ceremonies, exemplify the rituals skills of the three. Exemplary of the technical skills is the story of Śubhākarasiṃha casting a bronze stūpa that "surpassed in technique any [previous work] of men or gods."

Chou Yi-Liang's essay is a foundational work for the study of East Asian tantra. The fundamental information it provides about three figures considered to be the founders of tantric Buddhism in China has molded the way the subject has been studied ever since. By focusing on Śubhākarasiṃha, Vajrabodhi, and Amoghavajra, Chou's essay replicates the "founder school" model of religion in general and of Buddhism in particular. This viewpoint reinforces the Shingon school's scholastic distinction between heteroprax and orthoprax tantrism. Shingon scholastics consider only those forms of praxis introduced by these three "founders" to be orthopractic. Any forms that preceded, and implicitly any that followed, are considered heteropractic.

Chapter 2, "Esoteric Buddhism in Korea," is the first of two essays by Henrik H. Sørensen included in this collection. As Sørensen notes, the study of tantric Buddhism in Korea is relatively young, but his overview establishes that esoteric practices have long been present in the peninsula. Although long dominated by the study of Sŏn (Ch. Ch'an; Jpn. Zen), the study of Korean Buddhism has recently turned its attention to the tantric (Kor. *milgyo*) tradition. Because of this long-standing inattention, the materials on Korean tantra are very limited, sporadic, and in some cases inferential. Sørensen, however, outlines the presence of tantric practices from the early period of Buddhism on the peninsula, the Three Kingdoms period (extending from the fourth to the mid-seventh century), up to the twentieth century.

In chapter 3, "On Esoteric Practices in Korean Sŏn Buddhism during the Chosŏn Period," Sørensen focuses on the premodern Chosŏn dynasty (1392–1910). Despite allegations of decadence, Sørensen finds that the Buddhist culture of the Chosŏn period—its literature, art, and architecture—is quite rich and demonstrates the depth of the tradition. Early in the Chosŏn period the seven Buddhist schools, including the two tantric schools, Sinin and Ch'ongji, were regrouped into two, Sŏn (meditation) and Kyo (doctrinal). After the merging, Pure Land and tantric practices ceased as separate schools but became pervasive in later Korean Sŏn.

A key concept in the development of tantric Buddhism in Japan is "attaining buddhahood with the present body" (Jpn. *soku shin jō butsu*). This is the phrase used by Kūkai, who established the Shingon tradition of tantric Buddhism in Japan, in the work translated in chapter 4 by Hisao Inagaki. In contrast to classic models of the path to awakening, which projected countless aeons of heroic effort, the idea of attaining buddhahood with the present body is part of a rhetorical strategy found in Japan that Paul Groner has called "shortening the path."[110] Some renderings of *soku shin*, which Inagaki translates here as "the present body," have used the phrase "this lifetime." While capturing part of what I understand to be the intended meaning—the shortening of the path—this latter rendering overlooks the radically embodied character of the human situation and its potential as understood by Kūkai. The attention Kūkai gives to the theory of six elements and the projection of these onto the body of the practitioner suggests this emphasis on the embodied character of awakening.

The next set of chapters presents information about tantric deities and rituals. Vajrasattva is one of the most frequently encountered figures in

Vajrayāna Buddhism. In chapter 5 Ian Astley examines a ritual known as the Five Mysteries of Vajrasattva, which is intended to provide the practitioner with experience of the central Vajrayāna concept that the passions (kleśa) are themselves awakening (bodhi). This is another version of the shortening of the path mentioned above. While the history of this treatment of the path to awakening has yet to be studied, it seems clear that it is rooted in Nāgārjuna's famous identification of nirvana and samsara.

Another of the key texts of the Shingon tradition, the Tattvasaṃgraha, is the source of a visualization practice known as the five stages of realization. In chapter 6 Dale Todaro introduces this practice, gives us a translation of the sūtra text, and examines the history of the practice in Japan. This is followed by a discussion of the stages of the practice and its exposition by commentators, both Japanese and Indian.

Pol Vanden Broucke examines the scriptural sources for the cult of the "Great Victorious Vajra" (Daishō Kongō) in chapter 7. This is a cult that emerged in Japan, for which there is no record in China. The cult of Great Victorious Vajra employed rituals described in the Yugikyō, one of the five scriptures considered central by the Shingon tradition.

The final set of essays examines the ways in which Vajrayāna praxis has influenced other religious traditions in Japan. Chapter 8, James H. Sanford's study of esoteric interpretations of the practice of reciting the name of the Buddha Amitābha, himitsu nembutsu, gives evidence of the spread of tantric practices and ideas throughout East Asian Buddhism. Discussing first what he calls normative Pure Land Buddhism, that is, the Pure Land thought formulated by Hōnen and Shinran, Sanford then goes on to discuss nembutsu practice in the Shingon tradition, focusing on Kakuban (1095–1134).[111] Kakuban promoted a nondual position, known as fu ni (not two), against a dualist one, ni ni (yet two). Sanford also examines the views of Dōhan, another important Shingon figure in the medieval period. After discussing the later development of the himitsu nembutsu tradition, he also examines the influence of himitsu nembutsu in Tendai, Zen, Pure Land, and the Gonaishō cult.

Shugendō, a religious tradition focused on ascetic practices in the mountains of Japan, was deeply influenced by Vajrayāna Buddhism (mikkyō). In chapter 9 H. Byron Earhart discusses the origins of Shugendō, also known by the name of its practitioners, yamabushi, by focusing on the legendary founder of the tradition, En no Gyōja. This history reveals the complexity of the development of Japanese religion, drawing not only on

Buddhist traditions from India filtered through China but also on Daoism, Chinese popular religion, and indigenous Japanese religious culture.

In chapter 10 Helen Hardacre discusses the significance of the division of a Shugendō pilgrimage into male and female pilgrimages and the tensions created by the presence of Korean women on the pilgrimage. The women pilgrims enter a cave, which homologizes both with a womb and with the maṇḍala of the womb world *(garbhakośa dhātu)*. Hardacre then expands her study to other mountain pilgrimages in Asia. Also of theoretical importance is Hardacre's feminist critique of the idea that all religions seek the union of opposites *(coincidentia oppositorum)*. Instead, she makes it clear that the study of religion must take into account the differences between women's and men's experiences—the one involving a return to the source of one's identity as a woman, and the other involving a merging with the opposite in a quest for wholeness.

The intent of this collection is twofold: to contribute to ongoing discussions about the problems raised in this introduction, and to assist in the recognition of esoteric Buddhism in East Asia.[112] There are many aspects of East Asian Buddhist practice and thought that I believe can be traced directly back to tantra, once scholars are sensitized to this possibility and learn to recognize tantra when they see it.

The question of what is esoteric Buddhism, and tantra generally, will continue to be a source of scholarly inquiry—and perhaps consternation—for the foreseeable future. Are we talking about a specific, clearly delineated lineage of transmission? A more general movement? A ritual technology? Or a diffuse set of practices and doctrines that permeate Buddhism throughout its East Asian history?

This is not to suggest that critical, self-reflective inquiries about what we mean by esoteric Buddhism, and tantra generally, are not productive. However, as we have seen from the discussions surveyed above, there is perhaps little to be gleaned from attempts to define esoteric Buddhism and tantra in the abstract. Rather, discussions rooted in the examination of specific instances, and particularly of marginal cases, would seem to be productive lines of inquiry.

In the case of East Asian Buddhism, the other key question is that of defining what is meant by the influence or effect of esoteric Buddhism on other forms of Buddhism and local religions. For example, does the use of a dhāraṇī for a *lokarāja* (lit., "king of the land," i.e., a protective deity) constitute an appropriation from esoteric Buddhism when that practice is found in a Zen context?

In considering such future research, however, we would be well advised to keep in mind the art historian Michael Baxandall's "excursus against influence." Baxandall asserts that the concept of influence is a curse,

> ... primarily because of its wrong-headed grammatical prejudice about who is the agent and who is the patient: it seems to reverse the active/passive relation which the historical actor experiences. ... [If we get the relation of agency properly arranged, then] the vocabulary is much richer and more attractively diversified: draw on, resort to, avail oneself of, appropriate from, have recourse to, adapt, misunderstand, refer to, pick up, take on, engage with, react to, quote, differentiate oneself from, assimilate oneself to, assimilate, align oneself with, copy, address, paraphrase, absorb, make a variation on, revive, continue, remodel, ape, emulate, travesty, parody, extract from, distort, attend to, resist, simplify, reconstitute, elaborate on, develop, face up to, master, subvert, perpetuate, reduce, promote, respond to, transform, tackle . . . —everyone will be able to think of others. . . . To think in terms of influence blunts thought by impoverishing the means of dif-ferentiation.
>
> Worse, it is shifty. To say that X influenced Y in some mat-ter is to beg the question of cause without appearing to do so. After all, if X is the sort of fact that acts on people, there seems no pressing need to ask why Y was acted on: the implication is that X simply is that kind of fact—"influential." Yet when Y has recourse to or assimilates himself to or otherwise refers to X there are causes: responding to circumstances, Y makes an intentional selection from an array of resources.[113]

Tantric Buddhism was one of the vast array of resources available to East Asian Buddhists almost throughout the entire history of Buddhism in East Asia. The ways in which it was propagated, developed, appropriated, sub-verted, occluded, and so on, are manifold and deserving of further research.

Tantrism in China

CHOU YI-LIANG

Introduction

THE AGE of the T'ang dynasty (AD 618–907) was a period when various
foreign religions were flourishing in China. Among these the most
important by far was Buddhism. As a result of the development of Buddhist
philosophy and theology during the Six Dynasties, there arose in the early
part of the T'ang period different sects such as Ch'an and T'ien-t'ai. These
represented the higher form of Buddhism, the value of which was not easily appreciated by ordinary people. On the other hand, the tantric form of
Buddhism, in which magic played a principal role, was quite popular
among the upper classes during the eighth and ninth centuries. It was during the seventh century that tantric Buddhism began to be systematized and
reduced to a philosophical basis in India.[1] Nevertheless, even before this
time there existed latent tantric elements in China, although it was not until
the eighth century that the sect was officially introduced there. This essay
is devoted to the study of the biographies of three Indian monks who
brought tantric Buddhism to China. Before dealing with them, however,
it will be profitable to examine the work of their more obscure predecessors, whose efforts, in translating and teaching, left the earliest vestiges of
this doctrine on Chinese soil.

TANTRISM IN EARLY CHINESE BUDDHISM

Chu Lu-yen, a monk from Central India, translated in AD 230 a text called
Mo-têng-ch'ieh ching. Besides directions for the worship of stars and some
simple rites for sacrificing to them,[2] this sūtra contains six dhāraṇīs which all
begin with the word *oṃ* and end with *svāhā*,[3] including instructions for necessary ceremonies during the recitation of the dhāraṇīs. One of these rites is
performed by lighting a great fire and throwing flowers into it at the end of
the recitation.[4] This ceremony, most likely influenced by Brahmanism,

seems to be a link between it and the homa rite taught in later tantric sūtras. Among the translations of Chih Ch'ien (d. after AD 253) several texts[5] consist of dhāraṇīs, but no rites accompanying them are described.

In the early fourth century the great Master Dharmarakṣa (d. after AD 313) made many translations. Quite a few of his sūtras consist of dhāraṇīs.[6] It is characteristic of Dharmarakṣa to translate the meaning of dhāraṇī instead of transcribing the sound. Examples may be found in two dhāraṇīs in the *Hailung-wang ching*.[7] In the fourth century two other masters from Central Asia were particularly famous for their magic, which they used effectively to strengthen the people's faith. The first, Fo-t'u-ch'êng (d. AD 348), is the subject of many legends.[8] He was said to be particularly proficient in dhāraṇīs and could employ spirits as he wished. By applying oil to his palm he was able to see what was happening a thousand miles away. Another of his accomplishments which no later monk possessed was the ability to tell fortunes by listening to the sound of bells hanging from the eaves of the temples.[9] Śrīmitra (d. between AD 335 and 342) was another monk who practiced the art of dhāraṇī with brilliant results wherever he went.[10] He translated some dhāraṇīs in a text now lost, called *K'ung-ch'uehwang ching*.[11]

Shê-kung (d. AD 380), a monk from Central Asia, obtained Fu Chien's favor because he could summon dragons and make rain.[12] This is one of the earliest occasions on which a Buddhist monk in China prays for rain. Later masters of the esoteric sect were all supposed to be able to do this. T'an-wu-ch'an (*Dharmakṣema, d. AD 433) was learned in dhāraṇī and showed his magic power by causing water to spring from a rock.[13] In the *Ta-chi ching*, which he translated, one passage declares that a bodhisattva has four kinds of ornaments, among which dhāraṇī ranks with śīla, samādhi, and prajñā.[14] *Suvarṇaprabhāsa*, also translated by T'an-wu-ch'an, gives instructions for making offerings during prayers for worldly benefits,[15] but the rite is by no means so elaborate as those practiced in later days.

T'an-yao, the monk who suggested the building of stone cave-temples in Ta-t'ung, translated the *Ta-chi-i shen-chou ching* in AD 462 with the collaboration of Indian monks.[16] It describes the method of making an arena where Buddhist images arranged in a circle receive the offerings of their votaries.[17] The arena seems to be a rudiment of the maṇḍala, or altar, the construction of which is taught in later texts. The same sūtra also teaches all kinds of siddhis {extraordinary powers}. There are siddhis to win a war, to stop a storm, to obtain rain, to conceal one's form, or to secure a wish-jewel. For different purposes different deities as well as different ways of worshipping are assigned.[18] The sūtra on siddhis translated by Shan-wu-wei in the time of the T'ang dynasty apparently is a more elaborate text of the same type. Emperor Yuan of the Liang dynasty, son of Emperor Wu, who was the most famous Buddhist emperor in Chinese history, says that he had learned several dhāraṇīs in his childhood,[19] indicating that at that time they were popular among the upper classes. A text called *Mo-li-chih-t'ien ching*, considered a translation of the Liang dynasty (AD 502–56), specifies the method of cleaning the hall of the temple and making offerings to the deity Marici.[20] A considerable amount of this sūtra is also devoted to the benefit which one would receive from reciting this dhāraṇī. A later version of the text translated by Amoghavajra adds some new elements which are not found in this one. It says that in reciting the worshipper should make the proper mudrās,[21] and carry small images of the deity on the head or on the arms as amulets.[22] Amoghavajra's version also mentions the building of a maṇḍala during the recitation of the dhāraṇī.[23] These additions would suggest that during the two hundred years between the early sixth century and the early eighth century tantric Buddhism gradually took its final shape in India.

In the early T'ang dynasty a Chinese monk, Chih-t'ung, translated several texts with dhāraṇīs. His biography says that he studied zealously the esoteric teaching.[24] Atigupta, who arrived in China in AD 652, translated the *T'o-lo-ni chi ching*, which consists of many rites similar to those taught in sūtras translated by Shan-wu-wei and Vajrabodhi.[25] Punyodaya, who came to China in AD 655, tried to introduce some texts of the tantric Buddhism then popular in India. But, because Hsüan-tsang, the promulgator of the idealistic school {Yogācāra} in China, was so influential at that time, Punyodaya was unsuccessful.[26] According to his biography by Tao-hsuan, when he returned from a trip to the South Seas, "les textes sacrés qu'il avait [précédemment] apportés avaient tous été emportés par Hiuan-tsang vers le Nord. Il avait bien l'intention de traduire [quelques textes] pour convertir [les Chinois], mais comme il n'avait plus de matériaux à sa disposition, il ne traduisit que trois Sūtra: *l'Octuple Maṇḍala, la Méthode pour adorer les Buddha,* et *l'Āṭānāṭiya;* ses traductions sont exactes, concises, et minutieuses, et parfaitement aptes à être toujours étudiées et mises en pratique."[27]

I-ching was also interested in the tantric form of Buddhism when he studied in Nalanda;[28] but he could not devote much time to it, as he had many other occupations. Nevertheless, among his translations the *Ta k'ung-chüeh-chou-wang ching*, with its appendix on methods for making altars and painting images, is a well-developed text of the tantric school. It is in this sūtra that the dhāraṇī is first deified and called a *vidyārāja* {"king of knowledge"}.[29]

These, then, were the earliest teachers of tantric Buddhism in China. Their work, though it achieved some degree of popularity, cannot be said to have established the cult as such. Besides these there were other monks who, we know, went to India to study the esoteric doctrine; but they all died in India before they could return to China to promulgate it.[30] Thus, it was not until the arrival of the three famous monks of the eighth century that this doctrine began to form a distinct and even dominant sect of Chinese Buddhism.

Shan-wu-wei arrived in Ch'ang-an in AD 716. Later he was allowed to translate the texts which he had brought along with him. Hence he became the first great master of this school in China. Soon after Shan-wu-wei came Vajrabodhi and his disciple Amoghavajra, who in later years made this school one of the important sects of the T'ang dynasty. Although this school of Buddhism did not have great influence on Chinese thought, it was closely associated with the court as well as the ordinary people who were interested in praying for their own welfare in the present and future life but not so keen on the discussion of profound doctrine. After Amoghavajra's death in AD 774 this school gradually declined. No more eminent masters are known to us except a few names mentioned in the diaries of Japanese pilgrims. During the early part of the Sung dynasty some Indian monks also translated quite a few texts of this school[31] and performed esoteric rites.[32] When Jojin, a Japanese monk, visited the palace of Emperor Shen-tsung in AD 1073, he found many images of deities who belonged to this sect exclusively.[33] This sect as a whole, however, did not prosper any more and was even held in contempt by the world.[34] Therefore, it would be safe to say that the esoteric school of Buddhism, about two and one-half centuries after its introduction into China and about one hundred and eighty years after its most flourishing period, died out in China before it was revived through the introduction of Tibetan Buddhism[35] in the Yüan dynasty some three centuries later.

This essay consists in the translation and study of the biographies of Shan-wu-wei, Vajrabodhi, and Amoghavajra, who are the only masters of this sect, in its proper sense, included in Tsan-ning's *Sung kao-sêng chuan*. My first aim is to check Tsan-ning's accounts with the scanty available sources which he failed to use or used erroneously. The second aim is to find some information in Indian and Chinese literature which may help us to understand the Indian background in these biographies. Although no reference to the three monks is found in any Indian books, a few facts, such as the Turkish rule in Northern India, the center of education in Kāñcīpura, King Narasiṁhapotavarman of that country, and the taming of the elephants, are proved by Indian sources. Thus we understand these biographies more thoroughly and can distinguish between historical facts and fanciful legends contained therein.

The third aim of this essay is to use these biographies as a framework around which to gather some material relevant to various phases of this sect, such as its rites, its relationship to the court, and its popularity among the masses. It is hoped that the position of this sect in the time of the T'ang dynasty will thus be made clear.[36]

TSAN-NING AND HIS SOURCES

Tsan-ning (AD 919–1001)[37] was born to a family named Kao which emigrated from Po-hai to Wu-hsing in the end of the Sui dynasty.[38] According to Wang Yu-ch'eng he became a monk in the T'ien-ch'eng period (AD 926) and in the early years of the Ch'ing-t'ai period (AD 934–35) he entered into Mt. T'ien-t'ai where he was fully ordained.[39] Being particularly proficient in the Vinaya texts, he earned himself the nickname Tiger of Vinaya. In AD 978 when Wu-Yueh was incorporated into the Sung empire, Tsan-ning was sent by the king to the Sung court where he was honored by Emperor T'ai-tsung with a purple robe and the title T'ung-hui. At the same time he was appointed to the Han-lin, which served as the Emperor's secretariat. In AD 991 he became an editor of the National Archives.[40] In AD 998 he was appointed the sêng-lu of the Right Road, which was in charge of half of the monks in the capital.[41] He held both positions until he died in AD 1001.

It is said that he was widely read in both Buddhist and non-Buddhist books. Scholars such as Hsu Hsuan, Wang Yü-ch'êng, and Liu K'ai were his good friends.[42] In Wang's work we find a preface to Tsan-ning's *Wen-chi*[43] and three poems presented to him,[44] in all of which Wang referred to Tsan-ning's scholastic achievements, particularly the contribution of the *Kao seng chuan*. In Hsu Hsuan's *Wen-chi* there is also a poem presented to Tsan-ning when he was returning to his home in the South. Since Hsu was famous for his study of palaeography, it is interesting to notice that in this poem he asked Tsan-ning to find for him the stele erected by Shih-huang of the Ch'in dynasty and inscribed by his renowned prime minister Li Ssū.[45] Ou-Yang Hsiu records a story of Tsan-ning which would show how tactful he was. When he, as a seng-lu, accompanied Emperor T'ai-tsu[46] to the Hsiang-kuo Temple in the capital, the latter was hesitating about whether he should kneel down to pay obeisance to a Buddha's image. Thereupon Tsan-ning said, "The present Buddha would not pay obeisance before a past Buddha." The emperor was highly pleased and it thus became a rule that the Emperor should not kneel before any Buddhist images. *Liu-i shih hua* also has a story revealing that Tsan-ning was witty and quick in reply.[47]

In the year AD 982 he received the imperial order to compile the *Sung kao-sêng chuan*. He obtained permission to return to the temple in Hang-chou where he came from and there he worked on the book, which he completed in AD 988.[48] The book is divided into thirty chapters, and composed of five hundred thirty-three biographies. There are also hundred thirty monks who have no biographies of their own but their lives are briefly recorded in the biographies of others.[49] As for the sources of this book, he acknowledges in his preface that he has made use of the biographies as well as the tomb inscriptions written by other people.[50] It is also affirmed by Chih-p'an in his *Fo-tsu t'ung-chi*.[51] This accounts for the difference in style, even within one biography.

The first half of Shan-wu-wei's biography is very elaborate in style and language because it is entirely taken, with very few changes in wording, from the work of Li Hua, who was considered a good prose writer. The latter half of the biography dealing with Shan-wu-wei's legend is based chiefly on the *Yu-yang tsa-tsu*, and hence the style is clearly different from the first half. For Vajrabodhi's biography Yuan-chao's work probably is the chief source, but Tsan-ning did not make use of all the information in his *Chêng-yüan shih-chiao lu*. The chief sources for Amoghavajra's biography are Chao Ch'ien's *Hsing-chuang* and Fei-hsi's *Pei-ming*. The style of the biographies of Vajrabodhi and Amoghavajra is more unified than that of Shan-wu-wei's biography. When Tsan-ning started the compilation of this book, he was already an old man. His preface says that besides himself several others took part in this work.[52] It is most likely that Tsan-ning only acted as the chief editor while other monks really did the compilation. This is why the style was considered poor, and Huang T'ing-chien even tried to revise it.[53]

Among other books which Tsan-ning wrote[54] only two are still preserved today. The first one is the *Sêng-shih-lüeh* in three chapters,[55] which is a general history of the sangha in China. The second book is a short treatise in one chapter called *Sun-p'u* dealing with bamboo shoots. It has five headings: the various names of bamboo shoots, the places where bamboo shoots are produced, the way of cooking them, the stories about bamboo shoots, and miscellaneous notes.[56] Probably it was due to this kind of knowledge that Liu K'ai called Tsan-ning the Chang Hua[57] of the day, as Chang was a well-known scholar with encyclopaedic knowledge.

The Biography of Shan Wu Wei of the Shang Shan Temple of Lo-Yang of the T'ang Dynasty

The monk Shan-wu-wei was by origin a native of Central India[58] and a descendant of Amṛtodana,[59] Śākyamuni's uncle. His Sanskrit name was Śubhakarasiṃha, in Chinese, Ching-shih tzū, which was translated as Shan-wu-wei. By another tradition his name was Śubhakara which also means Wu-wei in Chinese.[60]

Because of unrest in their own country, Central India, his ancestors had left it and gone to reign over the country of Oḍra.[61] Shan-wu-wei's father's name was Fo-shou wang [King *Buddhakara]. From his birth he appeared like a divinity and was endowed with virtues and accomplishments. Therefore his father tested him in a successive variety of positions.

At the age of ten he was in command of the army; and at thirteen he succeeded to the throne. He won the affection of both soldiers and civilians; but his brothers, being jealous of his ability, organized an armed rebellion. The resulting fratricidal struggle was so severe that Shan-wu-wei himself had to take active command. He was struck by a stray arrow and a flying discus[62] bruised the top of his head. Even so, when, in accordance with martial law, his brothers upon their defeat had incurred the penalty of death, he indulgently forgave them, despite the requirements of strict justice. Then, with tears in his eyes, he said to his mother and ministers: "When I led my army against my brothers, that was the end of any love between us. In order, however, to perfect my duty as a brother, I must now abdicate."[63] He thereupon gave the throne to his elder brother and earnestly requested that he might become a monk. Sadly his mother gave consent.[64]

She secretly gave Shan-wu-wei the pearl without price, which was the emblem of inheritance of the throne, just as correspondingly the vessels distributed among the feudal lords [identified them]. He went southward to the sea where he came to a superb monastery and there obtained the *saddharmapuṇḍarīka samādhi*.[65] He piled up sand to form stūpas, to the number of almost ten thousand, and even when a black snake bit his finger, he would not give up.

He then found accommodation on a merchant ship[66] by traveling on which he visited several countries, and while on board he recited [sūtras] and meditated in secret, emitting all the while a white light from his mouth. There were three days when the wind did not blow and yet the ship sailed onwards a vast distance. The merchants' lives were once in danger when they encountered pirates. Filled with compassion for his comrades, Shan-wu-wei whispered a dhāranī in silence. Seven koṭis of deities appeared in full glory, and finally the pirates were destroyed by other bandits who appeared. These bandits then confessed their sin and became his disciples.

They became his guides over the country, which was now easy and now difficult. Only after passing through many a weary wilderness and crossing stinking rivers did they reach Central India, where Shan-wu-wei met a king who was married to his elder sister. The king asked Shan-wu-wei why he had abdicated and could not repress his admiration. They walked into the palace hand in hand. Like sheltering clouds, Shan-wu-wei's presence comforted the whole country. Shan-wu-wei had grace of person and surpassing intelligence.

He understood the five ways[67] of Buddhism and the three disciplines.[68] He plumbed the meaning of both the dhāraṇīs and meditations and was an artist and expert craftsman [in the making of Buddhist images and stūpas]. When he first visited Nālandā Monastery (meaning "untiring generosity" in Chinese) from which the counterfeit doctrine[69] was derived, and which was the pole of all the saints, Shan-wu-wei presented the pearl of inheritance to be set in the forehead of the great statue of Buddha. By day it was like the moon, at night, like the sun.[70]

There was a certain monk named Dharmagupta[71] in the monastery. He held the mystic key to the gate of meditation and possessed the secret seal of Tathāgata. He appeared over forty years old, but was really eight centuries old. Hsüan-tsang had once met him. With great reverence, Shan-wu-wei made obeisance at Dharmagupta's feet[72] and recognized him as his master.

One day when Shan-wu-wei was acting as attendant for a meal, there was a monk from China present. Shan-wu-wei showed him the master's bowl, and the monk saw in it a fried cake and boiled millet which were still warm. Being astonished, he exclaimed, "But China is an uncountable number of miles away from here, and yet this Chinese food was cooked this morning and brought here!" Whereupon Dharmagupta said to Shan-wu-wei, "Since you have made no remark, you are really qualified to learn."

Then Dharmagupta imparted to Shan-wu-wei the dhāraṇīs, yoga,[73] and the doctrines of the three secrets.[74] Surrounded by dragons and divinities in a circle about him, he learned at one sitting to make the mudrās.[75] On that very day he received abhiṣeka and was made a master of men and devas, and received the title of Tripiṭaka {i.e., one who has mastery of all three sections of the Buddhist teachings}. The Tripiṭaka deal with moral conduct, meditation, and wisdom, while formally they are known as sūtra, vinaya, and śāstra. The dhāraṇīs are used to epitomize them; they are the shortcut to enlightenment and the lucky sea to release. The Buddhas of the three worlds were born through this gate [method?]. The illumination of [buddha's] intelligence bequeathed only one source of light. But it was forever and everywhere sufficient to meet the needs of diversified human nature. Therefore there have been innumerable buddhas, and meditations as numerous as grains of sand. A bodhisattva, having epitomized all the meditations in one string [i.e., dhāraṇī], would suddenly be elevated in rank and approach supreme enlightenment. This was the essence of Dharmagupta's doctrine.

Then Shan-wu-wei fearlessly wandered through the wild plains and made pilgrimages to all the sacred spots. If he went to a place once, he went three times. He entered Kukkuṭapāda Mountain, where he cut [the arhat] Mahākāśyapa's hair[76] and Avalokiteśvara laid hands on his head. Once when he spent the rainy season at Gṛdhrakūta Mountain, a wild animal guided him into a deep mountain cave in which it was as light as day. There he saw a vision of Śākyamuni with attendants on both sides as if they were bodily present.

Central India once suffered from severe drought and Shan-wu-wei was asked to pray for rain. In a short while Avalokiteśvara was seen in the sun's disk, with a water jar in hand pouring water on the ground. The people were delighted and deeply moved as they had never been before. He cast gold into the shape of pattra leaves on which he wrote the *Mahāprajñāpāramitā Sūtra*. He also melted silver to make a stūpa as tall as a buddha.[77] Because he had wandered for quite a long time, his mother thought he might be dead. She wept day and night so that she lost her eyesight; but when he sent a letter to inquire after her health, her eyes recovered their function as before.

Since the death of Buddha, heretics had prevailed in India. Ninety-six schools[78] held their respective particular views. With his opponents' own viewpoints as basis of argument, Shan-wu-wei attacked their mistakes and analyzed their doubts. He caused the heretics to free themselves of their mental fetters and also to abandon chaos for the road of enlightenment. The dharma,[79] like the clouds, benefits all people evenly without distinction, and meditation is good for all. The banners of the heterodox were overturned, and the victorious standard of Vairocana Buddha was set up. He caused the heretics to free themselves of their own bewilderment by concentration, and taught them to look for the Buddha within themselves.

Dharmagupta said to him, "You good man! You have a predestined call to China. Now you may go." Shan-wu-wei then reverently bade him farewell and left. When he arrived in Kashmir, he came at dusk to a river over which no bridge was built. He crossed it by floating through the air. One day he was invited to dine in a rich man's home. In a short while an arhat descended, saying, "I belong to Hīnayāna. You are a bodhisattva who is traversing the bhūmis." Thereupon the arhat yielded the [higher] seat to him and honored him. Shan-wu-wei presented an excellent robe to the arhat, who then departed into the sky.

Later Shan-wu-wei arrived in Udyāna. White mice ran up to him each day and brought presents of gold coins. He lectured on the *P'i-lu [chê-na ch'êng-fo shên-pien chia-ch'ih ching]* in the court of a Turkish [khan] and meditated under the khatun's tree. The dharma appeared in golden letters displayed in the sky. At that time a female attendant in the Turkish [khan's] palace pressed her hand to her breast from which three streams of milk flew out and poured into Shan-wu-wei's mouth. He, clasping his hands, said solemnly, "She was my mother in a former birth."

On his way, he met bandits who struck at him three times with a sword, yet he was not hurt. The man who wielded the sword heard only the sound of copper being struck. He went on and climbed the Snow Mountain. There he fell ill on reaching a large lake. Dharmagupta came from the sky saying: "While in the world a bodhisattva does not escape transmigration; but you have long understood the world. How can you be sick now?" After he had said this Dharmagupta ascended to the sky and Shan-wu-wei recovered [his strength completely] as though washed.

When he passed through Tibet, he stayed with some merchants. The barbarians, being greedy for money, came in large numbers to surround and waylay them. Shan-wu-wei secretly applied mudrās by heart, so that the chief of the Tibetan robbers [was defeated by his magic power and] begged for pardon. When he reached the western border of the great T'ang country, a god told him one night: "Eastward from here the country is not my domain; Mañjuśrī is guarding that heavenly land." The god vanished after having made obeisance at his feet. This was like Kapila's protection of Master Dharmamitra. Shan-wu-wei loaded his books on the back of a camel, which, when crossing the river at Hsi-chou[80] was pulled down into the river by the dragon. Shan-wu-wei also fell into the water and stayed three days in the palace of the dragon and propagandized them on the dharma, so that many were converted. When he led the camel out to the shore, the books were still not damp.

While Shan-wu-wei was still in the region of North India, his fame already had spread as far as China. Emperor Jui-tsung[81] ordered Jñāna and General Hsien to go out the Jade Gate[82] to welcome him. In the early years of the K'ai-yuan period [AD 713–41] Emperor Hsuan-tsung [r. AD 713–55] dreamed that he had met an eminent monk of unusual appearance. The Emperor, applying the paints himself, portrayed the dream monk on the wall of his hall. When Shan-wu-wei arrived, he was found to be identical with the monk of the dream. Rejoicing at this miraculous meeting, the Emperor decorated the temple in the palace [for Shan-wu-wei] and honored him as Master. Beginning with the princes of Ning and Hsüeh {the Emperor's brothers}, all knelt down before him and waited on him. As a bodhisattva might be received in the celestial palace, so this Indian monk was seated next to the Emperor who honored him as the Teacher of the Country, just as Huang-ti honored Kuang-ch'eng. Shan-wu-wei, on his part, caused the Emperor to enter the way of Tathāgata. This sublime doctrine was then at the peak of its popularity.

At that time there was an astrologer who could manipulate supernatural spirits and was learned in the mechanism of [cosmic] changes. When Shan-wu-wei and the astrologer were ordered to engage in a test of their rival miraculous powers in the presence of the Emperor, he was calm, but the astrologer who tried to worst him was at a loss to know what to do.

In the fourth year of K'ai-yuan, the year of ping-ch'en [AD 716] Shan-wu-wei first arrived in Ch'ang-an,[83] bringing with him some Sanskrit texts. He was stationed in the southern quarter of the Hsing-fu Temple {in north-western Ch'ang-an} by the Emperor's order. Later on he was ordered to stay in the Hsi-ming Temple {in western Ch'ang-an}. Messengers were sent repeatedly from the Emperor to inquire after his health and the presents given him were unusual. In the fifth year, the year ting-ssu [AD 717], by imperial order he made translations in P'u-t'i-yuan {a sub-temple of the Hsi-ming}. He asked the Emperor to invite noted monks who should discuss with him both the Chinese and the Sanskrit texts. He first translated in one chapter the *Hsu-k'ung-tsang ch'iu-wen-ch'ih fa*.[84] The monk *Siddhartha made an oral translation. Wu-chu wrote down and composed the text. It was copied and presented to the Emperor, who accorded it high praise. Thereupon an edict was issued that Shan-wu-wei should present to the Emperor all the Sanskrit texts he had brought along.[85]

Previously the monk Wu-hsing had gone to visit India. After he had finished his studies, he tried to return to China, but unfortunately died on reaching North India. All the leaves of the Sanskrit texts which Wu-hsing had obtained were preserved in the Hua-yen Temple in the capital. From these Shan-wu-wei and Master I-hsing selected for translation several texts and dhāraṇīs which had never been translated before. In the twelfth year [AD 724] he accompanied the Emperor to Lo-yang. There he received the edict ordering him to translate the *Ta-p'i-lu-chê-na ching* in the Fu-hsien Temple {in the eastern part of Lo-yang}. The complete Sanskrit text of that sūtra contained one hundred thousand stanzas, and what Shan-wu-wei translated was only a summary of essentials. It was put in seven chapters and called *Ta-p'i-lu-chê-na ch'êng-fo shên-pien chia-ch'ih ching*.[86] The monk Pao-yueh made the oral translation. I-hsing wrote down and composed the text with some omissions and additions.[87] It was written in a style well balanced between ornamental and simple language, and was in exquisite harmony with the profound doctrine it contained. On the one hand, it befits the Buddha's intention, and, on the other hand, it suits the inclination of the people. This text was the most essential means for the benefit of all the people.

He also translated the *Su-p'o-hu t'ung-tzū ching*[88] in three chapters, and the *Su-hsi-ti chieh-lo ching*[89] in three chapters. Both sūtras were complete vinayas for the Dhāraṇi sect. The prohibitions of the Secret sect are found therein. Those who had not entered the maṇḍalas were not allowed to read them, just as those who had not received full ordination should not overhear [the lectures on] discipline. The *Hsü-kung-tsang p'u-sa nêng-man chuyüan tsui-shêng-hsin t'o-lo ni ch'iu-wên-ch'ih fa*, which Shan-wu-wei rendered in one chapter, was simply abstracted and translated from the *Ch'êng-chiu i-ch'ieh-i t'u [p'in]*, part of the Sanskrit text of the *Chin-kang-ting ching*.

Being fond of quiet and simplicity, Shan-wu-wei was accustomed to tranquilizing his mind and calming his thoughts. From time to time he withdrew from his meditations to encourage the initiates. Those who saw him felt as if a lotus flower were blooming before their eyes. Those to whom he talked felt as if sweet dews were moistening their hearts. Every day someone was unexpectedly enlightened by him. When his fellow monks asked for an audience, he addressed himself only to the elder monk Ratnacinta.[90] All others honored him [with the humility] suitable to disciples. Master I-hsing was greatly esteemed by the Emperor and admired by the scholars of the day. In addition to [questions about] meditation and wisdom, I-hsing also consulted Shan-wu-wei on the profundities of yin and yang [i.e., astrology][91] before he made decisions.

Once, in his own quarters, Shan-wu-wei cast a bronze stūpa. He himself designed the model, which surpassed in technique any previous work of men or gods. Since the place required for smelting was extremely large, and the yard [of his quarters] was deep and narrow, the monks of the temple worried lest a wind might come up and the flame might rise and set fire to the temple. He said, laughing, "Don't worry. You'll see soon enough." On the day appointed for the casting, as he had predicted, heavy snow was falling. When the divine stūpa was taken out of the molds, lucky flowers [made of snowflakes] grew up on the mat spread in the yard. All the people shouted in admiration.

Once there was a great drought in the summer and the Emperor sent the eunuch Kao Li-shih in haste to ask Shan-wu-wei to pray for rain. He said: "It is destiny that there should be a drought now. If we summon the dragon by force, the rain thus invoked will be a deluge and only cause damage. That must not be!" The Emperor, urging him, said, "The people have been suffering from heat and are sick. Even some wind and thunder would be enough to satisfy them." Thus Shan-wu-wei's refusal was ineffectual. The officers showed him the implements used in making rain: banners, standards, conch shells, and cymbals were all available. Shan-wu-wei laughed and said, "Those things can't make rain. Have them removed quickly." He filled a bowl with water, stirring it meanwhile with a small knife and reciting a Sanskrit dhāraṇī of several hundred syllables. Soon an object, like a dragon, about the size of a finger and red in color, lifted its head above the surface of water, but dived back to the bottom of the bowl again. Shan-wu-wei went on stirring and reciting. After a while, a white smoke rose from the bowl and went straight up into the air for several feet, and was slowly dissipated. Shan-wu-wei told Li-shih, "Hurry back to the palace. It is going to rain!" Thereupon Li-shih rode away at full speed. When he looked back, he saw a white cloud rapidly blowing westward from the lecture hall, like a long strip of white silk flying across the sky. Soon it became dark and a great wind and thunder came. Li-shih scarcely reached T'ien-chin bridge {over the Lo River to the south of the imperial city} when the wind and rain caught up with his horse. Most of the large trees on the streets were uprooted. When Li-shih went into the palace to report, his clothes were all wet. The Emperor later welcomed Shan-wu-wei with his head bending to the ground and thanked him repeatedly.

Then at Mt. Mang a giant serpent appeared,[92] which Shan-wu-wei saw and addressed as follows: "Are you going to flood the city of Lo-yang?" He recited a dhāraṇī of several hundred syllables in Sanskrit. In a few days the serpent died. It was the omen indicating that An Lu-shan was going to occupy Lo-yang.

One tradition says that Shan-wu-wei once lived in the room of Tao-hsuan, the Master of Vinaya, at Hsi-ming Temple. He behaved rather rudely so that Tao-hsuan disliked him and had contempt for him. At midnight, when Tao-hsuan smashed a flea and threw it on the ground, Shan-wu-wei yelled repeatedly, "The Master of Vinaya struck the son of Buddha to death!" Now Tao-hsuan knew that Shan-wu-wei was a great bodhisattva. The next morning Tao-hsuan, holding his robe reverently, paid homage to Shan-wu-wei. If we examine this tradition closely, it was almost fifty years from Tao-hsuan's death to the middle of the T'ai-yuan period. Shan-wu-wei's unexpected appearance and disappearance are things that cannot be imagined by ordinary persons.

In the twentieth year [AD 732] he asked permission to return to India. The Emperor was sympathetic but did not grant his request. In the twenty-third year [AD 735], on the seventh day of the tenth moon, lying with his right side down and two feet overlapped, he died quietly. He was ninety-nine years old, or as the religious counted, he was eighty years of age. His fellow monks felt sad and lonely and the Emperor was shocked and grieved. The title of Director of the Court of State Ceremonial was bestowed on him. The Emperor ordered Hsien, First Secretary of the Court for State Ceremonial, and Vinaya Master Ting-pin, the master of rites of the temple, to superintend the funeral ceremony. In the twentieth year [AD 740], on the third day of the tenth moon, he was buried in the yard of the Kuang-hua Temple in the Western Hills of Lung-men. Because of his holiness, his body suffered no decay. On the day of his funeral the capital was the scene of [the people's] deep sorrow. Mountains and rivers changed their color. His disciples, both monks and laymen, Dhyāna Masters Pao-wei and Ming-wei of the Chêng family of Ying-yang and the Wang family of Lang-yeh, all were as grieved at the loss of the master as if they had lost their own fathers and mothers. In the beginning of the Ch'ien-yuan period [AD 758] the power of T'ang rose again [after the rebellion of An Lu-shan]. The two masters engraved a verse on a memorial stone and the lay believers dug the burial cave. His disciples went to live beside it just as Confucius's pupils had done to show their love for their master.

Shan-wu-wei's body, which can still be seen, has shrunk with time.[93] The black skin has dulled and the bones have become visible. Whenever a drought or flood has occurred in subsequent dynasties, people have gone to pray at the cave and have gotten results, so that many gifts of gratitude were laid there. The remains are covered with sheets of embroidered brocade as if he were asleep. Every time the remains are taken out of the cave, they are placed on a low couch and bathed with a fragrant unguent. The rich people in Lo-yang compete to give *ch'an-po*,[94] cleaning towels, and the toilet peas[95] used in the bath. The present Emperor,[96] when propitiating or praying for something, usually sends messengers to present gifts, and his desires have always been fulfilled.

The Biography of Vajrabodhi of the Kuang-Fu Temple of Lo-Yang of the T'ang Dynasty

The monk Vajrabodhi, [namely] Chin-kang-chih in Chinese, was a native of Malaya{kuṭa} (meaning brightness in Chinese) in South India. It was a district located near Potalaka Mountain, where Avalokiteśvara's palace was situated. His father, a Brahman, was proficient in the five kinds of knowledge and a teacher of the king of Kāñcī. Vajrabodhi was able to read ten thousand words every day when he was a few years old. He quickly comprehended whatever he saw and retained it throughout his life. At the age of sixteen, he was enlightened by Buddha's doctrine and therefore did not wish to learn the treatises of the Niganthas.[97] He cut his hair and put on a dyed robe and became a monk. This conversion was probably the result of good seeds planted during a former existence. Later he accompanied his teacher to Nalanda Monastery in Central India where he studied the sūtras, abhidharmas, and so on. When he was fully ordained, he heard the lectures on the vinayas of the eighteen schools.[98] Again he went to West India to study the nikaya treatises and the doctrine of yoga, three secrets, and dhāraṇīs. By the time ten years had passed he had become conversant with all the three piṭakas.

Then he visited Ceylon {presently Sri Laṅkā} and climbed Laṅkā Mountain. Traveling eastward, he visited twenty countries or more, including Bhoja {presently Palembang in Sumatra} the country of naked people, and others. Having heard that the buddhadharma was prospering in China, he went there by the sea route. Because of frequent mishaps, he took several years to get there.[99] In the year of chi-wei in the T'ai-yuan period [AD 719] he reached Kuang-fu {Canton}. An imperial edict ordered him to be welcomed to the Tz'u-en Temple in {southwestern} Ch'ang-an. After a short while he was transferred to the Chien-fu Temple {located in the K'ai-hua fang, to the south of the imperial city}. Whatever temple he stayed at, he always caused an altar to be erected for the abhiṣeka ceremony, on which a great maṇḍala was painted, and he converted the four assemblies of Buddhists {monks, nuns, laymen, and laywomen: bhikṣus, bhikṣuṇīs, upāsakas, upāsikās}. Dhyāna master Ta-chih {I-fu; d. AD 732 }, Ta-hui {I-hsing}, and Amoghavajra all honored him with courtesy becoming to disciples.

Later he accompanied the Emperor to Lo-yang. Since the first moon of that year it had not rained for five months. Prayer was offered at the sacred temples of mountains and rivers without result. The Emperor ordered Vajrabodhi to set up an altar for prayer. In consequence, he adopted the scheme of Pu-k'ung kou-i p'u-sa {Bodhisattva}.[100] An altar of four hastas {about eighteen inches} in height was erected in the hall of the temple, where he lived. He himself painted the image of the Bodhisattva of Seven Koṭis and set the date that when the eyes of the image should be drawn it would rain. The Emperor sent Master I-hsing to observe it secretly. It was still so hot in the morning of the seventh day that there was not a single cloud floating in the sky. But in the afternoon, when the eyes and brows of the bodhisattva were barely drawn, northwest winds began at once to blow so heavily that the tiles on the roofs were lifted and trees were uprooted. The clouds dropped their rain. The people far and wide were astonished. A hole was torn in the roof above the altar and heavy rain poured into the hall. Next morning, people of high and low degree in the capital asserted that Vajrabodhi had seized a dragon which had jumped up through the roof of the hall, and thousands of people daily sought to see the place. Such is the miraculous effect of the use of altars.

At that time the Emperor [Hsüan-tsung] was interested in Taoism and had no time for the [Buddhist] doctrine of śūnyatā. The officials, sensing the Emperor's intention, asked that the barbarian monks of foreign origin should be sent back to their own countries, and the date of departure was fixed forthwith. An attendant asked Vajrabodhi about his plans, and Vajrabodhi said: "I am an Indian monk, not a Tibetan or Central-Asiatic monk. I am not affected by the imperial order. Anyhow, I shall not leave." After a few days he suddenly decided to go to Yen-men by post-horse. When he bade the Emperor farewell, the latter was much surprised. An autographed order was issued to retain him.

The Emperor's twenty-fifth daughter was very much beloved by the Emperor. She had been ill for a long time and could not be cured. She was removed to rest in the Hsien-i Wai-kuan, where she lay with closed eyes, not having spoken for more than ten days. Previous to Vajrabodhi's plan of departure, an edict was issued ordering Vajrabodhi to be her preceptor in making vows to observe the Buddhist ordinances [śila]. This order was issued because the Emperor anticipated that the princess was certainly going to die. Nevertheless, Vajrabodhi went there. Having chosen two girls seven years of age from the palace, he had their faces wrapped with red silk and had them laid out on the ground. He had Niu Hsien-t'ung write an edict, which was burned elsewhere, and an incantation was said over it by Vajrabodhi. The two girls recited it from memory without omitting one word. Vajrabodhi then entered into samādhi. With inconceivable force he sent the two girls with the edict to King Yama. Within the time required for a meal, King [Yama] ordered the princess's dead nurse, Liu, to accompany the princess's spirit back with the two girls. Thereupon the princess sat up, opened her eyes, and talked as usual. Having heard of this, the Emperor started for the Wai-kuan on horseback without waiting for his guard. The princess said to him, "It is very hard to alter destiny as fixed in the other world. King [Yama] has sent me back to see you only for a short while." About half a day later she died. After that the Emperor began to have faith in Vajrabodhi.

Wu kuei-fei, who alone among the queens enjoyed the particular favor of the Emperor, presented treasures to Vajrabodhi. Vajrabodhi urged the queen to have made in haste a statue of Chin-kang shou-ming {Bodhisattva}.[101] He also advised the Prince of Ho-tung to paint an image in the stūpa of Vairocana. He told his disciples, "These two persons will not live long." In a few months both died as he said. All his predictions were in general similarly exact.

There was no principle with which he was not conversant, and there was nothing he did that was not effective. He could analyze and answer questions on sūtras, śāstras, the vinaya texts, secret dhāraṇīs, and other books whenever anyone asked, just as a bell would ring when struck. Whoever came to visit, if Vajrabodhi met him once, he never forgot him. In speech and behavior he was always solemn. His expression remained unchanged whether he was glad or angry, pleased or offended. Those who interviewed him, even though not knowing the scope of his mind, naturally expressed their admiration for him.

From the seventh year of K'ai-yuan [AD 719], when he first arrived at P'an-yu and then came to the capital, he was untiring in his propagation of the doctrine of the esoteric scriptures and in the erection of properly constructed maṇḍalas. Each effort was rewarded with a divine omen of approval. The monk I-hsing respected this doctrine [of esoteric Buddhism] and frequently asked Vajrabodhi questions, which he answered without concealing or omitting any detail. I-hsing himself had an altar erected where he received abhiṣeka and made vows to follow this doctrine. Since he recognized it to be profitable, I-hsing asked the master to translate some texts for promulgation. In the eleventh year [AD 723] Vajrabodhi, by imperial edict, translated in the Tzŭ-shêng Temple {in northwestern Ch'ang-an} the *Yu-ch'ieh nien-sung fa*[102] in two chapters and the *Ch'i-chu-ti t'o-lo-ni* in two chapters. *Īśvara, an officer of the Imperial Secretariat and a great Brahman chief of East India made the literal translation. The monk Wen-ku from Mt. Sung wrote it down.

In the eighteenth year [AD 730] at the Ta-chien-fu Temple he also translated the *Man-shu-shih-li wu-tzŭ-hsin t'o-lo-ni*[103] and the *Kuan-tzŭ-tsai yü-ch'ieh fa-yao*, each in one chapter. The monk Chih-tsang {Amoghavajra} made the literal translation. I-hsing wrote it down and composed the text with some omissions. Vajrabodhi also noticed that some passages and sentences were lacking in the old translation of the text of the [Mahā]pratisarā[dhāraṇī] and completed it by adding the missing part. All the dhāraṇīs and mudrās translated by Vajrabodhi were effective whenever they were applied. The mystic doctrine was at the height of its popularity. Many of those who studied under Vajrabodhi in both capitals were saved by him. Both lay and clerical disciples transmitted his doctrine from one generation to another.

On the fifteenth day of the eighth moon in the twentieth year, the year of jên-shên [AD 732],[104] he told his disciples at the Kuang-fu Temple in Lo-yang: "When the white moon becomes full {middle of the lunar month},

I shall go." Then he made obeisance to the image of Vairocana Buddha, walking around it seven times. Having withdrawn to his own quarters, he burned perfume and made vows. After he paid homage to the Sanskrit texts and confided the new translations on the doctrine [to his disciples], he died calmly.[105] His secular age was seventy-one and his religious age, fifty-one.

On the seventh day of the eleventh moon of that year he was buried on the right bank of the I River to the south of Lungmên. A stūpa was erected in his memory. His disciple Amoghavajra, his religious heir, made recommendations to the Emperor, who accordingly bestowed upon Vajrabodhi the posthumous title Master of the Country. Tu Hung-chien, the Assistant Secretary of the Imperial Secretariat, a disciple who had received abhiṣeka from Vajrabodhi and believed in him ever since, composed an inscription on the stele to record his virtue.

The author says: "According to the scheme of the maṇḍala of five divisions,[106] young boys or virgins must be used as media to summon spirits. It was once extremely easy to cure illness or exorcise evils. People in modern times, however, use this method to profit their body or mouth, therefore little result is obtained. Generally these methods are held in contempt by the world. Alas that the deterioration of the good dharma has gone so far as this!"

The Biography of Amoghavajra of the Ta-hsing-shan Temple of Ch'ang-an of the T'ang Dynasty

The monk Pu-k'ung's Sanskrit name was Amoghavajra of which the Chinese translation is Pu-k'ung-chin kang; but he was known for the sake of brevity by [the abbreviated name consisting of] two characters. He came of a Brahman family of North India and his father died in his childhood. Later he visited China with his uncle. At the age of fifteen he became Vajrabodhi's disciple. The master first introduced to him a Sanskrit text of Siddham {script},[107] and a treatise on the science of sounds [i.e., grammar],[108] which he mastered in ten days. The master was surprised and ordained him as a bodhisattva.[109] Having led Amoghavajra to the Vajradhātu maṇḍala and tested him by observing the place where he threw a flower on the maṇḍala,[110] the master knew that Amoghavajra was going to advance the doctrine greatly.

By the time he was fully ordained, he became an expert in expounding the vinaya texts of the Sarvastivadin school and was conversant with the writings and languages of several foreign countries. When the master translated sūtras, he was frequently ordered to collaborate. He completed the twelve years' course in six months when he studied the science of sounds. He learned the *Bhadracarī praṇidhāna*[111] in two evenings, while others would have spent one year. His quick comprehension was always like this.

Amoghavajra had wished for three years to learn the method of the five divisions and the three secrets of the new yoga doctrine; but since the master did not teach it to him, he thought of returning to India. The master then dreamed that all the images of buddhas and bodhisattvas of the temples in the capital went off toward the east. When he awoke he realized that Amoghavajra was a real recipient of the dharma and gave his assent to the latter's request. Thereupon the master imparted to him the method of abhiṣeka of the five divisions, the homa rites,[112] and the rites an ācārya should know. He also taught Amoghavajra in full detail the *Vairocana Sūtra* and the manuals of siddhi and so forth. Later Amoghavajra accompanied the master to Lo-yang, where the latter died in the twentieth year of K'ai-yuan [AD 732].[113] After the portrait hall[114] was finished and a posthumous title was conferred on the late master, Amoghavajra planned to make a long journey to India and Ceylon, as the late master once ordered him to do.

He first arrived at Nan-hai-chün, where Governor-General Liu Chu-lin made an earnest request for abhiṣeka. In the Fa-hsing Temple he converted in succession hundreds, thousands, and myriads of people. Amoghavajra himself prayed to the chief deity; and ten days later Mañjuśrī, constrained by his faith, put in an appearance. Before he boarded the ship the Governor-General summoned the great chiefs of the barbarians in the region of P'an-yu, I-hsi-pin, and elsewhere and warned them: "Now the Master of Tripiṭaka is going to South India and Ceylon. You are to warn your captains to see to it that they—the master and his twenty-one disciples, including Han-kuang and Hui-pien—get there safely, and that the nation's credentials [which they bear] are not lost."

In the twelfth moon of the twenty-ninth year [AD 741] he left Nan-hai on board a K'un-lun ship. When they reached the boundary of Kaliṅga[115] they met with a heavy storm. Each merchant, being terrified, tried to propitiate the gods by the method of his own country, but without result. All of them knelt down to pray for help and protection. Hui-pien and other disciples also wept bitterly. Amoghavajra said, "I have a plan. Don't worry." Thereupon, with a five-fingered vajra of Bodhicitta in his right hand and the *Prajñāpāramitā Sūtra* in his left hand, he recited once the

Mahāpratisarā dhāraṇī and performed the rite required for this dhāraṇī. The wind subsided immediately and the sea became calm and clear. Later they came across a large whale, which, emerging out of the sea, emitted jets of water like a mountain. It was even more threatening than the previous calamity, and the merchants were ready to give up their lives. Amogha-vajra performed the rites as before, and told Hui-pien to recite the *So-chieh lung-wang ching.* At once all the dangers disappeared.

When he arrived in Ceylon, the king sent a deputy to welcome him. The guardsmen on foot and on horse were stationed in ranks along the street when he entered the city. The king, having made obeisance at his feet, invited him to stay in the palace to be entertained for seven days. The king himself bathed Amoghavajra daily, using a golden barrel full of fragrant waters. The crown prince, the queens, and the ministers acted similarly.

When Amoghavajra first met the ācārya Samantabhadra he presented gold, jewelry, brocade, and embroideries and requested the master to expound for him the doctrine of yoga in the *Chin-kang-ting ching* of eight-een chapters and the method of erecting an altar in accordance with the Mahākaruṇā-garbhadhātu maṇḍala in the *Vairocana Sūtra.* He also per-mitted Han-kuang, Hui-pien, and other disciples to receive the abhiṣeka of five divisions together.

Amoghavajra, after that, had no regular teacher for his studies. He sought everywhere for the scriptures of the Esoteric sect and obtained more than five hundred sūtras and commentaries. There was nothing that he did not go into thoroughly as, for example, the samaya,[116] the various deities' secret mudrās, forms, colors, arrangements of altars, banners, and the literal and intrinsic meanings of the texts.

One day, for entertainment, the king ordered some wild elephants to be tamed. Everybody climbed up the high places to watch, but no one dared come near. Amoghavajra stood in the middle of the street in *maitrī samādhi reciting a dhāraṇī and making mudrās with his hands. Several mad elephants suddenly tumbled down. People all over the country were aston-ished by the story.

Then he visited India, where he caused auspicious omens many times. In the fifth year of T''ien-pao [AD 746] he returned to the capital and pre-sented a letter from King Sīlamegha of Ceylon, and ornaments of gold and jewels, the Sanskrit text of the *Prajñāpāramitā Sūtra,* miscellaneous pearls, and white cotton cloths. The Emperor ordered him to stay temporarily in the office of the Court of State Ceremonial. Later he was summoned to the palace to erect an altar for the Emperor's abhiṣeka ceremony. Then he moved to the Ching-ying Temple.

It was very dry all through the summer of that year and the Emperor ordered him to pray for rain. The imperial edict said: "The rain must not last too long, neither must it be too heavy." Amoghavajra asked to erect an altar [at which to pray] to the Peacock King. Before three days had passed it had rained sufficiently. Being very much pleased, the Emperor bestowed on him a purple kaṣāya robe[117] in a jeweled case and helped him into the robe. In addition, he was granted two hundred p'i of silk.

Once a great gale came on suddenly. The Emperor ordered Amoghavajra to stop it by praying. He asked for a silver bottle and applied some magic to it. Soon the wind calmed down, but when a goose in the lake accidentally bumped the bottle and tipped it upside down, the gale blew again with even greater velocity and violence. For the second time he was ordered by the Emperor to stop it and the same result was obtained with the same celerity. A style {name} Chih-tsang was then bestowed on him by the Emperor.[118]

In the eighth year of the T'ien-pao period [AD 749] he was permitted to return to his native country. When he arrived at Nan-hai-chün, having used five post-horses,[119] an imperial edict was issued to detain him again. In the twelfth year [AD 753], upon the request of the Military Governor-General of Ho [-hsi] and Lung [-yu] Ko-shu Han, the Emperor ordered him to go to Kansu. He arrived at Wu-wei in the thirteenth year [AD 754] and stayed in the K'ai-yuan Temple.[120] The Military Governor-General and his subordinates all wanted to receive abhiṣeka. Several thousand people of high and low degree attended the ceremony. Han-kuang and other disciples were also instructed in the method of the five divisions. The Commissioner of Religious Affairs and K'ai-fu, Li Yüan-tsung, was also taught the same method and the Vajradhātu maṇḍala. An earthquake occurred that day in the temple where the ceremony was held, and Amoghavajra said, "It is due to the concentration of the audience's faith!" In the fifteenth year [AD 756] he was ordered by the Emperor to return to the capital, where he stayed in the Ta-hsing-shan Temple.

During the early days of the Chih-te period [AD 756–57] the Emperor was in Ling-wu and Feng-hsiang [to prepare for the recapture of the two capitals]. Amoghavajra often presented memorials to him, inquiring after the Emperor's health, while in his turn Emperor Su-tsung secretly sent messengers asking for secret methods. When the capital was recaptured and the T'ang dynasty reestablished, the date was exactly as Amoghavajra had predicted.

During the Ch'ien-yüan period [AD 758–59], he was invited to the palace to perform the homa sacrifice, and then the Emperor received the abhiṣeka of a cakravartin possessing seven jewels.[121] Once at the end of the Shang-yuan period [AD 760–61] the Emperor was ill. Amoghavajra exorcised the evil spirits by reciting the Mahāpratisarā dhāraṇī seven times; and as a result the Emperor was well the next day and paid even more respect to him than before.

Amoghavajra asked for the Emperor's permission to go to the mountains. Li Fu-kuo conveyed orally the edict which ordered him to recite sūtras in the Chih-chu Temple in Mt. Chung-nan. One night when he was in the middle of his recitation, Mahāsukhasattva[122] was so moved that the deity's hair [between his eyebrows] stretched out and emitted a light. It was thus proved that Amoghavajra had ascended to the stage next to that of siddhi.[123] Amoghavajra said, "How can I seek my own release with the people still unsaved?" [So he put off his own release.]

After Emperor Su-tsung died, Emperor Tai-tsung succeeded to the throne and showed him even greater favor. When he had finished the translation of the Mi-yen-ching[124] and the Jên-wang-ching,[125] the Emperor wrote prefaces to them. On the very day when these texts were officially announced, auspicious clouds appeared unexpectedly in the sky. The ministers of the whole court expressed their congratulations. On the first day of the eleventh moon of the year Yung-t'ai [AD 765], he was promoted by an imperial edict to the rank of T'e-chin and the office of Probationary Director of the State Ceremonial. He was also given the title Ta-kuang-chih san-tsang.

In the third year of Ta-li [AD 768], a ceremony of Buddhist recitations was held in Hsing-shan Temple. The Emperor on that occasion presented him with twelve quilts of embroidered brocade and thirty-two embroidered gauze banners, and also provided meals for fourteen days for those monks who took part in the recitation. The eunuch attendants, the ministers, and the commanders of the imperial army were all ordered by the Emperor to go there for abhiṣeka. In the winter of the fourth year [AD 769], Amoghavajra asked the Emperor to issue an order that Mañjuśrī bodhisattva was to be worshipped as the guardian deity in the refectories of the temples all over the country. The request was granted. This was because Amoghavajra did not have high respect for Kauṇḍinya, who was an arhat. In the summer of the fifth year [AD 770], when a comet appeared, an imperial order was issued to invite Amoghavajra to Mt. Wu-t'ai to recite sūtras. After the religious ceremony was over, the comet vanished immediately. In the autumn, when Amoghavajra returned from Wu-t'ai, the Emperor sent a eunuch to welcome him outside of the city with a "lion-horse" curbed by the Emperor's own bridle and bit. Provisions for the journey were granted by the Emperor.

On the second day of the tenth moon of the sixth year [AD 771], which was the Emperor's birthday, Amoghavajra presented as gifts the sūtras which he had translated and a memorial saying: "I followed and attended the late Master of Tripiṭaka [i.e., Vajrabodhi] for fourteen years ever since my childhood, and was instructed in the doctrine of yoga. I also visited India where I sought for the doctrine that I had not been taught and I found sūtras and commentaries which amounted to five hundred–odd works. In the fifth year of T'ien-pao [AD 746] I returned to the capital. Emperor [Hsüan-tsung] ordered me to go to the palace and erect an altar for abhiṣeka. The Sanskrit sūtras which I brought back were all permitted to be translated. Emperor Su-tsung performed the homa sacrifice and abhiṣeka in the palace. The two emperors repeatedly ordered me to collect the Sanskrit texts [brought back] in the previous periods, to repair those pattra leaves of which the binding strings were lost, and to translate those texts which had not yet been translated. Your Majesty followed reverently your deceased father's intent in ordering me to continue translating and promulgating for the benefit of the people of all classes. From the T'ien-pao period up to the present, the sixth year of Ta-li, in all I have translated one hundred and twenty–odd chapters, seventy-seven works. In addition, the catalogue of names of monks and laymen who helped in composing the texts and the abridged manuals for recitation were all copied. As it happens to be Your Majesty's birthday, I reverently present them to you." An imperial edict was issued to allow those sūtras to be promulgated in the capital and the provinces, and they were also to be listed in the official catalogue of the Tripiṭaka. Li Hsien-ch'eng read the imperial edict granting Amoghavajra eight hundred rolls of brocade, colored cloth, and silk. The ten monks who helped him to translate sūtras were each granted thirty rolls. The monk Ch'ien-chen presented a memorial to express their gratitude. Other monks and lay disciples were rewarded with cloth in accordance with their merit.

Once because of drought in the capital during the spring and summer season, the Emperor ordered Amoghavajra to pray, saying: "If it rains within three days it will be due to your magic power. If it rains after three days, the credit will not be yours." Amoghavajra, having received this order, erected an altar [to perform the rite], and on the second day it rained heavily and sufficiently. The Emperor bestowed on him a purple gauze robe and one hundred rolls of miscellaneous colored cloth. Seven robes were granted to his disciples and a feast to feed one thousand monks was provided as a reward for his achievement.

Amoghavajra presented a memorial asking the Emperor to build a pavilion for Mañjuśrī [in the Hsing-shan Temple].[126] He obtained the imperial permission as well as contributions from [Tu-ku] kuei-fei, Prince of Han, and the Princess of Hua-yang. About thirty million ch'ien from the imperial treasury were donated.

Amoghavajra again translated the *Nieh-lu-t'u-wang ching*. Gifts were granted by the Emperor one after another and the messengers were busy on the streets. In the ninth year [AD 774], from spring to summer, he kept on promulgating the subtle dharma and encouraging his disciples. He talked frequently about the *Bhadracarī praṇidhāna* and the *Ch'u-shêng wu-pien fa-men ching*,[127] which he, praising and admiring, repeatedly advised his disciples to recite. To those who had previously been taught the doctrine, he told them particularly to pay attention to the following things: the contemplation on Bodhicitta, the chief deity's mudrā, the intuitive comprehension of the letter "a," and the realization of the *anutpāda* {nonorigination} of the dharmas.[128] [Then, according to Amoghavajra, they] would reach Mahā-bodhi. The disciples were told again and again in such a lucid way as if he were showing them everything in his palm.

One night he told his disciple Chao Ch'ien to bring him a brush and an ink-slab: "I will make an abridged version of the manual on nirvāṇa and cremation for posterity and my funeral ceremony should be held in compliance with it." Ch'ien knelt down and requested three times: "Will you be so merciful as to stay in this world forever? Otherwise whom should the people rely upon?" Amoghavajra simply smiled. Before long he became ill, whereupon he presented a memorial in which he bade farewell to the Emperor. Imperial messengers were sent to inquire after his health, and both physicians and medicines were sent from the Emperor. He was made K'ai-fu i-t'ung san-ssū and invested with the title of Duke of Su. Three thousand households were assigned as his fief.

Amoghavajra earnestly declined the honor, but [the Emperor] did not permit. Being quite displeased, he said: "The saints seem to have extended their hands to console me. When the white moon {i.e., new} is full, I shall go. Why should I steal more titles and positions when I am dying?"

Thereupon, through the eunuch Li Hsien-ch'eng, he presented to the Emperor as a token of farewell the five-fingered bell and vajra which were inherited from his deceased master, a silver plate, and rosaries made of seeds of the bodhi tree and crystal beads. On the fifteenth of the sixth moon, he bathed and shampooed in fragrant water and lay with his head toward the east and facing the north in the direction of the imperial residence. While making a great mudrā, he died in the midst of meditation at the age of seventy. His religious age was fifty. His disciple Hui-lang succeeded him as the master of abhiṣeka. There were several others who knew the dharma.

Having heard of his death, the Emperor put off his daily interview [with his ministers] for three days. He also appropriated silk, cloth, and miscellaneous fabrics, in addition to four hundred thousand ch'ien for the funeral ceremony, and two million–odd ch'ien for building a stūpa. The Commissioner of Religious Affairs, Li Yuan-tsung, was ordered to supervise the funeral ceremony.

Shortly before Amoghavajra's death, the monks in his temple dreamed that a precious balcony of a thousand jen had fallen down and the new pavilion for Mañjuśrī had become dilapidated. They also dreamed that a vajra had flown up to the sky. The pond at the rear of the Hsing-shan Temple dried up without any evident cause. Fruits were produced on the bamboos and the flowers in the gardens withered.

He was cremated on the sixth of the seventh moon. The Emperor sent the kao-p'in, Liu Hsien-ho, to make offerings to him at the temple. The official title Ssū-k'ung, and the posthumous title Ta-pien-chêng kuang-chih san-tsang were bestowed on him. When the fire of the pyre went out, several hundred grains of relics were found and eighty grains were presented to the Emperor. The bones of the crown of the head did not burn and on them there was a relic partly hidden and partly exposed. The Emperor ordered the erection of a separate stūpa in his own quarters.

Whatever Amoghavajra did benefited the world, but he showed superiority particularly in dhāraṇī. If we try to examine his stage of kṣanti,[129] we should fail to ascertain his rank. Emperor Hsüan-tsung previously had special respect for him. Once when a drought occurred, the Emperor ordered Amoghavajra to pray for rain. He said: "We may have rain after a certain date, but if we obtain it by force now, there will be a terrible storm." The Emperor then asked his Master Vajrabodhi to erect an altar to pray. Just as he had said, the wind and rain thus brought about would not stop. Some residential districts and markets were flooded; trees were uprooted or felled. An edict was immediately issued asking Amoghavajra to stop the storm. Amoghavajra kneaded five or six earthen [dolls in the shape of] old women {another version says "dragons"} which he scolded in Sanskrit in the court of the temple where water was accumulated. Soon it cleared up.

Hsüan-tsung once summoned the astrologer Lo Kung-yüan to have a tournament of magic power with Amoghavajra in the hall for casual affairs. Amoghavajra often turned his hand to scratch his back. Lo said, "May I lend you my backscratcher?" There was a piece of decorative rock in the hall then. Amoghavajra struck the backscratcher at the rock and smashed it into pieces. Lo tried several times to pick up the broken backscratcher but failed. To the Emperor, who was about to arise and get it, Amoghavajra said, "Third Master,[130] you don't have to get up. This is merely an image." Then he raised his hand to show Lo that the backscratcher, intact, was again in his hand.

In North Mang Mountain there appeared a great serpent which the woodcutters frequently saw. Its head, when turned up, was like a hill, and it usually inhaled the air with dew at night. Once when the serpent saw Amoghavajra, it spoke in human tongue: "I am a victim of my bad conduct. How could you save me? I often want to stir up the water in the river to destroy the city of Lo-yang for my own satisfaction." Amoghavajra taught it the Buddhist precepts and explained for it the doctrine of karma. Besides, he said: "You receive punishment because of your hatred of others, how can you now hate the people and kill them again? My power, however, is supreme. You ought to think of my words and then this body of a serpent will be abandoned." Later on the woodcutters saw the serpent dead in the valley and the evil smell spread out several li.

Whenever Amoghavajra was ordered by the Emperor to pray for rain, he had no particular rites. Only one embroidered seat was to be set. He would turn with his hands a wooden image of [a certain] deity a few inches tall, and then throw it while reciting a dhāraṇī. When it stood up on the seat itself, Amoghavajra would observe the corners of its mouth. As soon as its teeth were exposed and its eyes winked, it would rain.

During the period of T'ien-pao [AD 742–55] Tibet, Ta-shih [Arabia], and K'ang [Samarkand] sent armies to surround Hsi-liang-fu. The Emperor summoned Amoghavajra to the palace [to perform some rites], and the Emperor himself attended the ceremony. Amoghavajra, holding an incense-pot, recited the secret words from the *Jên-wang [Sūtra]* twice seven times. The Emperor then saw approximately five hundred divine soldiers appearing in the court. Being surprised, he questioned Amoghavajra. The latter said: "The son of Vaiśravaṇarāja is going to rescue An-hsi with his army. Please make offerings right now and send them away." On the twentieth day of the fourth moon, as one would have expected, the local government reported: "On the eleventh day of the second moon, about thirty li to the northwest of the city appeared giant divine soldiers among the clouds and mists. The sounds of drums and horns were heard as if mountains and earth were exploding or trembling. The barbarian troops were astonished and collapsed. In their camps gathered many golden-colored mice, which bit asunder the strings of their bows and cross-bows. {Vaiśravaṇarāja is often represented together with the mouse.} The pavilion above the northern gate of the wall was illuminated, and there stood the divine king staring angrily at the barbarian commanders who ran off pell mell." Having read the report, the Emperor thanked Amoghavajra. After that the Emperor ordered an image of this king to be placed in the pavilion above the city gates all over the country.

After Amoghavajra's death, all the autographed edicts of the three emperors were turned in [to be preserved] in the palace. Honored in his lifetime and lamented at his death, Amoghavajra was not rivaled in former or present times by any western monks who came to promulgate the dharma. It was Hui-lang who succeeded him. A stele of which the inscription was composed by the Censor General Yen Ying and inscribed by Hsu Hao was erected in his own quarters in the temple.

The author says: "Among those who promulgated the Wheel of Teaching and Command in China, Vajrabodhi is regarded as the first patriarch, Amoghavajra the second, and Hui-lang the third. From him on, the succession of patriarchs is known to everybody. As time went on minor schools were separated one from another and formed many different sects. They all claim to teach the great doctrine of Yoga. Though they are many in number, I wonder why so little effect has been shown. The development of this school can be compared to the myth that Yü-chia produced Ying-lung, Ying-lung in its turn produced the phoenix. From the phoenix onward only common birds are produced. How can we escape a change?"

Esoteric Buddhism in Korea

Henrik H. Sørensen

Introduction

IN RECENT YEARS the study of the esoteric and Tantric Buddhist tradition has become a very popular topic among Buddhologists and historians of religion around the world. In the case of Korea it is interesting to note that it is the growing interest in Tibetan Buddhism which has stimulated the inquiry into Korea's own esoteric Buddhist heritage. For some reason the study of esoteric Buddhism (Kor. *milgyo*) has lagged behind the study of other aspects of Korean Buddhism, which is otherwise a rather developed field within the humanities. However, from the mid-1970s scholarly works on Milgyo and related topics have increased sharply and as recently as 1986 a symposium with the title "Milgyo sasang ŭi Hanguk chŏk chŏngae" (The Development of Korean Esoteric Thought) was held at the Tongguk University in Seoul.[1]

Interest in Milgyo studies in Korea has concentrated on how it developed as a distinct denomination of Korean Buddhism on a par with the other Korean Buddhist schools, its importance within the larger tradition of Buddhism as national protector (Kor. *hoguk pulgyo*), the liturgical tradition with its rituals, its literature, and its presence as an undercurrent in both Koryŏ (936–1392) and Chosŏn (1392–1910) Buddhism. The study of Korean esoteric Buddhism has hitherto captured little interest among Western scholars, and we have even heard of scholars who claim that there is no such thing as esoteric Buddhism in Korea. However, this situation may well change in the near future as research in the field of Korean Buddhism is experiencing a steady expansion in both the United States and in Europe.

One of the major problems encountered in the study of Korean esoteric Buddhism is the lack of historical sources, something which is especially acute with regard to its presence and role during the early phase of Buddhism in the Three Kingdoms period (from the fourth century to 668) and in Unified Silla (668–936). As a matter of fact even for the first half of the Koryŏ dynasty it is hard to come by substantial and reliable material of a historical nature. Only when we come to the latter part of the Koryŏ do we have sufficient material at our disposal to establish a relatively complete historical stratification for the esoteric tradition based on both literary and material evidence.

That the problem of historical documentation for early Korean esoteric Buddhism is rather significant in contemporary Korean studies should not come as a surprise, since it is a common one for Korean Buddhist scholarship in general. It cannot be denied that our understanding of the historical development and impact of Buddhism in general during the Three Kingdoms period and to some extent under the Unified Silla has been severely hampered by the fact that the majority of Korean scholars working in the field have relied uncritically on such works as the *Samguk yusa* (The Memorabilia of the Three Kingdoms),[2] a compilation and adaptation of miscellaneous Buddhist tales, accounts, and scattered notes by the Koryŏ monk Iryŏn (1206–89), and the *Haedong kosŭng chŏn* (Lives of High Korean Monks),[3] compiled by the monk Kakhun (n.d.) in 1215, in their presentation of early Korean Buddhism.[4] To a lesser extent the *Samguk sagi* (The Historical Records of the Three Kingdoms)[5] has also been used as a primary source. Such an approach to the early history of Korean Buddhism has effectively muddled the perspectives of the study of the esoteric tradition and has resulted in a rather distorted picture of its historical development. The reason for the exaggerated importance with which the *Samguk yusa* has been credited in relation to early esoteric Buddhism is the fact that it is virtually the only literary source that mentions the first introduction of esoteric Buddhist practices from Tang China to Korea and also the only source which connects this with the names and activities of a number of monks whose names are not documented in the contemporary records. It goes without saying that unless the various strata which make up the *Samguk yusa* are properly identified and placed in a chronological and cultural context, the work should not be accepted as other than a thirteenth-century composition. This means that its contents should be used with caution and only in concert with primary material.

Furthermore there is a general tendency among contemporary Korean scholars to view the rise of the esoteric Buddhist tradition in Korea as isolated sectarian developments. The reason for this may lie in their more or less conscious attempt at constructing a Korean parallel to Japanese Shingon

Buddhism; however, this is not confirmed by the extant sources. On the contrary these indicate that esoteric Buddhism was an integrated part of the general makeup of Korean Buddhism across sectarian divisions from early on. In other words esoteric doctrines and practices were present within the structure of most Buddhist denominations and as such followed the same syncretic development that took place in China and Vietnam. There is also a tendency among Korean scholars to borrow from the doctrines of Shingon Buddhism in order to fill out gaps in their reconstruction of the history and doctrines of Korean esoteric Buddhism. Such an approach inevitably leads to misconceptions and distortions, since it conflicts with the literary evidence as well as with the different cultural and historical developments that took place in the two countries.[6]

The purpose of the present chapter is to establish a plausible historical framework for the esoteric Buddhist tradition in Korea, to show its characteristics and developments, and finally to give an idea of the literary material which the tradition has handed down to us.

Early Esoteric Buddhism on the Korean Peninsula

As to when esoteric Buddhism or rather esoteric practices were first introduced to Korea, we can only speculate. Buddhism is traditionally thought to have entered Korea in 372, and although this figure may or may not be correct we can safely assume that Buddhism was present on the Korean Peninsula by the end of the fourth century at the very latest.[7] It is common knowledge that esoteric teachings as known from contemporary Indian and Chinese sources normally formed a part of a number of canonical sūtras[8] including those belonging to the so-called dhāraṇī-sūtra class.[9] For Korea there is virtually no information to be had concerning the number and types of canonical Buddhist scriptures that were available in the country before the early seventh century, and even then it is not until well into the eighth century that a clearer picture of what the early Korean Tripiṭaka actually looked like emerges. Sūtras such as the *Saddharmapuṇḍarīka Sūtra*,[10] *Suvarṇaprabhāsa Sūtra*,[11] *Renwang banruoboluomi jing* (Prajñā-pāramitā Sūtra of the Benevolent Kings),[12] and the *Bhaiṣajyaguru Sūtra*[13] as well as a number of dhāraṇī-sūtras were among the earliest known scriptures with an esoteric content to be widely circulated in the Three Kingdoms.[14]

In terms of cultural material, archeological findings have revealed that the erection of stūpas was related to the doctrines of *hoguk pulgyo* in the early history of Korean Buddhism. Hence it seems highly plausible that the early practice of erecting stūpas was somehow connected with esoteric teachings, much as it was later on. In any case the existence of cults dedicated to the worship of the so-called eight classes of beings (Kor. *palbu ch'ŏnyŏng*), the Twelve Spirits of the Zodiac (Kor. *sipyi sin*), and *vajrapālas* (Kor. *kŭmgang*) are clearly indicated by the numerous reliefs found on stone stūpas from the seventh and eighth centuries.[15] Despite the material evidence for the prevalence of esoteric practices or rituals in Silla before the unification in conjunction with the *Bhaiṣajyaguru Sūtra* and the zodiac we still do not know how widespread they were, how they were practiced, or how they related to the rest of Korean Buddhism.

The *Samguk yusa* mentions an *Inwang toryang* (Benevolent Kings Bodhimaṇḍa) sponsored by the Silla King Sŏngdŏk (702–37), in which the *Jenwang jing* was employed. This may be yet another example of the use of esoteric Buddhism in connection with *hoguk pulgyo*, but as our information is based on the *Samguk yusa*, it should be seen as little more than an indication.[16]

After the unification of the realm by Silla in 668 esoteric Buddhist materials become more prevalent. Among the most important early items directly connected to esoteric Buddhism is the woodblock print of a dhāraṇī-sūtra, namely the scroll of the *Raśmivimalaviśuddhaprabha Dhāraṇī Sūtra*,[17] which was found in the Śākyamuni Stūpa (Sŏkka T'ap) in Pulguk Temple on the outskirts of the old Silla capital Kyŏngju in 1966. This woodblock print is dated to 751 and is considered the oldest extant woodblock printed sūtra in the world.[18] The presence of the copy of this dhāraṇī inside the stūpa is evidence of the belief in the divine protection of dhāraṇīs in conjunction with stūpa worship and is an important example of the functioning of esoteric Buddhism as a national protector in Unified Silla.[19]

It has been claimed by some Korean scholars that the creation of the Sŏkkuram, the artificial Buddhist cave sanctuary on Mt. T'oham above Pulguk Temple in Kyongju which was completed in 750, is a product of esoteric Buddhism.[20] However, the general outline of the shrine as well as its iconography do not distinctively signal an esoteric Buddhist affinity.[21] The only carving which may be said to be an esoteric figure, at least from the point of view of iconography, is the relief of the Eleven-Headed Ava-lokiteś-vara, Ekādaśamukha. The appearance of this form of the bodhisattva is in itself not sufficient proof that the cave shrine was inspired by esoteric

Buddhism, and in lieu of wanting historical sources we must consider it a bit farfetched to see Sŏkkuram as a monument of esoteric Buddhism.[22]

It is interesting to see that the few esoteric Buddhist texts of pure Korean origin from the early period were produced by great monks generally known for their great scholastic merits. Among these works are *Taesŏng taejip Chijang sip non kyŏngsŏ* (The Preface to the Mahāyāna Great Collection Kśitigarbha Ten Wheels Sūtra)[23] by Sinbang (n.d.), *Kŭmgwang myongch'wi sŭngwang kyŏng yakch'an* (An Outline of the Suvarṇaprabhāsa Sūtra)[24] attributed to Kyŏnghŭng (n.d.), the *Kŭmgwang myŏngch'wi sŭngwang kyŏngso* (Commentary to the Suvarṇaprabhāsa Sūtra)[25] by Sungjang (n.d.), and finally the *Yaksa ponwŏn kyŏng kochŏk* (The Record of the Old Methods [Pertaining to] the Sūtra of the Original Vows of Bhaiṣajyaguru)[26] by T'aehyŏn (fl. 8th cent.).[27] In addition a number of now lost works, thought to have contained esoteric Buddhist teachings and methods, are attributed to important Silla monks, among whom is Wŏnhyo (617–86), the great scholiast.[28]

Korean monks with affinity to the Chinese Tiantai school have been documented from relatively trustworthy Chinese sources, and it is not unlikely that they brought esoteric scriptures and practices of the Tiantai brand with them back from China.[29] However, the available sources are too scanty to yield anything substantial, and it is highly doubtful whether we shall be able to find new materials which may further our understanding in regard to this. In this regard we must conclude that there is a fair possibility that esoteric practices as they were cultivated by the followers of the Tiantai school during the late Sui and Tang dynasties are likely to have been known in Korea as well.[30]

According to the *Samguk yusa* there appeared during the reign of Queen Sŏndŏk (632–47) a monk by the name of Milbon (n.d.) who taught esoteric practices.[31] This master is credited with a number of miracles, mainly exorcistic in nature in connection with the use of a magic wand (possibly a vajra) and the recitation of the *Bhaiṣajyaguru Sūtra*. Consequently he has been considered one of the founders of Milgyo by the Koreans.[32] The account is what may be termed a stereotype of a thaumaturge and as such fits nicely with standard accounts of other high monks found in compilations of the *Gaoseng chuan* type. In order to give an idea of what constitutes the image of this particular esoteric wonder worker we shall give a full translation of the section in question as follows:

Queen Sŏndŏk [called] Tŏkman had become terminally ill. The monk Pŏpch'ŏk from Hŭngryŏn Temple was ordered to stop the disease but after [having tried for] a long time there was no result. At that time there was the Dharma master Milbon whose virtuous cultivation was known in the land and everywhere he was praised. The queen ordered that he be invited to enter the palace. [However, Mil-]Pon remained outside the royal palace, where he recited the *Bhaiṣajyaguru Sūtra*. Having recited the entire text he threw a wand with six rings into the [queen's] bedchamber where it penetrated an old fox and Pŏpch'ŏk. He [then] threw them into the courtyard, whereupon the queen's disease was cured. At that time there issued forth five-coloured spiritual rays from the top of Milbon's head and those who witnessed it were all astonished.[33]

The story of Milbon continues with an account of how he exorcises a horde of demons from the house of the Silla nobleman and thereby saves young Kim Yangdo. The perceptive reader will note that there is considerable resemblance with the *Sŏng gaoseng chuan*'s (The Sŏng History of High Monks)[34] account of the Indian esoteric master Vajrabodhi (669–741) curing the daughter of Tang emperor Xuan Zong (r. 712–56) and the account of Milbon curing Queen Sŏndŏk.[35] It would seem that Iryŏn had taken over the healing element from this account and used it in the Milbon story just as it appears in the section discussing Hyet'ŏng (n.d.), another esoteric master from Korea.

As it is, there are no Silla records of Milbon, no surviving scriptures that bear his name nor anything that a person with a realistic historical view can accept as factual. It is not utterly impossible that there could have been a monk with this name who functioned at the Silla court sometime before the middle of the seventh century, but beyond the mere name, there is nothing with which we can possibly substantiate him as a historical figure, much less gain an insight into his supposed esoteric teaching.

Hyet'ŏng is another Silla monk associated with esoteric practices. He also figures in the *Samguk yusa* only and therefore belongs together with Milbon to the transhistorical category of Korean Buddhist lore.[36] Hyet'ŏng is supposed to have traveled to Tang during the middle of the seventh century, where he is said to have cured the daughter of Emperor Gao Zong (649–83) by using dhāraṇīs.[37] Note again the similarity with the account of

Vajrabodhi as mentioned above. As is the case with Milbon there are no contemporary records, either Chinese or Korean, with which we may substantiate him as a historical figure.

Lastly the *Samguk yusa* contains a few passages on Myŏngnang (n.d.), also a practitioner of esoteric lore.[38] Like Hyet'ŏng, Myŏngnang went to China and later participated in Silla's struggle for independence from the Tang. He is credited with conjuring up a storm which capsized the invading Chinese fleet by employing a ritual involving the "Images of the Spirits of the Five Directions."[39]

Summing up the above it is obvious that the early history of esoteric Buddhism in Korea is rather sketchy. Beyond the archaeological material, which is itself meager at least from the period before the eighth century, there is in fact very little substantial material on which we may establish a historical development. If we choose not to dismiss the information from the *Samguk yusa* entirely but accept its tales as pointers, then we may tentatively consider that esoteric Buddhist practices became gradually popular on the Korean Peninsula from the seventh century onward.

The Transmission of the Zhenyan School to Korea

When it comes to Korean monks with connection to the Zhenyan tradition of Tang China descending from the three great patriarchs, Śubhakarasiṃha (637–735), Vajrabodhi, and Amoghavajra (706–74), we are on firmer ground. It is interesting to note that whereas there are no contemporary Korean records available on these monks, both the Chinese and Japanese sources document Korean monks among the disciples of the great masters of this tradition including Huiguo (?–805), a disciple of Amoghavajra and the teacher of the celebrated Japanese founder of the Shingon school, Kūkai (774–835), in addition to the dual transmission of the teachings and ritual procedures relating to the Garbhadhātu and Vajradhātu maṇḍalas.[40]

As regards the Zhenyan transmission to Korean monks, the *Liangdu da faxiang cheng shizi fufa ji* (The Record of the Great Dharmalakṣaṇa[41] Generations of Masters and Disciples Transmitting the Dharma in the Two Capitals),[42] from 834, records that Śubhakarasiṃha had a Korean disciple by the name of Hyŏnch'o (n.d.), to whom he transmitted the methods of the Garbhadhātu Maṇḍala.[43] Another Silla monk who is said to have studied under Śubhakarasiṃha was Yirim (n.d.). This monk is neither found in the Chinese nor in the Korean material but is referred to in the Japanese record *Naishō hossō ketsumiaku* (The Record of the Blood Line of the Inner Realization of the Dharmalakṣaṇa),[44] dated to 819. Here it is said that Yirim received the teachings of the Garbhadhātu maṇḍala (lit., Great Wheel) and subsequently spread the dharma, that is, the esoteric teachings in Silla.[45] It is interesting to note that Yirim also figures in the lineage of patriarchs presented in the picture scroll Kōsō zō (Images of the High Monks).[46]

The most important of Śubhakarasiṃha's Korean disciples, however, was Pulga Saui (n.d.).[47] The reason for his importance lies not so much in the position he may have had among the disciples of the Indian master but in the fact that he is the only Korean monk who has produced a substantial work that gives clear evidence of the doctrinal transmission of Zhenyan Buddhism to Silla. The work in question is the *Tae Piroch'anakyŏng kongyang ch'adung pŏp so* (The Outline of the Progressive Methods of Making Offerings [based on] the Mahāvairocana Sūtra), an extensive exposition in two chapters.[48] This lengthy work is a combination of a ritual manual and a commentary on the last five ritual sections (Ch. *pin*) of the sūtra in question. It contains quotations from the sūtra focusing on how to make offerings with mantras and hymns (Kor. *chisŏng*).[49] Some parts of the text are in the form of a dialogue between the author and an imaginary interlocutor. Furthermore, the text is important for its detailed interlinear comments on the meaning of the major mantras of the sūtra.[50] Details on Saui's activities in Korea are not known, except the name of the temple in which he is said to have dwelt.[51]

Vajrabodhi and later Amoghavajra are known to have had one Korean disciple in common, namely the celebrated pilgrim monk Hyech'o (fl. 8th cent.), who is famous for his journey to India. The Chinese records referring to Hyech'o's connection to the Zhenyan tradition are extremely brief and generally do not provide much more than his name.[52] However, we have two short works from his hands, the *Taesŏng yuga kŭmgang sŏnghae Munsusiri ch'ŏnbi ch'ŏnbal taegyo wang kyŏngsŏ* (Preface to the Mahāyāna-yogavajra Prakṛtisāgara Mañjuśri–Sahasra Bahusahasrapatra Mahātantra-rāja Sūtra)[53] and the *Ha Oknyŏ tamgi u p'yo* (Presenting the Jade Woman with a Fervent Prayer for Rain to Fall).[54] The preface does not provide us with further information on Hyech'o's connection to the Zhenyan tradition but simply affirms his affinity to Vajrabodhi. The second piece is a short tract in the form of a petition to the Jade Woman asking her to allow rain to fall. Both texts provide us with enough information to establish Hyech'o in the orthodox line of Zhenyan Buddhism. Finally we may add that his achievements as a disciple of Vajrabodhi and Amoghavajra in China and as the author of the *Hyech'o wang o Ch'ŏnch'uk kuk chŏn* (Hyech'o's Diary of a Pilgrimage to the Five Regions of India)[55] have tended to overshadow his importance for Buddhism in Korea as such.

The last great master in the orthodox Zhenyan transmission, Huiguo, is recorded to have had two Korean disciples: Hyeil (n.d.) and Ojin (n.d.).[56] Huiguo transmitted to Hyeil the methods relating to both the Vajradhātu and the Garbhadhātu maṇḍala in 781, and to Ojin he transmitted only the Garbhadhātu maṇḍala, which took place in 789.[57] Hyeil is stated to have returned to Silla upon the completion of his studies in Tang, whereas Ojin is said to have continued to India. None of these monks appear in the contemporary Korean records and at least in the latter case we can be fairly certain that Ojin never returned to Silla.

The last Silla monk with spiritual affinity to the Zhenyan school is one Kyŭnyang (n.d.). He is said to have been a second-generation disciple of Huiguo and a dharma brother of Haiyun (n.d.), the compiler of the *Liangdu da faxiang cheng shizi fufa ji*.[58] There are no other records on Kyŭnyang, and there is no way to know whether he remained in Tang or returned to Silla. He is also not mentioned in the contemporary Korean records.

More or less contemporaneous with Amoghavajra and his Korean disciples, Sŏn Buddhism (Ch. Ch'an) was starting to become popular in Unified Silla. Contemporary records tell us about the large numbers of Korean Sŏn pilgrims who went to Tang in search of an enlightened master.[59] One of the most prominent of these Korean Sŏn monks was Hyeso (774–850), who on his return to Silla settled in Mt. Chiri, where he founded the renowned Ssanggye Temple around 835.[60] Hyeso's epitaph, which is dated to 887, mentions that the master introduced the use of *pŏmp'ae*, ritualized chanting in Sanskrit in the liturgy, and that he used secret methods handed down by Śubhakarasiṃha as protection against wild animals.[61] Although the inscription is not clear as to which esoteric methods Hyeso employed, we must assume from the context that the secret methods referred to were various dhāraṇīs and mantras probably used as part of a larger ritual. Hyeso's esoteric Buddhist connection in China is not mentioned explicitly, but he probably came into contact with esoteric practices while studying in the famous Shaolin Temple in 810.[62] Mt. Song, where Shaolin was situated, had been a center of Ch'an Buddhism since the late Northern Wei (386–535), and we have documentation from the first half of the eighth century that esoteric Buddhism was cultivated by the Ch'an adepts there.[63]

Another tradition within Korean Sŏn postulates a connection between the cultural hero Tosŏn (827–97),[64] who is credited with introducing the *p'ungsu* system {feng shui, geomancy} and the founding of numerous temples based on the principles of this system. Tosŏn is said to have inherited the *p'ungsu* instructions from the Chinese esoteric master Yixing (673–727), who also imparted esoteric teachings to him.[65] Much of the written material on Tosŏn and his achievements is clearly fictitious and of a much later date, and I shall not go further into a discussion of that here except to note that at the time of the middle Koryŏ there was a widespread tradition linking Sŏn Buddhism of the late Unified Silla with esoteric practices.[66]

Esoteric Buddhism under the Koryŏ

One of the problems we encounter in working with esoteric Buddhism from the Koryŏ is the appearance of the name "Sinin school" (the Mudrā school) used to indicate a sect of esoteric Buddhism.[67] This sect is claimed by tradition to have been founded by Myŏngnang during the middle of the seventh century, but as we have previously pointed out the *Samguk yusa*, the main source for this tradition, is not reliable.[68] However, the *Samguk yusa*'s account of the establishment of this sect in Hyŏnsŏng Temple under King T'aejo (r. 918–43) of Koryŏ may have some truth in it.[69] For historical verification of the existence of this sect we shall have to turn to the *Koryŏ sa* (The History of the Koryŏ Dynasty),[70] which mentions esoteric rituals conducted in temples supposedly under the control of members from this denomination.[71] More will be said about these rituals in the following.

The other esoteric Buddhist sect the name of which appears in Koryŏ records is the Ch'ongji school, or Dhāraṇī school, which takes its name after its headquarters, the Ch'ongji Temple.[72] Again, the *Samguk yusa* presents us with a wholly fictitious line of transmission extending back to Hyet'ŏng, mentioned previously. The *Koryŏ sa* abounds in references to rituals conducted in temples belonging to this school, but none of these records predate the twelfth century.[73] It appears that several of the Ch'ongji monks achieved prominence during the later part of the dynasty.[74] Unfortunately detailed historical and doctrinal source materials are wanting. Neither the Sinin school nor the Ch'ongji school survived the Koryŏ dynasty as individual denominations, although Korean Buddhist rituals as such had been largely esotericized by the beginning of the fifteenth century. In 1407, when King T'aejong (1400–1418) of the Chosŏn dynasty effected the merging of all the Buddhist schools in the country into the two denominations, Sŏn and Kyo (doctrinal Buddhism), the Sinin school became part of the former while the Ch'ongji school became part of the latter.[75]

Having dealt briefly with these two esoteric denominations, about which we know very little, it would be in order to turn our attention to the esoteric Buddhist scriptures current in the Koryŏ dynasty. As is commonly known it was during the Koryŏ that the Koreans made a printed Tripiṭaka of their own, and, as we shall presently see, this event gave a considerable impetus to esoteric Buddhist practices. In 991 the Koreans were able to import a copy of the *Shu Tripiṭaka* from Song China, and in 1029 they began the carving of their own version of the Buddhist canon. The *Shu Tripiṭaka* introduced numerous hitherto unknown canonical and other scriptures to the Koreans, and part of this new material included a large amount of esoteric texts. During the following two centuries the Koreans were quick to collect whatever new translations and texts they could lay their hands on. Not only did they compile Chinese works but they also had access to works and translations produced in the states of Liao (907–1125) and Jin (1115–1234). The *Shinp'yŏn chejong kyojang ch'ongnok* (The Catalogue of the New Compilation of the Treasury of Teachings of All the Schools)[76] by Yich'ŏn (1055–1101), the founder of the reformed Korean Ch'ŏnt'ae school, testifies to the great zeal with which the Koreans compiled Buddhist scriptures. Incidentally there is some indication of esoteric practices within the confines of the Ch'ŏnt'ae school, but the exact nature of these practices beyond public rituals is not known. The restored *Koryŏ Tripiṭaka* from 1251 reveals that nearly all the late translations of esoteric Buddhist scriptures made by Dharmapāla (963–1058), Dānapāla (n.d.), and Dharmarakṣa (Ch. Hufa; n.d.) were available in Korea during that time. A large number of the so-called dhāraṇī-sūtras and other esoteric scriptures are known to have been employed during the Koryŏ mainly for rituals. However, the mere presence in the *Koryŏ Tripiṭaka* of texts relating to esoteric and tantric Buddhism does not necessarily indicate the study and practice of these scriptures and their doctrines, and for this we need additional documentation. In this context it is important to note that we have no evidence to show that the higher *yoga* and *anuttaratantras*[77] such as the *Guhyasāmaja Tantra*[78] and the *Śrivajramaṇḍalaṃkāramahā Tantrarāja*,[79] both of which are found in the *Koryŏ Tripiṭaka*, gained any real popularity. In any case they have left no lasting imprint on Korean Buddhism. In fact it is hard to come by any reference to the tantras as such in the Koryŏ material.

That esoteric Buddhism was an important aspect of Koryŏ Buddhism can hardly be denied. The sources tell us of numerous esoteric Buddhist rituals held by the court as part of its spiritual "defense" against the invasions from the Khitans, the Jürchen, and the Mongols, which swept the country at intervals throughout most of the dynasty. Thus, "hoguk pulgyo" was a persistent and important factor in the Koryŏ dynasty's fight for independence. This is also documented in the *Koryŏ sa*, where we learn that most of the ritual practices connected with the protection of the nation had esoteric Buddhist implications. Among the strictly esoteric Buddhist ceremonies sponsored by the court are rituals dedicated to the protectors Marīci, Mahāmayūrī Vidyarāja, Aparājita Vidyarāja, Avataka (Ch. Da Yuanshuai), and even to Yamāntaka.[80]

There has been some speculation on the influence of Tibetan Buddhism on Koryŏ Buddhism, especially during the Mongol occupation of Korea from 1251 to around the 1350s, when the Mongols started to lose control of the peninsula. It is known that Tibetan tantric rituals were practiced at the Koryŏ court during the late thirteenth and early fourteenth centuries, although few records are available to substantiate this. One interesting account found in the *Koryŏ sa*, and dating from the reign of King Chŭngyŏl (r. 1275–1308), tells about a Tibetan lama who practiced sexual rites, although covertly, and who later organized a large-scale tantric ritual in the royal palace in which a special three-dimensional *maṇḍala* with numerous deities made of dough was used.[81] Likewise in the reign of the following king it is recorded: "In King Chunghyŏn's first year (i.e., 1309) in the fifth month, the Tibetan Palapsa (Bakasi) and nineteen men arrived, and the king received them."[82] Whatever the case, Tibetan tantric practices appear to have been limited to the royal court. There is no direct evidence of its influence on Korean Buddhism as such, which in any case must have been relatively minor if not negligible.[83]

Late in the Koryŏ dynasty we find evidence of esoteric influence in the newly introduced Imje Sŏn (Ch. Linji Chan), the main school of Chinese Chan Buddhism. This took place via the relationship between the Indian Tantric master Dhyānabhadra (1236–1363),[84] who is known in Korea as Chigong, and Naong Hyegŭn (1320–76), who is one of the most important Korean Sŏn masters from the late Koryŏ.[85] The exact nature of this relationship and its doctrinal and practical implications await further research.

However, it is obvious from a cursory glance at the source material, which is relatively substantial, that there was an influence from late Indian Buddhism on Korean Sŏn through the transmission of certain esoteric practices and teachings.[86]

There are three esoteric works in the Tripiṭaka attributed to Dhyāna-bhadra, two of which are ritual texts related to the worship of Avalokiteśvara and a late translation of the Uṣṇīṣavijaya-dhāraṇī.[87] Naong wrote a few addresses in connection with water and land festivals (Kor. *suryŭk che*), eso-teric rituals which seek to liberate the ghosts of the dead that have not been able to find rebirth. These include the *Kuk haeng suryŭk chae kisi yŭkdo posŏl* (Address on the Six Gati at the Opening of the National Water and Land Fes-tival)[88] and a similar speech given in connection with another *suryŭk* ritual held in 1374 on the occasion of the death of King Kongmin (r. 1351–74).[89]

Esoteric Buddhism during the Chosŏn Dynasty

During the Chosŏn dynasty, Buddhism gradually lost its influence as the national creed due to the rise of Neo-Confucianism, which gained effec-tive political and social control in Korea in the course of the fifteenth cen-tury. The suppression of Buddhism did of course not happen overnight, and, especially during the early reigns of the dynasty, Buddhist masters with knowledge of esoteric lore functioned as royal preceptors (Kor. *wangsa*) as previously. By the late fifteenth century the anti-Buddhist movement had gained momentum and the Buddhist institutions were subjected to various restrictive measures in addition to the confiscation of much temple land.[90] Later, during the seventeenth century, monks and nuns and their temples were banned from the capital of Seoul.[91] Partly due to this situation Buddhism went back to the countryside and the moun-tains and in a sense can be said to have been prompted by external circum-stances to rid itself of some of the worst excesses from the Koryŏ.[92]

Despite the suppression and staunch opposition from the Confucian officials, the royal house and the Chosŏn government continued to support various projects relating to Buddhism, including the esoteric tradition. Thus we read in the official dynastic records (Kor. *shillok*) from the fifteenth century of several instances in which the state sponsored the publication of esoteric Buddhist works. We find in the *Sejong shillok* (Veritable Records of Sejong's Reign) an entry from the fifth year (1423) in which it is recorded that the entire collection of esoteric Buddhist scriptures from the canon were carved and printed together with the *Avataṃsaka Sūtra*.[93] From the sixth year there is a reference to the carving and printing of the esoteric *Mahāprajñā Sūtra*,[94] and again in the same year it is mentioned that the wooden blocks containing the esoteric Buddhist scriptures written in Siddham script as contained in the Tripiṭaka were printed and compiled into one section.[95]

Esoteric practices continued to thrive and may have attained an even higher status in general Buddhist practices than they had under the Koryŏ. Since the importance of esoteric Buddhism and its literature is relatively well documented from the early sixteenth century onward, our knowledge in this respect can be said to be rather comprehensive. We do not find any traces of the tantras in this material however. Esoteric literature from the Chosŏn period is characterized by original Korean compositions and only occasionally inspired by or directly based on Chinese models.[96]

The extent to which esoteric practices had penetrated Korean Buddhism during the Chosŏn can perhaps best be seen in the degree to which it influenced nearly all aspects of ritual practice and liturgy. In fact the majority of ritual texts from this period contain mudrās and mantras, and it is interesting to see how esoteric practices were combined with both Pure Land and Sŏn Buddhism. Sŏn was clearly the most dominant denomination of Chosŏn Buddhism, and we find esoteric practices in the writings of both Houng Pou (1510?–66)[97] and Chŏnghŏ Hyujŏng (1525–1604),[98] two of the great masters of that time. Pou's significant work *Suwŏl toryang konghwa pulsa yŏhwan pinju mongchung mundap* (Questions and Answers in a Dream between Guest and Host [concerning] the Imaginary Water-Moon Bodhimaṇḍa and Illusory Buddhist Affairs),[99] written in the form of a dialogue, discusses the integration and compatibility of Sŏn and esoteric practices. In this connection mention should also be made of Hyŭjŏng's works, a number of which deal specifically with esoteric practices. They are the *Sŏlsŏn ŭi* (The Ritual for Explaining Sŏn)[100] and the *Unsŭ tan* (The Cloud and Water Altar).[101] His most popular work, the *Sŏnga kwigam* (The Hand Mirror of the Sŏn Tradition),[102] contains an interesting passage which reads:

> As regards the practice of recitation of mantras, it is done because former karma is difficult to cut off, although present karma can be regulated through self-cultivation. For this reason it is necessary to avail oneself of their spiritual power (i.e., that of the mantras).

Comment: Mātaṅga's obtaining of the fruits [of cultivation] is true and not false. Those who do not recite the spiritual mantras will not be able to remove themselves from the affairs of Mara.[103]

Despite the fact that this is a quite unusual argument to hear from a master of Sŏn, it goes to show just how important esoteric practices had become in Korean Buddhism by Hyŭjŏng's time. The integration between esoteric practices and Sŏn/Ch'an can also be seen to have taken place in Ming China, where we find it prominently in the teachings of Hanshan Deqing (1546–1623), one of the great Buddhist masters of that time.[104] The proliferation of ritual works and manuals is perhaps the most significant aspect of esoteric Buddhism during the Chosŏn period and gives ample testimony to the importance of the tradition.[105] Our knowledge about Buddhist rituals in Koryŏ times is limited to those sponsored by the court, and very few texts are extant. Hence what we know does not provide us with sufficient information with which we may compare the situation during the Chosŏn period. It appears that the monks in nearly all the larger temples published their own textbooks on rituals such as that of feeding the ghosts in water and on land, cremation, supplication of the Ten Kings of the hells, etc. Furthermore, the period also saw the large compilations of the texts for the main ritual procedures and mantra manuals in vogue during the day. Most important among these ritual manuals are the *Chinon chip* (The Collection of Mantras),[106] the *Cheban mun* (The Zhipan Text),[107] a compilation from 1659,[108] the *Pŏmum chip* (The Collection of Sanskrit Sounds)[109] from 1709, and finally the *Chakbŏp kwigam* (Manual of Essential Ritual Procedures),[110] compiled in 1828, which has been the main ceremonial manual of Korean Buddhism since.

Esoteric Buddhism in Korea Today

That elements of esoteric practices are still alive in contemporary Korean Buddhism is evident in the rituals of most of the Buddhist denominations. In the case of the Chogye Order, the largest of the Korean Buddhist schools, esoteric elements such as the use of dhāraṇīs and prayers in connection with exorcism, cremation, and memorial services are still common. In addition, although its ritual meaning has been all but forgotten, Siddham script is still widely used as ornaments on altars and on ceilings in temple buildings and as topics for calligraphy, for example, in the form of the *Yukcha Mantra* (Six

Character Mantra, i.e., "Oṃ maṇī padme hūṃ").[111] Furthermore, such ritual manuals as *Sŏngmun ŭibŏm* (The Ritual Codex of Buddhism),[112] *Pulgyo pŏpyo kugam* (The Manual of the Essential Methods of Buddhism),[113] and *Pulgyo hŏngbŏm* (Extensive Manual of Buddhism)[114] currently in use in the Chogye Order contain much esoteric Buddhist material.

Although it was not formally established until 1970 the T'aego Order is in actual fact the real inheritor of the esoteric tradition in Korea.[115] This is evident in the elaborate rituals accompanied by the chanting of *pŏmp'ae* still practiced and transmitted by this Buddhist denomination. There are a number of ritual manuals which are unique to this tradition, and their contents mostly consist of dhāraṇīs and hymns, often in Hangul with the sounds based on transcribed Sanskrit. As with the Chogye Order, the *Sŏngmun ŭibŏm* is the major ritual manual employed. As such, the ceremonies of the T'aego Order appear to be the most living continuation of the thriving esoteric ritual tradition of the Chosŏn dynasty.[116]

Among the new Buddhist schools that arose in Korea after the Japanese occupation are two with a distinct esoteric program. The Chinon (Mantra) Sect, claiming the Silla monk Hyet'ŏng as its original founder, was established in 1948 by the monk Sŏn Haebong. This sect endeavors to restore what it believes was the original Milgyo of Unified Silla, but in fact it is a Korean version of contemporary Japanese Shingon Buddhism, although it does not follow quite the same ritual procedures and differs on minor doctrinal interpretations. The other esoteric school is the Chingak (True Enlightenment) school, which was founded by Sŏn Kyŭsang (d. 1963) in 1947 under the name Simin Pulgyo.[117] It claims Vairocana as its principal Buddha and teaches a mixture of esoteric doctrines largely based on Shingon Buddhism including the dual maṇḍalas of the Garbhadhātu and Vajradhātu and a revised form of its teaching on the elements. In many ways it bears the characteristics of a "new religion" in the sense that it greatly stresses the role of the founder and his highly personal interpretation of the Buddhist tradition.[118]

On the basis of the information that has been presented here we should now have a relatively clear overview of the contents and development of esoteric Buddhism in Korea. It should be clear that with the exception of a very brief period during the eighth to ninth centuries, when Korean monks connected to the orthodox Zhenyan school in Tang China taught in Silla, esoteric Buddhism did not exist as a distinct sectarian movement. On the contrary, esoteric Buddhism, which may have been present on the Peninsula very early, has been a steady and persistent undercurrent in Korean Buddhism and has occasionally surfaced to take on a leading or influential role within the various aspects of Korean Buddhism. With regard to ritual and liturgy it would seem that esoteric practices have dominated as far back as we are able to document these practices.

One aspect of Korean esoteric Buddhism, which I have briefly touched upon here is the possible connection between esoteric Buddhism and the rise of *p'ungsu*, the practice of geomancy. There are strong indications in the epigraphical source material from the late ninth century and slightly later that Korean *p'ungsu* of the late Silla was partly based on Chinese esoteric Buddhist teachings. I have not, however, gone into this question to any length. Another significant aspect of esoteric Buddhism not mentioned here is its direct and indirect influence on Korean linguistics and semantics. While it is difficult to trace this influence in the pre-Koryŏ and to some extent in the Koryŏ material, we have abundant sources from the Chosŏn period to show that the "science of words," that is, the lore of the dhāraṇī and mantra, played a significant role in the formulation and development of the Korean language.

Future research on the esoteric Buddhist tradition in Korea could take several directions, and I shall limit myself to indicating a few of them here. First, it would be a major task to work on the early esoteric Buddhist tradition in Korea, including Unified Silla, from a strictly historical point of view. A primary task would also be to account for the importance and prevalence of esoteric rituals during the Koryŏ dynasty. Another significant topic would be the study of esoteric beliefs and practices during the Chosŏn period with special emphasis on rituals. Another would be to investigate the nature and extent of esoteric teachings in Chosŏn and Chongt'ŏ (Pure Land) Buddhism during the Chosŏn, and yet another important task would be to account for the amount and typology of esoteric elements in traditional Korean Buddhist votive paintings, the so-called *t'aenghwa*.

On Esoteric Practices in Korean Sŏn Buddhism during the Chosŏn Period

HENRIK H. SØRENSEN

KOREAN BUDDHISM during the Chosŏn dynasty (1392–1910) has often been designated as an inferior and degenerated form of Buddhism, supposedly blemished by superstitious beliefs and practices. This popular description should undoubtedly be seen as a modern reflection of the massive Confucian abuse and social denigration to which the Buddhist religion was subjected during the greater part of the dynasty's reign of over five hundred years. In fact Buddhism was relatively vital during long periods of the Chosŏn during the sixteenth and seventeenth centuries, its most flourishing phase. Characteristic of Chosŏn Buddhism is its great penchant for syncretism among its various denominations, including their doctrines and practices. Furthermore, in the Buddhist literature from this period we also find evidence of a considerable interest in harmonization with Confucianism and the Daoist philosophy of the Lao-Zhuang type.[1]

In terms of Chosŏn Buddhist culture, its literature, art, and architecture is extremely rich, which testifies to a deep-rooted and multifaceted tradition. Especially in the field of literature, Buddhism was highly prolific and showed a far greater compatibility with secular learning and lore than was the case during the Koryŏ dynasty. It cannot be denied that Chosŏn Buddhism was considerably reduced from the Buddhism of the preceding dynasty in terms of diversity of practices, hermeneutics, philosophy, cultural developments, and economic strength. That it was much more than a degenerated and declining religion is abundantly clear from the extant materials.

The purpose of the present study is to throw light on a hitherto little-studied aspect of Sŏn Buddhism under the Chosŏn, at least outside Korea, namely, the presence and significance of esoteric Buddhist *(milgyo)* practices evident in Sŏn literature from that period.[2] The material investigated here consists mainly of the collected writings of famous monks, the so-called *chip* (collected writings) containing miscellaneous literary output, commonly including whole chapters of poetry, letters, individual doctrinal compositions, exhortations, and ritual writings composed by the Sŏn monk-author in question. The last of these, ritual writings, became extremely popular during the Chosŏn dynasty due to the increasing interest in liturgy and esoteric practices, and Buddhist ritual texts from this period amount to several dozen individual works.[3]

Sŏn and Esoteric Buddhism during the Late Koryŏ Dynasty

Before embarking on the designated theme of this presentation, it would seem in order to have a brief look at the relationship between esoteric Buddhism and Sŏn in the previous dynasty. The history of esoteric Buddhism during the Koryŏ is to a large extent shrouded in obscurity. It is known that there were two denominations of esoteric Buddhism, the Sinin school and the Ch'ongji school, which are mentioned in the sources from the middle of the Koryŏ.[4] However, apart from the traditional myths contained in the *Samguk yusa* (The History of the Three Kingdoms),[5] we have nothing solid as to their origin or historical transmission.[6]

The teachings and practices connected with the Ch'ongji school and the Sinin school are largely liturgic in nature and were mainly based on the use of mantras, dhāraṇīs, and mudrās in connection with elaborate rituals.[7] Most probably the Chinese translations of Indian esoteric scriptures by Amoghavajra (705–74) and others served as the core of the Ch'ongji school's spiritual inheritance. If this assumption is correct, it may indicate that it was modeled on a late Tang form of Zhenyan Buddhism, which is likely to have been augmented by the "new" esoteric material translated during the early Song, and eventually brought to Koryŏ prior to the carving of the first Korean Tripiṭaka.[8] The importance of the Ch'ongji and the Sinin schools during the Koryŏ can be inferred on the basis of the rather voluminous esoteric material, which we have from the beginning of the Chosŏn period, as well as information contained in the *Koryŏ sa* (History of the Koryŏ Dynasty).[9] However, it remains a fact that there are very few primary sources with sufficient information available for us to establish a proper historical context for both of these esoteric Buddhist denominations.[10]

Sŏn Buddhism of the late Koryŏ was dominated by monks such as Naong Hyegŭn (1320–76),[11] T'aego Poŭ (1301–82), and Paekun Kyŏnghan (fl. 14th cent.), all of whom taught in accordance with orthodox Linji Chan (Kor. Imje Sŏn) imported from Yuan China during the first half of the fourteenth century.[12] In China there had been very little if any connection between that school and esoteric Buddhism; however, in Korea the development appears to have taken a somewhat different turn. In the writings of either T'aego or Paekun there is virtually no evidence of esoteric elements; in the case of Naong, however, a few pieces among his writings are of interest in the present context.

Like the two other Sŏn masters, Naong had journeyed to Yuan, where he arrived in 1348. While in Dadu (Beijing), Naong became acquainted with the Indian monk Dhyānabhadra (Chigong; 1236–1363) who was a master of Tantric Buddhist lore and practices.[13] Having traveled about for some time, he went to study under the Ch'an Master Fulong Qianyan (1284–1357),[14] from whom he eventually received transmission. Later he lived in the Guangji Temple in Dadu and is said to have had an audience with the Yuan emperor Temür (Shun; r. 1333–42).[15] Despite Naong's Sŏn affiliation it is abundantly clear from his own statements that he foremostly considered himself a disciple of Dhyānabhadra and that he received instructions from this Indian master in esoteric Buddhism. After Dhyānabhadra died in Dadu in 1363, some of his relics were brought to Korea, where Naong had them enshrined in a stūpa at Hoeam Temple.[16]

According to Dhyānabhadra's stele inscription, the *Sŏch'ŏn Chenambakt'a chonja pudo myŏng* (The Pudo Inscription of the Indian Ven. Dhyānabhadra),[17] which is composed in the form of an autobiography, we learn that he was well versed in the *vinaya*, the teachings of *prajñā* (this probably should be taken as indicating madhyamaka), and that he mastered a whole range of esoteric teachings including various dhāranīs.[18] However, he was clearly opposed to the practice of sexual yoga (Skt. *karmamudrā*), which he considered a perversion.[19]

There are two short translations, or rather transcriptions, of esoteric Sanskrit Buddhist texts into Chinese, from Dhyānabhadra's hand. The texts in question are the popular *Nilakanthaka Dhāranī* and an appendix entitled *Kwanseŭm posal sisik* (Offering Food to Avalokiteśvara Bodhisattva), both of which consist entirely of dhāranīs in transliterated Sanskrit.[20] The extent of Dhyānabhadra's influence on Naong's Sŏn can only be guessed at, since few real esoteric elements show up in the latter's teachings. Despite this, it is highly likely that Naong was familiar with esoteric practices and that he may have employed them in the various ritual contexts over which he presided. It is known that Naong wrote a few addresses on esoteric rituals of the *suryŭk che* type (water and land rituals), which are performed in order to seek the liberation of the ghosts of the dead that have not been able to be reborn. Rituals of this type require a complex esoteric procedure in which altars, mantras, invocations, and offerings are extensively used. Among these are the *Kuk haeng suryuk chae kisi yukdo posŏl* (Address on the Six Gati at the Opening of the National Water and Land Festival)[21] and a similar speech given in connection with another water and land ritual held in 1374 on the occasion of the death of King Kongmin (r. 1351–74).[22]

Naong's successor, the Royal Preceptor Muhak (1327–1405),[23] who also studied under Dhyānabhadra and became a trusted advisor to the first Chosŏn King T'aejo (r. 1392–98), appears to have shown some interest in esoteric practices, but as no written works have come down from him, the nature of his teachings remains largely obscure.[24] Despite this lack of sources throwing light on the extent of esoteric Buddhist practices in late Koryŏ Sŏn, Dhyānabhadra certainly must be considered a key figure in this development, a position that he retained throughout the rest of the dynasty within the school of Sŏn.[25]

The Merger of Esoteric Buddhism and Sŏn during the Early Part of the Chosŏn Dynasty

A significant aspect of the early Yi kings' efforts to control Buddhism were the decrees concerning the merger of the various Buddhist schools which had come down from the Koryŏ.[26] At the time of the founding of the Chosŏn dynasty Korean Buddhism consisted of twelve schools: the Chogye school (which in effect was divided into two distinct traditions—the Susŏn Temple tradition from Chinul (1158–1210) and the Imje tradition introduced to Korea from Yuan China during the fourteenth century, as mentioned above),[27] the Ch'ŏnt'ae school,[28] the Ch'ongji school, the Pŏpsa school,[29] the Sŏja school,[30] the Hwaŏm school,[31] the Tomun school,[32] the Chungdo school,[33] the Chaŭn school,[34] the Sinin school, the Sihŭng school,[35] and the Namsan school.[36] According to the decree formulated by King Taejong (r. 1401–18)[37] and his ministers, these Buddhist schools were ordered to merge into seven denominations in 1407 (on the second day in the twelfth month of the seventh year during the reign of King Taejong). The seven schools were the Chogye school, the Ch'ŏnt'ae school, the Hwaŏm school, the Chaŭn school, the Chungsin school,[38] the Ch'ongnam school,[39] and the Sihŭng school.[40] While the merger had a far-reaching impact on the subsequent development of Korean Buddhist doctrines and practice, the major reasons behind the king's decree should be seen as an attempt at gaining economic and administrative control of the Buddhist sangha including its extensive temple lands.

In 1424 (the sixth year of King Sejong's reign) the Ch'ŏnt'ae school, the esoteric Ch'ongnam school, and the Chogye school were merged into the school of Sŏn under the general aegis of Sŏn Buddhism. The other schools of doctrinal Buddhism—the Chungsin school, the Hwaŏm school, the Chaŭn school, and the Sihŭng school—were merged into the school of Kyo dominated by Hwaŏm Buddhism.[41] For Sŏn Buddhism, which at that time was more or less dominated by orthodox Imje Sŏn, with its stress on sudden enlightenment according to the so-called Patriarch Sŏn, this meant an unavoidable reversal to a form of Sŏn integrated with doctrinal Buddhism much like that which had been expounded by Chinul during the early thirteenth century.[42] It is difficult to establish to what degree the Ch'ŏnt'ae teachings influenced the practice of Sŏn at that time,[43] but as we shall see below, it remains a fact that practices related to both esoteric Buddhism and the Pure Land tradition would eventually become pervasive influences on Korean Sŏn. The esoteric element which begins to show up in Sŏn Buddhist writings from the thirteenth century onward undoubtedly reflects the influence of the integration with the Ch'ongji school, which, as we have seen, was one of the two esoteric schools of the Koryŏ dynasty. As time wore on the contact between the schools of Sŏn and Kyo became quite intimate, and it is more than likely that the practices of the Chungsin school gradually became accepted in the Sŏn tradition as well. In any case, I find little reason to doubt that both of the esoteric denominations were relatively vital by the time of the mergers during the first three decades of the fifteenth century. That esoteric ritual practices would become a prominent aspect of this syncretic form of Korean Buddhism from the early fifteenth century onward is fully documented by the extant sources.[44]

Esoteric Buddhism in the Teachings of Hŏ ung Pou

Among the important Buddhist masters of the early part of the Chosŏn dynasty we find Hŏ ung Pou (1510?–66),[45] who was a leading figure in the short-lived Buddhist restoration during the reign of Queen Dowager

Munjŏng (?–1565).⁴⁶ Strictly speaking, Pou was not a master of Sŏn in any of the recognized lines, but a disciple of an obscure master who resided in Yŏngmun Temple in Yangju, Kyŏnggi province.⁴⁷ Later in life Pou rose to become a leader within the school of Sŏn due to his great personal charisma, deep insight, and close connection to the queen. He actively advocated the harmonization of Sŏn and Kyo, as well as that of Buddhism and Confucianism.⁴⁸ Pou was responsible for reestablishing the Buddhist examination system *(sunggwa sŏnsi)*, which had been defunct since the early days of the dynasty. While this system lasted, it benefited many of the great Buddhist masters who rose to prominence during the latter half of the sixteenth century.⁴⁹ Pou's main residence was the Pŏngun Temple, situated to the east of the capital in Kyonggi province, and it was here that he composed the majority of his works and poetry.⁵⁰ His extant writings, relatively numerous, are represented by the *Hŏung tang chip* (The Collected Writings of Master Hŏung),⁵¹ the *Nanam chapchŏ* (The Miscellaneous Writings of Nanam),⁵² the *Kwŏnyyŏm yorok* (Essential Record of Encouragement to [Practice] Invocation [of the Buddha]),⁵³ and the important *Suwŏl toryang konghwa pulsa yŏhwan binju mongchung mundap* (Questions and Answers in a Dream between Guest and Host Concerning the Imaginary Water-Moon Bodhimaṇḍa and Illusory Buddhist Affairs).⁵⁴

Scattered throughout Pou's writings we find evidence of esoteric Buddhism, mainly in the form of dhāraṇīs and mantras. Due to the leading role he played as royal advisor to Queen Dowager Munjŏng during her fifteen years in power, he had to preside over a number of important ceremonies and wrote the texts for the ritual proceedings of two *suryuk* rituals dedicated to the two former kings Chungjong (r. 1506–44) and Injong (r. 1544–45) respectively.⁵⁵ There is extensive use of mantras evident in the accompanying ritual text. However, Pou also wrote smaller occasional tracts and addresses for a variety of ceremonial occurrences such as "eye-opening" rituals (*kaegwang,* lit., "opening the light") for the inauguration of Buddhist images and paintings, the carving of scriptures, and so on, all of which involved elements of esoteric lore and practice.⁵⁶

The most clear-cut example of esoteric practice within the general teaching of Pou is, however, found in the above-mentioned *Suwŏl toryang konghwa pulsa yŏhwan binju mongchung mundap.* This work, which is written in the form of a dialogue with an imagined questioner, is basically a discussion of the true meaning and value of Buddhist rituals. In some places of the text there is a certain feeling of Buddhist apologetics, and even though the dialogue is artificial, we may partly see it as an indication that Buddhist ritual practices were being condemned, probably by the Confucian officials in the government. The holding of large communal ceremonies was especially criticized as an expression of superstition and for being a costly drain on the local economy. It should be remembered that Pou was one of the primary leaders of the Buddhist revival under Queen Munjŏng, and that it was necessary for him to defend the position of Buddhism against the antagonistic Confucian bureaucrats.

In the course of his explanation Pou integrates the basic Sŏn Buddhist doctrines on nondualism and the mind with esoteric practice. While the basic trend of this work is wholly Sŏn in that it stresses the undivided mind of the adept, it is in fact a highly conscious attempt at extending this vision to include the realm of liturgical practice in both theory and practice. As we shall presently see, this work treats a wide range of topics related to esoteric lore, including the establishing of an altar, extensive use of mantras, and *bījas* {literally "seeds," referring to usually single syllable mantras considered to be the condensed form of a deity's power} written with Siddham script.

From the very beginning of the *Suwŏl toryang konghwa pulsa yŏhwan binju mongchung mundap*, Pou sets out to place Buddhist rituals and the use of mantras within the accepted realm of Sŏn. The opening section reads:

> In an imaginary location among the white clouds there is a guest. One day he asked the Mindless Man of the Way in Mt. Dharma Nature, saying: "I have heard that commoners arrange maigre feasts *(chae)* when worshipping the Buddha. As a further mystery they rely on mantras, which certainly is far from abiding by the complete vision *(wŏngwan)*.[57] Is it so?" The Man of the Way said: "It is so! Those of the four classes of *danapati* with very sincere minds establish dharma assemblies, and create bodhimaṇḍas *(toryang)*, noble and pure. They make altars precious and clean (lit., white). With incense, flowers, lamps, and candles they join in the arrangements. Tea, fruit, and rare foods they arrange in order, including the thousand pendant silken streamers. The multitude of immortal music is arranged on the side. A hundred thousand kinds of music, and limitless, wonderful offerings, nothing which cannot be imagined, widely and orderly arranged. If this is not the complete vision,

how can it carry out the ten thousand dharmas and yet illumine the One Mind? [How can it] abide in one thing, and yet manifest the multitude of principles? Through the offerings it transforms the few and changes the many, and with nothing it makes something, causing the impure to become pure. This mind-dharma is unobstructed, phenomena *(sa)* and principle *(ri)* are completely fused, large and small are harmonized, existence and nonexistence are not two, and the impure and the pure have the same essence. Do not think that the great assemblies are [just] superior feasts, but participate in them from this day on. For this reason it is necessary to rely on the complete vision so that you will be able to adorn the worldly truth (i.e., the relative plane) and [thereby] complete the offerings of the wonderful dharma."[58]

Further on in the text, Pou turns to a discussion of Buddha nature *(Pulsŏng)* or Buddha mind as the origin and foundation for all phenomena. The text further reads: "Now, as regards the One Mind *(ilsim)*, it is the wondrous essence of the ten thousand phenomena. The ten thousand phenomena are the spiritual activity of the One Mind. Outside the mind there are no phenomena, and outside phenomena there is no mind, hence mind is phenomena, and phenomena are mind. Essence and function are completely fused. Since the Mind Mirror is without obstruction, the spiritual activity of the three wisdoms *(samban)* accords with the complete vision of the One Mind."[59] Here the most noteworthy passage is that which makes a full identification between mind and phenomena. In effect this means that the physical appearances are actually made of "mind-stuff," that is, insubstantiality. Somehow this takes the basic Yogācāra tenet of "mind only" to its logical extreme, and beyond its original meaning. However, to a Korean Buddhist of the sixteenth century it is precisely such a doctrinal reduction, no matter how simplistic, which makes the identification between the mind cultivation of Sŏn and ritual practices compatible.

The text goes on to say:

The mind-dharma is nondual, wondrously transforming, and eternal, and therefore, it cannot be grasped by the intellect. Then

one-pointedly hold and intone the dhāraṇī called "Limitless
Majestic Virtue, Self-so Brilliance and Victorious Wonder and
Strength," which our Buddha taught.[60] What are the three
virtues that this one food-transforming mantra commands? As
regards the "Limitless Majestic Virtue, Self-so" it is the liberating virtue. "Brilliance" is the virtue of *prajñā*, and as for "Victorious Wonder," it is the virtue of the Dharmakāya concerning
"Strength," it is the strength and function of these three virtues.
Dhāraṇī means to control and hold *(ch'ongji)*. The controlling
and holding of the three virtues simply rests in the One Mind.
The three virtues of the One Mind, the dharma, and Complete
Wonder *(wŏnmyŏ)* do not have a different essence. Hence the
mind is the mantra, and the mantra is the food.[61]

Following the same logical reduction as we saw above, Pou explains how
the practitioner's undivided mind and the mantras he intones are not something apart from it. Hence his mind and the mantras are not only unified
through the sharing of the same essence, they are actually identical! In this
way Pou succeeded in establishing a doctrinal justification for the combination of Sŏn soteriology and esoteric Buddhist practices. As such it is
undoubtedly one of the most obvious examples of the degree to which the
integration between Sŏn and esoteric practices was achieved during the
Chosŏn period.

It is probably correct to say that esoteric Buddhism was not a major feature in Hŏung Pou's teachings, but its presence can nevertheless be felt in
much of his writings. Hence, we may conclude that during his time esoteric practices were in the process of becoming fully absorbed into Sŏn
Buddhism to such a degree that they were no longer seen as a foreign element. This development of course reflects the general harmonization and
compatibility which was achieved between the doctrines and practices of
both Sŏn and Kyo during the Chosŏn period, a feature that, as we shall see
below, was further strengthened toward the end of the dynasty.

Hyūjŏng and Esoteric Buddhism

Chŏnghŏ Hyūjŏng (1520–1604), better known as Sŏsan Taesa, and one of the
most highly venerated Sŏn monks in the history of Korean Buddhism, was
also a master of esoteric practice and liturgy. This aspect of his personality

is normally not so well known, and has in any case received little attention hitherto.[62] One possible reason for this neglect may be the traditional
high status he has enjoyed, and still enjoys, as a leading figure in the Sŏn
tradition. However, by taking a closer look at his writings, it soon becomes
obvious that he was not a Sŏn master in a narrow sectarian sense of the word,
but encompassed both esoteric and Pure Land practices in his career as well.

Hyŭjŏng's interest in esoteric practices even shows up in his most important Sŏn work, the *Sŏnga kugam* (The Magical Mirror of the Sŏn Family),[63]
where we find the following statement regarding the necessity of using
mantras.

> [The reason why] we recite mantras is although
> present karma can be regulated and avoided through
> self-cultivation, former karma is difficult to cut
> off. Therefore it is necessary to avail oneself
> of spiritual power.

> Commentary: Mātaṅga obtaining the fruits [of
> her cultivation of mantras] is true and not false.
> Those who do not recite spiritual mantras
> will not be able to remove themselves
> from the affairs of Māra.[64]

Here Hyŭjŏng gives a standard explanation based on the traditional
Buddhist view of karma as to why mantras are indispensable tools. The
individual patterns of karma accumulated by sentient beings over many
lives are so deeply ingrained that even self-cultivation in the present life is
likely to fail in rooting out the retribution. Hence, the practitioner of Sŏn
will need the divine assistance that the mantras are said to generate in order
to overcome the obstacles from previous karma.

The reference to the girl Mātaṅga in the commentary relates to the celebrated passage found in the *Dafoding rulai miyin xiu chengliao yi zhu pusa
wanxing shoulengyan jing* (Śūraṅgama Sūtra),[65] where Śākyamuni Buddha
saves his disciple Ānanda from the clutches of the harlot Mātaṅga, who had
employed a dhāraṇī with which to ensnare him.[66]

Elsewhere in the *Sŏnga kugam*, Hyŭjŏng goes into detail regarding the
use of a certain class of mantras. It is found in a rather curious section on
personal hygiene which mainly deals with the correct behavior of a monk

while in the communal latrine. Although the practical aspects such as washing one's hands are dealt with, it is obvious that the metaphysical purification is even more important. To this end Hyŭjŏng recommends the use of a set of five mantras for purification and for control over various evil powers traditionally thought to dwell in latrines. The text reads:

... Upon entering the latrine one should first snap
one's fingers three times in order to warn the demons,
who dwell in the filth. Silently intone each of the
[following] spiritual mantras seven times. First
intone the Mantra for Entering the Latrine:
Om hanro taa sabaha.[67]

Thereupon [one should intone] the Mantra of Purification:
Om hana mirite sabaha.

Holding the [water] pitcher with the right hand [one should use]
the nameless finger of the left hand to wash oneself.
This is called true purification. After this one intones
the Mantra for Purifying the Hand:
Om chuga raya sabaha.

And then one intones the Mantra for Getting Rid of Filth:
Om siri ya pahyŏ sabaha.

Following this one intones the Mantra of the Pure Body:
Om paje ranoa kadak sabaha.

These five spiritual mantras possess a great majestic
power (dŏk), and upon hearing [them] all evil
demons and spirits will certainly pay their respects
with palms brought together (Skt. añjali).[68]

For some unknown reason this interesting section has been discarded from all modern editions of the Sŏnga kugam, probably because it appears funny or perhaps even embarrassing to contemporary Korean Buddhists. However, it is important because it sheds light on old patterns of belief and behavior within the Buddhist sangha in traditional Korea.[69] Another reason may be that contemporary Korean Buddhists have a problem understanding how Hyŭjŏng, an enlightened Sŏn master and cultural hero, could teach such seemingly strange beliefs. In any case, it remains a fact that belief in evil spirits was an integral part of the life and customs of people under the Chosŏn, and that the communal latrine was considered a particularly unclean place for more than one reason. In the Buddhist vinaya traditionally followed in East Asia there are numerous rules on behavioral patterns of conduct for monks and nuns in connection with the easing of nature. Even in the writings of the celebrated Japanese Sōtō Zen master Dōgen (1200–1253) we find descriptions, down to pedantic details, on how to wash the hands repeatedly with various substances after having eased one's nature, etc.[70] However, as we have seen above, in Korean Sŏn temples in Hyŭjŏng's time a modified form of the traditional vinaya rules on how to deal with hygienic details in the latrine was taught. Interestingly, in the Sŏnga kugam, Hyŭjŏng is actually quoting verbatim from a Chinese text, the Deng si guishi (The Regulations for Entering the Latrine),[71] as contained in the Chan manual Zimen jingxun (Admonitions for the Black-Robed Fellows).[72] Hence we find that in early Ming China, the traditional regulations of the vinaya had been supplanted by a mixture of esoteric practices, folk customs, and beliefs concerning toilets, combined with the ever-prevailing fear of ghosts, which had become accepted within Chan Buddhism. Eventually these beliefs were introduced to Chosŏn, undoubtedly in conjunction with the Zimen jingxun, and there accepted as an integral part of the general Korean Buddhist makeup.

Among the other works authored by Hyŭjŏng that show direct evidence of esoteric practice and beliefs, the Sŏlsŏn (The Ritual for Explaining Sŏn)[73] and the Unsŭ tan (The Cloud and Water Altar),[74] which are both liturgical works, contain numerous mantras as an integral part of their respective ceremonial proceedings. The ritual of the Sŏlsŏn is a distinct Sŏn Buddhist ceremony carried out in order to commemorate the "Holding of the Flower," the wordless teaching said to have been given by Śākyamuni Buddha to his senior disciple Mahākaśyapa, a scenario which has traditionally been considered the origin of "the transmission of the mind," that is, the very foundation of Sŏn orthodoxy.[75] The ritual set forth in the latter text is in the form of a more general Buddhist ceremony including the invocation of the triratna (the "three jewels": buddha, dharma, and sangha), all the buddhas and bodhisattvas of the ten directions, the Sŏn patriarchs, offering of food, feeding the pretas (hungry ghosts), and so forth, as well as a section on repentance *(ch'amhui)*. The ritual of the *Unsŭ tan* was meant to be held as a sangha ceremonial event, and each of its sections contains mantras to go along with the prayers.[76] Common to both rituals are the establishment of a special altar used as the focus of the spiritual power invoked. The extent of Hyŭjŏng's esoteric practice even included the worship of the seven stars of the Great Dipper *(paekdu ch'il sŏng)*,[77] a practice normally carried out as a means of attaining worldly blessings and the prolongation of one's life span.[78]

Despite his reputation as a leading master of Sŏn, Hyŭjŏng nevertheless was considerably influenced by esoteric Buddhist practices and lore. And as we have seen, his interest in liturgy and the use of mantras and dhāraṇīs made him a rather active author as well as a compiler of ritual manuals. In fact, Hyŭjŏng's liturgic manuals were to have a continuous influence on the subsequent development of ritual and esoteric practices within Korean Sŏn, an influence which was felt well into the present century. Hence, in his role as preserver and transmitter of these esoteric practices, he may also be considered a major figure in the later phase of esoteric Buddhism in Korea.

Esoteric Buddhism and Sŏn during the Late Chosŏn

By the beginning of the seventeenth century the distinctions between the two schools of Sŏn and Kyo had become so blurred that it was no longer possible to distinguish one from the other. Many Sŏn monks took a great interest in the doctrinal aspects of Buddhism, and especially in the teachings related to the Pure Land and Hwaŏm, which greatly influenced the Sŏn community. Monks affiliated with the school of Kyo also practiced meditation and studied Sŏn doctrinal and historical works. As a natural consequence of this development, esoteric Buddhist practices, especially those connected with communal rituals, were no longer seen as something apart from Sŏn.

Examples of esoteric practice in the teachings of Hyŭjŏng's first-generation disciples and their successors are relatively frequent, and we no longer encounter writings that attempt to justify their presence within Sŏn. Samyŏng Yujŏng (1544–1610),[79] who is usually considered the foremost of Hyŭjŏng's successors, authored a short prayer to accompany an esoteric ritual, the *Mita chos ŏng chŏman so* (Prayer for Completing [a statue of] Amitābha and Painting the Pupils).[80] P'yunyang Onggi (1581–1644),[81] one of Hyŭjŏng's youngest disciples, wrote a couple of occasional prayer forms, including the *Suryuk so* (Prayer for the Water and Land Ceremony)[82] and the *Sip wang so* (Prayer for the Ten Kings [of the Hells]).[83] Both of these prayers are for rituals which use mantras and mudrās. Kiam Pŏpgyŏn (fl. 17th cent.)[84] composed several prayers and addresses for esoteric ceremonies, such as two different pieces both entitled *Saengjŏn yesu so* (Prayer for Arrangements before Rebirth),[85] *Sŏngsu ch'ŏ nch'o so* (Thanksgiving Prayer to the Constellations in Heaven),[86] an occasional text for a water and land ritual, and the *Yŭryŭng sa pogwang chon kige kaech'uk nak sŏng suryuk kwŏsŏn mun* (Text for the Inducement of Goodness [in the form of] a Water and Land [ritual] on the Completion of the Foundation Stones of the Yuryung Temple's Universal Light Hall).[87]

Also the *Pŭhyu tang taesa chip* (The Collection of the Great Master Pŭhyu Tang),[88] in five chapters and containing the works by Hyŭjŏng's dharma brother Sŏnsu (1543–1615),[89] features a number of short texts and prayers indicating this master's use of esoteric lore. The texts in question include such pieces as *In Hwaŏm kyŏng kyŏm suryuk sŏ* (Prayer [on the occasion of] the Prince of the *Avataṃsaka Sūtra* together with a Water and Land [ritual]),[90] *Pŏnwa suryuk sŏ* (Prayer [on the occasion of] a Burning Clay, Land and Water [ritual]),[91] *Pak Tiaebi ku cha sŏ* (Prayer [on behalf of] Pak Taebi, Who Wishes to Have a Son),[92] etc.

In the material related to later monks we find examples of esoteric lore in the writings of Wŏljŏ Toan (1638–1715),[93] who authored the *Yaksa hyeso* (Prayers for Bhaiṣajyaguru Assembly),[94] and in those of Ch'ŭbŭng Solam (1651–1706),[95] who wrote several prayers for esoteric rituals such as the *Amita toryang so* (Prayer for the Amitābha Bodhimaṇḍa),[96] *Chijang toryang so* (Prayer for the Kśitigarbha Bodhimaṇḍa),[97] *Haengmin sojau chejil Kwanŭm toryang so* (Prayer for Good Fortune, the Dispersing of Calamity and Getting Rid of Disease at the Avalokiteśvara Bodhimaṇḍa),[98] and the *Sokae toryang so* (Prayer for the Dispersing of Calamity Bodhimaṇḍa).[99] Lastly we have information on the Sŏn monk Yŏngp'a Sŏnggyŭ (1728–1812)[100] from Unhae Temple, who is said to have recited the *Taebi chu* (Great Compassion Dhāraṇī) ten thousand times.[101]

Sŏn and Esoteric Buddhism in the Chinon Chip

Ritual texts were one branch of Korean Buddhist literature which flourished during the Chosŏn period, and esoteric elements and practices can be found in the vast majority of them. In the course of the esoteric Buddhist manifestation, which by the middle of the sixteenth century had become a fully accepted part of Sŏn Buddhist rituals, we start to encounter examples of a conscious attempt at integrating esoteric meditation practices with Sŏn. In addition to Pou's exposition in the *Suwŏl toryang konghwa pulsa yŏhwan binju mongchung mundap*, as discussed above, one of the best attempts at showing the common goal of Sŏn and esoteric practice is found in the comprehensive manual of mantras, the *Chinon chip* (The Collection of Mantras).[102] The edition referred to is the one with a colophon by the Sŏn monk Sŏrun (n.d.)[103] and which was first published at Ansim Temple in 1569. This manual has long since captured the interest of Western philologists working on the medieval Korean language and on the early version of Hangul, the Korean alphabet. However, very few have noted the highly illuminating introduction attributed to Yongam Chŭngsuk (n.d.),[104] which is appended to the Manyŏn Temple edition from 1777.[105] As we shall see below, this introduction, including the prefaces and postfaces, is particularly illuminating in relation to the practical harmonization of esoteric Buddhism and Sŏn during the later part of the Chosŏn dynasty.

The primary intent of the introduction to the revised edition of the *Chinon chip* is a discussion and formulation of what may be called "the science of sound and letters," a Buddhist hermeneutic presentation of the significance and usage of mantras, dhāraṇīs, and Siddham script. Although the focus of this introduction is on the spiritual meaning of the "true words," including their relation to the canonical scriptures, we find lengthy passages in which the relationship and correspondence between mantric lore and Sŏn practice are set forth. Here it is interesting to note that the overall tone of the introduction is replete with Sŏn, Chŏngto, and Hwaŏm terminology such as "One Mind" *(ilsim)*, "accomplishing awakening" *(yoŏ)*, "empty stillness" *(kong jŏk)*, "bodhi of great emptiness" *(taegong poje)*, "the complete and sudden gates" *(wŏndon mun)*, "mind contemplation" *(simguan)*, and "the sixteen wonderful visualizations" *(sipyuk myŏgwan)*.[106] A central passage from the introduction entitled *Ajanon* (A Discussion of the Character "A") reads:

The verse on the character "A" in the *Vairocana Sūtra*[107] says:

An eight-petaled, white lotus flower suddenly opens,
brightly manifesting the character "A,"
its color [being of] a white brightness.[108]

When contemplating the form of this character, wisdom will make one realize that *bodhi* is fundamentally unborn. Complete and perfect, it is similar to a moon disk. This is the meaning of contemplating the character ["A"]. Only those who cultivate *yoga* (i.e., esoteric Buddhism) [may] contemplate the moon disk of the *bodhi* mind. Inside the moon disk, arranged in revolving order from the right, are the forty-two Sanskrit Siddham letters, all being of a golden color with a brightness extending to the ten directions. From this, one will be able to realize Vairocana's body of wisdom, which is the perfection of the contemplation of the character "A." Tripiṭaka [Master] Amoghavajra[109] instructed his followers saying: "You should all contemplate the *bodhi* mind of the Original Worthy (i.e., Vairocana), the great being. This is the *bodhi* mind of the Original Worthy, the great being!"[110] Having [himself] accomplished the dharma of the unborn, and realized the great enlightened body he (i.e., Amoghavajra) handed down the [method] of the contemplation of the character "A" to his followers.[111] The above way of contemplation is not different from the Sŏn path outside the established norm *(kyŏgoe sŏnmun)*. In the Sŏn path they teach men through the characterless *kongan*, which is similar [in essence] to the character "A." The dharma method of contemplating the mind is not apart from the detailed investigation of the principle of the abstruse [whereby] the evident and the mysterious are completely fused. By constantly contemplating the character "A," one is fundamentally working on the *hwadu*[112] (lit., head of the word).[113]

Of immediate interest here is that the author invokes the authority of an important esoteric scripture, the *Jingang ding jing yujia xiuxi pilushena sanmodi fa* (Vajra Uṣṇīṣa Sūtra's Methods of Yoga Practice [for the achievement of] Vairocana Samādhi), as well as Amoghavajra and the classical Zhenyan tradition of Tang China. This shows that traditional Zhenyan material was still in vogue in Korea at this time, and that it was being actively propagated within a Sŏn context. The meditation on the character "A" is of course one of the most common forms of contemplation within the East Asian esoteric tradition.[114] In his recommendation of the contemplation of the character "A," the author endeavors to show its identity and compatibility with the *hwadu* practice common in Korea Sŏn. His rationale for this is that the *kongan* is fundamentally identical with the character "A," that is, the essence of *prajñāpāramitā*.

Further on in his discussion of the value of the contemplation of the character "A" we read:

> It is like the [method] of *chegwan* (Ch. *zhiguan*) in the Ch'ŏnt'ae [school] which teaches people, saying that when they are deeply absorbed they should visualize the character "A" in front of the nose. The beginning of the visualization of the round disk with [the character] "A" is just like the way the Sŏn School instructs people to contemplate the white-colored "A" character in the center of the disk, and then to enter *samādhi*.[115] This is also called to visualize in the mind a moon disk with the character "A." [Then] visualizing the character "Kwa," intone the mantra, whereupon you will obtain the Three Mysteries *(samhyŏn)*. They mutually correspond like the out and in breath, and the matching halves of a talisman. All the seventeen hundred odd *kongan* of the Sŏn school moreover do not go beyond the one character "A," and hence they (i.e., the two kind of practices) are unified as the shortcut method.[116]

In this passage we find Chŭngsuk including the *zhiguan (chegwam)* practice of Ch'ŏnt'ae Buddhism in his apologetic for the esoteric practices of the *Chinŏn chip*. As will be remembered, the Ch'ŏnt'ae school was the other important denomination of Korean Buddhism, which had become absorbed into the school of Sŏn at the time of the merger in 1424, and it is likely that specific practices related to this tradition were still in vogue in Chŭngsuk's time. In any case it should be borne in mind that esoteric practices had been part of the general curriculum of Ch'ŏnt'ae Buddhism long before it was formally introduced to Korea, so it is not so surprising to find great similarities between esotericized Ch'ŏnt'ae and esoteric Buddhism. Again the identity between the *kongan* practice and the Aja contemplation is brought up, and both are stated to coalesce into the shortcut method, a designation usually reserved for the *kongan* or *hwadu* practice alone.

The introduction to the Manyŏn Temple edition of the *Chinŏn chip* offers, as we have seen, a highly interesting perspective on the relationship between Sŏn *kongan* practice and classical *milgyo* as seen in a seventeenth-century Korean Buddhist context. Whether the practical grounds for making contemplation of the character "A" and *hwadu* practice compatible are present or not, it is a clever move on the part of the author of the introduction to utilize the doctrine of universal emptiness, symbolized by the character "A," as the link to the "characterless" Sŏn meditation. Through this hermeneutical feat he succeeds in establishing a plausible ideological basis for both types of practice. Hence we may see Chŭngsuk as following in the footsteps of Houng Pou in the process of making esoteric practices compatible and eventually identical with Sŏn meditation.

Sŏn and Esoteric Practices in the Buddhist Ritual Manuals

The extent to which the integration of Sŏn and esoteric Buddhism had been achieved toward the end of the Chosŏn dynasty is best illustrated by the ritual manuals compiled and edited by Sŏn monks. Among the most important ritual manuals from the seventeenth century is the new edition of the *Pŏ mŭm chip* (The Collection of Sanskrit Sounds).[117] This manual was originally compiled by Chisŏn (n.d.) and first published in 1661. It was later revised and published by the monk Chinwan (n.d.) in Torim Temple in 1709, and later two prefaces were added.[118] Although this manual cannot be attributed to one particular Buddhist denomination, it is quite evident from the contents that it was primarily meant for use in the Sŏn temples, or rather in communities where Sŏn dominated. Perhaps the best example of the Sŏn affiliation of the *Pŏ mŭm chip* is the fact that it contains the full text of the *Sŏnmun chosa yech'am mun hwajang sŏ* (The Text of the Flower Store Book of the Patriarchs of the Sŏn Sect's Ritual of Repentance),[119] a major ritual text which invokes the orthodox Sino-Korean Sŏn lineage.[120] Although not containing any esoteric elements as such, the very fact that this important Sŏn ritual text is included among purely esoteric material shows beyond any doubt that the manual was designed for use in a Sŏn Buddhist environment where esoteric rituals were practiced. Noteworthy is also the minor *Sŏlsŏn chakpŏp chŭggyŏl* (The Sequential Methods for a Sŏn Discourse),[121] which gives the ceremonial proceedings accompanying a formal Sŏn address by the spiritual head *(pangjang)* of a Sŏn community to the assembly of monks. The chanting of a mantra is part of this ritual.[122]

A later edition of the *Pŏ mŭm chip*, the so-called Osan edition,[123] contains two ritual texts in connection with presenting food offerings. They are the *Kongyang mun* (Text for Receiving Offerings)[124] and the *Chosa kongyang mun* (The Text on the Offerings to the Patriarchs),[125] which invoke the major patriarchs of Sŏn, here represented by three Worthies: Dhyānabhadra (Chigong), Naong, and Muhak. This ritual involves the chanting of the *Taebi sinju* (Great Compassion Mantra) as well as the *Śurangama Mantra*. Both of these rituals give a clear indication of the Sŏn Buddhist context.

In 1827 the Sŏn master Paekp'a Kunsŏn (1767–1852) compiled the *Chakpŏp kugam* (Manual of Methods),[126] which is a comprehensive collection of liturgic material based on most of the older ritual texts from the Chosŏn, including major parts of the above *Pŏ mŭm chip*, which were still in use during his day. Although the ritual elements directly bearing on Sŏn Buddhism are relatively few in this compendium, the *Chakpŏp kugam* nevertheless shows us the large amount of esoteric liturgy which was practiced in Sŏn temples during the first half of the nineteenth century. Contained in this manual is the text for a ritual called *Chongsa yŏngbap* (The Spiritual Rice [offering] to the Masters of the School),[127] in which the whole lineage of Sŏn masters of a given temple is invoked. As such, this ritual deals with one of the most central aspects of Sŏn Buddhism, namely that of lineage. The last item of the *Chongsa yŏngbap* dealing with Sŏn in an esoteric ritual setting is the treatise *Kandang non* (Treatise on Inspecting the Hall),[128] which gives an explanation of the Sŏn ritual *Kandang*.[129] Like the previous ritual it also involves the use of mantras.

The twentieth-century ritual manual *Sŏngmun ŭibŏm* (The Ritual Codex for Buddhists),[130] which is based in large part on the *Chakpŏp kugan*, contains the *Sam kwasang ch'ong* (The Invocation of the Three Venerables).[131] The Three Venerables of this invocation, which combines Sŏn lore with esoteric methods, are the masters Chigong, Naong, and Muhak, whom we have just met in connection with another liturgical text. In addition, the *Songmun ŭibŏm* includes a section of "pure" Sŏn material such as guidelines for sitting in meditation, Sŏn verses, and songs.[132]

Korean Buddhism underwent a general doctrinal and practical coalescence during the Chosŏn dynasty in the course of which clear-cut sectarian distinctions became blurred or even disappeared. One of the main features of Chosŏn Buddhism was the high degree of "esoterification" of its liturgy and the various aspects of ceremonial life. As Sŏn was undoubtedly the leading element within Chosŏn Buddhism, it naturally absorbed a considerable amount of esoteric practices and eventually came to regard them as a natural part of the Sŏn communal life.

Despite the multifarious aspects of esoteric Buddhist practices within Korean Sŏn of the Chosŏn, it is apparent that the main esoteric element was the use of mantras. Common to the use of mantras and dhāraṇīs within Sŏn Buddhism was their general application as "tools" of power or associated means of spiritual efficacy, rather than as primary means to achieve the goal of the religious life. Despite this we have also seen that some monks attempted to popularize them as methods equal to *kongan* practice. That the belief in the power of these esoteric incantations and practices was rather widespread within Sŏn circles is evident, since several important Sŏn masters such as Pou, Hyŭjŏng, and Paekp'a composed or compiled works containing esoteric material. Perhaps the degree of esoteric influence is most obvious in the liturgical manuals used by the Sŏn communities from the middle of the Chosŏn dynasty on.

Esoteric practices are still carried out in Sŏn temples in modern Korea, but they are now mostly limited to cremation rituals, the *ch'ilchae* ceremonies, and occasional rituals for the empowerment of statues and altar paintings *(t'aenghwa)*. It is also not uncommon for sick monks to practice the *Tabei chu* as a means of being healed. A few decades back it was still possible to find Sŏn monks who were very skilled at writing Siddham for ceremonial purposes. Today it is extremely rare to find anyone within the Chogye Order, the main Buddhist denomination in Korea, who knows Siddham at all, not to mention being able to write it. The T'aego Order of married priests, in which Sŏn is also practiced, is known to preserve many ritual traditions of Korean Buddhism and much of the old esoteric lore. Only a small number of the senior priests of that order have more than a superficial knowledge, however, and apparently they have great difficulty in transmitting it to their disciples. In fact, as the general liturgical aspects of Korean Buddhism steadily decline, in one or two generations the last vestiges of traditional esoteric Buddhist practices will be only a memory.

Kūkai's "Principle of Attaining Buddhahood with the Present Body"

TRANSLATED WITH AN INTRODUCTION AND ANNOTATION BY HISAO INAGAKI

Introduction

CHINESE ESOTERIC BUDDHISM entered a new epoch in the eighth century when Śubhakarasiṃha (637–735) and Vajrabodhi (671–741) produced Chinese translations of the *Mahāvairocana Sūtra* and the *Diamond Peak Sūtra*, respectively, thereby promulgating what is called "genuine esotericism" as distinguished from "mixed esotericism."[1] Furthermore, Amoghavajra (705–74), Vajrabodhi's disciple, actively engaged in the dissemination of the teaching while translating a large number of esoteric texts which he had brought from India. It was his disciple Huiguo (?–805) who transmitted the teaching to Kūkai when the latter visited China.

After returning to Japan, Kūkai (774–835),[2] popularly known by his posthumous title "Kōbō Daishi," propagated the esoteric teaching in Kyoto and elsewhere while writing a number of works. Being a faithful follower of the esoteric tradition, he based his system of thought on the teachings of Indian and Chinese masters and attached especially great importance to the sūtras of genuine esotericism and two treatises attributed to Nāgārjuna, namely, *Treatise on Bodhi-Mind* and *Commentary on the Treatise on Mahāyāna*. He further developed and systematized the doctrine with his extensive knowledge and religious ingenuity.

Of all the works of Kūkai, the following six are considered the most important in the Shingon sect:

1. *Ben-ken mitsu-nikyō-ron*, 2 fascicles, T. vol. 77, no. 2427, a treatise which compares exoteric and esoteric teaching and shows that the latter is superior because it was expounded by the Dharmakāya Buddha.[3]
2. *Sokushin-jōbutsu-gi*, 1 fascicle, T. vol. 77, no. 2428.

3. *Shōji-jissō-gi*, 1 fascicle, T. vol. 77, no. 2429, a treatise which establishes the doctrine that Mahāvairocana's preaching of dharma is heard through phenomenal existences.

4. *Unji-gi*, 1 fascicle, T. vol. 77, no. 2430, a discourse on the significance of the mystic letter "hūṃ," saying that it contains deep and boundless significance of the absolute truth and that one can attain the state of Mahāvairocana by contemplating on it.

5. *Hizō-hōyaku*, 3 fascicles, T. vol. 77, no. 2426, a discourse on the ten stages of spiritual progress, which correspond to the ten categories of Buddhist and non-Buddhist paths.

6. *Hannyashingyō-hiken*, 1 fascicle, T. vol. 57, no. 2203, a commentary on the *Prajñāpāramitā-hṛdaya Sūtra*.

These six works in 9 fascicles and the *Treatise on Bodhi-Mind*, 1 fascicle, are collected in "The Ten-Fascicle Books" explaining the fundamentals of the Shingon doctrine. The theory of the ten-stage spiritual progress is more extensively discussed in the *Himitsu-mandara-jūjūshin-ron*, 10 fascicles, T. vol. 77, no. 2425.

In Kūkai's system of thought, attainment of buddhahood with the present body occupies the most important place. Ordinarily, buddhahood is to be attained after three "incalculable aeons" *(asaṃkhya-kalpa)*, during which one gradually accumulates merit, removes evil passions, and cultivates wisdom. All exoteric teachings, Kūkai claims, more or less follow this pattern of practice, but esoteric teaching which is the direct and spontaneous revelation of the ultimate truth by the Dharmakāya Buddha presents a mysterious, transcendental means whereby one attains Buddhahood very quickly, even in the present life. This doctrine, however, was not Kūkai's dogmatic elaboration. There is evidence that Amoghavajra and Huiguo had the same view.[4] The theory of quick attainment of Buddhahood, it must be added, is not peculiar to esoteric Buddhism. The Tendai and Kegon schools have a similar doctrine, and Zen advocates instant realization of enlightenment. Kūkai's contemporary and the founder of the Japanese Tendai sect, Saichō (767–822), in fact, promulgated the teaching of quick realization of buddhahood based on the *Lotus Sūtra* against the Hossō teaching that expounds gradual progress toward enlightenment over a period of three incalculable aeons. In Kūkai's view, Tendai and Kegon talk only about theoretical possibilities of attaining buddhahood quickly and lack an actual experience of realization.

It is not known exactly when Kūkai wrote the *Sokushin-jōbutsu-gi*. It is presumed that he wrote it during the Tenchō period (824–33).[5] It is also suggested that since the theory of the six elements is frequently mentioned in the works written after the first year of Tenchō (824), he must have written this work in the late Kōnin period (c. 820–24).[6] There is still another assumption placing the date of compilation between the eighth and the ninth year of Kōnin (817–18) based on an investigation into the relationship between Kūkai and Tokuichi, his contemporary and scholar of the Hossō doctrine.[7]

The treatise consists of three parts: scriptural evidence, verse, and exposition of the verse. In Part I, eight passages are quoted from the *Mahāvairo-cana Sūtra*, sūtras belonging to the Diamond Peak {*Vajraśekhara*} group, and the *Treatise on Bodhi-Mind* as the scriptural evidence for establishing the principle of attaining buddhahood with the present body. The verse, consisting of two stanzas in eight lines, is attributed to the "Great Ācārya of Tang," namely Huiguo, in a different text of the *Sokushin-jōbutsu-gi*,[8] but this ascription is not generally accepted because the text in question is thought to have been composed by some other person. The verse, indeed, forms an integral part of the *Sokushin-jōbutsu-gi*, presenting the essentials of the doctrine of attaining buddhahood with the present body, and so it can be considered as the most important part of the entire system of Shingon esotericism. The first stanza explains the meaning of "sokushin," and the second one that of "jōbutsu."

It is important to note that in Parts II and III Kūkai follows the pattern of discourse adopted in the *Treatise on the Awakening of Faith in Mahāyāna* and the *Commentary on the Treatise on Mahāyāna*, namely, (1) presentation of the essence of all things, (2) phenomenal manifestations of the essence in concrete forms, and (3) activity and function of the essence. The essential substance of the universe, according to Kūkai, is the six elements (six *mahābhūta*s), namely, earth, water, fire, wind, space, and consciousness. In ordinary Buddhist teaching, these six are regarded as constituent elements of the phenomenal world *(saṃskṛta)*, and the very essence of things is shown in Mahāyāna by such terms as "dharma-nature" *(dharmatā)*, "true thusness" *(tathatā)*, and "emptiness" *(śūnyatā)*. Kūkai's view of the universe is that the six elements are its essence and are identical with the Dharmakāya Buddha Mahāvairocana. As in other aspects of his esoteric doctrine, Kūkai presents the ultimate essence of things in positive and concrete terms, whereas those familiar with Zen may expect a negative expression. These six elements and all phenomena, including all sentient beings and even buddhas, are in the relationship of "producing" elements and "produced" things, but in reality it is not a relative relationship, and a popular concept of "creation" does not apply here. Though the first five are treated as material elements and the last one as the mental element, they are basically of the same nature. They penetrate one another and are mutually unhindered. Hence, what is material is mental, and what is mental is material. This provides the basis for universal, mutual unhinderedness through which the esoteric principle of the unity of man with buddha is established. Kūkai further demonstrates that the first five elements represent the noumenal principle and the last one signifies perfect wisdom. This means to say that the whole universe produced from the six elements is the embodiment of Mahāvairocana's noumenal principle and wisdom. In their original state, the six elements are "unproducing" and "unproduced." The "original unproducedness" (ādyanutpāda), indeed, is the keynote of genuine esotericism and is represented by the syllable "a."

As we have seen above, phenomenal manifestations of the six elements can be considered as self-manifestations of Mahāvairocana Buddha. The universe as such is, therefore, a pictorial presentation (maṇḍala) of this original buddha. In terms of the four kinds of maṇḍalas, the universe is, first of all, a mahā maṇḍala, and various phenomenal existences can be considered as deities arising out of the original body, Mahāvairocana. Second, the universe is interpreted spiritually as a manifestation of his vows and ideas, and so various things in it are considered as swords, jewels, lotus flowers, and so on, held in the hands of the deities which represent their distinct vows and wishes. In this sense, the whole universe is a samaya maṇḍala. Third, the universe is a self-manifestation of dharma, and each phenomenal existence is a letter of dharma containing immeasurable meanings and merits. Also various letters signifying deities in the mantras are revealed as phenomenal existences in the universe. Hence, the whole universe is a dharma maṇḍala. Lastly, movements of things in the universe represent deities' actions; hence, the universe is a karma maṇḍala. The four kinds of maṇḍalas which are usually shown in pictorial forms, seed-letters (bīja), or act-signs have thus a cosmic significance. As it is said in the Sokushin-jōbutsu-gi, each of the four kinds of maṇḍalas is as immense as space, and they penetrate one another, being mutually unhindered.

The real religious significance of Kūkai's theory of origination from six elements lies in the spontaneous function of Mahāvairocana. He manifests himself in various forms of buddhas and deities, and reveals dharma to sentient beings. Since it is conceived that the activity of Mahāvairocana is displayed with his body, speech, and mind, one who seeks unity with him is required to take a specific physical posture and perform specific oral and mental exertions. Therefore, Kūkai attaches great importance to the three kinds of practice, namely, mudrā-sign, incantation of mantra, and samādhi-meditation. These three are called "the three mystic practices"—"mystic" because they are so profound and subtle that even the bodhisattvas of the highest rank cannot recognize them. The three mystic practices originally belong to the buddha, and the practitioner is only required to conform to them as they are transferred to him. It is further conceived ontologically that all sentient beings possess by nature the same mystic forms of action as the buddha's—as it is technically called *(musō no sammitsu)*—but they do not realize them until they successfully perform the prescribed method of practice and attain unity with the buddha.

The spiritual communication and unity between man and buddha which thus involves physical, oral, and mental correspondence is expressed by the term *kaji*. This word is originally a Chinese translation of the Sanskrit *adhiṣṭhāna* (power, authority, blessing) which refers to the buddha's power brought to bear on a bodhisattva to assist him in his spiritual progress. The term as Kūkai interprets it refers to this power on the part of the buddha and also to the practitioner's response to and reception of it. The terms "adding" and "holding" are given these two distinct meanings. In other words, as Kūkai notes, "adding" refers to the buddha's great compassion, and "holding" to man's faith. In his introduction to the *Mahāvairocana Sūtra*, Kūkai says,[9] "adding and holding" is favored by the Buddha and "adding and endowing" is an old translation. But these do not exhaust its implications. "Adding" is the term for "communication and penetration," and "holding" has the meaning of "holding and keeping something from dispersing." That is to say, the "Buddha entering into me and I entering into the buddha" is the significance of the term. In explaining the principle of attaining buddhahood with the present body, three kinds of "sokushin-jōbutsu" are distinguished: "intrinsic embodiment," "empowerment and respondence," and "manifest realization." First, all sentient beings intrinsically and spontaneously possess all the merit of the *vajradhātu* and *garbhadhātu* maṇḍalas, with their bodies containing the noumenal qualities of the five elements and with their minds embodying the enlightenment-wisdom of the consciousness element. Therefore they are in themselves dharmakāya buddhas. Second, one attains unity with Mahāvairo-cana Buddha through the three mystic practices of empowerment and respondence. In this stage of practice, the practitioner is identical with Mahāvairocana as long as he is in the mystic samādhi of yoga, but when he leaves it he returns to the state of an ordinary man still bound by evil passions and desires. Third, as the practitioner continues to perform the three mystic practices, he will attain the full realization of buddhahood, with all his actions always in harmony with the buddha's. Since he thus manifestly realizes the intrinsic virtue of Mahāvairocana, his body is now the buddha's body, and the buddha's body is his body.

The theory of the three kinds of attainment of buddhahood should not be attributed to Kūkai because it appears in a different text of the *Sokushin-jōbutsu-gi*[10] that was most probably composed by some other person, but it has been widely used in the Shingon sect to explain the deep meaning of this principle. In accordance with the three meanings of the principle, three distinct readings of "sokushin jōbutsu" have been devised. In the case of the intrinsic embodiment of buddhahood, the phrase is read *"sunawachi mi nareru butsu"* ("in itself one's body is an actualized buddha"). In the second case of realizing buddhahood through empowerment and respondence, it is read *"mi ni sokushite butsu to naru"* ("with the present body one becomes a buddha"). Third, with reference to the manifest realization of buddhahood, the reading is *"sumiyakani mi butsu to naru"* ("quickly one's body becomes Buddha's").[11]

There are a number of old and modern commentaries on the *Sokushin-jōbutsu-gi*,[12] of which the translator has chiefly availed himself of those written by Raiyu (1226–1304), Shōshin (1287–1357), Yūkai (1345–1416), and Donjaku (1674–1742).[13]

As Shingon esotericism is a highly sophisticated religious-philosophical system, it is impossible to discuss all aspects of the system here. I hope, however, that the above remarks on the "Principle of Attaining Buddhahood with the Present Body" will serve as an introduction to the whole system.

Principle of Attaining Buddhahood with the Present Body

I. SCRIPTURAL EVIDENCE

Question: Various sūtras and treatises expound attainment of buddhahood in three *(asaṃkhya)* kalpas.[14] What scriptural evidence is there to establish the principle of attaining buddhahood with the present body?

Answer: The Tathāgata expounds it in the esoteric piṭaka.[15]
What is the exposition in the sūtras?
(1) The *Diamond Peak Sūtra* says,[16]

> Those who practice this samādhi
> Will realize buddha's bodhi with the present body.

"This samādhi" refers to the samādhi of one letter (i.e., *bhrūṃ*) representing the Bhagavat Mahāvairocana incarnated as a Golden Cakravartin.[17]
(2) Again, it is said,[18]

> If there are beings who encounter this teaching
> And practice it diligently day and night, throughout the four
>   periods of a day,[19]
> They will attain the stage of joy in this life
> And realize enlightenment after sixteen lives.

I explain: "This teaching" refers to the great king teaching of samādhi realized inwardly by the dharmakāya buddha.[20] "Stage of joy" is not the first bhūmi mentioned in the exoteric teachings; it is the first stage of our buddha-vehicle,[21] as fully explained in the section on stages.[22] "Sixteen lives" refers to the lives of the sixteen great bodhisattvas;[23] they are fully explained in the section on stages.
(3) Again, it is said,[24]

> If one practices in accordance with this supreme principle,
>   one will attain the highest enlightenment in this life.

(4) Again, it is said,[25]

> You should know that your body
> Becomes the vajradhātu.[26]
> When your body has become vajra,
> It is firm, solid and indestructible.
> I have attained the vajra-body.

(5) The *Mahāvairocana Sūtra* says,[27]

> Without abandoning this body,
> One attains supernatural power over the objective world,[28]
> Wanders freely in the state of great emptiness,
> And, moreover, accomplishes the bodily mystery.

(6) Again, it says,[29]

> If you want to enter perfection *(siddhi)* in this life,
> Comply with (your buddha's) empowerment and contemplate
>   on it.
> After receiving the mantra (of your buddha) personally from your
>   reverend teacher,
> Meditate on it until you become united with it. Then you will
>   attain perfection.

The "perfection" mentioned in the sūtra refers to the perfection (of five supernatural powers, etc.) by holding the mantra and the perfection of the buddhahood of dharmakāya. "The state of great emptiness" means that dharmakāya is unhindered like the great space, contains all the phenomenal forms and is everlasting; hence, "great emptiness." It is the basis on which all existing things rest; hence, "state." "Bodily mystery" means that even bodhisattvas of the equal bodhi[30] cannot see the three mystic practices of the dharmakāya buddha; and so how can those of the tenth bhūmi[31] have a glimpse of them? Hence, it is called "bodily mystery."

(7) Also it is said in the Bodhisattva Nāgārjuna's *Treatise on Bodhi-Mind,*[32] "In the mantra teaching alone is found the theory of attaining buddhahood with the present body. Hence, it expounds the method of samādhi. It is not found or mentioned in the various other teachings."

"It expounds the method of samādhi" refers to the samādhi self-realized by the dharmakāya. "Various other teachings" refer to exoteric teachings expounded by the enjoyment body for the sake of others.

(8) Again, it says,[33]

> If a man seeking buddha's wisdom
> Attains bodhi-mind,
> He will quickly reach the stage of great enlightenment
> With the body born from his father and mother.

II. VERSE

This principle is established by the above passages of evidence in the scriptures. What are the distinct meanings of the words "attaining buddhahood with the present body" as expounded in these sūtras and treatises? A verse says,

The six elements are mutually unhindered, everlasting and in
   harmony with reality. [essence]
The four kinds of maṇḍalas are not separate from each other. [form]
Empowerment and respondence in the three mystic practices
   quickly reveal (the three bodies of buddha). [function]
Manifold relationships like Indra's net are shown as "present or
   identical body." [unhinderedness]

One spontaneously possesses all-wisdom,
With mental functions and mind-kings as numerous as the
   particles of the universe,
Each embodying the five wisdoms and boundless wisdom;
Because it functions like a clean mirror it is called Reality-
   Enlightenment wisdom. [enlightenment]

I explain: With these two stanzas in eight lines I praise the significance
of the four characters. These four characters contain boundless meaning.
None of the buddha's teachings go beyond this one phrase. Hence, I have
condensed them into these two stanzas to disclose the boundless virtue.

The verse is divided into two parts: the first stanza praises the significance of the first two characters, and the next one that of the second two
characters. The first part is further divided into four: the first line shows
essence; the second, form; the third, function; and the fourth, unhinderedness. The second stanza presents four things: first, attainment to the buddhahood of dharmakāya buddha; second, innumerableness; third,
perfection; and last, reason.

III. EXPOSITION

First line:

I explain: "The six elements" are the five elements[34] and consciousness. The
Mahāvairocana Sūtra says,[35]

I have realized the original unproducedness,
Gone beyond the path of words,
Attained liberation from various faults,
Freed myself from causes and conditions,
And realized that voidness is like space.

This is the significance of the six elements. A seed-mantra says, *a vira hūṃ khaṃ hūṃ*.[36] The syllable *"a"* signifying the original unproducedness of all dharmas represents the earth element.[37] The syllable *"va,"* signifying transcending verbal expositions, represents the water element.[38] Purity and nondefilement are referred to by the syllable *"ra,"* which represents the fire element.[39] That causal karmas are not to be grasped is implied by the syllable *"ha,"* which represents the wind element.[40] "Like space" is implied by the syllable *"kha,"* which represents the space element.[41] "I have realized" indicates the consciousness element.

The word *shiki* (consciousness) is used in the causal state, and *chi* (wisdom) in the resultant state.[42] And, since *chi* (wisdom) is also *kaku* (realization), "I have realized" indicates the element of consciousness. Sanskrit *"buddha"* and *"bodhi"* are derivatives of the same word (*budh*). *"Buddha"* is translated as *"kaku"* (realization), and *"bodhi"* as *"chi"* (wisdom). Therefore, *"samyaksaṃbodhi,"* used in various sūtras, was formerly translated as *"henchi"* (universally knowing), and later as *"tōgaku"* (equal enlightenment), for they have the same meaning. This sūtra refers to consciousness as *"kaku"* in accordance with the superior sense of the term. The only difference is whether it refers to the state of cause or of result, the original or the derivative state. The verse of this sūtra makes this statement with reference to the five buddhas' samādhis.[43]

Again, the *Diamond Peak Sūtra* says,[44]

> All dharmas are originally unproduced;
> Their substance is beyond verbal descriptions,
> Pure and without defilement;
> Though there are causes and karmas, they are like space.

This verse has the same context as the one in the *Mahāvairocana Sūtra*. "All dharmas" refers to all mental dharmas. The number of mind-kings and mental functions is immeasurable; hence, "all." "Mind" and "consciousness" are different words with the same meaning. For this reason, Vasubandhu and others established the principle of Consciousness Only {Yogācāra} based on the theory that the three worlds are merely (manifestations of) mind. The explanation of the rest of the verse is the same as above.

Again, the *Mahāvairocana Sūtra* says,[45]

I am in agreement with the mind-state,
Attaining freedom in reaching anywhere
And permeating universally various
Animate and inanimate beings.
The syllable *"a"* refers to the primordial life.
The syllable *"va"* refers to water.
The syllable *"ra"* refers to fire.
The syllable *"hūṃ"* refers to wind.
The syllable *"kha"* is the same as space.

In the first line of the passage of this sūtra, namely, "I am in agreement with the mind-state," "mind" refers to consciousness-wisdom. The last five lines refer to the five elements. The middle three lines explain the unrestricted function and the quality of unhinderedness of the six elements. The *Prajñāpāramitā Sūtras*,[46] the *Bracelet Sūtra*,[47] and others also expound the principle of the six elements. These six elements produce the four kinds of dharmakāyas[48] and the three kinds of worlds, such as all buddhas, all sentient beings, and receptacle worlds.[49] Hence, the Bhagavat Mahāvairocana sets forth a verse on the arising of Tathāgata and says,[50]

"(The six elements) produce various conformable shapes[51]
Of dharmas and dharma-aspects,
Buddhas, śrāvakas,
World-saving pratyekabuddhas,
Hosts of valiant bodhisattvas,
And the most honored man {bhavagat} as well.
Sentient beings and receptacle-worlds
Are produced in succession.
Dharmas which arise, dwell, and so on (i.e., change and perish),
Are thus produced perpetually."

What meaning does this verse reveal? It reveals that the six elements produce the four kinds of dharmakāyas, four kinds of maṇḍalas, and three kinds of worlds.[52] "Dharmas" refer to mental dharmas, and "dharma-aspects" refer to material dharmas. Also, "dharmas" is a general term, whereas "dharma-aspects" refer to distinctive aspects of dharmas. Hence, the following lines say that buddhas, śrāvakas, pratyekabuddhas, bodhisattvas, sentient beings, and receptacle-worlds are produced in succession. Also, "dharmas" refers to the dharma maṇḍala; "dharma-aspects" refers to the samaya maṇḍala bodies; from "buddhas" to "sentient beings" all are the mahā maṇḍala bodies; and "receptacle-worlds" refers to the lands on which they rest. "Receptacle-worlds" is a general term for the samaya maṇḍala. Also, "buddhas," "bodhisattvas," and sages of the two vehicles refer to the world of wisdom-enlightenment; "sentient beings" refers to the world of sentient beings; and "receptacle-worlds" refers to the world of receptacle. Also, the producing agents are the six elements; "various conformable forms" are the produced dharmas, namely, the four kinds of dharmakāyas and the three kinds of worlds.

Therefore, it says next,[53] "O Lord of Mystery, in laying out a maṇḍala, there are (proper) positions, seed-syllables, and samaya-signs of the sacred ones. You should listen carefully. I will now explain." Then he sets forth a verse and says,

> The mantra-practitioner should first
> Place a maṇḍala-platform in his own body.
> From the feet to the navel,
> Form a great vajra-layer.
> From there to the heart, imagine a water-layer.
> A fire-layer is above the water-layer;
> A wind-layer is above the fire-layer.

I explain: "vajra-layer" refers to the syllable *"a"*; the syllable *"a"* represents earth. Water, fire, and wind are to be known from the passage. "Maṇḍala-platform" refers to the space element. "Mantra-practitioner"[54] implies the mind element. "Sacred one" in the prose is a mahā maṇḍala body; "seed letter" is a dharma maṇḍala body; "samaya-sign" is a samaya maṇḍala body; each of the three bodies comprises a karma maṇḍala body. Detailed explanations are given extensively in the sūtras. They are to be known from the passages of the sūtras.

Again, it is said,[55]

> The Bhagavat Mahāvairocana says, "O Vajrapāṇi, the minds of various tathāgatas bring forth actions, as in sports and dancing, displaying various forms extensively. They embrace the four elements, dwelling in the mind-king, and are identical with space. They produce great results, both visible and invisible,

and produce various ranks of all śrāvakas, pratyekabuddhas and bodhisattvas."

What meaning does this passage reveal? It reveals that the six elements produce all things. How do we know? The reason is as follows: "mind-king" refers to the consciousness element; "embrace the four elements" indicates the four elements; "identical with space" refers to the space element. These six elements are producing agents. "Visible and invisible results" refers to the worlds of desire and form, and the world of non-form, respectively.[56] The rest are as shown in the passage. They are the produced dharmas.

Thus the passages of the sūtras all treat the six elements as the producing agents, and the four kinds of dharmakāyas and the three kinds of worlds as the produced (dharmas). Though the produced dharmas, extending from dharmakāya to the lower six realms, have the distinctions of fine and gross, great and small, they do not go beyond the six elements. For this reason, the Buddha expounds the six elements to be the essential substance of dharmadhātu.

In various exoteric teachings the four elements and so forth are treated as insentient things, whereas the esoteric teaching expounds that they are the samaya bodies of the Tathāgata. The four elements and so on are not separate from the mind element. Though mind and matter are different, their essential nature is the same. Matter is mind, and mind is matter; they are mutually unhindered and unobstructed. Wisdom is identical with object, and object with wisdom; wisdom is identical with principle,[57] and principle with wisdom; they are unhindered and free. Though there are two kinds of things, producing and produced, they are in reality entirely beyond active–passive distinctions. What creation is there in the principle of naturalness? Words, such as producing and produced, are all mystic symbols. Don't cling to the ordinary, superficial meanings and engage in various idle discussions.

The body, thus made of the six elements which are the essential substance of dharmadhātu, is unhindered and unobstructed, with the elements mutually penetrating and harmonizing with each other, everlasting and immutable, and equally dwelling in reality-end (bhūtakoṭi). Therefore, the verse says,

The six elements are mutually unhindered, everlasting and
in harmony with reality.

"Unhindered" means "freely penetrating." "Everlasting" means "immovable," "indestructible," and the like. "Yoga" (in harmony) is translated as "agreeing, uniting." Mutual agreement and penetration are the meaning of this verse.

Second line:

Concerning the line "The four kinds of maṇḍalas are not separate from each other," the *Mahāvairocana Sūtra* says,[58] "All tathāgatas have three kinds of mystic bodies, namely syllable, sign, and figure."

"Syllable" refers to the dharma maṇḍala. "Sign" refers to various ensigns, namely, the samaya maṇḍala. "Figure" is a body endowed with the marks and characteristics of excellence, namely, the mahā maṇḍala. Each of these three bodies has specific postures and act-signs; this is called the karma maṇḍala. These are the four kinds of maṇḍalas.

According to the exposition of the *Diamond Peak Sūtra,*[59] the four kinds of maṇḍalas are as follows.

First, mahā maṇḍala refers to each buddha or bodhisattva's body endowed with the marks and characteristics of excellence. A painting of his figure is also called mahā maṇḍala. It also refers to the main honored one with whom a practitioner attains unity through the five-aspect meditation for attaining the buddha's body.[60] It is also called mahā wisdom-seal.[61]

Second, samaya maṇḍala refers to things held in the hands, such as ensigns, swords, wheels, jewels, vajras, and lotus flowers. It is also a painting of such things. It also refers to a mudrā which takes its shape from the "diamond bonds"[62] formed by joining the two palms. It is also called samaya wisdom-seal.

Third, dharma maṇḍala refers to the seed-mantra of one's honored one, namely, the seed-letter written in the position of each deity. It also refers to all the maṇḍalas of dharmakāyas[63] and the words and meanings of all the sūtras. It is also called dharma wisdom-seal.

Fourth, karma maṇḍala refers to various postures and act-signs of buddhas, bodhisattvas, and the like and also to cast and clay images. It is also called karma wisdom-seal.

The four kinds of maṇḍalas and four kinds of wisdom-seals are immeasurable. Each of them is as immense as space. That is not separate from this; this is not separate from that; it is just as space and light are mutually unhindered and unobstructed. Hence it is said, "The four kinds of maṇḍalas are not separate from one another." "Not separate" is the meaning of the verse.

Third line:

"Empowerment and respondence in the three mystic practices quickly reveal (the three bodies of buddha)" is to be explained. "The three mystic practices" are bodily mystic practice, oral mystic practice, and mental mystic practice. The Dharmakāya Buddha's[64] three mystic practices are so profound and subtle that even bodhisattvas of the equal bodhi and the tenth bhūmi cannot perceive them; hence, "mystic." Each honored one equally possesses the three mystic practices, numerous as the particles of the universe; one gives empowerment to another, and another responds to one. So it is with the three mystic practices of sentient beings. Hence it is said, "empowerment and respondence in the three mystic practices." If a mantra-practitioner, after discerning this significance, holds his hands in the mudrā, recites the mantra with his mouth, and settles his mind on the samādhi, he will quickly attain the great siddhi through the mutual correspondence and agreement of the three mystic practices.

For this reason, a sūtra says,[65]

> These three mystic letters (i.e., *oṃ, bhuṃ,* and *khaṃ*)[66]
> Of Mahāvairocana Buddha,
> Each contains immeasurable (significances).
> If a man impresses his heart with (Mahāvairocana's) seal[67] and
>   mystic letters,
> He will realize the (great, perfect) mirror wisdom[68]
> And quickly obtain the bodhi-mind
> And the adamantine body.
> If he impresses his forehead with them, it should be known,
> He will realize the wisdom of equality
> And quickly obtain the body of the stage of sprinkling *(abhiṣeka),*
> With a mass of merits adorning his body.
> If he impresses his mouth with the mystic words,
> He will realize the wisdom of excellent discernment,
> Thereby turning the wheel of dharma,
> And obtain the body of buddha's wisdom.
> If he impresses his head with the recitation of the mystic letters,
> He will realize the wisdom of accomplishing metamorphoses
> And produce the buddha's transformed bodies,
> Thereby taming the beings difficult to tame.

If he impresses his whole body
With the seal and mystic letters,
He will realize the wisdom of essential substance of dharmadhātu,
The space body of dharmadhātu
Of Mahāvairocana Buddha.

It is also said,[69]

Entering the meditation on dharmakāya-thusness, one realizes the equality, like space, of the perceiving subject and the object perceived.[70] If a man practices it exclusively and without interruption, he will enter the first bhūmi in this life and acquire instantly the provision of merit and wisdom to be accumulated during the period of one asaṃkhya kalpa. Owing to the empowerment of many tathāgatas, he will soon reach the tenth bhūmi, the stage of equal bodhi and finally that of supreme bodhi,[71] thus attaining *sarvajñā* (all-wisdom), equality of self and others, and the same dharmakāya as that of all the tathāgatas. He will then benefit infinite sentient beings always with the unconditioned great compassion,[72] thereby fulfilling the great task of the buddha.

Again it is said,[73]

If a practitioner avails himself of the teaching arising out of the inwardly realized wisdom of self-enlightenment[74] expounded by the self-enjoyment body of Mahāvairocana Buddha and also avails himself of the wisdom of the enjoyment body for others' sake of Vajrasattva in the state of the great Samantabhadra,[75] he will meet a maṇḍala ācārya[76] and be able to enter the maṇḍala. That is to say, he will acquire the karma (for abiding by the precepts)[77] and, as the ācārya conjures up Vajrasattva in Samantabhadra samādhi, Vajrasattva will enter his body. Owing to the divine power of empowerment, he will instantly attain immeasurable samayas[78] and dhāraṇī-gates. The ācārya transforms with the wonderful dharma his disciple's seeds of innate self-attachment.[79] The disciple will immediately acquire in his body the merit and wisdom to be accumulated during the period of one great asaṃkhya kalpa, whereat he will be considered to have been born into the buddha family.[80] He has been born from the mind of all the tathāgatas, from the mouth of Buddha from the buddha dharma, and from the teaching of dharma, and has acquired the treasure of dharma. The treasure of dharma refers to the teaching of awakening bodhi-mind through the three mystic practices.

This shows the benefit which a practitioner gains from his ācārya's performance of the method of empowerment and respondence when he receives the precept of bodhi-mind for the first time.

By just looking at the maṇḍala, he produces the pure faith in a moment. As he sees it with joyful mind, the seeds of vajradhātu[81] are planted in his ālaya-consciousness.[82]

This passage shows the benefit he gains on seeing various honored ones in the maṇḍala-assembly for the first time.

He fully receives a vajra name as he is commissioned with the task (of succeeding to the status of a buddha) at the ceremony of sprinkling. After this he obtains the vast, profound, and inconceivable teaching, whereby he transcends the results of the two vehicles[83] and ten bhūmis. If a man fixes his thought on and practices this teaching of the five mystic yogas of great Vajrasattva[84] uninterruptedly, throughout the four periods of a day, whether walking, standing, sitting, or lying, then he will remove all attachment to self and things in the realm of visible, audible, and perceptible objects, thereby attaining equality of all things, and he will realize the first bhūmi in the present life and advance gradually (in the bodhisattva's stages). Owing to the practice of the five mystic yogas, he will not be tainted in saṃsāra or attached to nirvāṇa. He will widely benefit beings of the five states of existence[85] in the boundless saṃsāra. Displaying tens of billions of incarnate bodies, he will wander freely in various states of existence and bring sentient beings to perfection, enabling them to attain the rank of Vajrasattva.

This shows the inconceivable benefit of the teaching which one gains when practicing in accordance with the prescribed rite.

Again, it is said,[86] "With the three mystic adamantine practices as the contributing condition[87] one realizes the resultant stage of Vairocana's three bodies."[88]

The sūtras such as have been quoted above all expound this teaching of the samādhi with quick efficacy based on the inconceivable supernatural powers.[89] If a man practices diligently, day and night, in agreement with the prescribed rite, he will obtain with the present body the five supernatural powers.[90] If he practices on and on, he will advance and enter the Buddha's stage without abandoning the present body. Detailed explanations are given in the sūtras.

For this reason, it is said, "Empowerment and respondence in the three mystic practices quickly reveal (the three bodies of buddha)." "Empowerment and respondence" indicates the Tathāgata's great compassion and a sentient being's faith. "Empowerment" means that the sun of buddha is reflected in the mind-water of a sentient being. "Holding" or "respondence" means that the mind-water of the practitioner perceives the sun of buddha. If the practitioner meditates on this principle well, he will quickly reveal and realize the original three bodies with the present body owing to the correspondence of the three mystic practices. Hence it is said "quickly reveal." The meaning of "identical" or "present body" is the same as that of the secular words "instantly" and "on the same day."

Fourth line:

"Manifold relationships like Indra's net are shown as 'with the present or identical body'" shows with a metaphor that the three mystic practices, numerous as the particles of the universe, of various honored ones are perfectly fused and unhindered. "Indra's net" means the jeweled net stretched across the top of this world system above Indra's palace. "Body" refers to one's own body, buddha's body, and sentient beings' bodies; these are called "body." Also there are four kinds of bodies; namely, self-nature, enjoyment, transformed, and homogeneous bodies are also referred to as "body." Also there are three kinds of bodies: letter, mudrā, and figure. These bodies are in manifold relationships and are like a lamp and its images in the mirrors, penetrating each other. That body is this body; this body is that body. Buddha's body is sentient beings' bodies; sentient beings' bodies are Buddha's body. They are not-identical and identical, not-distinct and distinct.

Therefore, the mantra of three equals and unhinderedness reads, *asame trisame samaye svāhā*.[91] The first word means "unequal"; the next one means "three equals"; and the following one means "three equalities." "Three" refers to buddha, dharma, and saṃgha. It also refers to body, word, and mind, as well as to mind, buddha, and sentient beings. These three things are equal with each other, constituting oneness. They are one but innumerable, innumerable but one. And yet they are not in disorder. Hence it is said, "Manifold relationships like Indra's net are shown as 'with the present or identical body.'"

Fifth to eighth lines:
Concerning the line "One spontaneously possesses all-wisdom," the *Mahāvairocana Sūtra* says,[92]

> I am the primordial being of all,
> Called "the support of the world";
> I expound the dharma unparalleled;
> I am from the beginning tranquil and unsurpassed.

"I" is the word referring to the Bhagavat Mahāvairocana himself. "All" means innumerable things. "Primordial being" means the original forefather who has realized from the beginning and spontaneously all the dharmas which are thus unrestricted. The Tathāgata's dharmakāya and the dharma-nature of sentient beings possess this principle of original tranquillity. But since sentient beings do not realize and know this, Buddha expounds this principle and enlightens them.

Again, it is said,[93] "One who seeks various causes and effects, such a fool does not know the mantra and the characteristics of the mantra."[94] For what reason?

> Since it is expounded that a cause is not the agent (of the effect),
> The effect is unproduced.
> Since the cause is void,
> How can there be an effect?
> One should know that the effect of the mantra
> Is entirely separated from causes and effects.

The significance of the spontaneous possession (of all-wisdom) is equally revealed by the verses quoted above, that is, "I have realized the original unproducedness, . . . Freed myself from causes and conditions" and "All dharmas are originally unproduced; . . . Though there are causes and karmas, they are like space."

Also, the *Diamond Peak Sūtra* says,[95] "The kinsmen produced from the self-nature,[96] the sixteen great bodhisattvas such as Vajrapāṇi, and so forth,[97] each brings forth five hundred million koṭis[98] of subtle dharmakāyas, adamant bodies."

Passages such as this have the same import.

"Spontaneously" shows that all dharmas are naturally as they are. "Possess" has the meaning of "accomplish" and "without deficiency." "All-wisdom" *(sarvajña)* is Sanskrit. An older word is a corrupted abridgment. If spelled in full, it is "sarvajñāna," which is translated as "all-knowing wisdom." The final characters are "discernment" and "discretion." Each and every buddha possesses five wisdoms, thirty-seven wisdoms,[99] and wisdoms as numerous even as the particles of the universe.

The next two lines reveal this significance. In showing the quality of "discernment," the word "wisdom" is used. In showing the meaning of "collectively arising," it is called "mind."[100] To show the meaning of "rule and holding," we have the word "dharma-gate."[101] No word (of the above three) is separate from personality. Such personalities are more numerous than the particles of the universe. Hence, it is called "all-knowing wisdoms." The use of the appellation is different from that of exoteric teachings in which one all-knowing wisdom is set against all objects.[102] "Mind-kings" refer to the wisdom of essential substance of dharmadhātu and the other four wisdoms. "Mental functions" refer to the many-included-in-one consciousness.[103]

"Each embodying the five wisdoms" shows that each mind-king and each mental function has these five wisdoms. "Boundless wisdom" means exalted, extensive, and innumerable wisdoms.

"Because it functions like a clean mirror, it is called Reality-Enlightenment wisdom" gives the reason. For what reason are all buddhas called "Enlightenment-Wisdom"? The answer is: Just as all the forms are reflected in a clean mirror on a high stand, so it is with the Tathāgata's mind-mirror. The clean mirror of mind hangs high on the top of dharmadhātu, being serene and shining on all without perversion or mistake. What Buddha does not possess such a clean mirror? Hence it is said, "Because it functions like a clean mirror, it is called Reality-Enlightenment wisdom."

The Five Mysteries of Vajrasattva: A Buddhist Tantric View of the Passions and Enlightenment

IAN ASTLEY

Introduction

THE PRESENT STUDY is an offshoot of research on the Sino-Japanese version of the *Prajñāpāramitā in One Hundred Fifty Śloka*—commonly called the *Rishukyō* in Japanese. This is a little-known text which occupies an important position in the doctrines and practices of one of the main Japanese branches of Buddhist tantrism, Shingon-shū.[1] The *Rishukyō* is extant in ten versions: one Sanskrit/Khotanese fragment with a corresponding Tibetan text (P. 121), two extended versions in Tibetan (P. 119/120), and six Chinese. The last of these (T. vol. 8, no. 244, Chinese extended version, before 1000 CE) corresponds partly to the Tibetan extended versions; the first, Xuanzang, T. vol. 7, no. 220(10), before 664 CE) is quite lengthy and still mainly pre-tantric in character, whilst the remaining four (T. vol. 8, nos. 240, 241, 242, 243) are approximately one hundred fifty *śloka* in length and show varying degrees of tantric influence. It is T. vol. 8, no. 243, Amoghavajra's version, which is generally referred to as the *Rishukyō*, being the only consistently formulated tantric text among the shorter versions. It has also been an integral part of the Japanese Shingon tradition since its inception in the early ninth century.

In the Shingon sect the final section of the main body of the sūtra has come to be called "The Dharma-Gate of the Profound Mystery," and it is the strand of thought and ritual practice contained in this section and corresponding passages in related texts which is of interest to us here.

SOME NOTES ON METHOD

The primary purpose of this offering is to draw attention to a phenomenon within the esoteric Buddhist tradition in Japan which does not seem to have been kept alive elsewhere, but which nevertheless raises interesting questions concerning our understanding of the tantric tradition outside Japan. The present study attempts to give some background information and hints as to possible directions for further work. It also presents one of the key texts which incorporates material on the Five Mysteries of Vajrasattva.

In determining the ritual structure of the primary material, I have relied heavily on Hatta Yukio's *Shingon-Jiten* (SJT), taking the patterns evidenced by his index listings.[2] The significance of these patterns of mantra and dhāraṇī is that since they generally have a specific reference—to a buddha, bodhisattva, lesser divinity, and/or points of doctrine—by mapping the context and order in which they occur, one can build up a more or less accurate and coordinated picture of ritual patterns and their theoretical background. Having done this, one can start to piece together a picture of a tradition that constitutes a significant part of later developments in Buddhism in China and Japan, but which has so far received very little attention in the West.

In the section below describing the ritual in the *Gohimitsuki*,[3] I have first given the individual mantra an ordinal number, starting from the first transcribed mantra in the text.[4] These are, of course, the same numbers as in Hatta's index listings; they appear below within parentheses. The SJT number footnoted to each mantra refers to its number in the body of the dictionary, where the reader will generally find some explanation of the meanings and references of these cryptic utterances.

Concerning Sanskrit equivalents: while some can be stated with certainty to be accurate indications of the original, this is by no means always the case. I have marked with an asterisk those terms which are either doubtful, or simply tentative guesses for the benefit of those with a Sanskrit or Tibetan background. Some will doubtless feel that I should have been more liberal in my use of this device.

THE GENERAL CONCEPT

When a child first comes into the world, the first major step in its development is simply seeing a given object. A desire for the object gradually arises and with time the newly born child becomes capable of reaching out and touching it. Through continued touching the child develops a concrete relationship, a bond to the object, and with time—usually a matter of months—comes to an understanding of the object's characteristics and possible uses. Eventually he or she is able to use the object for the various purposes for which it was intended.

With a little imagination, we can see that this pattern—leading from simple perception through contact to involvement and finally to mastery and freedom in applying whatever is being dealt with—can be perceived in a wide variety of situations and processes. What we are concerned with here is a tantric reformulation of basic elements of Buddhist doctrine, expressed in a ritual form that in turn expresses the tantric view of yoga and enlightenment. Briefly stated, the teaching of the Five Mysteries is that the yogin on his way to enlightenment must first perceive the possibility of the goal and develop the desire, the resolve necessary for its attainment. He should then, as it were, come into direct contact with the path by performing the necessary practices, whereupon he develops an intimate involvement with the path revealed by the Buddha. Having gained insight into the truth *(dharma)* of the Buddha's teaching, he becomes capable of using this enlightenment for the benefit of sentient beings throughout the three realms.[5]

THE SPECIFIC FORMULATION

The precise configuration of the pentad under examination here is as follows:

> Vajrasattva (Kongōsatta)
> Surata/Iṣṭa-vajriṇī (Yoku-kongōnyo)
> Kelikilā-vajriṇī (Soku-kongōnyo)
> Kāmā/Rāga-vajriṇī (Ai-kongōnyo)
> Kāmeśvarā/Māna-vajriṇī (Man-kongōnyo)

The names of these deities may be translated respectively as the Thunderbolt (or Adamantine) Being[6] and the Adamantine Consorts of Desire, Touching,[7] Love, and Pride. It will be noticed that the first-named (and central) deity, Vajrasattva, is masculine, and that the remaining four are feminine. It might help here to look at some explanations typical of modern Japanese Shingon scholarship.

The *Mikkyō-jiten*[8] (MDJT) gives the following basic information about our topic:

> [The Five Mysteries are] Vajrasattva, who has the pure mind of enlightenment as his essence, and his immediate entourage, the four Bodhisattvas (Adamantine Desire, Adamantine Touching, Adamantine Love and Adamantine Pride) representing the four passions, and express in a thoroughly esoteric fashion the pro-

found mystery of the passions themselves being enlightenment.[9] The four Adamantine Bodhisattvas correspond to sentient beings and are the various taints of the passions, and [the Five Mysteries] indicate directly the fact that essentially they are originally endowed with the mind of enlightenment.[10]

The idea is, then, the commonly found Mahāyāna notion that enlightenment is to be found innate in all sentient beings, with the tantric formulation of the idea that the yogin arrests the samsaric influence of the passions by transmuting the raw energy inherent in them for the purpose of enlightenment.

A further permutation of this idea is that there is no duality between the beginning stage in the enlightenment process and final attainment. The former is commonly called the cause of enlightenment, the raising of the *bodhicitta*, which Vajrasattva primarily stands for. The latter is the effect produced by the yogic exercises which constitute the path. Since the pentad consists, on the one hand, of that which is pure and enlightened and, on the other, of the most basic passions, another principle found in our Japanese sources is that of sentient beings and the Buddha being of one essence. These two aspects come out in the various *bīja* assigned to the Five Mysteries as a whole. It will be sufficient to take two of these as illustrative: *stvaṃ* and *hhūṃ*, or double *hūṃ*.

Stvaṃ is analyzed[11] as *st* + *vaṃ*, the former being regarded as an abbreviation of *sattva*, "being," by implication also the Adamantine Being at the center of the Five Mysteries, i.e., Vajrasattva. The latter is the *bīja* of Mahāvairocana in the Vajradhātu maṇḍala,[12] and is thus the aspect of enlightenment. Joining these two together results in an expression of the principles indicated in the previous paragraph, which is formulated as *inka–fu'ni/shōbutsu–ittai*, "The motivation and the fruit are not dual / beings and the Buddha are of one essence."[13] The double hūṃ, generally transcribed as *hhūṃ*, expresses precisely the same ideas.[14] When written in the the Siddham script, the *bīja* appears as two graphs of the letter *h*, one above the other. MDJT assigns the top element to Mahāvairocana, that beneath to Vajrasattva, and gives the meaning as the same as the previous *bīja*.[15]

A further important aspect of the Five Mysteries strand of thought is the maṇḍala representations we have of the deities concerned. There are two main types, which differ according to the relative positions of the deities.[16] The most striking aspect of these maṇḍala, however, is the common characteristic, namely the fact that all five deities do not reside in their own separate parts of the maṇḍala but are grouped together on the same lotus dais and within the same lunar disc. In line with common Mahāyāna Buddhist symbolism, the lotus dais indicates compassion and the lunar disc wisdom, but the specific significance of this configuration is not only that both aspects have been achieved but that they have been integrated into one unit, which in turn represents the tantric ideal of man perfected.[17]

To give a reasonable account of where and how this idea of the Five Mysteries arose is a large undertaking, not least because a detailed examination of material in the Tibetan Kanjur would be required. To my knowledge, however,[18] it is only in Japan that there remains any living acquaintance with the concept of the Five Mysteries and the attendant ritual cycles, so limiting our enquiry to the Sino-Japanese tradition will not be wholly irrelevant. An indication of the textual basis for the present study is now in order.

Textual and Historical Background for the Five Mysteries

We may summarize the most important primary materials which apply to a study of the Five Mysteries from the Sino-Japanese sources as follows:

1. The following items in the *Rishukyō* literature are particularly relevant: T. vol. 8, no. 243, chaps. 1, 17 (784b1–29, 786a5–b4); T. vol. 8, no. 244 (the so-called extended version), pt. 1 (787a20–b22), pt. 14 (799b3–c17), pt. 21 (812a20–b4).[19]
2. Amoghavajra's commentary (T. vol. 19, no. 1003) on his own translation of the *Rishukyō* (T. vol. 8, no. 243) is also of some value in furnishing us with clues to the sūtra's historical and theoretical background.
3. The so-called Six Vajrasattva Rituals (*Rokushu-Kongōsatta-Giki*) found in T. vol. 20, nos. 1119, 1120a & b, 1121 (translator unknown), 1122, 1123, 1124, 1125.[20]

Some remarks on the last heading are in order, since the text we are concerned with comes under it. The Japanese scholar Fukuda Ryōsei has divided these Vajrasattva rituals into three groups: those with a direct relationship to a ritual tradition known as the *Srīparamādya* (i.e., the latter half of T. vol. 8, no. 244 and T. vol. 20, nos. 1119, 1120, 1123), those where the main theme of the *Rishukyō* is evidenced in the structure (T. vol. 20, nos. 1124, 1125), and those which may be placed somewhere between these two (T. vol. 20, nos. 1121, 1122). To Fukuda's opinions I would add my own suspicion—based primarily on a comparison of the mantra and mudrā sequences in the respective texts—that T. vol. 20, no. 1121 is very close to his first group, and that T. vol. 20, no. 1122 is rather much the odd man out in this sextet. T. vol. 20, nos. 1124 and 1125 have the same basic background as the *Rishukyō*, but, it should be remarked—as Fukuda does—that the material apart from the central motifs differs rather.[21]

The Diamond Peak Yoga Meditative and Recitative Ritual of the Practice of the Five Mysteries of Vajrasattva (Kongōchō–yuga–Kongōsatta-gohimitsu–shugyō–nenju-giki)[22]

INTRODUCTION

The text of the ritual begins with reference to the hundred thousand verses and eighteen assemblies of the *Kongōchōkyō*[23] and proceeds to passages in praise of the virtues of the teaching. "If one does not enter the Five Families/Five Mysteries maṇḍala *(go'bu-gohimitsu-mandara)*, one will not receive the threefold esoteric empowerment *(kaji, adhiṣṭhāna)*."[24]

There is then material concerning the following: the nature of the three realms and the way that leads out of them; the various paths within Buddhism itself, the significance of the bodhisattva's task, and the long path to enlightenment; the superiority of gaining entry to the samādhi of All-Pervading Goodness *(Samantabhadra)*, entry into the body of Vajrasattva, and receipt of supernatural powers through his empowerment; and the aspects of esoteric practice and realization that are revealed to the yogin in this state. Beginning at 535c8 there are references inter alia to the mind of joy *(kangi-shin)* and abiding in the *ālayavijñāna;* the various *bīja* of the Vajradhātu; receipt of *abhiṣeka* and the thunderbolt name *(kongō-gō);* and attainment of the extensive, profound, wonderful teaching *(kōdai-kanshin-fushigi-hō)* that transcends the two vehicles and the ten stages and is "This Great Dharma-Gate of the Yoga of the Five Mysteries of Vajrasattva" *(dai-Kongōsatta-gohimitsu-yuga-hōmon).*

In summary, the following themes, common to much of the esoteric tradition in China and Japan, are repeated in this opening section of T. vol. 20, no. 1125: the task of the bodhisattva in the esoteric vehicle as being to transcend the mundane and the supramundane spheres and attain to the inexpressible dharma which lies beyond, and the superiority of such a bodhisattva to those of the two vehicles *(ni-jō).*[25] Having attained his own enlightenment, the bodhisattva works unceasingly throughout the cosmos, bringing benefits—material, supernatural, and spiritual—to sentient beings.[26] Also discussed are the themes of the necessity of the constant expression of one's insight in one's everyday life, the identity of nirvāṇa and saṃsāra, and the absence of taints or attachments in one who has realized this state.[27]

REALIZING THE STATE OF VAJRASATTVA

This section[28] begins with observations on the type of place one should select for the performance of the ritual. The yogin then worships the tathāgatas of the four directions, and the text gives information on the effects of this worship on the body: it rids the body of the impurities in its three functions, and one comes to receive the ceremonial precepts of unhinderedness in the three worlds.[29]

The practitioner next contemplates the myriad assembly of all the buddhas and bodhisattvas in emptiness, and with the right knee touching the earth forms the seal {mudrā} of arousing the thunderbolt and intones that mantra.[30] One should also perform the appropriate meditation with the mind. After a reminder of the primacy of the original vow, the yogin repents before the holy assembly and gives forth the fivefold great vow (goshu-daigan). He then adopts the posture of Vajrasattva (right leg folded on top of the left) and forms the mudrā of concentration (jō, *dhyāna) and recites the mantra of unsurpassed, right, complete enlightenment (mujō-shōtō-bodai-shin shingon, *anuttara-samyak-sambodhi mantra), which runs:

(1) *oṃ sarva-yoga-cittam utpādayāmi*[31]

Through this mantra—which may be translated as: "Om! I awaken the mind which is in union with everything"—all the tathāgatas enable the yogin to overcome all demons and to rank equal with the buddhas and the bodhisattvas. The yogin also realizes Vajrasattva's great heart of courage and the fact that all sentient beings are endowed with the essence of the repository of all the tathāgatas (nyorai-zō-shō).[32] "Because Samantabhadra Bodhisattva pervades all sentient beings, I cause all the masses of beings to awaken and attain the state of Vajrasattva."[33]

Beginning with the phrase "The yogin performs this meditation . . . ," the next portion of the text[34] has five distinct parts: the first refers to Vajrasattva, the second to Ākāśagarbha, the third to Avalokiteśvara, the fourth to Viś-vakarman, and the fifth to the fact that sentient beings are all endowed with the bodies of these four great bodhisattvas. The specific natures or essences (shō, *bhāva) with which they are each associated are as follows:

Vajrasattva: all sentient beings endowed with the tathāgata-
repository-nature

Ākāśagarbha: all sentient beings' thunderbolt/adamantine {vajra}
repository-nature

Avalokiteśvara: all sentient beings' wonderful-dharma-repository-
nature

Viśvakarman: all sentient beings' karma-repository-nature

Body of the four great bodhisattvas: all sentient beings being thus
endowed with the four kinds of repository-nature

The practitioner then vows that all sentient beings shall quickly attain
the pure body of Mahāvairocana, and intones the mantra:

(2) *oṃ sarva-tathāgata-saṃsitāḥ sarva-sattvānāṃ sarva-siddhayaḥ
sam-padyantāṃ tathāgatāś-cādhitiṣṭhanām*[35]

This is a vow to complete all the mundane and supramundane *siddhi*, and
is used in conjunction with *vajrāñjali-mudrā*.[36] The mantra which follows
confirms this.

We now come to a series which is common to all the six Vajrasattva rituals.[37]

(3) *oṃ vajrāñjali*[38]

This mantra and the mudrā which accompanies it are commonly found as
an introductory action prior to a given ritual proper (or section of a ritual).
Being an ancient traditional gesture throughout the Buddhist world, it covers a wide variety of deities and functions. The designation *vajrāñjali* as
opposed to simply *añjali* is most commonly found in texts in the *Kongōchōkyō* lineage, which see one of the meanings of *vajrāñjali* as being the
starting point in the process of ascending through the various bodhisattva
stages. The mudrā simply has the fingers of the two hands stretched but
interlocking,[39] which symbolizes the perfect intertwining of the principles of wisdom and skillful means.[40]

(4) *oṃ vajra-bandha*[41]

In the first instance this mantra and its accompanying mudrā indicate the
lunar disc of the mind/heart,[42] which shows the inner locus whence the particular buddhas and bodhisattvas emanate. In the various ritual procedures
of the *Kongōchōkyō* texts, this mantra and mudrā combination commonly
follows directly on the preceding one.[43] The significance of *bandha* in this

context is twofold: first, it relates to the bond between the buddhas and bodhisattvas, on the one hand, and sentient beings, on the other;[44] second, it refers to the tantric idea of the transformation of the passions into enlightenment: the energy inherent in the passions has to be arrested and bound fast, lest it simply continue the round of saṃsāra. Hence the correct practice of this mantra/mudrā unit leads to the fulfillment of the ten perfections; and the two aspects of the mudrā—outer and inner—refer respectively to the buddha and to sentient beings.[45] The explanatory comment in the text should thus be seen in this light: "Through forming this mudrā one in fact brings about the thunderbolt wisdom which liberates."[46]

The next mantra in the series brings in a further element:

(5) *oṃ vajra-bandha traṭ*[47]

Hatta identifies this mantra as belonging to the function of wrath *(fun'nu)*.[48] This doubtless crops up here to ensure the safe passage of the practitioner through the various pitfalls and hindrances that confront him in the task ahead. The term *fun'nu*, here translated as "wrath," is used in Sino-Japanese esotericism to indicate the overcoming of hindrances to the practice of the way, generally depicted in the form of demons and other evil or unpleasant manifestations. Amoghavajra's text gives the effect of this seal as the conquering of the ten passions,[49] which in turn calls forth all the other seals. These seals come to reside in the yogin's body and mind, and he then perfects the various attainments that are part and parcel of his path. There are four seals referred to under the term *issai-in:*

1. The great wisdom seal *(dai-chi'in)*
2. The pledge wisdom seal *(sanmaya-chi'in)*
3. The dharma wisdom seal *(hō-chi'in)*
4. The karma wisdom seal *(katsuma-chi'in)*[50]

It will be seen that these seals correspond to the four types of maṇḍala that the Japanese founder of Shingon, Kūkai, enumerated; they are thus one of the many points of continuity between the Chinese and Japanese branches of the tradition.[51]

The theme of the next combination of mantra and mudrā is that of entering:

(6) *oṃ vajrāveṣa aḥ*[52]

Like the bell, whose sound penetrates everywhere, the wisdom of the

Tathāgata[53] is brought into the yogin's own body and illuminates his store-consciousness—the deepest level of his consciousness, which therefore affects his whole being. The *bīja* syllable *aḥ* indicates Trailokyavijaya (Gōzanze). According to the text, this mantra causes the four seals to manifest: further, it has tremendous power and can bring about perfection quickly.[54]

The final combination in this subsection is begun by the seal of the pledge of the thunderbolt fist *(kongō-ken-sanmaya-in, vajra-muṣṭi-samaya-mudrā)*, followed by the corresponding mantra:

(7) *oṃ vajra-muṣṭi baṃ*[55]

The four seals of the previous stage are now bound fast in the yogin's body and mind and cannot be lost.[56]

Up to now this section has dealt with a group of mantras common to most of these Vajrasattva rituals. Though the following combinations are not to be found in the other texts, they do form an integral part of the "Diamond Peak Yoga of the Five Mysteries of Vajrasattva."

(8) *samayastvaṃ*[57]

This mantra is intoned together with the *samaya mudrā* (both hands in the *vajra-bandha* position, middle fingers intertwined, hands then held in front of the chest),[58] and the practitioner is instructed to visualize Vajrasattva in a lunar disc of light.[59] The repeated performance of this seal and mantra has the effect of perfecting all the seals in all the families (or divisions, *bu, kula*). Hatta describes this mantra as one which incorporates the realm of Vajrasattva. The meaning of *samaya* in this context is that of equality *(byōdō, samatā)*, namely that the practitioner becomes one with the reality of the Thunderbolt.[60] The presence of the term *tvaṃ* ("thou [art]") indicates that this ideal has at this stage in the ritual assumed a human expression.

The following passage brings in the experience of bliss:

(9) *samaya hoḥ suratas tvaṃ*[61]

Surata is an ambiguous term, in that it not only refers to the mundane, deluded bliss of the ignorant,[62] but also—in its tantric usage—intends the absolute bliss of enlightenment.[63] We find in fact the themes we are dealing with here in Amoghavajra's commentary on the *Rishukyō*, where he explains the term as it appears in the first chapter of the sūtra: "Vajrasattva, moreover, is *surata*. Because the boundless, great compassionate pledge to the

inexhaustible realms of sentient beings—which are everywhere condi-
tioned—attains the benefits of peaceful bliss, and the assembly of the heart
takes no rest and is without duality in the equality of self and other, it is simply called 'surata.'"[64]

The *bīja* syllable *hoḥ* refers to *kangi*, "delight or joy," reminiscent as it is
of the laugh which comes forth upon the experience of great bliss *(dairaku,
mahāsukha)*. The result of this combination is that the essence of the thunderbolt *(vajrasattva)* comes to permeate the yogin's body and mind and that
one's desires and hopes are all attained.[65]

The practitioner now forms a thunderbolt fist *(kongō-ken, vajramuṣṭi)*
with each hand and adopts the characteristic posture of Vajrasattva: left fist
on the thigh, right fist grasping the thunderbolt, which is held before the
chest.[66] He then declares himself to be Vajrasattva:

(10) *vajrasatvo 'haṃ*[67]

Having intoned this, he should contemplate his own body as having
become Vajrasattva, abiding in a large lunar disc and seated upon a lotus
blossom, with the gemmed diadem of the five buddhas upon his head. He
has a smiling countenance and a body the color of the moon. Light perme-
ates inside and out, giving rise to great compassion, liberating innumerable
worlds of sentient beings and causing the attainment of the body of
Vajrasattva. Each of the yogin's three mysteries[68] is now as space *(kokū,
ākāśa)*.[69]

The text now goes on to explain that if one has perfected this seal, one
will be able to perform one's worship of the buddhas and bodhisattvas and
see the tathāgatas and Vajrasattva, even if one transgresses the teaching or
commits other grave offenses.[70] The yogin now visualizes the four seals surrounding Vajrasattva (that is, in their manifest forms as female deities), holding their respective emblems and wearing the diadem of the five buddhas.[71]
Totally absorbed in the vision, he should now recite the mantra:

(11) *vajrasatva aḥ*[72]

by means of which Vajrasattva should penetrate everywhere.[73]

(12) *vajrasatva dṛśya*[74]

occurs as a unit with the foregoing mantra in various Vajradhātu rituals.
While the former is a contemplation of one's own body as that of Vajrasattva,
the manifested wisdom body *(gen-chi-shin)*, the latter is a resolution to open

the eye of the heart *(shin-gen)* and embrace the true essence *(shin-zui)* of Vajrasattva.[75] Its effect is to cause a vision of Vajrasattva while one is in samādhi.[76] Then, with instructions to intone the mantra clearly and distinctly, the yogin is given the four most pervasive and typical *bīja* in the Five Mysteries cycle:

(13) *jaḥ-hūṃ-vaṃ-hoḥ*[77]

These are of course the *bīja* of the *saṃgraha* deities:[78] their function is a preliminary, even peripheral, one in the Vajradhātu rituals proper, but in the Five Mysteries cycles they assume a special significance on account of the particular emphasis that the latter give to the idea of arresting the perpetuating trend of the passions and transforming it into a trend toward enlightenment. The text describes the basic characteristics of the individual syllables as summoning-entering-binding-joy:[79] more precisely it is the wisdom-body of Vajrasattva which causes these four functions, which in turn bring about the fusion between the deity and the yogin.[80] The yogin then forms the seal of exquisite bliss *(sorata-in, surata-mudrā)* and recites another fundamental mudrā in the Five Mysteries cycles:

(14) *suratastvaṃ*[81]

The function of this mantra is to call forth the four *pāramitā*, to cause them to reside in their original positions.[82] These deities both protect and uphold the teaching.[83]

We have now come to a point where the general parallels to the other texts in the sextet finish for a while. The correspondences do in fact begin again later, thus presenting us with two distinct phases in the ritual procedure in these texts—one might term them the general (which establishes the traditional affiliation, i.e., with the *Kongōchōkyō* lineage) and the particular (which gives the specific Five Mysteries teachings). It is around these two subcycles that the various versions differ most, and it is here that the "Diamond Peak Yoga of the Five Mysteries of Vajrasattva" has most of its independent material. This material ends with the repetition of the mantra *suratastvaṃ*,[84] before the second of the two major groups that form the basis of these six texts.[85]

There now follows ritual adornment with the seal of the diadem of the five buddhas *(gobutsu-hōkan-in)*,[86] through which one attains the stage of consecration of the thunderbolt essence *(vajrasattva)* of all the tathāgatas *(issai-nyorai-kongōsatta-kanjō-i,* **sarva-tathāgata- vajrasattvābhiṣeka-pada)*.[87]

This theme of ritual consecration of oneself is continued in the next action, which is the consecration of the wig: *vajra-mālābhisiñca mām*.[88] This short section is then rounded off with the seal of joy *(kangi-in)*,[89] before the first mantra specific to the Five Mysteries in their entirety occurs.

The Five Mysteries Ritual Proper

(18) *oṃ mahāsukha-vajrasatva jaḥ-hūṃ-vaṃ-hoḥ suratastvaṃ*[90]

There then follow four laudatory verses pertaining to the four esoteric *karma-mudrā (shi-himitsu-katsuma-in)*,[91] after which there begin the mantra and mudrā specific to the four deities surrounding Vajrasattva:[92]

1. *Yokukongō-in* (Iṣṭa-vajriṇī-mudrā): to be visualized with bow in the left hand and arrow in the right hand. Mudrā: both hands in *vajramuṣṭi*. *Mantra:* (20, regarding this mantra, see note).[93]
2. *Keirikeira-in* (Kelikilā-mudrā): the hands are as in the previous stage, but crossed together and placed in front of the chest. *Mantra:* (21) *satvaṃ vajrasatva-parama-surata*.[94]
3. *Aikongō-in* (Rāga-vajriṇī-mudrā): same basic clasp, but the left hand supports the right elbow, such that the right arm points upward toward the shoulder in imitation of the banner or staff which this bodhisattva typically holds. *Mantra: sarva me mahāsukha-dṛṣṭiya ja*.[95]
4. *Kongōman-in* (Māna-vajriṇī-mudrā): the two *vajramuṣṭi* now rest on their respective thighs, and one inclines one's head to the left.[96]

Next follow the Pledge Seals *(sanmaya-in, samaya-mudrā)* of the Five Mysteries.[97] The first is that of Vajrasattva, accompanied by the mantra (24) *suratastvaṃ*, by means of which one's supernatural powers, length of life, majestic power, and bodily marks[98] come to be the same as those of Vajrasattva.[99] Then follow the mantra and mudrā combinations of the four consorts in order. The first dhāraṇī in this group of four (nos. 25–28) is said to be capable of removing passions which persist on account of subtle ignorance *(misai-mumyō)*,[100] and relates to adamantine desire. The dhāraṇī relating to Kelikilā is capable of liberating and preserving all realms of suffering sentient beings and fully attaining the samādhi of great peaceful bliss.[101] The dhāraṇī and seal of Rāgavajriṇī relate to liberation by great compassion *(daihi-gedatsu)*, in which one regards all sentient beings as one's child and arouses the heart/mind of peaceful bliss which liberates them *(bassai-anraku no shin).*[102] The final element, that of pride *(Kongō-man, Māna-vajriṇī),* enables the practitioner to attain the *pāramitā* of great vigor *(dai-shōjin-haramitsu, *mahā-vīrya-pāramitā)* and is further related to worship.[103]

The main purpose of the ritual now having been accomplished, the practitioner chants a supplicatory dhāraṇī of one hundred characters.[104] This ends with the *bīja* syllable *aḥ*, which has meanings and associations that integrate the various aspects of the process we are examining here.[105] The text at this point has what is obviously a misprint,[106] the characters *zu* (chant, intone) and *in* (seal) being inverted. The line should thus translate: "Next, residing in Vajrasattva's pledge seal *(Kongōsatta-sanmaya-in),* one chants the hundred-character dhāraṇī of Mahāyāna enlightenment *(daijō-genshō-hyakuji-shingon).*" The dhāraṇī brings about entry into the samādhi of Vajrasattva.

"Thus having entered the samādhi of Vajrasattva, one then forms the seal of great wisdom *(daichi-in)* and intones the dhāraṇī of the adamantine essence *(kongōsatta, vajrasattva)* of Mahāyāna enlightenment *(daijō-genshō),* saying: '*vajra-satva.*'"[107] Residing in the seal of great wisdom, one is now enjoined to continue recitation and contemplation without limit *(mugen-nenju).*[108] The practice of this combined samādhi and recitation ensures the attainment of innumerable samādhi in this present life, as well as attainment of the body of the main object of worship *(honzon no shin).* One is also rewarded with the manifestation of all the tathāgatas, the five *abhijñā* (supernatural powers), and the ability to course at will through all realms in the ten directions, bringing innumerable benefits to sentient beings. The final lines that pertain to the ritual proper run:

> The yogin—walking, standing, sitting or lying—is always with the four consorts, who moreover surround him, residing on a great lotus blossom within a common lunar disc. He who is the adamantine essence is the Bodhisattva of All-pervading Goodness (Samantabhadra-bodhisattva), that is, the first son of all the tathāgatas, all the tathāgatas' mind of enlightenment *(bodhi-citta),* the prime master *(soshi)*[109] of all the tathāgatas. It is for this reason that Vajrasattva is revered and loved by all the tathāgatas. As the sūtra explains:
>
> Vajra-sattva-samādhi: the name brings about the ritual of the buddhas. This ritual is able to bring about the buddha's path: if one is apart from this, then there neither is nor is not the buddha.[110]

Deities in the Five Mysteries

We are now at the end of the material pertaining to the ritual proper. The remainder of the text gives information on the deities found in the Five Mysteries.[111] The text may be divided as follows:

FOUR PĀRAMITĀS[12]

> Yoku: *prajñāpāramitā*
> Soku: *ākāśagarbha-samādhi ([mahā-]dhyāna-prajñāpāramitā?)*
> Ai: Tārā Bodhisattva, great compassion *([mahā-]karuṇa-*
> *prajñāpāramitā?)*
> Man: *mahāvīrya-prajñāpāramitā*

Yogācāra Analysis[113]

> Yoku: *ālaya-vijñāna* (with his bow and arrow he aims at all the
> defiled seeds in the *ālaya-vijñāna*); *dai-enkyō-chi (adarśajñāna).*
> Soku: *manas*, the pure seventh consciousness falsely grasping the
> eighth consciousness, the origin of deluded views concerning the
> self; *byōdōshō-chi (samatā-jñāna).*
> Vajrasattva: residing in the great wisdom seal, which encompasses
> the major deities of the Vajradhātu; the perfection of their wis-
> doms leads to the perfection of the self and other enjoyment
> bodies (*jijuyū-/tajuyū-katoku-shin;* probably the formulation of
> the buddha body formula found in the *Jōyuishiki-ron* by Hsüan-
> tsang).[114]
> Ai: *mano-vijñāna; myōkanzat-chi (pratyavekṣana-jñāna).*
> Man: the first five consciousnesses (i.e., the senses); *jōshosa-chi*
> *(kṛtyānuṣṭhāna-jñāna).*

The bodhisattvas here appear in their mode of transforming (purifying) the various defiled strata of consciousness.

THE VARIOUS EYES[115]

> Yoku: eye of wisdom *(e-gen)*, discriminating things according to
> their nature, but seeing them nevertheless as neither existing nor
> not existing.

Soku: through the wisdom which is without taints, knows that
things are neither identical nor different.

Vajrasattva: the dharmakāya itself, neither arising nor passing, and
as boundless as space.

Ai: the celestial eye of great compassion *(daihi-tengen)*.

Man: the pure fleshly eye, devoid of hindrances *(shōjō-muge-nikugen)*.

This body as a whole (i.e. all these virtues combined) is
Vajrasattva.[116]

FOUR PĀRAMITĀS[117]

Yoku: Kongō-haramitsu *(vajra pāramitā)*

Soku: Hō-haramitsu *(ratna pāramitā)*

Ai: Hō-haramitsu *(dharma pāramitā)*

Man: Katsuma-haramitsu *(karma pāramitā)*

THE FOUR TATHĀGATAS[118]

Vajrasattva himself takes on the aspect of each of the four tathāgatas in turn,
and as he goes through each of these manifestations, the consorts take on
corresponding forms of the bodhisattvas in the Vajradhātu:[119]

Akṣobhya

Yoku: Kongō-satta *(vajra sattva)*

Soku: Kongō-ō *(vajra* king)

Ai: Kongō-ai *(vajra* love)

Man: Kongō-zenshō *(vajra sādhu,* good victory)

Ratnasambhava

Yoku: Kongō-hō *(vajra* gem)

Soku: Kongō-nichi *(vajra* sun)

Ai: Kongō-dō *(vajra* banner)

Man: Kongō-shō *(vajra* smile/laugh)

Amitābha

Yoku: Kongō-hō *(vajra-dharma)*

Soku: Kongō-ri *(vajra* sword)

Ai: Kongō-in *(vajra* cause)

Man: Kongō-go *(vajra* language)

Amoghasiddhi

> Yoku: Kongō-go (*vajra* action)
> Soku: Kongō-go (*vajra* protection)
> Ai: Kongō-yakusna *(vajra-yakṣa)*
> Man: Kongō-ken (*vajra* clasp/fist)

THE GATHERING (SAṂGRAHA) DEITIES[120]

Note that the inner worshipping deities are in fact the following group *(ken-zoku)* of four, as are the outer worshipping deities (that is, the group performs both functions).[121] In this mode, the bodhisattvas have the following correspondences:

> Yoku: hook, setting sentient beings on the path of the buddha.
> Soku: rope (by implication, since the text mentions only the seal of
>   the embrace—as a rope is tied around someone).
> Ai: chain.
> Man: bell, which awakens sentient beings to enlightenment.

THE FAMILIES[122]

There follow brief remarks on maṇḍala pertaining to the various families *(bu, kula):* "The Samantabhadra maṇḍala is not separate from the five bodies.[123] The Trailokyavijaya maṇḍala is in fact the same as the Vajradhātu.[124] The Lotus Family maṇḍala of all-pervading subjugation accords with the sequence here. The Gem Family and the Accomplishment of all Purposes,[125] moreover, are the same as this explanation. The Five Mysteries of Vajrasattva are themselves the Tathāgata Family, and this in fact embraces the Vajra Family, the Lotus Family, and the Gem Family."

MISCELLANEOUS TEACHINGS[126]

The five bodhisattvas together on the same lotus dais has the meaning of liberation through great compassion *(daihi-gedatsu),* while the lunar disc indicates great wisdom *(daichi).* Because of the latter, the bodhisattva remains untainted while in birth and death; because of the former, he refrains from entry into nirvāṇa.

Three kinds of *sattva* are distinguished in the sūtras: deluded beings *(gu-satta),* wisdom beings *(chi-satta),* and adamantine (or thunderbolt) beings *(vajrasattva).* The difference lies in practice.

The next section consists of material found verbatim in the one-hundred-character verse of the *Rishukyō*, along with short explanations of selected lines.[127]

Conclusion

The complexity of the textual sources for the Five Mysteries is balanced by the relative simplicity of the concept itself. This very simplicity is in turn the reason for its inclusion in the context of tantric teachings, in that it implies the direct attitude to the struggle with man's passionate nature, which is the hallmark of the tantric's religious endeavor.

In the foregoing, I hope that I have given the reader some idea of the way in which the topic is dealt with in sources that are still the subject of concern in the modern Shingon sect in Japan. I should also be very happy if the reader has seen the manner in which the ancient authors of these ritual documents attempted to formulate their religious and philosophical perceptions of the world, for it is all too easy to dismiss these cryptic scriptures as just so much mumbo jumbo. There also remains a great deal of work of a purely text-critical nature, which may contribute significantly to our knowledge of the esoteric Buddhist tradition in East—and possibly also in Central and South—Asia. The above account will hopefully go some way to providing the stimulus for such research.

An Annotated Translation of the
Pañcābhisaṃbodhi Practice of the *Tattvasaṃgraha*

Dale Todaro

THE *Pañcābhisaṃbodhi*[1] (five stages of realization) visualization practice which Kūkai introduced to Japan and established as a hallmark of Shingon Buddhist practice is based on the *Tattvasaṃgraha*.[2] It constituted an integral part of the required *Vajradhātu vidhi* (Jpn. *kongōkai shidai*, ritual manual for the vajra realm) undertaken by all Shingon adherents. In the tenth stage of Kūkai's *Hizō hōyaku*, Kūkai states this visualization practice should be perfected by Shingon followers.[3] The following English translation of that part of the *Tattvasaṃgraha* discussing the *Pañcābhisaṃbodhi* practice is based on the authoritative, 1983 romanized edition of the complete Sanskrit text in five parts by Kanjin Horiuchi.[4] Horiuchi based his edition on the two Sanskrit manuscripts of the sūtra discovered in Nepal in 1932 and 1956 by G. Tucci and D. Snellgrove respectively. As Horiuchi follows the commentaries of Ānandagarbha[5] and Śākyamitra[6] (both tenth century), these also will be referred to below in addition to the major Japanese commentary on the *Tattvasaṃgraha* by Donjaku (1674–1742).[7] The initial questions to be answered in the following are, How faithful were Kūkai and his early followers to the original practice? What, if any, changes can be discerned in known writings of Kūkai and his disciples? How did they understand this practice?

Translation[8]

Then all the tathāgatas filled this buddha realm like sesame seeds.[9] At that time all the tathāgatas formed a great assembly and approached the Sarvārthasiddhi Bodhisattva Mahāsattva seated on the seat of enlightenment. Approaching, they appeared with saṃbhoga-type bodies of bodhisattvas and spoke thus: "Son of a noble family, you who endure all austerities, how will you realize the supreme, perfect enlightenment without knowing the truth of all the tathāgatas?"

THE PAÑCĀBHISAMBODHI[10]

(1)[11] Then the Sarvārthasiddhi Bodhisattva Mahāsattva, upon being exhorted by all the tathāgatas, rose from the *āsphānaka* samādhi. Prostrating to all the tathāgatas he said: "Blessed ones! Tathāgatas! Teach (me)! How should I practice? What is this truth?" Thus speaking, all the tathāgatas addressed this bodhisattva in accord and said: "Son of a noble family, you should proceed with the mantra, muttered at will, which is naturally successful and which composes and thoroughly masters your own mind: *Om* I perform thought penetration."

Then the Bodhisattva spoke thus to all the tathāgatas: "I have been taught. Blessed ones! Tathāgatas! I see the form of a moon disc in my own mind." All the tathāgatas said: "Son of a noble family, this mind is naturally luminous. As one cleanses it, so it becomes. It is just like dyeing with color a white garment."

(2) Then all the tathāgatas, for the increase of the knowledge of the naturally luminous mind, for this Bodhisattva, also produced the mind of enlightenment with this mantra which is naturally successful: *Om* I produce the mind of enlightenment.

Then the Bodhisattva again, by the command of all the tathāgatas, generated the mind of enlightenment and said: "That form of a moon disc I see just as a moon disc."

(3) All the tathāgatas said: "The mind of all the tathāgatas, Samantabhadra, the mind arisen, has become consistent.[12] Practice it well! For the strengthening of the arisen mind of Samantabhadra of all the tathāgatas imagine a vajra form in the moon disc in your own mind with the mantra: *Om* Stand up, oh thunderbolt!"

The Bodhisattva said: "Blessed ones! Tathāgatas! I see a thunderbolt in the moon disc."

(4) All the tathāgatas said: "Stabilize this thunderbolt of the Samantabhadra mind of all tathāgatas with this mantra: *Om* I consist of thunderbolt!"

Now these body, speech, and mind vajradhātus of all tathāgatas, assembling as far as all of space, entered that sattvavajra completely by the empowerment of all tathāgatas. Then the Bhagavat Sarvārthasiddhi Mahābodhisattva was consecrated with the thunderbolt named initiation "Vajradhātu, Vajradhātu!" by all the tathāgatas.

Then the Vajradhātu Mahābodhisattva spoke thus to all the tathāgatas: "Blessed ones! Tathāgatas! I see myself as the body of all tathāgatas."

(5) All the tathāgatas replied: "Now, great being! Visualize yourself as the *sattvavajra*, the buddha form endowed with the best of all forms, reciting at will with this naturally successful mantra: *Oṃ* As all the tathāgatas are, so am I."

Having been so addressed, the Vajradhātu Mahābodhisattva knew himself to be a tathāgata. He prostrated to all the tathāgatas and spoke thus: "Empower me! Blessed ones! Tathāgatas! May you strengthen this enlightenment!"

Having been so addressed, all the tathāgatas entered this *sattvavajra* of the Vajradhātu Tathāgata.

Japanese Examples of the Pañcābhisaṃbodhi Practice

The five stages of meditation identified above are outlined by Kūkai in his *Hizō hōyaku:*

> Next, I will clarify the five stages of perfecting the body. The first is to penetrate the mind. The second is generating the mind of enlightenment. The third is the thunderbolt mind. The fourth is the thunderbolt body. The fifth is realizing unsurpassed enlightenment and obtaining a firm body like that of a thunderbolt. When these five stages of meditation are perfected then one attains the body of the principle deity of worship. Your radiance will be that of the body and mind of Samantabhadra identical with that of all Buddhas in the ten directions. Also, although there are those who are early or late in their perfection of yoga in the three periods, once achieving enlightenment they experience no past, future, or present.[13]

This brief description by Kūkai closely follows that of the *Tattvasaṃgraha*. Fuller descriptions of these stages, using Kūkai's terminology, which are nearly identical with the *Tattvasaṃgraha*, are found likewise in all of the following sources (listed here for easy reference). These are *Vajradhātu vidhis* incorporating the *pañcābhisaṃbodhi* practice.

1. Kūkai (?) (774–835): *Kongōkai kigami shidai;* also called *Kongōkai bonji shidai* and *Kongōkai ōshi shidai;* dated 1226.[14]

2. *Mujin sōgonzō shidai;* written by either Kūkai, Shūei (809–84), or Genjō (active AD 900).[15]

3. *Kongōkai daigiki,* copy dated 1167; written either by Kūkai or Shūei.[16]

4. Jichie (AD 786–847): *Kongōchō yuga rengebu daigiki.*[17]

5. Uda Tennō (Kanpyō: AD 867–931): *Kongōchōkyō rengebu shinnenju shidai.*[18]

6. Jōkei (Chōkei: AD 866–900?): *Kongōkai nenshidai shiki.*[19]

7. Junnyū (AD 890–953): *Kongōchō rengebu shinnenju shidai.*[20]

8. Shingō (AD 938–1004): *Kongōchō rengebu shinnenju giki shiki.*[21]

9. Yūkai (AD 1345–1416): *Chūinryū shido kuden; Kongōkai shidai.*[22]

10. Shinzei (AD 800–860): *Gobukanjinki.*[23]

11. Gengō (AD 914–95): *Kongōkai nenju shiki.*[24]

These sources testify to the uniformity in the early Shingon tradition of the *pañcābhisaṃbodhi* practice. The only obvious difference from the *Tattvasaṃgraha* in all the above sources is the addition within the third stage of a secondary visualization practice. This involves the visualized expansion and contraction of a thunderbolt. Sources 1, 6, and 11 above state this visualization is based on an oral tradition. The Shingon monk Saisen (1025–1115) tells us they were added to clarify to the yogin the characteristics of the container world of the Dharmakāya Buddha.[25]

Commentary

It should be remembered that the Vajradhātu recitation manuals used in the Shingon school in Japan are based by and large on the *Chin kang ting lien hua pu hsin nien sung i kuei [Jin gang ding lian hua bu xin nian song yi gui],* translated by Amoghavajra.[26] As indicated by the term *lien hua pu,* this meditation manual is said to correspond to the lotus family among the five families of the *Tattvasaṃgraha* lineage texts[27] and to the mystery of speech among the three mysteries of the body, speech, and mind.[28] It is also said that this manual was translated by Amoghavajra because it is with the flower of the mind of enlightenment as cause that Buddhahood is achieved.[29] This correspondence with the lotus family is indicated by the Amitābha samādhi mudrā first formed upon entering the *pañcābhisaṃbodhi* practice and the lotus visualized in the moon.[30] Also, discriminative knowledge among the five knowledges corresponding to this family is suggested by the Japanese term *kansatsujishin* samādhi, which is first entered when practicing the *pañcābhisambodhi* meditation (discriminative knowledge or wisdom = observing one's own mind).

According to F. Edgerton,[31] *āsphānaka* samādhi doubtlessly is the same as *āsphāranaka* samādhi. While both manuscripts of the *Tattvasamgraha* have *āsphānaka* samādhi, the Tibetan[32] and both Chinese translations of Amoghavajra and Sego[33] have *āsphāranaka* samādhi. The latter is translated as "space-filling" by Lessing.[34]

Ennin interprets *āsphānaka* samādhi as breath-counting meditation *(ānāpāna).*[35] He writes that in this meditation the mind and body should be still. The lips and teeth are closed and both eyes are slightly opened. Mindfulness of breathing is practiced to stop the obstructions of confusion, dissipation, and the like. This is practiced by the slow-learning Mahā-yānists, Hīnayānists, and heretics. If one can quickly enter the path of this sūtra there is no need to rely on this meditation.[36]

According to Donjaku, it is through *āsphānaka* meditation that one enters the first of the five stages of religious practice known in Japanese as *tsūdatsushin.* Quoting from the *I kuei,*[37] he writes: "On *āsphānaka, ā* means the absence of. *Spānaka* means consciousness. This is a samādhi where the mind is held in equilibrium. *Ka* means body. One should say (this is a samādhi where) there is absence of the consciousness and the body is held in equilibrium."[38] Donjaku clearly states this is not breath-counting med-itation.[39] Rather, in this meditation, one should abide in quietude and equilibrium, and by the knowledge of the absolute truth, visualize count-less buddhas in space, as numerous as sesame seeds. Through this samādhi one realizes that all defilements and obstructions are like a ring of fire, an echo in an empty valley. In such a meditation one does not perceive the body-mind complex and one knows all things are without an intrinsic nature.[40]

Donjaku also says Sarvārthasiddhi is another name for Samantabhadra.[41] This is the mind of enlightenment. The seat of enlightenment is the devo-tee's own mind. The *sambhogakāyas* are the devotee's bodies of equality knowledge.[42] When the Shingon practitioner first undergoes an initiation into the Vajradhātu mandala he/she receives the bodhicitta precepts and practices this visualization of five features. While *āsphānaka* cannot be inter-preted as Ennin does strictly as breath counting, it is clear that the Shingon tradition orally taught a preliminary practice prior to the *āsphānaka* samādhi which involved stilling the breathing process as described by Ennin. This is explained, for example, in sources I and II above. First the breath is quieted. Then the letter *hūṃ* is visualized (a symbol of the mind of enlightenment) entering and exiting the body with the breath. During this visualization the tongue is held stationary touching the roof of the mouth, and the body is held erect and still in a lotus position. While identifying with the letter *hūṃ*, consciousness of the body and mind subsides. Hereafter one enters the *āsphānaka* samādhi and cultivates the wisdom that observes the objects of the mind free from discrimination. All *kleśas, skandhas*, and so on, are known to be without an abiding, intrinsic nature and are likened to various illusions. Jichie (source 4) says that the objects of mind are thus known to arise from the *ālaya* consciousness; one hereby knows they all arise based on one's own mind. This visualization practice leads to a state of profound quietude and equilibrium, which, however, must not be attached to. This is followed in our text by the *pañcābhisaṃbodhi* practice, which leads to the realization of the intrinsic nature of the mind and body (recall that, as explained above, consciousness of the mind and body is absent). While abiding in this samādhi countless numbers of sambhogakāya buddhas are visualized filling the air. One abides in the tenth *bhūmi* gained by the enlightened bodhisattvas of the three vehicles (one has yet to enter the buddha stage). After being exhorted by the sambhogakāya buddhas and leaving the *āsphānaka* samādhi one moves into the causal stage of the Shingon school and beyond the ten *bhūmis*.[43]

Donjaku gives the following names for these five stages of religious practice: *tsūdatsuhonshin, shubodaishin, jōkongōshin, shōkongōshin*, and *busshinenman*.[44] His discussion of these stages is as follows.

First, *shin* in *tsūdatsuhonshin* means the mind of enlightenment. *Tsūdatsu* means to see the path, that is, the practice of visualizing the mind of enlightenment symbolized by the moon. He says that visualization of the letter *A* is a means to perfect the visualization of the moon. In regards to the latter he quotes from the *Bodaishinron*:

> The mind of the common person is like a closed lotus. The mind of a buddha is like a full moon. . . . The practitioner should visualize a sun or moon disc in the mind. By practicing this visualization one will radiate the original mind's natural purity. Moreover, this should be like the full moon's light which pervades space without distinctions. . . . This is called the pure dharmadhātu and also the sea of prajñāpāramitā and truth. It can encompass manifold and countless precious gem samādhis.

... Why is the example made with a moon disc? To create the round, bright form of a full moon is similar to encouraging the mind of enlightenment.[45]

The devotee should practice this visualization for a long time. Cultivating and perfecting it, it should not be ignored and forced.[46]

Second, the next stage is where the visualized moon is seen constantly. Nondiscriminating knowledge is hereby cultivated. Quoting again from the *Bodaishinron*, Donjaku writes, "If one, just for a moment, visualizes it, this is called seeing reality. ... If one constantly sees it this is to enter the first bodhisattva bhūmi."[47] Here one first should attain a stable mind whereby joy is experienced; this is the *pramuditā* bhūmi.[48] Donjaku says this stage includes all practices from the first bhūmi up to the tenth bhūmi.[49]

Third, now one attains mastery of the tenth bhūmi, although the mind is still affected by the impressions of the storehouse consciousness. The thunderbolt is visualized to strengthen the mind of enlightenment which has been awakened. This thunderbolt visualized in the moon disc has five prongs which emit rays of light. This represents the unstained, pure Buddha knowledge. Here one attains the initial stage of *tōgaku,* or enlightenment.[50]

Fourth, the next stage of realizing the thunderbolt mind is the stage where one receives an *ācārya* consecration {Jpn. *ajari kanji,* dharma transmission ceremony that confers the status of master of tantric Buddhism}, equivalent to the thunderbolt samādhi. The crown placed on the head during this consecration consists of the five buddhas, and the thunderbolt one holds in the hand indicates one is the lord of the teaching. The consecration is called "vajradhātu" because all the deities of the *Vajradhātu* maṇḍala enter the body. *Sattvavajra* means to realize the thunderbolt at the time of the consecration.[51]

Fifth, in the final stage one's body becomes a maṇḍala body; that is, one becomes fully enlightened. The buddhas of the five quarters enter the body. These are endowed with the three mysteries and perfect the devotee. Being thus endowed with the three mysteries and reciting the mantra, one perfects realization gained in stage four.[52]

Buddhaguhya and other Indian commentators also give an explanation of the *pañcābhisambodhi* practice.[53] The devotee first practices breath meditation whereby the six senses are quieted and concentration can begin. The tongue is placed against the palate, the eyes are half closed, and the body should be sitting in an upright posture. Once the body and mind are still, one is to concentrate the mind with the mantra "*Oṃ* I perform thought penetration."

In regards to breath meditation, Padmavajra says *prāṇa* (wind or breath) issues from all openings of the body and the perceptive consciousness usually rides on these winds. By stopping the inhalation and exhalation process it is possible to gain concentration: the flow of consciousness to the external world then stops.

When the moon disc is seen in the mind, Buddhaguhya says, the devotee realizes the principle of śūnyatā, or emptiness. The moon disc at first is not constantly seen because in the next stage the mahā-bodhisattva is made to say, "That form of a moon disc I see just as a moon disc." This is because habitual mental patterns have not been completely purified and one's merits and insight are immature. Buddhaguhya says the mark of the moon disc that appears is a sign of the devotee appearing as the principle deity of worship.

In the second stage the moon is made to shine brightly like a full autumn moon. Padmavajra, like Donjaku, says the accomplishments of this stage correspond with the first nine bhūmis. According to Ānandagarbha the mantra "*Oṃ* I produce the thought of enlightenment" increases the light of the moon. Śākyamitra says the moon visualized here is like the full moon of the fifteenth day of the [lunar] month. He also says the first stage corresponds with mirrorlike knowledge and the self-nature of Akṣobhya, while the second stage corresponds with equality knowledge and the self-nature of Ratnasambhava. (In his *Gosojō shingi montōshō* Saisen likewise makes these same correlations of the five buddhas and the five stages.)[54]

In the third stage, Buddhaguhya says, a five-pronged thunderbolt should be visualized in the moon disc to strengthen the mind of enlightenment. This symbolizes the five wisdoms. Both Śākyamitra and Ānandagarbha say this practice is correlated with discriminative knowledge and Amitābha.

Ānandagarbha and Śākyamitra both equate the fourth stage with the self-nature of Amoghasiddhi. Buddhaguhya says that by the correct and long visualization of the thunderbolt in the moon it becomes clear and stable and thereby the practitioner becomes the vajradhātu consisting of the body, speech, and mind mysteries of all the tathāgatas.

Buddhaguhya says that the final stage is a means the devotee has of unifying the radiating light of the moon. That is, with the body becoming the radiant moon one illumines all worlds as the Bhagavat Vairocana. Padmavajra adds that now one appears as a niṣyandakāya with radiant marks.

Conclusion

In general terms Kūkai comments as follows on the effects of this practice:

> If this visualization is perfected, visible are the pure and impure
> lands in the ten directions; all sentient beings in the six transmi-
> gratory paths; the practitioners of the three vehicles; the creation
> and destruction of the worlds in the three times; the differences
> of karma of sentient beings; the activities of bodhisattvas in
> stages leading to enlightenment; and all buddhas in the three
> times. By realizing the body of the principle deity of worship
> one will fulfill all the acts and vows of Samantabhadra. . . . Thus,
> it is this samādhi which enables one to perfect the self-nature of
> all buddhas, to realize the dharmakāya of all buddhas, to realize
> the innate wisdom of the dharmadhātu, and to perfect the sva-
> bhāvakāya, sambhogakāya, nirmāṇakāya, and niṣyandakāya of
> Mahāvairocana Buddha. Since the yogin has not yet realized this,
> it is fitting that this be cultivated.[55]

It is clear from this that Kūkai taught that this samādhi would lead to
complete enlightenment as understood in the Shingon school. That it is
unquestionably difficult to perfect, however, is indicated in different ways.
First, Kūkai urges his followers to cultivate it—that it could lead to enlightenment does not obscure the fact that it was a practice only for those who
had earlier mastered meditation practices associated with the other
Buddhist schools (these are outlined in Kūkai's *Hizō hōyaku*). As Saisen and
even Ennin put it, it was a practice for those in the fast lane, fast learners,
those who had gone beyond the traditional bodhisattva realizations (in former lives perhaps) and entered the buddhayāna.[56] This practice is found in,
and still remains an integral part of, all Vajradhātu vidhis, so it would be
continuously "practiced" over the life span of the Shingon adherent initiated into its ritual-visualization order. One reason, perhaps, for the numerous examples of abbreviated Shingon vidhis in Japan,[57] soon after Kūkai
introduced vidhis, is that much time, indeed, could be spent mastering similar "short" visualizations in any context. Long rituals accompanying these
visualization practices weren't always the rule.

Common to both the Japanese and Tibetan interpretations of this practice are their correlations of the five stages with the five buddhas. Also, both

associate intimately a mantra recitation with each visualization practice—
it is the mantra that encourages the success of the visualization. This emphasis on mantra recitation is true to the correlation of this text traditionally
with the mystery of speech.

The perfection of this practice leads to an enlightenment characterized
by five wisdoms. Saisen states that whoever quickly attains this enlightenment is not aware of there being five stages of practice as such. This practice here is divided into stages for those requiring time to perfect it. He also
goes on to say that after the *pañcābhisaṃbodhi* practice is completed in the
Vajradhātu vidhis, the yogin becomes a self-oriented sambhogakāya buddha
since one abides on the seat of enlightenment in the vidhi. The exact
ramifications of Padmavajra's statement (and the statements of other
Indian and Tibetan commentators on the results of this practice) that the
yogin becomes a niṣyandakāya should be investigated to see if his teachings
differed as to the results or effects of this practice.

It is remarkable that after so many centuries this tradition of the
pañcābhisaṃbodhi practice is so little changed and still continues. After an
early canonization of the Shingon teachings related to this practice, the
promise of enlightenment by the master of this practice is still maintained.

The Twelve-Armed Deity Daishō Kongō and His Scriptural Sources

Pol Vanden Broucke

Introduction

THE TWELVE-ARMED DEITY Daishō Kongō,[1] "Great Victorious Vajra," belongs to the rich pantheon of the Japanese Shingon school of esoteric Buddhism. In Japan, this deity was mainly invoked to gain victory in warfare *(senshō kigan)*. We do not have any evidence of a Daishō Kongō cult in China. His image is found only in a few Japanese paintings and drawings.[2] As far as we can ascertain there is no image of this deity in the Chinese, Indian, and Tibetan Buddhist pantheons. Daishō Kongō is included neither among the deities explained in the two main texts of Shingon *(Vairocanābhisaṃbodhi* and *Tattvasaṃgraha)*[3] nor in the pictorial representations of these scriptures (Taizō mandara, Skt. Garbha maṇḍala; Kongōkai mandara, Skt. Vajradhātu maṇḍala).[4]

Since there is no Indian deity parallel to Daishō Kongō, the Indian designation of this twelve-armed figure remains problematic. In his *Introduction to the Maṇḍala*, Yamamoto Chikyō renders Daishō Kongō into Mahājayavajra ("Great Victorious Vajra") but gives no further explanation or attestation for this Sanskrit name.[5] Apparently he reconstructed the Indian name of Daishō Kongō by translating the Sino-Japanese name word by word into Sanskrit. Up to now we have not yet found any Indian deity called Mahājayavajra. The outer circle of the Durgatipariśodhana maṇḍala described in the Nispannayogāvalī contains a deity called Vijayavajra, "Victorious Vajra."[6] Although the Indian name of this deity is reminiscent of the Sino-Japanese name Daishō Kongō, there is no iconographic resemblance at all. Vijayavajra is another name for Vasanta, a Hindu deity associated with spring and related to Kāma.[7] Vijayavajra is described as a white deity sitting on a frog and holding a sword in the left hand and a vajra in the right hand. The sword is also one of the attributes held by Daishō Kongō, but many other deities hold this object. As we will see below Daishō Kongō is apparently an abbreviated appellation.[8] This problem will be further treated in the discussion of the scriptural sources of Daishō Kongō.

In the Japanese commentarial tradition there has been a lot of speculation on the identity of this deity.[9] In the *Yugikyō* (see below) he is presented as a manifestation of Dainichi. But there are different explanations according to the schools and sub-schools in Shingon and also in Tendai. According to the esoteric Buddhism of the Tendai school (Taimitsu) he is a direct manifestation of Dainichi (Vairocana), the so-called Twelve-Armed Dainichi (Jūnihi Dainichi).[10] In Tendai, Daishō Kongō is also equated with Shōissai Butchō, "All Comprising Buddha Crown" (Kinrin Butchō, "Golden Wheel Buddha Crown").[11] This deity belongs to a group of speculative deities who are a deification of Buddha's *uṣṇīṣa*, the protuberance on the crown of his head which is one of the thirty-two characteristics of a Buddha.[12] According to the Hirosawa branch (Hirosawa-ryū) of the esoteric Buddhism of the Shingon school (Tōmitsu), Daishō Kongō is explained as a transformation of Aizen Myōō, "King of Esoteric Knowledge (called) Tinted by Lust" (Skt. *Rāgarāja), who, in his turn, is regarded as a transformation of Kongōsatta (Skt. Vajrasattva).[13] In the Daigo branch he is identified with Daibutchōson, "Great Buddha Crown Honored One."[14] In the Mii branch (Mii-ryū) he is considered as the main deity of the *Yugikyō*. According to this branch his twelve arms represent the twelve chapters of this scripture.[15] Because of his complicated character Daishō Kongō is difficult to classify in the pantheon of Sino-Japanese esoteric Buddhism. Depending on the iconographic or ritual handbook, he is classified either as a deity belonging to the Butchō-bu, "Buddha Crown Section";[16] the Bosatsu-bu, "Bodhisattva Section";[17] or the Myōō-bu, "Vidyārāja Section."[18]

The purpose of the present study is to provide a translation of the texts in which the iconography and ritual of Daishō Kongō are described.

The Scriptural Sources of Daishō Kongō

The iconography and ritual of Daishō Kongō are based on chapter 8 of the *Chin-kang-feng Lou-ke I-ch'ieh Yü-chia Yü-ch'i Ching* (Jpn. Kongōbu rōkaku issai yugayugi kyō, "The Scripture of All the Yogas and Yogīs of the Vajra Peak Pavilion," T. vol. 18, no. 867).[19] This scripture is traditionally considered to be a Chinese translation from the T'ang dynasty (618–907). This esoteric Buddhist text is extant only in Chinese and not in Sanskrit or Tibetan versions. It is better known by its abbreviated Japanese title *Yugikyō*. The *Yugikyō* is a major text in the Japanese Shingon school and is included in the *Gobu no hikyō* ("The Five Secret Scriptures"), a set of five texts which constitute the Shingon canon.[20] Kūkai (774–835), the founder of the Shingon school, named the temple complex on Mt. Kōya after the first three characters of the title of this text, i.e., Kongōbuji, "Vajra (or Diamond, Adamantine) Peak Temple."[21] Nowadays, however, Kongōbuji refers to the single temple which is the headquarters of the Kōya branch of the Shingon school.

According to the Shingon tradition, the *Yugikyō* explains the deep meaning of the "Non-Duality of the Two Sections" (Ryōbu Funi), a central Shingon tenet.[22] This interpretation of the text became the basis for the construction of a unique Japanese stūpa, the Yugitō, built in 870 near the Ryūkōin (or Chūin) on Mt. Kōya.[23] The term *ryōbu* refers to the two complementary aspects of the ultimate reality: the Taizō (Skt. Garbha, "Womb") and the Kongōkai (Skt. Vajradhātu, "Vajra Realm"). The Taizō represents the enlightened universe from the viewpoint of compassion and is symbolized by the lotus. Kongōkai represents the realm of knowledge in which illusion and passion are crushed. It is symbolized by the vajra ("thunderbolt," "diamond"), which is indestructible like diamond and which destroys all delusion. In Shingon these two aspects are considered as a unity. The Taizō and Kongōkai are represented graphically in the Taizō mandara and the Kongōkai mandara respectively, the two main maṇḍalas in Shingon Buddhism.[24] These maṇḍalas depict the teachings of the two fundamental Indian texts of Shingon: the *Vairocanābhisaṃbodhi* and the *Tattvasaṃgraha*. In Shingon, these two maṇḍalas are pictorial representations of the two complementary aspects of the ultimate reality. This reality is embodied in Vairocana (Dainichi), also known as Mahāvairocana in the Sino-Japanese tradition.

The *Yugikyō* also occupies an important position in the Tendai school and forms part of the Tendai version of the *Gobu no hikyō*.[25] It is also regarded as canonical in the heterodox Tachikawa school (Tachikawa-ryū), where it is included in the *Sangyō ichiron* ("The Three Sūtras and the Treatise"), a set of four canonical texts.[26]

We have no idea in what degree the *Yugikyō* was important in China. The Chinese translation is usually attributed to Vajrabodhi (671–741) or

Amoghavajra (705–74).[27] But the question whether the text is a translation of a lost Indian original or was fabricated as a Chinese apocryphal text, and then spuriously attributed to one of the founders of the esoteric Buddhist tradition in China, cannot yet be answered with certainty. The text was first introduced to Japan by Kūkai in 806. The *Yugikyō* is not included in any catalogue of the T'ang. It is first listed four centuries after its introduction in Japan, in the sixth chapter of the *Chih-yüan Fa-pao K'an-t'ung Tsung Lu,* abbreviated *Chih-yüan Lu.* This is a comparative Chinese-Tibetan catalogue of the Chih-yüan era, compiled by Ch'ing Ch'i-hsiang in Peking between 1285 and 1287.[28]

Whatever the position of this text in China, it became a major text in the Japanese Shingon and Tendai schools. Through the centuries, the text has been the subject of highly speculative interpretations in Japan. This resulted in numerous commentaries written from the first half of the Heian period through the Edo period.[29] The *Yugikyō* is also the scriptural source for the iconography and the ritual of Aizen Myōō, another deity with no Indian or Tibetan parallel.[30]

A twelve-armed deity with an appearance similar to Daishō Kongō is also described in a short ritual text titled *Daishō Kongō Butchō nenju giki* (T. vol. 19, no. 980). The translation of this text is also attributed to Vajrabodhi. Of this text there is only one manuscript extant, a manuscript copied by the Japanese scholar-monk Shinson of the Daigoji and dated Kōgen 11 (1257).[31] It is again unclear whether this text is a translation of a lost Indian original or was fabricated elsewhere as an apocryphal text. Moreover, the *Daishō Kongō Butchō nenju giki* is not named in any Chinese Buddhist catalogue.[32] In this short text Vairocana explains to Vajrapāni the formula *(mantra)* and the hand-gesture *(mudrā)* of a deity called Daishō Butchō ("Great Victorious Buddha Crown"), the effect of reciting his mantra and the way of drawing his figure. The text bears a strong resemblance to chapter 8 of the *Yugikyō.*

Translation of Chapter 8 of the Yugikyō

The Great Samaya[33] of the Highest Truth of the Great Victorious
Vajra Crown of All Tathāgatas

Then[34] the Universally Shining Bhagavat (Dainichi, Skt. Vairocana) manifested furthermore various kinds of light. From the top of his crown he sent out adamantine fierce light illuminating the bodhisattva Vajrapāni (Jpn. Kongōshu)[35] and others. They were all silent. He further manifested a body and hands.[36] He was provided with twelve arms and made the hand-gesture of the Knowledge Fist.[37] Furthermore, he possessed a five-pronged vajra,[38] a lotus, a jewel, a karma[vajra],[39] a hook (Skt. *aṅkuśa*), a rope, a chain, a bell,[40] a knowledge sword,[41] and a wheel of the dharma,[42] the twelve great hand-gestures.[43] His body was dwelling on a large white lotus with a thousand petals. The color of his body was like the sun and the light of the five locks of hair[44] spread regally in the ten directions.[45] His face smiled and he expounded the formula of the great samaya of the highest truth of the Great Victorious Vajra Crown, saying:

oṃ mahāvajroṣṇīṣa hūṃ traḥ hrīḥ aḥ hūṃ[46]

After he had explained this esoteric wisdom,[47] he explained in gāthās:[48]

In the pure and wondrous lands of the ten directions,[49] in the three periods[50] as well as in the three realms,[51] he is the most honored one, unique and unequaled, this great wheel-turning king.

He destroys the buddha crowns[52] and comprises those who are equally enlightened. Those who honor him are his entourage. They will quickly realize the great siddhi.

When the people of the latter dharma recite this formula for a long time, the sword or the soldier will not hurt them, and water and fire will not burn or sweep them away.

The Lotus and Vajrapāni[53] will shelter and guard them. When one recites one hundred and eight times, one will eliminate the sins of a hundred kalpas.

When one recites one thousand times, one will realize one's wishes. When one recites one lakṣa, one will obtain the great vajra body.[54] When one recites one koṭi, one will realize the Universally Shining Honored One.[55] The thousand Buddhas will surely and without doubt come to protect us.

Now,[56] I furthermore explain the hand-gesture, the adamantine supreme thought. Bind the ten degrees[57] internally[58] and stretched. Bend the patience and the vow {fingers} like a crown.[59] This is called the fundamental thought,[60] the supreme wheel-turning hand-gesture [mudrā].[61]

If one always forms this hand-gesture, the honored Vajrasattva,[62] the Lotus[63] and Jewel King,[64] the honored Viśvakarman,[65] and all the noble honored ones will come and increase their protection.

This person is like a vajra[66] and cannot be destroyed by the unwholesome. This body is like a beam of light and can penetrate the darkness of the three realms.

This person is like a lotus and cannot be tainted by the various dust particles. This body is like karma and largely brings forth the activities of the buddhas.

The body is like the Universally Shining Honored One. The buddhas will not abandon you. The body is like Mañjuśrī and can realize the endless wisdom.

The body is like the vajra-wheel and can turn the wheel of the leading principle.[67] Possessing this formula and hand-gesture one can realize such things.

If one relies on a pure abode of contact, if one only forms the supreme hand-gesture and recites the fundamental thought, then there will be nothing that will not be accomplished.[68]

Whatever one does, it will all be realized. All wishes will be fulfilled.

The esoteric knowledge of the Vajra Crown which realizes the Supreme Honored One, says:[69]

oṃ vajrasatvakośa hūṃ[70]

The supreme mani (i.e., jewel) which realizes Vajrapāni, says:

om vajraratnakośa trah[71]

The supreme thought of the lotus which realizes Vajrapāni, says:

om vajradharmakośa hrīh[72]

The supreme thought of the skillful acts which realizes Vajrapāni, says:

om vajrakarmakośa ah[73]

The supreme one who realizes the vajra-hook, hooks:[74]

om vajrasatvāmkuśa jjah[75]

The supreme one who realizes the vajra-rope, leads:

om vajraratnapāśa hūm[76]

The supreme one who realizes the vajra-chain, binds:

om vajrapadmasphota vam[77]

The supreme one who realizes the vajra-bell, makes happy:

om vajrakarmagamt hoh[78]

Because one possesses the eight great esoteric knowledges,[79] one can realize a hundred thousand things. The hand-gestures are like those of the Vajra Realm[80] and the formulae should be known.

[Against] all the invincible ones one must use these hand-gestures and esoteric knowledges.

Next the secret word of the vajra-sword should be known:

oṃ vajrasatvatīkṣṇa hūṃ[81]

It destroys the walls of ignorance and produces the wisdom of all the Buddhas. The hand-gesture is the same as the *Mañjuśrīkarmasamaya.[82] Next the secret word of the vajra-wheel should be heard:

oṃ vajracakra hūṃ jjaḥ hūṃ vaṃ hoḥ hūṃ[83]

[Form with] the two wings[84] the vajra-fist[85] and hook the four degrees—charity (symbolized by the right little finger), wisdom (left little finger), energy (right index), and power (left index)— into one another. This is called the secret hand-gesture.[86]

If the disciple of the formula does not make a maṇḍala but only possesses these hand-gestures and formulae, then this is equal to installing all the maṇḍalas to a great degree.

In all parts of one's own body one will realize the multitude of buddhas completely.[87] This will be matchless, wonderful, and, moreover, of an unsurpassed taste. Furthermore, the secret word of the four converting esoteric knowledges[88] will be explained:

oṃ sarvatathāgatāṃkuśe hūṃ jjaḥ[89]
oṃ sarvatathāgatāpāśe hūṃ hūṃ[90]
oṃ sarvatathāgatāsphote hūṃ vaṃ[91]
oṃ sarvatathāgatāveśa hūṃ hoḥ[92]

When one recites these secret formulae a little, the sixteen great bodhisattvas will be born from the dharma realm. They will all possess their fundamental emblems.

Next one recites the eight offerings *(pūjā)*, and with the four converting esoteric knowledges one will realize the great maṇḍala.[93] Next one recites the verse of the main honored one.[94] The secret words of the eight offerings and the four means of conversion will be explained next:

oṃ sarvapūja jaḥ hūṃ vaṃ hoḥ[95]

Next, O Secret Lord, I shall in addition explain in the supreme thought of this thought the secret method. Buddha is called the five yogas.[96]

One should visualize the Universally Shining Lord.[97] The own-body is completely equal.[98]

Furthermore, one should visualize in front of oneself the Victorious Vajra-Jewel.[99] He dwells in a blazing sun and grasps a wonderful great precious flag.

Next, to the right, one should visualize the Adamantine Lotus-Hook.[100] He dwells in a yellow wheel, grasps a hook, and smiles greatly.

Next, to the left, one should know the Adamantine Precious Great Storehouse.[101] He dwells in a green wheel and grasps a great round mirror.

Next, in the back is the Adamantine Great Tainted Lotus.[102] He dwells in a red wheel and grasps a wondrous[103] great red lotus.

These are called the five yogas. They are the secret supreme taste.

All wishes will be fulfilled completely. Always form these yogas and recite the aforementioned eight great esoteric knowledges.[104]

With the power of the secret hand-gesture[105] they will realize all the wishes completely. Even if one does not rely on the summoning hand-gestures and on the recitation of the esoteric knowledge of Incense and Flower,[106] one will attain the highest perfection. One will attain this quickly in the present period.

Then all the bodhisattvas of the assembly and all the vajra-holders[107] visualized in one thought the buddha-thought. They rejoiced and dwelled in peace.

Translation of the Daishō Kongō Butchō Nenju Giki

The Ritual of the Mindful Recitation of the Great Victorious Adamantine Buddha Crown[108]

By Imperial Mandate, Vajrabodhi, Tripiṭaka Master from South India, received the honor of translating this text.

Then the World Honored One manifested fivefold radiance[109] for all the sentient beings in the latter period of the dharma. From his crown he emitted firelight and illuminated the devils and the demons in the three worlds, those who have no faith in Buddhism. At the same time he burnt them completely.

When the bodhisattva Vajrapāni saw these characteristics, he said to the World Honored One: "The *devamāras*, the demons, those who do harm to the sentient beings are burnt by the knowledge-fire of the Tathāgata. They are all frightened and do not obtain ease. What teaching do you want to explain? I only want that you, O Tathāgata, explain it."

Then the Great Vairocana Buddha told the bodhisattva Vajrapāni:

There is an esoteric knowledge king[110] called the Heart Formula of the Great Victorious Buddha Crown. By reciting it one time, one's wishes will be fulfilled. It is the superior king of esoteric knowledge among the Buddhas of the ten directions. If there is a vajra-disciple[111] who recites it a full fifty thousand times, then all the buddhas, the great bodhisattvas, the divine nāgas, and the goddesses will all protect him day and night and fulfill the wishes.

Then the Tathāgata expounded the esoteric knowledge:

oṃ mahāvajroṣṇīṣa hūṃ traḥ hrīḥ aḥ hūṃ

Bind the two hands internally and bend the patience and the vow {fingers} like a crown. This is called the fundamental great hand-gesture. If in the transformations in the latter period of the dharma there are sentient beings who constantly form this hand-gesture and recite the formula, then all the military forces will not harm them, water and fire will not burn or sweep them away. All the devils and demons will feel inconvenience. The noble multitude of the Vajra and the Garbha[112] will come and increase protection, whether sitting or lying down.

Next I will explain the ritual of drawing the image.[113] Take a pure silk cloth during the dark half of the month under the constellation Anurādhā.[114] Draw the Great Victorious King of Esoteric Knowledge[115] wearing the five buddha crown.[116] He manifests twelve arms and abides in the gesture of the knowledge fist. He grasps a five-pronged vajra, a blue lotus, a jewel, a karma[vajra], a hook, a rope, a chain, a bell, a sharp sword, and a wheel. He dwells on a white lotus with one thousand petals. The color of his body is like white light. His whole body produces firelight. In the four corners draw four vidyārājas. In the southeastern corner draw Acalanātha Vajra.[117] In the southwestern corner, Hayagrīva Vajra.[118] In the northwestern corner, the Six-Legged Vajra.[119] In the northeastern corner, Yakṣa Vajra.[120] Draw these four wrathful kings all holding weapons. They manifest an extremely fierce appearance. Next draw the divine kings of the eight directions.[121] They will all be attendants, respectful and surrounding. If there is a practitioner of the formula who wants to pay worship, then in a pure room or a quiet place in a mountain grove he must burn incense, scatter flowers of the season, and recite the formula five hundred thousand times. Myself, the eight buddha crowns,[122] the innumerable gods, bodhisattvas, and adamantine gods will manifest their body and permanently serve you as you please. If there are sentient beings who recite this formula every day, they will surpass all the heavenly beings in this life. In the future period their body will be like the Universally Shining Honored One. He who possesses this hand-gesture and formula will be able to realize a thousand million wishes. If there is a practitioner, someone who performs the various subjugations of devils and all the āveśa rituals, then I will produce innumerable vajra youths.[123] They will always dwell (near) the one who recites at will. If you feel compassion, if you do not hate, and if you visualize the syllable hūṃ on the heart, then you will abide in the samādhi of the main deity, whether you are walking, standing, sitting, or lying. You will realize all wishes. The seeing among the sentient beings will all be happy and feel affection. This person will be like the Universally Shining Honored One. The innumerable Buddhas will come and protect you without abandoning you. If the practitioner of the formula does not cause attachment, hatred, or delusion, if he takes deeply refuge in the three treasures[124] and transfers merit with good acts in the six paths,[125] then he will quickly realize the unsurpassed bodhi.[126] The practitioner should use the formula and the gesture of ucchuṣma vajra[127] in impure places and empower the five places.[128] Make a fist with the four fingers of the right hand and erect the thumb. The secret word is:

oṃ krodhana hūṃ jaḥ[129]

Collated
The 29th day of the 2nd month of Kōgen 2 (1257).
Copied in the Kakudōin
Adamantine Buddha Disciple Shinson 22 [years old][130]

The Cult of Daishō Kongō in Japan

In Japan, the ritual described in chapter 8 of the *Yugikyō* was performed to avoid natural calamities *(sokusai)*, to obtain the affection of others *(keiai)*, and to gain success on the battlefield. As a matter of fact, the *Yugikyō* proclaims that by reciting the formula of Daishō Kongō one will not get hurt by the sword and one will not be destroyed by fire or swept away by water.

The *Kakuzenshō*[131] reports the performance of this ritual by the monk Ninsei:[132] "I dedicate the foregoing[133] to his Majesty the Regent *(kanpaku)*,[134] the former Chief Advisor to the Emperor *(zen-daishōkoku)*,[135] for appeasing, increasing fortune and life, and to realize his wishes. I started from the seventeenth day of the tenth month of Kyūan 6 [1150] and continued till today, in total two hundred twenty-four days and nights."

In a note written at the back *(uragaki)* of the *Yugikyō kuden*,[136] a commentary on the *Yugikyō* by the Shingon monk Dōhan (1178–1252), it is stated that the ritual of Daishō Kongō was performed for easy childbirth: "Around the eighth month of the sixth year of Kenpo [1218],[137] the ritual of Daishō Kongō was performed to pray for the easy childbirth of the chūgū."[138]

The same text contains also a note which refers to Minamoto Yoritomo's (1147–99) reverence for Daishō Kongō:[139] "The Great Shōgun Yoritomo of Kamakura wrote the formula of Daishō Kongō in the battle. He hid it on a metal object under the sleeve of his armor *(yoroi)*. On his sleeve he fixed a charm on which the character *shō* (to win, victory) was written."

The *Sanbōin-ryū Dōsen sōjō kuketsu*,[140] a collection of oral transmissions compiled by the monks Dōchō (1709–95)[141] and Unjo (n.d.),[142] states that Minamoto requested the monk Shōken (1138–96)[143] to perform the ritual of Daishō Kongō for him. We also read that Minamoto triumphed because of the character *shō* of Daishō written on his armor. The text also states that this ritual was executed to empower *(kaji)* weapons. Takeda Kazuaki[144] mentions in his study of a painting that depicts Aizen Myōō sitting inside a stūpa that the ritual of Daishō Kongō was performed in the Tōji Temple for Ashikaga Takauji (1305–58) in the third year of Kenmu (1336).[145]

In a contemporary note on the *Usuzōshi* included in the *Kokuyaku mikkyō* it is stated that the ritual of Daishō Kongō was also effective in horse races *(keiba)*.[146] Unfortunately the author of this note does not refer to any source or text.

Breath of Life: The Esoteric Nembutsu

James H. Sanford

You are a man of Tendai training. Therefore you will divide the Nembutsu practice into three forms. First is the nembutsu of Makashikan. Secondly, there is the nembutsu of the *Ōjō yōshū*. And thirdly is the nembutsu of Shan Tao.

Hōnen (1133–1212), to a disciple[1]

THE JAPANESE PURE LAND tradition is often considered to derive directly—or solely—from the Tendai school and to present a form of Buddhism that constitutes a rather close analogue to Western dualistic forms of religion. This dualism is characterized by a series of oppositions that include Amida's[2] distant paradise, the *Jōdo* ("Pure Land") versus *edo* (this dirty world of unsaved mortals); *busshin* ("buddha mind"), versus *bonshin* (our corrupt minds; the differentiation between *tariki*, the grace-like "other power" bestowed by Amida, and *jiriki*, the be-lights-unto-yourselves "self power" that has lost all efficacy in these latter, dark days of the dharma *(mappō);* and a parallel differentiation of the Jōdo path versus an older, and now irrelevant, Shōdō (Way of the Saints). Humanity's only hope in this dismal age is to do the *nembutsu*[3] to call out to Amida in the hope that this august being will turn his compassion toward us and allow us, in spite of all our sins and our wholly undeserving nature, to be reborn, not here or in some Buddhist hell, but in his Pure Land Paradise of the West (*Gokuraku*, the Land of Joy).

This study briefly outlines the tantric Shingon school's *himitsu nembutsu* (esoteric *nembutsu*)[4] counterversion of the usual Pure Land teachings, a monistic, this-worldly, immanental variant that had great impact across a wide range of Buddhist venues, from its foundations in the late Heian within Shingon proper, through certain aspects of medieval Tendai and Zen, and on into Pure Land "heresies" that survived as underground popular movements into the twentieth century, and probably persist in some venue somewhere in Japan even today.

The "Normative" Vision of the Pure Land

The differences between the *himitsu nembutsu* tradition and the orthodox Pure Land schools centered on three major issues: (1) the nature of Amida and his relationship to human beings; (2) the nature of the Pure Land and of *ōjō*, or rebirth in that land; and (3) the nature of the *nembutsu* itself. These issues of dispute were, of course, the basic constituents of Amidism. The last of them, the *nembutsu*, was in many ways the most important, since the manner in which the *nembutsu* was understood was often crucial to a coherent understanding of the other elements. Before examining the *himitsu nembutsu* alternative, we ought first to take a brief look at these core elements as they were seen in "normative Pure Land."[5]

Though individuals within what I have called the normative Pure Land tradition disagreed among themselves over particular meanings and interpretations, the school in general held to something like the following set of doctrines on the three main issues:

AMIDA AND HUMANITY

In a former age of the universe there was a monk called Dharmākara. Lokeśvararāja, the buddha of that age, predicted—infallibly, since he was a buddha—that Dharmākara too would one day become a buddha. In response to this prediction, Dharmākara vowed that when that event took place he would establish a Pure Land for the salvation of all beings. Dharmākara, of course, became the Buddha Amida. And though he was in a certain sense once a man like any other, he has for eons been a full-fledged Buddha presiding over his Pure Land of the West. There he and his attendant bodhisattvas work for the welfare of worldlings trapped in the realms below, aiding them to be reborn in this Pure Land until, at the end of all time, all beings will be bodhisattvas or buddhas and we will at last, all together, all at once, take one giant step into nirvāṇa.

The beings in the lower realms are trapped there by delusions that breed bad actions, which in turn breed further delusion. The arrival of Śākyamuni in India may have allowed for a brief respite, in which his immediate followers were able to apply his teachings directly and attain salvation by themselves, but the world has long since drifted into the age of decay of the dharma during which, according to most wings of normative Pure Land, only the saving compassion of Amida drawn by the *nembutsu* (or perhaps simply given free of all conditions by Amida) can be efficacious.

THE LAND: ŌJŌ

Amida's Pure Land of the West is an arena which seems to retain form and diversity. Indeed, as its very name, Gokuraku, implies it is a place of endless (or ultimate) joy. Nonetheless, it is a place unlike our world. For in the Pure Land all is, as its name suggests, pure.[6] The joy of the Pure Land is not a hindrance to the attainment of nirvāṇa but perhaps something like a foretaste. There are in fact other, similar Pure Lands among the "universes without number," but due to Amida's vow to bring undeserving worldlings to rebirth in his Pure Land, it is the most easily attained of these.

If one insists on talking of Gokuraku in terms of conventional space, then it is located in the West, but its location is so far removed from our own dirty, impure land, that even to talk of Gokuraku in terms of distance or space is almost an absurdity. If it were not for the compassion of Amida, Gokuraku would be wholly unreachable. The application of the Western term "transcendent" for the location of this Land and for the nature of its master, Amida, may be slightly anomalous, but it is not wide of the mark by much.

Rebirth in the Pure Land, or *ōjō*,[7] is, as is implicit in the vows taken by Dharmākara, available to virtually all beings. Even great sinners, would they but make the effort of uttering the *nembutsu*, could slough off *kalpas* of deserved punishment for their past and present sins. Not all would, however, immediately become as pure as the land in which they were reborn. Normative Pure Land posits nine levels of rebirth. The truly pure and spiritually wise are born there to become, as it were, instant bodhisattvas. But others must first spend long purgatorial ages within the calices of lotus flowers, gradually leaching the dross of their former lives. For those of the ninth and lowest layer this could be a very long process indeed, but even the lowest state in the Pure Land is happier than the highest earthly throne—to say nothing of the torments of the awful hells that surely await most of us.

THE NEMBUTSU

Ōjō to the Pure Land normally follows utterance of the *nembutsu* (though not until the end of the believer's current lifetime). This does not necessarily mean that the call has any coercive effect on Amida. To insist on such a suggestion would imply that Amida's actions might in some way, shape, or form be dependent upon our attentions to him. This would be tantamount to taking a *jiriki* (self-powered) position. In fact, salvation is better understood to be wholly the gift of Amida (and thus *tariki* or "other" powered). Amida could if he chose to—though, of course, he would not so choose—ignore our cries for help. The *nembutsu,* then, is not really a form of worship at all—albeit its most common form "Namu Amida Butsu" may be translated "Hail the Buddha Amida." It should, rather, be understood as a cry of thanksgiving for the fact—practically certain if not technically so—that Amida has heard and will save.

I have in the paragraphs above represented a generalized understanding of the logic of the normative Pure Land position on the *nembutsu.* Specific understandings much worried normative Pure Land thinkers. Hōnen, for instance, was even open to the partial utility of practices other than the *nembutsu.* But the tradition of his followers—however much they argued over the required number of *nembutsu,* the preferred form of their utterance, or even the exact nature of the practice—was constantly drifting in one direction. That is, toward sole reliance on a *nembutsu* that was a sui generis salvational fact quite beyond the terms of devotion, worship, or meditation as those had been understood by earlier schools of Buddhism.

History of the Himitsu Nembutsu *Tradition: Kakuban and His Precursors*

The central figure in the *himitsu nembutsu* tradition is unarguably the Shingon prelate Kakuban (1095–1134, a.k.a. Kōgyō Daishi). Prior to Kakuban's time Pure Land views had hardly begun to crystallize into a systematic perspective, but this does not mean that neither Amida, the Pure Land *(ōjo)* nor the *nembutsu* was unknown to the Japanese Buddhist tradition. It simply indicates that they were still nonproblematic features, similar to a number of other elements of Buddhism. Within Tendai and Shingon alike, Amida was seen as one of a number of Buddhas. And while rebirth in his Pure Land was possible, such a rebirth was seen not so much as a way station to final enlightenment and nirvāṇa as a procedure that utilized meditation on Amida to see the emptiness of all dharmas, to finally come to grips with the ultimate nature of the universe, and to become enlightened.

Typically this meditation might take place on one's deathbed as a sort of meditation of last resort, but in theory it was little different from any of a number of other visualization exercises. In Shingon and Tendai visualizing Amida was most often assimilated to the potent stimulation of *bodhicitta*[8] that could be brought on by the *Aji kan*, or visualization of the syllable "A."[9] One's meditative encounter with Amida was less an attempt to gain rebirth in the Pure Land than to evoke one's own *bodhicitta*, to enter a state of perfect oneness with Amida and to forestall rebirth in any land, save to the extent that enlightenment even at the very end of one's life could always be seen in a Shingon context as a form of that school's most distinctive promise, *sokushin jōbutsu*, or "bodily buddhahood."[10]

At this stage we are talking about the kind of *nembutsu* that Hōnen refers to in our epigraph as "the *nembutsu* of *Makashikan.*" From our point of view Hōnen's *"nembutsu* of the *Ōjō yōshū"*and his *"nembutsu* of Shan Tao" were simply two hardly distinguishable stages of an emergent normative Pure Land view.

With Kakuban (who, it should be kept in mind, was born almost thirty years before Hōnen) we see something else. This something was sufficiently distinct that it would eventually be singled out for special attention and a particular name. That name is *himitsu nembutsu*. This kind of *nembutsu* is first mentioned in works written after Kakuban's death, where it is presented as a fourth form in addition to the three kinds of *nembutsu* that Hōnen speaks about. Thus we can suspect that the term developed primarily as a result of Kakuban's teachings. Initially, the impact of the *himitsu nembutsu* interpretations was limited to Mount Kōya and other Shingon centers—especially important was Negoro, the site of Kakuban's last years. Gradually, however, this countertradition evolved and spread beyond those confines. And, as we will see below, it was felt well beyond the pale of *mikkyō*.[11]

Kakuban was born in Bizen in Kyūshū. He studied with the noted monk Kanjō (1052–1125) at the Ninna-ji. Later, having attracted the support of Emperor Toba, he established the Denbō-in at Shingon's main stronghold on Mount Kōya—and is thus counted the founder of Shingon's Denbō-in sub-school. He was also invited to become abbot of the main temple of Kōya, Kongōbu-ji, but due to internal opposition he was not able to accept this post. Kakuban eventually left Kōya to settle at Negoro-ji, later the center of Shingi Shingon, the largest school of Shingon after the main branch on Kōya. He is, thus, deemed the founder of Shingi Shingon, though this attribution is in some ways more honorific than substantive.

Kakuban is generally considered to be the founder of the *himitsu nembutsu* movement, though in point of fact he had precursors and collaterals as well as intellectual descendants. Nonetheless, Kakuban's role in blending the tantric ideas of Shingon proper with the central elements of the then still emergent Pure Land ideology was major, and in terms of historical impact his fusion of Amidist and mikkyō themes constitutes the most important single contribution to the *himitsu nembutsu* tradition.

Kakuban was a partisan of the radically nondual *fu'ni* (not-two) wing of Shingon, from which perspective he wrote a number of diatribes against the alternative, gradualist *ni'ni* (yet-two) school. It was, in fact, doubtless only Kakuban's radical unwillingness to validate discriminations of any sort that allowed him to combine the this-worldly immanentalism of *fu'ni* Shingon and the implicit dualism of emerging Pure Land ideology; to construe the Pure Land message as obviously this-worldly; and to consider Amida, the principal figure of the Pure Land texts, and Mahāvairocana (Jpn. Dainichi, lit. "Great Sun"), the central Buddha of Shingon, as virtual co-avatars.

Though elements of this program can be found in a number of Kakuban's works, his major contributions toward a *fu'ni* interpretation of Amidism were the *Gorin kuji myo himitsu shaku* (Secret Explication of the Mantras of the Five Wheels and the Nine Syllables), the *Amida hishaku* (Secret Explication of Amida), the *Ichigo daiyō himitsu shū* (Secrets of the Crucial Moment of Death), and several short texts on *A-ji kan*, the visualization of the syllable "A." The *Gorin kuji myo hishaku* is the best-known work in Kakuban's large oeuvre (for in spite of his rather short life span, Kakuban was a highly prolific writer) and was widely copied and read in later times. The *Amida hishaku* was possibly a bit less familiar, as well as less radical in its outlook, but it too had fairly wide currency, perhaps because it was written not in classical Chinese but in Japanese of a reasonably accessible style and was quite short into the bargain. The *Ichigo daiyō himitsu shū* was also relatively well known, in part, one must suppose, because as a guide to a good death it had considerable practical appeal. The interpretations of the Pure Land posed by Kakuban in his various texts will be considered in more detail presently.

Kakuban's precursors fall into two groups. There are first of all several mainline monks whose interpretations of Amida prefigure those of Kakuban. The second line of influence is that of the so-called *Kōya hijiri* (ascetics of Mount Kōya), a somewhat disparate group of self-regulating, and to a large degree self-styled, holy men who had by the eleventh century gathered in substantial numbers on the numinous slopes of Mount Kōya. One contemporary text estimates that in the late twelfth century there were two thousand of these *hijiri* on the mountain, as against only three hundred regularly ordained monks.[12] Many of these informal ascetics were devoted to, among other things, the Buddha of the Western Pure Land, Amida. Though some of them maintained an interest in Amida that was no more than simple devotion, others of the Kōya *hijiri* held notions that were already moving to incorporate more innovative ideas about the Pure Land into the body of Shingon thought. In particular they were prone to see Mount Kōya itself as an earthly Pure Land, a sort of geographical avatar of the Mitsugon Pure Land associated with Vairocana in numerous Shingon texts. From this point of departure, it was no great step to further equate the Mitsugon Jōdo not only with Kōya but with Gokuraku, the Pure Land of Amida. Kakuban, unlike some monks associated with official Shingon institutions, maintained close relations with many of these independent Kōya *hijiri*.

More formal precursors of Kakuban would include Yōkan (1033–1111), a member of the Sanron school. In his *Ōjō jūin* (Rebirth's Ten Causes), Yokan expounds on the themes of nirvāṇa's identity with saṃsāra, the equation of bodhi (enlightenment) and the passions, and the specification of the heart as the locus of buddha-nature. His *Ōjō kōshiki* (The *Ōjō* Ritual) states that holding the *nembutsu* in the mouth gathers buddhas into the heart and that the *nembutsu* replaces other rituals. Another Sanron monk, Chingai (1095–1151), argued in his *Bodaishin shū* (On Bodhicitta) and *Ketsujō ōjō shū* (On Certain Rebirth) that the generation of bodhicitta was a kind of ōjō rebirth.

The figure who had the deepest influence on Kakuban was, doubtless, the Hosso monk, Jitsuhan (?–1144). A number of Jitsuhan's writings, whose titles suggest that they were primarily concerned with Amida and the Pure Land, have been lost, but surviving works include his *Byōchū shugyō ki* (The Practice to Be Done in the Grip of Illness), which was almost certainly the prototype for Kakuban's *Ichigo daiyō himitsu shū*, both texts being outlines for the use of the *nembutsu* at the hour of death. However, Jitsuhan's interpretation seems to flow uneventfully from a straightforward, if thoroughly *mikkyō*, reading of the *Kan muryōju kyō* (Visualization of the Buddha of Endless Life),[13] whereas Kakuban's text clearly takes the ideas of emergent normative Pure Land into account.

Further History of the Himitsu Nembutsu *Tradition: Kakuban's Immediate Followers*

Later figures who followed Kakuban's lead and who continued to develop and propagate the *himitsu nembutsu* ideology from within the confines of Shingon proper include Kakukai (1142–1223),[14] Myōhen (1142–1224), and Jōhen (1165–1223). Myōhen spent the years 1171 to 1174 with Hōnen, the founding father of orthodox Pure Land, before permanently settling on Mount Kōya. Because the Pure Land school was becoming a fairly well defined entity by his day, Myōhen tried to eliminate the implicit tension between Shingon and the new school by calling the *nembutsu* a practice belonging "neither to the exoteric schools nor to the esoteric school, an incomprehensible practice."[15] In this, the attempt to maintain room for the increasingly untenable conflation of mikkyō and Pure Land notions, Myōhen differed from most subsequent Shingon adherents of the *himitsu nembutsu* ideology, who more and more insisted on subsuming the Pure Land elements under an explicit Shingon orientation. Myōhen died, we are told, chanting the *nembutsu,* presumably in accordance with the intent of the *Kan muryōju kyō,* though in accordance with what vision of that text is not so clear. The next main figure, Jōhen, moved a bit further from Hōnen, making an essentially mikkyō reinterpretation of Hōnen's views.

The major *himitsu nembutsu* figure after Kakuban was Dōhan (1178–1252). Dōhan wrote voluminously on a multitude of topics. Among his many writings was the *Himitsu Nembutsu shō* (Compendium on the Esoteric Nembutsu), the most influential work on *himitsu nembutsu* thought after Kakuban's writings. If Kakuban can be considered the founder of the *himitsu nembutsu* lineage, then Dōhan must be accounted foremost among his descendants.

The ensuing history of the *himitsu nembutsu* tradition will be briefly examined later in this study. At this point we turn to the doctrinal core of the tradition, the ideas of Kakuban and Dōhan. In each case I outline their views on the same key issues under which normative Pure Land was treated above: first, the nature of Amida, second, ōjō and the Pure Land, and third, the nature of the *nembutsu.*

The Himitsu Nembutsu *Vision: Kakuban*

KAKUBAN'S VIEW OF AMIDA

Kakuban's view of Amida varies. To a degree this variance may simply reflect texts from different dates: Kakuban's ideas seem in general to have become more radical as he grew older. But it may also be a case of differing moods or differing intended audiences. Usually Kakuban's view of Amida and humanity seems in close harmony with Jitsuhan's consistent, if for mikkyō fairly conventional, position that all beings, including buddhas and humans, are fundamentally alike.

In his *Byōchū shugyō ki* Jitsuhan conflates the visualization of Amida and the visualization of *A-ji*. For Jitsuhan, Amida is the *honzon*, or chief object, of both of these exercises. On his deathbed the practitioner visualizes Amida, does a mudrā appropriate to Amida, and intones a call to Amida that is far more a mantra than a *nembutsu* in the normative Pure Land sense of the word. The purpose of this exercise is to awaken the dying person's *bodhicitta*, to awaken the latent Buddhahood that is his essential nature, for in the final analysis Amida and humans are of one nature, or in Jitsuhan's vocabulary *shō-butsu ichinyo*, "beings and the Buddha are of one suchness."

Kakuban, also, took the *A-ji kan* meditation as crucial. And, like Jitsuhan, he associated the "A" of *A-ji* with the initial syllable of Amida. But Kakuban went further. If "A" linked *A-ji* and Amida, then it also linked Amida and Vairocana, for *A-ji* was preeminently the *bīja* of Vairocana in his Garbha-dhātu aspect.[16] Therefore, Kakuban concluded, Vairocana and Amida were one and the same. Not surprisingly from a monk of Shingon training, this tended to come out, unconsciously perhaps, as a co-option of Amida into Vairocana, rather than as an Amidist rereading of Vairocana. But at the level of overt expression and probably at the level of his own understanding, Kakuban's words were intended simply to mean what they said. For Kakuban, Amida and Vairocana were nondually one. And humans were beings on the way to, or returning to, the same state of buddhahood. Intermediary distinctions were, in the final analysis, of only marginal importance. As with Jitsuhan, human beings were buddha, but the buddha that they were was ultimately a singular buddha, the nondual Vairocana of Shingon.

KAKUBAN'S VIEW OF THE PURE LAND

For Jitsuhan the visualization of Amida on the deathbed is just like the standard *A-ji kan* visualization; that is, it serves to raise bodhicitta. Like normative Shingon use of the *A-ji kan*, it opens one to the awareness of primordial nonbirth *(honbushō)* and emptiness. This practice done at death is, thus, more the summation and purification of a life than a translation from this world to a new life in another land. Though one may use the proto-normative Pure Land term *junji ōjō*, or immediate rebirth, the immediacy in this case is from latency to enlightenment rather than from this world to the distant Gokuraku paradise. Since Amida and our own bodies are equally absolute, it is within the body that this procedure culminates. The contents of an afterlife do not concern Jitsuhan, primarily because it does not even occur to him that such descriptions could be more than metaphorical *upāya* for a rebirth that actually takes place within the human spirit itself. (Though, as usual in Shingon contexts, "spirit" is here to be seen not in contrast to but in conjunction with "body.")

Kakuban, too, held that the normative Pure Land idea that the Pure Land lay across a gap millions of miles beyond our world was wholly incorrect. As he says in the concluding lines of his *Amida hishaku:* "To hate this world and take joy in Paradise, to hate one's 'dirty body' and revere some Buddha-body, this we may call ignorance or delusion. Even if this world were eternally impure, how, if one always sees it as a Dharma-realm, can he fail to enter the path of Buddhahood?"[17]

For Kakuban the locus of the Pure Land is simply our own body; Gokuraku is as close as our own heart. In the *Ichigo daiyō himitsu shū*'s segment on Gokuraku we are asked: "Where is Gokuraku? How could it be across the ten directions, in some place other than the meditating adept? To meditate properly does not lift one out of this world, does not bring rebirth in Gokuraku. My body enters Amida, but it does not return to Amida. Rather I am transformed into Vairocana. My body evokes Vairocana. This is the wondrous realization of *sokushin jōbutsu*."[18] This is all perfectly clear. The view is quite close to normative Shingon. Here Amida, who in many of Kakuban's passages is at least nominally interchangeable with Vairocana, is put clearly in third place, second not only to Vairocana but even to the individual self (as buddha) as well.

In another passage from the *Amida hishaku* Kakuban seems even more tendentious: "Again, this heart and these Buddhas are, from the outset, of one substance. This heart needs not seek transformation into a Buddha. If one withdraws from delusion, Wisdom will emerge of itself, and one will attain Buddhahood in this very body. To conclude that there is a Buddha-body outside of one's own body, or to seek some Pure Land beyond this soiled world, is to encourage great fools and to bring profit to the evilest of men."[19]

KAKUBAN AND THE NEMBUTSU

If Kakuban was fairly predictable in his treatment of both Amida and the Pure Land, his views on the *nembutsu* were considerably less conventional. There was a progressive series of logical steps in his understanding. The first is Kakuban's reduction of the three secrets *(sanmitsu)* of ordinary Shingon[20] to a single secret, the secret he calls *ichimitsu jōbutsu* or "one-secret buddhahood." Under Kakuban's theory, the usual three secrets can all be subsumed under the aegis of the secret of speech.

This apparently novel collapse is not, in all fairness, unprecedented. Kūkai advocated *de jure* the necessity of all three secrets, but his persistent stress on the crucial importance of *sokushin jōbutsu* amounted to a *de facto* privileging of the secret of body. But Kakuban's shift to speech and his insistence on the idea of a single, crucial practice are a notable departure, and in the overall context of Japanese Shingon a departure that seems worthy of being characterized as radical, especially inasmuch as it specifically depreciates two of the orthodox mainstays of normative Shingon.[21]

Atop this already complex nexus of associations, Kakuban superimposes the linkage of "A" to Amida. "A" is, of course, the first syllable of Amida's name and thereby the core of the six-character *nembutsu* invocation, *Namu Amida Butsu*, "Hail the Buddha Amida." It is as well the first syllable of the key word *amṛta*, in the nine-syllable mantra to Amida, *Oṃ amṛta teja hara hūṃ*. And, as noted before, "A" is a *bīja* of Vairocana. The identity of all these "A"s is, to Kakuban, self-evident and is but a further testimony to the identity of Amida and Vairocana.

Kakuban, however, takes his reduction of all mantras to "A" yet another step. The carrying vehicle of all sound is breath. Breath is also the focal object of those yogas that depend on counting in-breaths and out-breaths. Kakuban combines these two ideas and sees that every in-breath is the substantiation of "A" and every out-breath is the substantiation of "hūṃ." Every full cycle of in-breath and out-breath completes the mantra "A-hūṃ."[22] Inasmuch as every utterance of "A-(hūṃ)" is an invocation (or evocation) of Amida's essential being, breath is, in and of itself, both the mantra of Amida and Amida himself. At the same time, "A" is also equated by Kakuban with the great element air (or wind), and air is taken to be the quintessence of the five material elements earth, water, fire, air, and space.

Furthermore, since hūṃ is the *bīja* syllable of Shingon's sixth element, spirit or mind, this allows A-hūṃ to represent the two great Womb and Vajra maṇḍalas, emblematic of the body-spirit dual unity of the universe (i.e., the transcendent embedded within the immanent) and the parallel dual unity of the human mind-body complex. Thus, the "A-hūṃ, A-hūṃ" of the organic body is a constant regeneration of the identity of the six elements as well as a *nyūga ga'nyū* consubstantiation of Amida and Dainichi (Amitābha and Vairocana) and the individual self.[23] In a word, I breathe Amida and Amida breathes me.

In his *A-ji kan* in Japanese Kakuban tells us:

> Breath is *A-ji*. To say that whenever the mantras of the various Buddhas of the ten directions and three times are chanted there is a Nembutsu is a shallow interpretation. If we think of a victorious mantra which by in-breath and out-breath calms the mind, then the one and only example that brings all others to a halt must be this one dharma, *A-ji*, which quiets the mind. Nothing else will put one on the rapid path to *bodhi*. The precious name, *A-mi-da*, surpasses other rites.[24]

In this passage, the *nembutsu* is a samādhi-engendering mantra to Amida, as are the three syllables *A-mi-da* themselves. But Kakuban once again takes his argument further and reduces the sound-bearing breath that reduces A-mi-da to breath alone. "The spiritual power of my body is the living breath of the Buddha-lands in every direction. This breath continues without pause whether I walk, stand, sit, or lie down, day and night even when I sleep, all without my exerting the least effort. There is no more efficacious act than just contemplating one's breath, in and out."[25]

At this point we have come a long way both from standard Shingon ideas up to Kakuban and from early normative, or proto-normative, Pure Land thought. Kakuban has not only foreclosed seeing the *nembutsu* as a salvific call to some transcendental divinity who sits kinglike in his distant realm of western purity but has also moved a considerable distance from the mikkyō rituals (more or less *ni'ni* in tone) that utilize mantra to awaken bodhicitta. In their stead we find the claim that the autonomic, purely instinctive, totally innate, entirely unconscious—and therefore absolutely immanental—process of breathing is, in and of itself, in all its materiality, the deepest form of spiritual activity. Here we are at a level that is neither *tariki* nor *jiriki*, but something beneath or beyond both.

Though any fully nondual perspective might tend toward such a position, the framing of the position in terms of breath is a fresh invention which seems to have come late in Kakuban's life. (Some of his early treatments of *A-ji* hardly prefigure, much less express, this radical view.) Certain linguistic features, however, make it a less arbitrary move than we might at first imagine. A good deal of the symbolic power of the conflation of Amida, breath, and *A-ji* comes from the fact that the translation equivalent of *namu* in the "Namu Amida Butsu" form of the *nembutsu* is *"kimyō,"* a compound whose constituent characters literally mean "return" and "life."[26] Since Kakuban has made air emblematic of Amida and also the primal element of the universe, since the sounds of the *nembutsu* ride on air, and since air in the human body is life breath, life too must consist of the essence of Amida's true nature. That this is so becomes even more certain when we recall that Amida's alternate name, Muryōju Nyorai, literally means "the Tathāgata Endless Life." True enlightenment to Amida is, then, a form of *naishō* or "inner enlightenment"[27] to the fact that Amida is breath, is life. Amida is the source of our every inhalation and with every exhalation we "return our life" (breath; *kimyō*) to Amida.

According to the doctrines of Normative Pure Land, Amida will come to rescue us from our deathbeds if we but recite the *nembutsu* ten times (or for ten moments). This visitation is called Amida's *raigō* ("coming to meet"). But, following Kakuban, we can now see that breathing in and out brings us a perpetual *raigō* or *ōjō* that renews itself from moment to moment. Another term for this endless miracle is *sokushin ōjō* or *"ōjō* in this very body." This bodily *ōjō* is not, of course, limited to human beings. In a passage from Kakuban's prose *Aji-kan gi* [Meaning of the A-ji Visualization] he likens the heart to a lunar orb:

> *A-ji kan* is an oral teaching concerning breath-count yoga. This is what it is. Eyes opened or eyes closed, simply concentrate on *A-ji.* In the center of our moon-disc heart is an innate, natural syllable "A." This is the principle of original nonbirth. From the self-existent Dharmakāya on high,[28] to the four kinds of mortal beings below, down to the soil, trees, tiles, and stones, there is not one thing that lacks the principle of original non-birth. Therefore, when we speak of the innate essence of all beings, this is what we mean. The heart that visualizes "A" and the "A" being

visualized must be seen as an originally nondual singularity. Further, the "A" of my moon-disc heart goes out for the benefit of others in my out-breaths. The out-breaths of all living beings and my out-breaths go out for the benefit of us all. And when the "A" in the moon-disc heart of all the Buddhas goes out from them, it settles into our moon-disc hearts. Thus, out-breath and in-breath have not, from the beginning of time to this very day, either increased or decreased. Nor will they into the endless future. When in this visualization the breaths are crystallized one by one, the principle of original nonbirth of all beings and the essence of original nonbirth of all the Buddhas must be gathered together in your own heart. When breath leaves your breast and stirs the dust beneath your nostrils, you must open your mouth slightly and realize "A" sounding in your in-breath and your out-breath. And when you open your eyes, you must see yourself drawing the "A" before you into your moon-disc heart. . . . "A" is in all things. It is the natural *bīja* endowed by the *Dharmakāya*. Therefore, good *dharmas* and bad *dharmas*, the natural world and its kingdoms, the mountains, the rivers and the great earth, sand, stones, birds, and beasts, all alike sound this note, are all the "A" of this innate dhāraṇī. This is the *samādhi* of natural principle.[29]

Kakuban's writings show more variety and explore many more themes than the schematic outline just provided suggests. Some of them verge on the ecstatic, and even the more conventional works display more than a few contradictions and probable changes of mind. Beyond that, Kakuban developed other inventions that, while not as important in the long run as his idea of *kimyō*, are just as striking as intellectual constructs. Nonetheless, even in this outline we can see that his view of Amida, the Pure Land, and the *nembutsu* is one in which syncretism both co-opts and resists elements of the emerging normative Pure Land worldview. This indicates, of course, that between Jitsuhan's *Byōchū shugyō ki* and the late works of Kakuban a general normative Pure Land position was becoming an ever clearer alternative to older understandings of Amida's nature and uses.

The Himitsu Nembutsu *View: Dōhan*

If Kakuban was given to largely, though not entirely, unproblematic syncretism of mikkyō and emergent Pure Land ideas, Dōhan marks a different
stage in the development of the *himitsu nembutsu* tradition, one in which
real concessions to normative Pure Land views were made mostly in the
breach, and serious measures were taken toward supplanting normative
Pure Land interpretations altogether and replacing them with perfectly self-
conscious Shingon understandings.[30]

Dōhan, accounted one of the "eight geniuses of Kōya," came to Mount
Kōya in his fourteenth year and studied initially with Myōnin (1148–1229)
of the Shōchi-in. In 1216, having taken tonsure and having received esoteric
initiation, Dōhan left Kōya to study with Jōhen. He was also in the inner
circle of Kakukai and is sometimes considered a disciple of that master as
well. Eventually he returned to Kōya to serve for a time as abbot of the
Shōchi-in. In 1243 he was exiled to Sanuki and did not return to Kōya until
1249. When he died in 1252 he left behind a formidable reputation and a
prodigious number of writings. His works are especially noted for the
scholastic rigor he applies to his arguments.

Though Dōhan studied with a number of teachers and doubtless had
many conversations with their peers and disciples, the most immediate
influence on his views of the Pure Land was probably Jōhen, whose ideas it
will be useful to consider briefly here. Jōhen, too, studied widely and wrote
much. While abbot of Zenrin-ji in Kyoto, he met one of Hōnen's disciples
and became familiar with Hōnen's *Senchaku hongan Nembutsu shu* (On the
Nembutsu of the Selected Original Vow). He also knew Myōhen and like
Myōhen was almost as much a part of the Pure Land tradition as of Shingon, though his ideas about the Pure Land carried a heavy burden of Shingon ideology. Jōhen held, for example, that if the common Mahāyāna tenet
"*saṃsāra* is *nirvāṇa*" were true, then the *nembutsu* also equaled *nirvāṇa*. He
denied any difference between this world and the Pure Land and held the
doctrine that this present body is buddha *(genshin soku butsu)*.

DŌHAN'S VIEW OF AMIDA

By the time Dōhan was developing his own systematic presentation of *himitsu nembutsu* ideas, Pure Land had become a substantial spiritual force
in Japan. Dōhan was obliged thereby to take basic (and now actively normative) Pure Land doctrines pretty much as they came and to address them

in a serious and careful fashion. His writings are, in fact, an apologia for the *himitsu nembutsu* view, written directly against the normative Pure Land view.

When Dōhan talks of Amida he says that there are exoteric and esoteric understandings and that while ordinary Pure Land views are not exactly false, they at best can represent the first, or possibly first and second, levels of a four-layer structure of understanding and interpretation. These four levels of esoteric explication are:

1. The surface meaning: things just as they seem; the literal meaning.
2. The profound secret meaning: the inner, Buddhist, meaning.
3. The profound secret-within-secret meaning: the mikkyō understanding, incomprehensible to followers of other schools.
4. The secret meaning of the profound secret-within-secret meaning: the deepest mikkyō reading; examples here would include such notions as "the passions themselves are enlightenment," "phenomena are themselves absolute," and "mortal beings and the buddha are not two."

Stages 1 and 4 often look exactly alike.

When Dōhan applies this paradigm to an understanding of Amida, the four stages develop as follows:

1. Holding the notion that Amida is the Buddha Ratnagarbha.
2. The realization that Amida is the Dharmakāya Buddha, Vairocana.
3. The realization that Amida is Vairocana as eternally manifest within this universe of time and space.
4. The innermost realization that Amida is the true nature, material and spiritual, of all beings, that he is the omnivalent wisdom-body, that he is the unborn, unmanifest, unchanging reality that rests quietly at the core of all phenomena.

One could hardly imagine a more complete reversal of the dualistic and transcendental thrust of normative Pure Land. The Amida of this vision is almost indistinguishable from the first and third forms of *sokushin jōbutsu* enumerated in the *Ihon* recension of Kūkai's *Sokushin jōbutsu gi* (On Bodily Buddhahood).[31] Here Amida is simply an alternate term for Vairocana. At other points Dōhan suggests that Amida is an intermediary figure between beings and the Mitsugon Paradise (n.b.: Vairocana's Mitsugon, not the normative Pure Land's Gokuraku).

DŌHAN ON THE PURE LAND

As with the other issues he takes up, here too Dōhan subjects his theme to a four-layered hermeneutic. And again the deepest, most secret layer is quite the opposite of the "superficial glimpses" afforded adherents of the normative Pure Land view. The shallow understanding of Pure Land and *ōjō* is as rebirth into some distant world. But actually *ōjō* is rebirth into Gokuraku only in the sense that all "paradises" are really located in the heart. Gokuraku or Tuṣita (the paradise of Maitreya, the Buddha of the Future) are but alternate names for Vairocana's Mitsugon Jōdo, the Buddha-land of the heart. Journeys to the Pure Land are journeys inward. Further, if there were a literal rebirth with Amida in Gokuraku as suggested by the normative texts, that could only amount to joining Amida; enlightenment even in that Pure Land would still take *kalpas*. By contrast, Shingon is rapid; enlightenment (the real meaning of rebirth) is in this lifetime in this body, in this heart.

THE NEMBUTSU AS SEEN BY DŌHAN

Though Dōhan's underlying hermeneutic is fourfold, his specific treatment of the *nembutsu* seems to come, oddly enough, in tripartite structures. In part this follows from the fact that Amida's name consists of three syllables; Dōhan, unlike Kakuban, who reduced the *nembutsu* to a single syllable "A," gives value—albeit not equal value—to all three syllables. Dōhan relates Amida to a series of parallel structures. "A-," "-mi-," and "-da" are the germ syllables of the "three families": buddha, vajra, and lotus. They also stand for *dharmakāya, sambhogakāya,* and *nirmāṇakāya.* They correspond to the three secrets of body, speech, and mind and therefore to the three consequences of these secrets, the three wisdoms. Individually and as a whole these three syllables are articulated in three stages. These are: as latent sounds in the throat, as subvocalization on the tongue, and as externalized and audible sounds when they leave the lips. These are the three stages of beginning, middle, and end and thus emblematic of totality.

Seen as a form of samādhi, there are, again, three kinds of *nembutsu.* The *nirmāṇakāya nembutsu* samādhi is reliance on the Pure Land as the sole way. (Why reliance is to be construed as a form of *nembutsu* is not quite clear to me.) The *sambhogakāya nembutsu* samādhi sees the *nembutsu* as a calling out (as per normative Pure Land). The highest form, the *dharmakāya nembutsu* samādhi, however, is to take the *nembutsu* as an esoteric dhāraṇī.

Two parallel triplicities suggest that Dōhan has in fact made a significant departure from Kakuban. The first of these is his arrangement, in what now appears to be an ascending order, of the homology of three buddhas and the three secrets. According to this paradigm, Śākyamuni is to be equated with the secret of body, Amida with the secret of speech, and Vairocana with the secret of mind. The second paradigm is a parallel analysis of "lands." The secret of the body is to be equated with this dirty land *(edo)*, the secret of speech with Amida's Gokuraku Jōdo, and the secret of mind with Vairocana's Mitsugon Jōdo. In part this is a strategic de-syncretization. Kakuban's nearly identical Amida and Vairocana are teased apart in order to restore Vairocana to uncompromised preeminence. We might also begin to suspect that, if for Kūkai the secret of body was the most equal of three equal secrets, and if Kakuban put his whole emphasis on the secret of speech, then Dōhan seems to betray a clear preference for mind.

All of this leaves us still wondering, however, what became of Dōhan's four-level hermeneutic. Why doesn't it apply to *nembutsu?* A plausible answer to this worry can be made, I think, if we consider Dōhan's *nembutsu-as-dhāraṇī* to be a third-level esoteric secret, and thus beyond the ken of normative Pure Land, but not the final, innermost, secret secret-of-secrets. That secret, of the fourth degree, is *nembutsu* as *himitsu nembutsu.* And here Dōhan reflects rather than departs from Kakuban.

One of the criticisms that Dōhan makes of the orthodox Pure Land understanding is lodged against its common tenet that the *nembutsu* should be a perpetual *nembutsu.* This, if taken literally in a normative Pure Land sense, is, Dōhan argues, impossible. One cannot constantly utter the spoken *nembutsu.* To put it as simply as possible, some time or another we all have to sleep. And even when awake, we have enough things to say other than "Namu Amida Butsu." Within the confines of normative Pure Land, then, perpetual *nembutsu* is an absurdity. But from the position of the *himitsu nembutsu* it is not only possible, it is even easy. Here Dōhan reverts to Kakuban's equation of Amida, *nembutsu,* life, and breath.

> The intoning is Wisdom; the chant is Principle. Wisdom and Principle are the twin *maṇḍalas.* The practitioner always ceaselessly breathes, in and out. Breath is the name-body of Amida. In-breath and out-breath are the twin *maṇḍalas.* Out-breath is the Vajra Maṇḍala and reaches out, in-breath is the Womb Maṇḍala of inner enlightenment. Therefore, out-breath is the Wisdom of the Calling [Out] and in-breath is the Principle of

Nembutsu as [inner] realization. Thus, the breath of the practitioner constitutes a ceaseless Nembutsu.[32]

This mode of *nembutsu* is also called the *hōni nembutsu*. *Hōni* is a term that refers to phenomena as latent, innate, spontaneous, or simply natural. From this wholly immanental understanding of the *nembutsu* we can know that all breath, and all sounds, human or otherwise, are in fact *nembutsu*. So too life. So too Amida. The universe is a *maṇḍala*, and Amida, like us, is but a figure in its midst.

Decline of the Himitsu Nembutsu *Tradition*

In 1413 Yūkai, the great champion of Shingon's *ni'ni* wing, managed to drive many of the *hijiri* (whose position would have been taken as supportive of the *fu'ni* view, and whose very nature was anathema to the more organizationally inclined Yūkai) off Mount Kōya. At the same time he managed to prohibit the building of new *hijiri* retreats on Kōya and to outlaw several sorts of dancing or singing *nembutsu* practice. This event should probably be taken as the downturn of the *himitsu nembutsu* tradition as well. Though it did not bring an actual end to the school's influence, which persisted in a much more informal, even underground, fashion both within and without the Shingon school, the "housecleaning" on Kōya did signal the end of the *himitsu nembutsu*'s period of creativity and growth. The politically motivated destruction of Negoro by Hideyoshi in 1585 probably erased most of such lingering traces of the formal movement as still survived at that time.

By the Edo period (1600–1867), texts dealing with the *himitsu nembutsu* were mostly repetitive of earlier redactions, but even some of these "reruns" had fairly wide popular circulation, as for example the *Himitsu Nembutsu shiki* (Private Notes on the Himitsu Nembutsu) of Donjaku (1674–1742) and the *Himitsu Nembutsu kōwa* (Discussions on the Himitsu Nembutsu), the *Himitsu anjin ryakusho* (Outline of the Esoteric Settled Mind), and *Himitsu Nembutsu ryakuwa* (Brief Notes on the Himitsu Nembutsu) of Hōjū (1723–1800).

Throughout this period the works of Kakuban and Dōhan continued to hold their place as well, as can be attested by the listings of Shingon-related works appropriate for lay readers that are specified in the *Shinsen shoseki mokuroku daisen* (The Great Newly Selected Index of Writings) of 1681 and its supplement of 1698, which includes Dōhan's *Himitsu Nembutsu shō*,

Kakuban's *Ichigo daiyō himitsu shū,* and *Gorin kuji myō himitsu shaku;* Echō's *Shingon Nembutsu shū;* Rentai's *Shingon kaiko shū;* a biography of Kakuban, the *Kōgyō Daishi gyoji ki* (Acts of Kōgyō Daishi); and a contemporary work on *himitsu nembutsu,* the *Kōya ōjō den* (Legends of Ōjō on Kōya) by Kaiei (1642–1727).[33] Perhaps the last of these well-known treatments was the *Misshū anjin kyō shishō* (Chapter on the Settled Mind of the Esoteric School) of Besshō Eigon (1814–1900).

Himitsu Nembutsu *beyond the Orbit of Shingon*

We have seen that the *himitsu nembutsu* tradition began within the confines of Shingon, rose to a certain height under the aegis of Kakuban and Dōhan, and then fell into decline—at least at the level of institutionalized, sectarian Buddhism. Nonetheless, before this downturn, the tradition had a considerable impact on other schools of Buddhism, and both within institutionalized contexts and within the far less regulated structures of folk practice it had continuing impact well after its formal decline. The range and depth of these effects can only be lightly sketched here, but without such a sketch the full import of the *himitsu nembutsu* tradition's place in Japanese religious history would remain only half told. The following depictions—which are truly no more than sample outlines—proceed in terms of sectarian categories. The fugitive remnants and hints of *himitsu nembutsu* thought in purely popular contexts are, as one would expect, harder to come by. But in several of the cases given below I think we can sense that the outer limits of sectarian belief are already congruent with popular belief and ritual. This is certainly the case with the Gonaishō.

TENDAI

Since normative Pure Land had deep organic connections with Tendai, and since Tendai—at least its Taimitsu wing—was at times hardly distinguishable from Shingon, it is simply to be expected that the *himitsu nembutsu* ideas would be picked up by at least some Tendai monks. And, indeed, so they were. In his 116-chapter *Keiran jūyōshū* (Leaves from a Storm-Blown Valley[34]) the Tendai monk Kōshū (early 1300s) outlines four kinds of *nembutsu,* including *himitsu nembutsu,* which he allowed was more profound than those of the regular Pure Land position. Tendai texts also talk of five kinds of *nembutsu* empowerment *(kanjō)* that seem to be derived from the *himitsu nembutsu* tradition. An Eshin-ryū school text called the *Goju sōden kōsetsu kōshaku* (General Explication of the Five Sorts of Transmission) tells us:

> Amida, Lord of the Western Quarter, uses the air *cakra* to form his body and the element metal for his substance. The *Vairocana Sūtra* says, "Life is breath." Breath is an esoteric Amida, an esoteric *nembutsu*. In-breath and out-breath naturally return to a sea of breath that is Amida or Vairocana—whether one intones the *nembutsu* or not. Whether the Name is uttered or not, breath is the yoga of the Three Secrets.[35]

This passage is practically a direct lift from Dōhan's *Himitsu Nembutsu shō:*

> The four kinds of being of the six realms, all the voices of the ten realms of illusion and enlightenment are alike Dharma-realm bodies of Amida. Their voices are all manifestations of the Great Element, Air; are the in-breath and out-breath of living beings. This breath is the root of life of these beings. The *Vairocana Sūtra* says, "Life is breath." The *Yugi kyō* [Yoga Sūtra] says, "Vajra is the root of life." Both texts take breath to be the root of life.[36] Therefore, Amida is, in verity, the life of all beings. Since the living beings of the world are endless, we call Amida "Endless Life."[37]

A particularly notable use of Kakuban's idea of *kimyō* as life-breath is that made by the Danna-ryu cult of Genshi Kimyō-dan (the Occult Altar of Breath). The altar of this cult is arranged as if it were a three-*honzon* altar with Amida at the center and Avalokiteśvara and Mahāsthāmaprāpta at either side. But in the place of Amida is the god Matara (a god of less than clear provenance, sometimes identified with Mahākāla, or as a *ḍākiṇī*). In spite of its outward appearance, this Matara is considered a form of Amida, in fact possibly the original form. The basic doctrine that connects the Genshi Kimyō-dan to *himitsu nembutsu* is its equation of Amida with wind, human breath, and life. Amida is the endless chain of phenomenal lives and our own life-breath is the Tathāgata of Endless Life. As a passage from a text called the *Kimyō-dan denju no koto* [Transmission of the Kimyō-dan] puts it: "The breath that passes through our mouth and nostrils is the *raigō*. Out-breath is, indeed, *ōjō*. The breath that passes out of the two nostrils is Avalokiteśvara and

Mahāsthāmaprāpta. The breath that exits from the mouth must, then, be the Tathāgata Amida. This understood, we see a perpetual *raigō* and an ever-present *ōjō*."[38]

Later in its history the Genshi Kimyō-dan cult seems to have become saturated with the ideas of Shingon's infamous left-handed school of tantra, the Tachikawa-ryū. At that point the idea that in-breaths and out-breaths were a natural *nembutsu* was extended yet another step. The in-and-out thrusts of sexual intercourse were considered a natural generation-regeneration of life-stuff and enlightenment.[39] (Tachikawa was, of course, like the *himitsu nembutsu* tradition, based on a radically uncompromising *fu'ni* philosophy of nondualism.)

ZEN

Traces of *himitsu nembutsu* in Zen are less easy to demonstrate. I think part of the reason is that, in spite of Zen's great simplicity and Shingon's great complexity, these two schools are very close in basic attitudes. Thus neither has very often to resort to the metaphors of the other. Each school has its own fully adequate symbol system to express the many intuitions they hold in common. One can, however, point to an instance or two. When I first published a translation of Ikkyū Sōjun's (1394–1481) short prose piece, *Amida hadaka* (Amida Stripped Bare),[40] I thought it was a fairly original Zen critique of Pure Land ideas. At this point, I would argue rather that it is directly dependent on the ideas of Kakuban and Dōhan. A few brief quotations may illustrate this point. About the location of Amida's Pure Land Ikkyū says: "The very body of the awakened person takes on the aspect of the West and is called the Pure Land. For the Buddha Amida resides within it."[41] And in a second place, ". . . the ultimate, ineffable joy. It is a state called by those fully awake to it the Pure Land Paradise."[42] Of Amida himself Ikkyū says: "The essence of the Universal Buddha—of the various Buddhas and bodhisattvas—has been condensed in the word Amida. . . . All the various Buddhas and bodhisattvas of the ten directions and the three ages are, in fact, Amida."[43] Ikkyū also talks of "the Pure Land simply in the heart" and states, "my own heart is Amida."

In similar fashion, Hakuin (1686–1769), like Ikkyū a monk of the Daitoku-ji lineage, takes a decidedly nondual, though not necessarily Shingon-derived, view of the Pure Land. In the *Orategama zokushū* (The Continued *Orategama*) Hakuin says:

The true practitioner of the Pure Land doctrine. . . . Reciting the name of the Buddha constantly, he has reached the state where the mind is undisturbed. . . . His own body is the limitless body of Amida, the treasure trees of seven precious gems, the pond of eight virtues. He has penetrated to the understanding that mountains, rivers, the great earth, all phenomena are the rare and mysterious Sea of Adornment. The ultimate, in which there is complete concentration in calling the name, in which not an instant of thought is produced, and in which the body and life are cast aside is known as "going to" (ō). The place where *samādhi* is perfected and true wisdom makes its appearance is known as "being born" (jō). The welling-forth of this absolute principle in all its clarity, the immovable place in which he stands, not one fraction of an inch apart, is "the welcoming of Amida" (raigō). When the welcoming and the rebirth are then and there not two things—this is the true substance of one's own nature.[44]

THE PURE LAND SCHOOL

Although the *himitsu nembutsu* took deliberate steps away from normative Pure Land views, it also affected the development of Pure Land ideology. This influence naturally tended to be deepest on those groups that were already moving in directions different from those of the Pure Land mainstream. Indeed, as we shall see below, when the influence becomes deep enough such groups attract the ascription "heretical."

Among the orthodox schools of Pure Land Buddhism the Seizan-ha borrowed much from *himitsu nembutsu,* and did so with no particular embarrassment. A passage from a text called the *Chikurin shō* (The Chikurin Compendium) should make this debt clear enough.

Life [breath] resolves back to Endless Life. . . . The intoning breath that is drawn from a heart that dwells within the realm of the three poisons is the Buddha-body. Breath is life itself. . . . Amida, who is called the Buddha of Endless Life, consists of numberless lives. Thus when the beings of the ten directions intone his name they attain ten *kalpas* of endless, truly enlightened long life. Thus our breath intoning the Nembutsu and the Buddha's long life are like the moon's reflection as it floats in the pool that is our heart.

In Shingon the secret of the body is primary. The mantras that resonate in the mouth, the *maṇḍalas* realized *[nen]* in the mind, and the mudrās incorporated in the body are all the Buddhas of Shingon. The core activity in the Pure Land school is to rely on the six-syllable *nembutsu*, "Namu Amida Butsu," to bring Buddhahood through *ōjō*.

In the mouth, life attains endless enlightenment. In the body, life attains endless awareness. When one sits in the sacred precincts, the triple activities of the bodhisattvas enter the endless awareness and become part of the efficacy of the six-syllable Nembutsu. These six syllables, Namu Amida Butsu, are usually considered a *samādhi* of the activity of speech. Thus the Nembutsu is a practice centered in speech. Even in the Shingon school speech can be seen as primary among the three secrets.[45]

Traces of *himitsu nembutsu* thought, at times perhaps mediated through Tendai, can be found even in such orthodox figures as the Shinshū patriarchs Zonkaku (1290–1373) and Kaku'nyo (1270–1351). Generally, however, they show up in Shin contexts only as aspects of the *hiji* ("secret business") heresies. Rennyo (1415–99), the great revitalizer of Jōdo Shinshū, for example, warns against these teachings, saying, "The so-called Hiji Hōmon is not Buddhism; it is simply a fearful heresy."[46]

An early example of such a Hiji Hōmon text is the *Hachimanchō no nuki-gaki Aji-kan no honmi* (Extract from Hachiman's Banner: The True Essence of Aji-kan). This forged text, which purported to be a direct transmission from Shinran to Nyoshin, was produced in late Kamakura or early Ashikaga. At its end is a fragment called "Shinran shōnin osode no moto" (From the Sleeve of Saint Shinran) which was supposed to pass secretly from master to disciple.

> This is to be whispered only into the ears of those directly in the bloodline. Maintain it carefully. This is for the ears of Nyoshin alone. . . .
>
> The Dharmakāya of expediency is produced by the twin syllables A and Un [a and hūṃ]. The yang aspect of an instant *(nen)* of life-breath is the "A-" breath. In an instant this approaches Emptiness and transforms into "-mi-." Since this comes from the heart, it is the Dharmakāya. The yin instant, which is "A-,"

receives the syllable Un and transforms into the syllable "-da." The locus of the union of the red and white[47] is called the Triple Body (Dharmakāya, Sambhogakāya, Nirmāṇakāya). This constitutes the three truths, Empty, Provisional, and Middle. Thus the twin Vajra and Womb realms are the twin red and white truths. Since this is born from the place where yin and yang unite, these two, the nature of Principle of the Dharmakāya and the content of Wisdom of the Sambhogakāya, ought ultimately to be called Amida of a single instant/thought [or of a single *nembutsu?*].[48] It further follows that the two characters *"na"* and *"mu"* represent the *hun* and *p'o* souls,[49] mind and thought. Beyond this, *nan* is father and *mu* is mother. Therefore, the father that can be named may be called "the mother of Light" *(kōmyō)*. There is no Bhūtatathatā apart from the Dharmakāya of expediency. To awaken to and fully realize this truth is to be a Buddha. . . .

When the practitioner's power is not adequate and he asks that his affairs be taken into divine hands, [this power manifests as] life-breath. And life is Amida. Amida returns *(ki-)* to that instant of thought that manifests as sun and moon. . . . When one recalls this, unspeakable tears of gratitude should be engraved in memory. Thereafter the person who realizes that the moon is of one substance, that the sun is of one substance, and that the self is of one substance, will speak of one substance with various bodies.[50] Therefore, his life *(-myō)* is unborn, undying, and selfless. For such a person to say *"kimyō"* is to *kimyō* with selfless *namu*. Such a person is the veritable dispenser of the enlightened wisdom of the monk Dharmākara's ancient vow. Maintain this secret; maintain this secret![51]

The Hiji Hōmon, and other similar groups anathematized by Rennyo, survived official Shinshū disfavor well into the Tokugawa era, and even if they did not exactly flourish, neither did they expire. Doubtless they were comforted by their certainty that their own lay leaders were the true followers of Shinran (or even Rennyo), and that orthodox claims to the contrary were no more than self-serving lies. In the texts propagated by these leaders, their followers could discover such truths as the fact that "when we chant 'Amida Butsu,' Amida is just another name for our own heart," that "Paradise is no longer far away," and that "to say the *nembutsu* is to recall one's own fundamental heart, which is pure and illuminated."[52]

Adherents of these unorthodox groups might be introduced to passages such as the following from the *Rennyo Shōnin hisho* (Secret Book of Saint Rennyo):

> Due to the loving kindness of Sun and Moon, Water and Fire, of all beings, both the sentient and nonsentient, even down to the grass and trees, there is not one but that participates in the virtues of water and fire. The Western Paradise is spoken of as being ten trillion worlds away, but when darkness is dispelled by the single, thought-free heart, the moon of the Single Heart of the Western Quarter appears at once. This is to know that the Pure Land fills all ten quarters of the heart. When we say, "Namu Amida Butsu" or "Namu Muryōju Nyorai," Amida is nowhere else but here. . . . Amida is in my four limbs and head. . . . When one contemplates the Pure Land of Amida as Mind-Alone, neither the Pure Land nor the befouled world is anywhere but here.[53]

As a final example of these texts I quote a segment of the so-called Ten Hiji supposedly transmitted from Shin'ei to Shinchi.

> Breath enters and leaves the Buddha Amida. The mouth is the altar of Amida. This is how you should understand *ōjō* "coming and going" [as in-breath and out-breath]. . . .
>
> This is something deep and darkly mysterious. However, when "Namu Amida Butsu" is uttered, Amida emerges out of "Namu."
>
> This is the mantra of natural self-enlightenment. All living beings are father and mother. And of these two, mother is A and father is Un. Mother produces A and father produces Un. And thus living beings produce Namu. Open the mouth and breath comes out, "A." Close the mouth and breath is drawn in, "Un." This is the *jōbutsu* (becoming Buddha) of breath.
>
> This great teaching is for one person at a time. It is a teaching in the lineage of Genshin Eshin. It is not to be given to nonbelievers. Do not trade it for a thousand pieces of gold, not for a thousand pieces of gold.[54]

An interesting feature of this text is the way in which its purported line of unbroken person-to-person transmissions parallels that of Shingon's transmission from the Buddha Vairocana to the bodhisattva Vajrasattva, on to a line of human patriarchs. The Ten Hiji transmission begins with Śākyamuni, passes to the bodhisattva Tenshin (Vasubandhu), then to Bodhiruci, Tan-luan, Tao-cho, Shan-tao, Hōnen, Shōkō, Nena, Jakue, on down to Shinjun, then to Shin'ei and Shinchi.[55] Though the names change, the structure is exactly parallel with the standard Shingon pattern.

THE GONAISHŌ

One of the most long-lived of Pure Land "heresies" was a group called the Gonaishō cult.[56] This movement combined elements of Tōzan Shugendō and Hiji Hōmon–like ideas into a complex fusion that lasted until at least the Second World War. In the overview that follows I will touch briefly on only three aspects of this movement: its literary sources, its ritual range, and its view of breath.

Although the Gonaishō cult was generally led by laypeople and supported primarily by peasants, and although it stressed the inheritance of purported "secret oral transmissions" from such notables as Kūkai and Shinran, it had a rather extensive textual base. In his broad investigation of the Gonaishō sources, Kikuchi Takeshi[57] analyzed the contents of one adherent's library and found that the forty-two texts owned included ten exclusively Gonaishō works, seven Hiji Hōmon works, five Shugendō texts, four works of Daoist provenance, one orthodox Shinshū piece, and eight untitled, miscellaneous works. Among the other texts that Gonaishō adherents commonly used, Kikuchi found, were many that provided unauthorized legendary materials about Shinran and Rennyo and many that retold the lives of famous Myōkōnin, the spiritual "idiot savants" of popular Pure Land. Clearly these were devised in part to place the Gonaishō within a recognizable, though unorthodox, Pure Land lineage. Interestingly, this lineage of individualistic hero figures included the Zen master Ikkyū—or at least a highly mythologized reflection of him as he is presented in the Tokugawa composition *Ikkyū Ninagawa: kyōka mondō* (Ikkyū and Ninagawa [Shinzaemon]: Their Contests of Mad Poetry). But the main authority figures elicited in support of the group's claims to true orthodoxy were Kūkai, Kakuban, and Shinran. Kakuban's *Gorin kuji myō himitsu shaku* was, in fact, held to be a sacred scripture. Shinran was understood to have been recipient from Kūkai of a secret *nembutsu* which is superior to ordinary *nembutsu* because "the exoteric *nembutsu* only saves monks, while the esoteric *nembutsu* can save monks and laypeople alike."

The textual complexity of the Gonaishō cult was matched by its ritual activities, which ranged from healing adherents and cursing enemies to procedures to effect an initiatory rebirth out of a dark cave or hut (at once a womb and a tomb) into the cult, and a highly involved ceremony to guarantee final salvation. This latter ceremony, in which a priest-psychopomp transfers his breath/*nembutsu* into the body of the dead person, seems to be largely based on the final sections of Kakuban's *Ichigo daiyō himitsu shū*. There are also some indications that the orgiastic "belt loosenings" and "group sleepings" that Hiji Hōmon groups were often accused of may have actually had a place in the Gonaishō—possibly via Tachikawa influence.

The Gonaishō view of breath was closely linked to its rebirth and death rituals. It also seems clearly derived from the *himitsu nembutsu* view. The *Gonaishō isshin ki* (On the Single Heart of Inner Enlightenment), for example, states: "The Heart of the Singular Buddha is the breath, 'A,' for this breath is the breath of the syllable 'A' in 'Amida.' This is the Dharma of the One Heart."[58]

Further, when a new convert was initiated, the Gonaishō master of ceremonies, who was a mortal representative of Amida, recited a *nembutsu* into the mouth of the neophyte and thus transmitted Amida from his breath to the convert as a variety of *sokushin jōbutsu*. (Perhaps this, like the initiatory death ritual above, was seen as both a death and a rebirth.)

Other *himitsu nembutsu*–like doctrines would include the assertions of one Gonaishō teacher that in-breath and out-breath constituted the deepest teaching of Shintō, of Confucianism, and of Buddhism. This teaching was called the Gozō Hōmon [Doctrine of the Five Viscera]. This last connection would lead us back once more to Kakuban, but also into a theme that we have not yet developed, Kakuban's adoption and adaptation of the Daoist "five viscera" motif. Rather than follow that temptation, I will instead bring to an end this already too diffuse introduction to the *himitsu nembutsu* and related esoteric immanentizations of Pure Land thought by quoting the opening lines of Gerard Manley Hopkins's "The Blessed Virgin Compared with the Air We Breathe":

> Wild air, world-mothering air,
> Nestling me everywhere,
> That each eyelash or hair

Girdles; goes home betwixt
The fleeciest, frailest-flixed
Snowflake; that's fairly mixed
With, riddles, and is rife
In every least thing's life.[59]

Shugendō, the Traditions of En no Gyōja, and Mikkyō Influence

H. Byron Earhart

SHUGENDŌ is a peculiar movement within Japanese religion which emerged from indigenous traditions in ancient times, accepted various religious elements such as religious Daoism (or Onmyō-dō in Japanese), but was organized especially around the forms of esoteric Buddhism. En no Gyōja (or En no Ozunu)[1] is the traditional founder of Shugendō, who is revered even today as setting the precedent of uniting both indigenous and imported religious traditions into a unique religious movement. In this essay we will introduce the religious movement of Shugendō and some traditions concerning En no Gyōja, with the purpose of demonstrating one example of *mikkyō* influence upon Japanese religion.

A Brief Sketch of Shugendō

As an expression of ancient Japanese religion, Shugendō is deeply involved in the various types of religious phenomena associated with Japanese mountains. So many such religious phenomena are associated with Japanese mountains that there is a special Japanese term, *sangaku shinkō* ("mountain belief" or "mountain creed"), which includes all such phenomena. For example, there is archaeological evidence proving that in early Japan rituals were performed on top of stones in the mountains. In addition numerous myths, rituals, festivals, and folk beliefs have enjoyed a long and intimate connection with mountains. The complex phenomena of sangaku shinkō cannot be treated here, but it is necessary to recognize the background of sangaku shinkō in order to comprehend the origins, development, and religious life of Shugendō.[2]

Although in ancient Japan there were indigenous forms of religion associated with mountains, these forms do not come down to us in a pure state today. For soon after Chinese civilization entered Japan, these indigenous forms became mixed both with religious Daoism (later known in Japan as Onmyō-dō) and with aspects of Buddhism. The problem of religious Daoism or Onmyō-dō and Shugendō will not be treated in this essay, but two major areas of this influence on Shugendō may be noted. First, in the origin of Shugendō, the Chinese traditions of hermits or wizards retiring into the mountains helped provide the rather speculative rationale for entering the mountains. Second, in the practice of developed Shugendō, the Japanese form of religious Daoism (Onmyō-dō) provided elements of doctrine, objects of worship, and magical charms or formulas.[3] In early Japan Buddhism was mainly the religion of the court and nobility, but even at that time there were individual Buddhist priests who entered mountain groves in order to perform more adequately their Buddhist meditation. Not only Buddhist priests but also *ubasoku* (Skt. *upāsaka*), unordained or lay believers in Buddhism, entered the mountains for practice. In the mountains the ubasoku carried out religious austerities including the memorization and recitation of sūtras or daranis (Skt. *dhāraṇī*). The ubasoku and other popular religious figures came to combine the mastering of magical formulas and acquiring of religious power with ascetic retreat into the mountains. In this manner, sangaku shinkō and "continental" traditions merged.[4]

The activity of ubasoku and other figures in learning daranis and entering the mountains for such purposes became quite conspicuous in Nara times. Not yet, however, was there an organized body of tradition which could shape such loose practices into a unified movement. Sometimes this early form of unorganized esoteric traditions is called *zōmitsu*, or "miscellaneous esoteric Buddhism." We shall see that the first historical reference to En No Ozunu occurs during this period. However, it is well known that the Heian period ushers in a new era in Japanese Buddhism. Saichō (posthumous title: Dengyō Daishi) and Kūkai (posthumous title: Kōbō Daishi) brought back from China new scriptures and rites, and founded on Mount Hiei and Mount Kōya, respectively, the new Buddhist sects of Tendai and Shingon. Incidentally, the fact that these new sects were founded on mountains, while reflecting Chinese models, in itself helped stimulate the earlier precedents for entering the mountains to carry out Buddhist training. But what was more important for Japanese Buddhism were the scriptures and rites so crucial for later developments.

In the Nara period the elements of zōmitsu had already become acclimatized to the Japanese mountains, and there were various types of ascetics *(genja)* or saints *(hijiri)* who carried out wandering careers therein. Especially the mountains around Yoshino at the east of the Yamato plain were considered to be ideal for such careers. Gradually the focus shifted to the Kumano area, where three centers of pilgrimage developed. Pilgrims to these sites were led by special "guides" *(sendatsu)*, who also directed the pilgrims in religious devotion along the way. Originally there was a distinction between the mendicant career and the ascetic career in one location, but gradually these types mixed together and blended with the leaders called sendatsu. In actuality these independent religious types presented a mixture of Shintō, Buddhist, and Onmyō-dō procedures at the end of the Nara period.[5]

In Heian times these independent figures and unorganized practices first began to take shape as Shugendō: the doctrine, rites, and formulas began to be standardized, and the individual practitioners came to be controlled by local mountain headquarters which appeared all over Japan. In brief, it was the new esoteric Buddhism of the Heian period which furnished the catalyst and framework for this organization. In fact, the two major Shugendō sects took shape around the two major esoteric traditions. Within the Kumano area, the Honzan sect of Shugendō was affiliated to the Taimitsu or Tendai branch of mikkyō through the temples of Onjō-ji and Shōgo-in. Centering around Ōmine, the Tōzan sect of Shugendō was affiliated to the Tomitsu or Shingon branch of mikkyō through the temples of Daigo-ji and Sanbō-in. In actuality, it was not until Kamakura times that Shugendō had digested the new Heian esoteric influence and achieved its definitive shape.

From Kamakura times on Shugendō played a very important role in Japanese religion. Shugendō "mountains" were opened up throughout all Japan, and the Shugendō practitioners, called *yamabushi*, were conspicuous in politics and art as well as in the religious life of the people. In the Edo period Shugendō came under the control of the Tokugawa *bakufu*, or Shogunate, and was on the decline when it was abolished in accordance with the new religious policies in the Meiji Restoration.[6] It is estimated that just before its abolition there were a hundred seventy thousand "sendatsu," and an untold number of other subordinate and special officers.[7] This short sketch of Shugendō will serve as the foundation for the remainder of this essay, which focuses on the traditions of En no Gyōja and mikkyō influence upon Shugendō.

Some Examples of Mikkyō Influence on Shugendō

The influence of mikkyō upon Shugendō forms one of the most important and conspicuous aspects of Shugendō's development and religious life.[8] Before discussing the mikkyō influence upon the traditions of En no Gyōja, it is well to suggest some general features of mikkyō influence upon Shugendō.

The religious life of Shugendō per se is too complicated to discuss here, but the basic principle is to gain religious or even magical power through retreat and asceticism within the mountains.[9] In connection with this basic principle, mikkyō influence is conspicuous, especially the Shingon traditions. It is well known that the *Dainichi-kyō* (Mahāvairocana Sūtra) is the primary scripture of Shingon, just as Dainichi-nyorai (Birushana or Vairocana) is the supreme figure of reverence.[10] Dainichi-nyorai is highly revered in Shugendō, and accordingly the formula (mantra, Jpn. *shingon*) of *on a bi ra un ken* corresponding to Dainichi-nyorai was highly favored. The crucial theory of the two mandara (Skt. *maṇḍala*) in the Dainichi-kyō pervades the complex symbolism of Shugendō. Indeed, often the mountains themselves are considered maṇḍalas: one mountain represents the "diamond" world, another mountain represents the "womb" world, and a third mountain represents the diamond and womb worlds together. These and other esoteric symbols prevail in the dress and tools of Shugendō.[11]

Perhaps the most striking influence of mikkyō upon Shugendō can be seen at the point of "Buddhology" or soteriology. Shugendō emphasizes actual asceticism in the mountains on the basis of the esoteric doctrine that all persons possess buddhahood and either may realize their identity with buddha or may "in this very body become buddha" *(sokushin jōbutsu)*.[12] In rites as well, Shugendō shows esoteric influence: the *saitō goma*[13] rite of Shugendō is a modification of the esoteric *goma* (related originally to the *homa)*; modified rites of esoteric ordination *(kanjō,* Skt. *abhiṣeka)* are also performed in Shugendō. The kaji (or *kaji kitō)* formed one of the indispensable procedures for the yamabushi. In summary, the esoteric influence upon Shugendō is quite obvious.[14] Esoteric elements of doctrine and rites provided the formal structure within which sangaku shinkō and elements of Onmyō-dō could be organized into a unified religious movement.

The Account of En no Ozunu in the Shoku Nihongi

The influence of esoteric Buddhism upon Shugendō can be understood better if the problem is limited to one aspect of Shugendō. Therefore we will take a closer look at the transformation of the traditions of En no Ozunu or En no Gyōja due to esoteric influence. At the same time, such an analysis provides insights into the early development of Shugendō.

Sufficient evidence has already been given to demonstrate that a religious movement such as Shugendō could have no one "founder." Rather, it emerged gradually out of the Japanese traditions of sangaku shinkō, early zōmitsu, and religious Daoism; then it increasingly became organized around esoteric Buddhist forms. As we shall see in the following discussions, the transformation of the traditions of En no Ozunu and his status as the founder of Shugendō is a direct result of the organization of Shugendō by esoteric influence.[15] Many documents reveal this development, but we will look only at three representative ones. First, the *Shoku Nihongi* will be quoted to present the earliest literary record of En no Ozunu in the Nara period. Second, the *Nihon Ryōiki* (or *Nihon Genpō Zenaku Ryōiki*) will be quoted to show how the tradition of En no Ozunu (or En no Ubasoku) developed on esoteric lines in the Heian period. Third, parts of the *En no Gyōja Honji* will be quoted to show how, by Kamakura or Muromachi times, En no Gyōja had become the founder of Shugendō with a thoroughgoing esoteric character.

The first recorded notice of En no Ozunu is found in the *Shoku Nihongi* (a record of the court from 697 to 791), and a continuation of the *Nihon Shoki* (also known as *Nihongi* in Aston's translation).

> En no Kimi Otsunu[16] was banished to the peninsula of Izu. Originally Otsunu had lived on Katsuragiyama and had been reputed as an adept in magic. Karakuni no Muraji, Hitotari, Gejugoige, took him as his professor. Later, jealous of his art, he slandered him that he led people astray by weird arts and therefore he was banished to a far-away place.
>
> It was said among the population that he often commanded spirits to draw water or to gather firewood for him.
>
> If they did not obey his orders, he bound them with magic.[17]

With this simple notice begins the long tradition of En no Ozunu. Even in this early notice he is described as a practitioner of magic in the famous mountain known as Katsuragiyama. Unfortunately, the content of this magic is not known, but some scholars have concluded that En no Ozunu was a "shaman" who practiced an indigenous Japanese form of divination.[18] However, even these scholars must depend in part on the *Nihon Ryōiki*, as the *Shoku Nihongi* account is very scanty in information concerning En no Ozunu. In fact, if he had not been banished, one wonders if he would have been mentioned at all.

For our purposes, several points within this account of the *Nihon Shoki* should be noted. First of all, Ozunu lived on the mountain called Katsuragi, and, second, he had mastered some form of "magic." These two points establish an early precedent for the relationship of some form of presence in the mountains and acquiring or performing the art of magic. Third, he is said to have control over spirits, indicating a superhuman power. This power included the ability to bind the spirits with his magic. Fourth, one aspect of his command over the spirits is to have them "draw water" and "gather firewood." This final point may be taken from the Lotus Sūtra.[19] However, except for this final point, the overall impression is remarkable for the lack of any explicit Buddhist influence. Furthermore, even though he possessed extraordinary powers, he is represented only as an exceptional individual. Indeed, his only pupil is said to have turned against him. In summary, we have no reason to believe that En no Ozunu will become the founder of Shugendō in the atmosphere of dominant esoteric influence.

The Tradition of En no Ozunu or En no Ubasoku in the Nihon Ryōiki

The next literary record of this figure occurs about a hundred years after he was supposed to have lived. In this short time a full-blown "tradition" has developed around him, and the tale in the *Nihon Ryōiki* is the main source of later references to him.[20] To the writer's knowledge this tale has not been rendered into English.[21] The text is not without its difficulties, and the writer does not feel competent to translate it. However, a tentative rendering is given here for the purpose of studying the tradition of En no Gyōja.[22]

Tale No. 28: Of Practicing the Magical Formula
of the Peacock King,[23] *and Thereby Becoming a Wizard*
in this World and Flying to Heaven

En no Ubasoku was of the family of E-no-kimi of the Kamo clan, at present the Takakamo clan of Asomi rank. He was a person of the province of Yamato, the district of Upper-Katsuragi, village of Chihara. By nature and from birth he was learned and full of enlightenment *(satori)*. He lived a life of reverent belief in the three treasures (Buddhism). Every evening he entered a five-colored cloud and flew beyond the sky, associated with the wizards, and played in the garden of eternity. He lay down to rest in the flowering garden, sucking up the spirit which nourishes one's character. Accordingly, at more than thirty (or forty) years of age he entered a rock cave, wore clothing of vines, and ate pine (needles), bathing in springs of pure water and rinsing away the filth of this world of desire. He practiced the magical formula of the peacock and was able to manifest wonderful magical arts. He achieved the ability to order about and use spirits and kami as he wished. He scolded the various devils *(oni)* and kami, and called a meeting, saying: "Make a bridge between the peaks of Kinpu (Kane no Mine or Kane no Mitake) and Katsuragi in the province of Yamato, and cross over." Then in the reign of the all-ruling emperor of the Fujiwara court, the great kami Hito-koto-nushi slandered him saying: "E no Ubasoku plans to overthrow the present reign." The emperor gave a command, dispatching his messengers to capture him. Now due to his magical power he could not easily be taken, so they captured his mother. Because they made his mother send for Ubasoku, he was taken. Thus, they exiled him to the island of Izu. One time his body went floating on the surface of the water as if he were treading on land. His body crouched down and he soared a thousand leagues, and his flying was like a (male) phoenix flying up.[24] In the daytime, in accordance with the emperor's command, he stayed on the island, but at night he retired to a cave of Mount Fuji in Suruga and practiced austerities. Nevertheless, he begged that the severity of his punishment be pardoned so that he might approach the capital, and he lay down on the blade of his sword and ascended to Fuji.[25] He grieved in exile for a period of three years. Then he was pardoned at New Year's, the first year of Taihō (701), under the star of metal younger brother, and he approached the capital. Finally he became a wizard and flew to heaven.

A person of the Japanese empire, the Buddhist priest (*hōshi*) named Dōshō, was commanded by imperial order to search out the dharma (Buddhism) in China (Tang). The priest went to Shiragi (Korea) on the request of five hundred tigers. Within the mountains there he lectured on the Lotus Sūtra. At that time there was a man among the tigers who offered up a question in the Japanese language. The priest asked, "Who are you?" He answered, "E no Ubasoku." The priest thought, "A Japanese saint *(seijin)*." He descended from his high seat and inquired of him. That great kami, Hito-koto-nushi, whom E no Gyōja previously bound with magic, even to this day cannot escape. The illustrations of his strange record abound in profusion. Therefore I shorten my tale. The person who knows the magical arts and the magnificent matters of the Buddha's Path (Buddhism), and believes in them, will without fail achieve this.[26]

The brief account of the *Shoku Nihongi* can hardly be compared with the elaborate tradition of the *Nihon Ryōiki*. The few details of the former account almost become lost in the full tradition of the latter. Even in the title we can recognize the fact that Buddhist and Daoistic elements have come to be associated with En no Ozunu. Before discussing this document, however, we will list in four points the new developments of the traditions of En no Ozunu as found in the *Nihon Ryōiki*. First, En no Ozunu is considered as an ubasoku (Skt. *upāsaka*), and has become an explicitly Buddhist figure. Second, En no Ozunu's magical technique has become magic of the Peacock King, important in esoteric Buddhism as a scripture and rite. Third, he has become a *shinsen* (Chinese sacred wizard), and the effect of his Buddhist magic has become linked with the thought of this wizard's magic (*hōjutsu*). Fourth, the reason for his exile is now considered to be the defamation of Hito-koto-nushi.[27] Other new features can be seen in his having a bridge built between the peaks of Katsuragi and Kinpu by the kami; and his journey into Korea is new.

The first question to arise in connection with this figure is his historicity. In this essay his actual historical existence is not of major consequence, but there is separate evidence that seems to verify the presence of a family named En which was attached to the Kamo clan in the area of Katsuragi. If this is the case, then it is possible that a historical figure named Ozunu served the Kamo clan in a hereditary office of worshipping Hito-koto-nushi. It follows that En no Ozunu could have practiced an indigenous form of "magic" or divination in a shamanistic career.[28]

The expansion of En no Ozunu's achievements in the *Nihon Ryōiki* does provide more material for inferring the "indigenous" character of his practice. However, the transformation of his career is much more conspicuous. The introduction of Daoistic elements is marked by such references as his change into a "wizard," or *sen*, who ascends to heaven, but the Daoistic element does not directly concern us. More important for our purpose is the Buddhist and esoteric coloring of this individual. Indeed, his very name of Ubasoku indicates that he has changed into a lay Buddhist of semi-magical character.[29] Even in the Nara period ubasoku are known to have memorized and used daranis for their magical power.[30] The noteworthy feature of "En no Ubasoku" in the *Nihon Ryōiki* is that his use of magic and daranis is no longer ambiguous, but is clearly specified as due to his mastery of the magical formula of the Peacock King. There are a number of "Peacock Sūtras" which have enjoyed a favored position in the history of esoteric traditions, possibly sanctioned by the historical Buddha, but at least preceding the historical emergence of Buddhism.[31] Already in the translation of the *Nihon Ryōiki* we indicated that "En no Ubasoku" himself appears to have assumed the form of a male phoenix. Tsuda and others have emphasized the fact that ascent to heaven as a wizard surely is evidence of Taoistic influence.[32] This evidence cannot be denied, but at the same time it is possible that Indian and Buddhist influence may be seen in such tales.[33]

Just as En no Ozunu cannot be considered the actual founder of Shugendō, likewise it is clear that he could not have possessed the Peacock Sūtra itself. There is unanimous scholarly opinion that the versions of this sūtra were brought to Japan after the time when he is supposed to have lived. Kōbō Daishi brought back one or more of these versions in 806, and the rite connected with the sūtra was performed mainly by Shingon priests.[34] However, the character of the "magic" of the Peacock King in the *Nihon Ryōiki* presents a contradiction with the fact that the rite of the Peacock Sūtra was ordinarily performed to bring rain, cure sickness, or gain an easy birth. En no Ubasoku's use of the magical power of the Peacock King for other purposes appears to be the result of adapting the religious character of the peacock to the tradition of the *Shoku Nihongi* and religious Daoist influence.[35] It should not be overlooked that the famous priest Shōbō (or Rigen Daishi, 832–909), the so-called "restorer" of the Tōzan sect of Shugendō, is said by some to have been the first in Japan to practice this rite.[36] At any rate the tradition that En no Ubasoku practiced the magic of the Peacock Sūtra establishes a major modification of his career due to the influence of esoteric Buddhism.

The Later Traditions of En no Gyōja, Especially the En no Gyōja Hongi

As Torao Sato and others have pointed out, the later traditions of En no Gyōja take as their main base the materials found in the *Nihon Ryōiki*. In this final section we will merely note some of Sato's conclusions, and then make some brief quotations from the rather late document entitled *En no Gyōja Hongi* in order to illustrate the thoroughly "Shugendō-ized" tradition of En no Gyōja.

Taro Wakamori and others have already recognized that the focus of developing Shugendō shifted from Katsuragi to Yoshino and the nearby mountain of Kinpu before proceeding to the area of Kumano and Ōmine. It was the increasing organization of Shugendō in the Kumano area which brought about these shifts. Probably the tradition that En no Gyōja had a bridge built between Katsuragi and Kinpu is a means of linking him with this central area of Shugendō.[37] Gradually "En no Gyōja," the name by which he is known throughout Japan as the founder of Shugendō, became associated primarily with the Kumano area. In the same fashion, Torao Sato has pointed out that by Kamakura times, when Shugendō was well established as a religious movement, the tradition of En no Gyōja became thoroughly transformed in a Buddhist and mikkyō manner.[38] And from Muromachi through Edo times many traditions were written about En no Gyōja as the founder of Shugendō.

Although En no Gyōja is remembered today mainly for his practice at Kumano, Ōmine, and Kinpu, in terms of literature this tradition is rather late. Satō notes that the tradition is not found in either the *Nihon Ryōiki* or the *Fusō Ryakki*, but first appears in the *En Kun Gyōshōki*, which was written in 1684.[39] Another relatively late development in the tradition of En no Gyōja as the founder of Shugendō concerns his connection with Zaō-gongen. The images of Zaō-gongen depict a fierce, menacing form that reminds one of Tibetan Buddhist sculpture; the identity of this figure in the Buddhist pantheon is still undetermined, but its esoteric origin is inferred from various indications, such as the vajra held in one hand.[40] These figures have been highly revered in the history of Shugendō, their early traces being found from Kinpu to Ō-mine. The most famous of all are the three large statues found in the main temple at Yoshino, the Zaō-do; within Shugendō En no Gyōja is considered to be responsible for the manifestation of Zaō-gongen and for the founding of Zaō-do. This problem is quite complex, but Satō quotes a number of Heian documents which refer to Zaō-gongen but do not mention En no Gyōja. The first document linking these two is the Kamakura writing *Konjaku Monogatari*. Thus, although faith in Zaō-gongen was active since Heian times, it was not until Kamakura times (when Shugendō was rather well organized) that En no Gyōja was linked to this thriving faith.[41] Many esoteric elements will be encountered in the quotations from the *En no Gyōja Hongi*.

En no Gyōja Hongi[42] or
The Authentic Record of En no Gyōja

Chapter 1: Birth

En no Ozunu was born on New Year's Day in the sixth year of the virtuous reign of Jomei, the thirty-fifth emperor. He was born in a family belonging to the Kamo clan in the province of Yamato, the district of Upper-Katsuragi, village of Chihara, Yahako. When he was born he held a flower in his hand. Even as he was born he could talk. His mother was surprised. She said, "This child does not need me to foster him." She placed him out in the field. This is a sign that even if no one gave him milk, he would not starve. Animals and birds were tame next to him. Dogs and wolves did not harm him at all. A purple cloud filled the sky of its own accord, and he did not get wet even in the rain and dew. In this way he grew up. His face was white and always full of rejoicing and smiling. His appearance was impressive and he carried out the four (Buddhist) commandments and was different from other people in the world. Always in his child's play his clothes never became wet from rain and dew. His feet never trod on the wriggling insects. He memorized naturally the *myōō* magic formula for rescuing from the suffering of snakes.[43] There were many wonderful instances of his granting magical power. Always he was apart from other children. Picking up rocks and rolling mud, he made Buddhist stupas and (simple) statues. He always played with the purpose of worship and reverence. He was certainly not an ordinary child.

In the first chapter from the *En no Gyōja Hongi* we can see that this figure has been turned into a thoroughly mythical character. His birth and childhood are accompanied by wonderful signs. The most remarkable feat is his "natural" mastery of the snake charm, which seems to be the same as the peacock charm. As mentioned in the note, "En no Gyōja" is reported as using the peacock formula in its generic sense as a snake charm, whereas earlier "En no Ubasoku" adopted it for his own magical aspirations. This should be seen as a "purification" of the tradition in accordance with more orthodox esoteric standards.

The second chapter has to do with En no Gyōja's descent from the kami, with the intention of establishing the identity of his mother and father. This chapter will be passed over for the third chapter.

Chapter 3, Part 1: Miracles of Ozunu

His mother Shiratarame had a dream on the night of the twenty-eighth day of the third month of the fifth year of the reign of Jomei. There was a thing in the air. Its form was like a kongōsho (Skt. *vajra*). Its brilliance was magnificent. It shone throughout the ten directions. It spread about and descended into her mouth, but there was no trace of it.[44] Afterward she remembered only a sweet taste on her lips. In her whole life she did not forget it. The aroma which it made was fragrant with scent. It was like a room of orchids. That child said this himself:

When I became thirteen years of age, every night I climbed the peak of Katsuragi. When the sun set I always returned home. When I became seventeen years old, I used wisteria leaves for a robe and ate pine needles. My austerities and difficult practices I never neglected. By myself I perceived the secret esoteric vehicle *(himitsujō)*,[45] I learned by heart (with no books or help) everything of the yoga of various Buddhas.

Furthermore, by myself I awoke to the inborn wisdom of Buddha. Alone I acquired the samādhi of Hoki Bosatsu. I became Jimyo-sen[46] and entered a cloud. I climbed to Toriten. I turned into Ryūgū-sen and traveled to the nether world.

(At this time Ozunu was twenty-five years old.) It was the fifth day of the fourth month of the fourth year of the reign of Saimei. He was gazing at a waterfall on the summit of Mount Mino-omote in Sesshū. He concentrated his heart and was striving earnestly. Immediately he ascended to the pure land of Ryūju Taishi (Nāgārjuna). A person there said, "Who are you?" He answered, "I am Ozunu." They went inside the temple. The temple was spacious and solemn. The towers and halls were high and lined up next to each other. The ground was made of lapis lazuli. There were gold platforms and jeweled stages. A pond of treasures with green, yellow, red, and white lotus flowers sent forth a fragrant aroma. Sacred trees were lined up in a row. A wonderful bird emitted a delicate sound and sang forth an exposition of the Law. A bright lantern of jewels shone brightly. A row of treasures, banners, and canopies stood there. A waft of incense of its own accord uttered a sound. It explained the subtle dharma of Mahāyāna. Other than that there were innumerable golden staffs, bells, and drums, which sounded of their own accord, manifesting the appearance of a Buddhist mass. He ate of the heaven's delicate sweet dew. A sea of clouds sprang up. They naturally provided a solemn altar as if offering up the central seven treasures. There was a treasure lotus. Above it there was Ryūju Bosatsu. His body was white. He was sitting with crossed legs. On his head was placed a treasure crown of the five wisdoms. In his right hand he held a kongōsho (vajra). In his left hand he held a treasure box of richi. Daibenzaiten was there. Tokuzen Daiō was there. (To wit this is Himyō Daiō.) Fifteen dōji of the diamond and womb maṇḍalas stood surrounding him to his right and left, front and rear. Since at that time Tokuzen Daiō was sitting, he stood and, holding the incense water, poured it over his head.[47] Ryaju Bosatsu conferred on him the greatest secret seal.[48] Immediately he passed over the nine worlds. Thus he arrived at the stage of wonderful enlightenment. Immediately he attained the secret doctrine. Receiving this, he returned. This was the seventh month, the third day. During this time more than eighty days had passed.

(In Ozunu's thirty-fourth year.) It was the fourth month of the sixth year of the reign of Emperor Tenchi. He first climbed Ōmine-san and reached the steep peaks. There was a skeleton here. Its five elements were not separated. Its height was nine and a half feet. He held in his left hand a kongōsho. He lay face up holding a sharp sword in his right hand. Ozunu wanted to take the things he was holding. But even though he shook the mountain he could not take them. Ozunu was sad and thought, "Is my asceticism ineffective? Moreover is this due to my karma?" He prayed to heaven and practiced austerities. This made him tired and exhausted. There was a voice which said, "You have passed seven lives in this mountain. This is the body of your third life. Also there are the bodies of two other lives. Chant the Senju (magic) formula five times and the Ke-ju three times and you will take them." He did as instructed and he took them. The skeleton stretched forth his hands and gave them to Ozunu. All his life he held to them and did not separate them from his body. After this he reached Nishi no Mukaino where there also was a skeleton. It was the body of his sixth life. Also at Shaka no Take there was a skeleton. This was from his fifth life. "Your first life was in the age of Ingyō, the thirtieth earthly emperor. Your third life was in the age of Emperor Ankō. Your fifth life was in the last years of the reign of Seimei. Your sixth life was in the second year of the reign of Ankan. By the merit of your past seven lives have you achieved this."

In the miracles of Ozunu we find more and more of Buddhist and eso-teric elements being associated with Ozunu. Indeed, there are so many diverse elements that it is difficult to identify them. In connection with mikkyō the appearance of a vajra to Ozunu's mother is quite significant; as Satō has suggested, it may link the vajra to the miraculous birth of Ozunu. In the chapter on birth he is described as learning the snake charm natu-rally, but in the chapter on miracles he learns the esoteric vehicle per se. He is associated with the highest and best of esoteric Buddhism. Again, the tale of Ozunu wresting a vajra from the skeleton emphasizes anew the supreme esoteric tool.

The above quotations from the *En no Gyōja Hongi* illustrate the esoteric influence upon this tradition in Muromachi times. From the remainder of this text, several additional examples may be cited. In the second part of chapter 3 is included a tale of how he received the mystical vehicle from Ryūju Taishi. In the first, "secret" part of chapter 3 is recorded that he installed a statue of Zaō-gongen in a cave. In the second part of this chapter, Zaō-gongen appears again, this time in connection with Hito-koto-nushi. The same part speaks of Ozunu's ordination, which later appears separately as chapter 5. In chapter 4 are treated Ozunu's visits to numerous mountains; often he practiced the goma at these mountains. Although these esoteric elements are not systematized, their occasional and natural appearances demonstrate their implicit acceptance in this tradition.

The development of the traditions concerning En no Ozunu depended to a great extent on esoteric influence. These traditions illustrate how Shugendō came to be organized around esoteric forms in Kamakura times and thereafter. The fact that the traditional founder of Shugendō was conceived in terms of esoteric models is the supreme example of esoteric influence upon Shugendō. However, this constitutes only one aspect of the esoteric coloration that pervaded all areas of Shugendō doctrine, rituals, and tools.[49]

The Cave and the Womb World

HELEN HARDACRE

THIS ESSAY delineates the different significance of a contemporary
Japanese rite for women and men.[1] It tries to show how women and
men experience the rite uniquely because of the way the symbolism of the
ritual interacts with their separate and differing psychological structures.
One of the conclusions reached in this investigation is that the meaning
of ritual frequently must be explained in terms of the gender of the participants.

The essay is divided into four sections. The first gives a description of the
rite of ascending the cave at the Oku no In peak of the Ōmine-san Shugendō
site. The second section considers the history of this rite and the nexus of
religious ideas it invokes. The third section focuses on the central psychological motif of the ritual, a return to the womb, and shows how the psychological significance of this motif differs for women and men. A fourth
section presents the conclusions reached.

The Ritual Ascent

This essay concerns the ritual ascent of Ōmine-san, a sacred mountain in
Nara Prefecture. Ōmine is an important site for Shugendō, the cult of sacred
mountains. Actually, Ōmine is the name not of a single mountain but of a
mountain chain stretching from Kumano to Yoshino. In this area there are
seventy-five *nabiki*, traditional sites designated for the practice of asceticism
by the *yamabushi* (mountain ascetics). Half of the Ōmine area, centering
on Kumano, is identified with the Womb World, while the other, Yoshino
half is identified with the Diamond World. This mapping of the maṇḍala
of esoteric Buddhism onto actual geography is a loose set of correspondences; it is not that each of the many compartments of the maṇḍala is
linked to a specific spot in the Ōmine territory. In these mountains there

are more than sixty caves, and legend has it that the founder of Shugendō, En no Gyōja, practiced asceticism in the dank recesses of one of them for three years. This cave, which cannot be positively identified with any of the sixty caves, is believed to have been a three-tiered cavern in which the first level represented the Pure Land, the second the Womb World, and the third the Diamond World.[2]

H. Byron Earhart summarizes the yamabushi's inspiration for performing asceticism in the mountains as the belief that "one can become a Buddha or equal to a Buddha by practice of mountain retreats combined with rituals."[3] Caves acquired a special importance for the yamabushi as places where it is possible to absorb the maximum spiritual power of the mountain and the deities who dwell there. Orikuchi holds that ascetics chose winter for their cave rites because of winter's close connection with motifs of purification. Purifying themselves of pollution, they entered the grottos in a state maximally capable of imbibing new powers. Hitoshi Miyake adds that since the kami are believed to pass the winter in the mountains in a state of semi-hibernation, if the yamabushi performs asceticism in the caves in that season, he may absorb the powers of the kami.[4]

Loosely affiliated with Shugendō orders are a number of informal confraternities *(kō, kōsha),* dedicated to the annual ascent of Japan's numerous sacred mountains. These societies host a pilgrimage to the mountain revered by the particular group once a year, and members ascend its peaks in the established order of worshipping at many small shrines along the route. Male members wear yamabushi attire or a white *happi* coat over white trousers, and women generally adopt the latter style. Usually men and women are separated along the route of march as well as in sleeping and dining facilities in those kō which have both female and male members. Through arrangements with the mountain's principal temple, the confraternity may sponsor group ritual within temple precincts or be assisted in ritual by temple personnel, including priests and acolytes. In June of 1982 I participated in the annual ascent of Ōmine-san with the Tsuruhashi Yamanashi-kō, a Japanese-led confraternity which is based in Osaka and includes many members of the Korean minority in Japan.

This assembly of the Yamanashi-kō lasted two days and included roughly 160 persons, of whom about 55 were Koreans (34 percent), 45 of them women and 10 men. There were 95 Japanese men and 10 Japanese women. The kō's leadership was entirely Japanese. Its eldest member was a Korean woman of seventy-one who ascended the mountain for the eighteenth consecutive occasion that year. Most of the female Korean members were making their second or third trip, and all reported that they had entered the kō through the recommendation of a Korean friend, usually an associate from one of many Korean temples in the Osaka area. No one can remember when or in what circumstances Koreans first joined the Yamanashi-kō beyond the recollection that their participation was notable even before World War II.

The entire group assembled at Osaka's Tennōji station at 6:30 a.m. and boarded a specially reserved train. From the beginning, seating arrangements were made by the Japanese leadership to separate Koreans from Japanese. The train arrived at the foot of the mountain around 8:30 a.m., and from there we boarded buses. In principle the rules of mountain worship prescribe complete separation of men and women from this point on, but this desideratum conflicted with that of maintaining a separation between Koreans and Japanese. The solution finally reached was to put all the Koreans and myself in one bus and, during the ascent to the Ryōsenji temple, to treat Japanese men, Japanese women, and Korean men as all equivalent.

The Korean women discussed this blatant discrimination against them rather heatedly and surmised that the Japanese women were at the bottom of it, not wanting to come near "noisy garlic eaters." The same explanation arose again when it was discovered that Korean women were to be housed in a smaller, less attractive inn than the Japanese women, who were treated as honorary males and housed with the men.

After lunch at the inn, the men departed to climb the main peak, while both Korean women and Japanese women set out for a lower peak, the Oku no In. Women are not allowed to climb the main peak. With the wife of the Japanese leader of the confraternity at the head, all the women walked to the trailhead, stopping to offer incense and candles at Shintō shrines along the way. In these devotional acts as well as in attire and decorum, the Korean women followed Japanese practice entirely. In spite of the energetic use of Shintō to colonize their homeland prior to 1945, they bowed piously and clapped before the shrines. Similarly, they also accepted the Japanese practice of barring women from the main peak, lest the foul pollution of a female body offend the mountain deity.

In the view of the Japanese leadership, the main object of female participation in the confraternity is to have them climb to the Oku no In, there to ascend a vertical shaft cave. Legend has it that this is the cave where the legendary founder of Japanese mountain worship, En no Gyōja, practiced austerities for three years. To reach the opening of the cave, a gaping hole high up in the rock wall, one climbs for about two hours along the steep path, finally entering the mouth by a swinging steel ladder. When all fifty-five women had struggled up to the cave opening, we were led in recitation of the Heart Sūtra by two acolytes from Ryūsenji; one of them led the way into the cave.

Climbing ten feet or so to reach the entrance, it is necessary to crawl through a narrow, muddy passageway into the first chamber. Here one is suddenly enveloped in icy air. This chamber is the opening to a vertical shaft of perhaps twenty meters, which is ascended by climbing horizontal steel bars pinned to the rock. The passageway is only large enough for one person to pass at a time, and a single misstep on the rusty bars would bring all crashing down in a helpless crush. Sensing the danger, the women stuck candles into crevices in the rock and cried out the Japanese pilgrims' proclamation of repentance, "Rokkon shōjō!" (Purify the six roots!), as they inched up the shaft. Fear and claustrophobia held all in their grip as freezing, putrid drops falling from the recesses above evoked startled cries. Finally we squeezed our way out of the shaft and into the second chamber of the cave. Now twenty meters above the first chamber, the second had the shape of a tetrahedron, with a small altar at each wall of the triangular base. These enshrined Acala, En no Gyōja, and the Eight Naga Kings.

Above the latter altar on the cave wall, a massive stalactite of fantastic, undulating shape represented the Naga Kings. Pitch-black except for votive candles, the chamber rose to a pinnacle some twenty meters or so above us. At the very top was a pinhole of light. Inside the air was frigid as all the women set fistfuls of incense and candles alight on the altars. Soon the sweet smoke was almost overpowering as all fifty-five women crowded into the triangular cavern no more than ten feet on a side. We recited the Heart Sūtra before the altar of Acala, then climbed down the tunnel and out into the light again.

Much has been written on Shugendō's rites of rebirth, achieved by climbing into mountains defined as a cosmic maṇḍala, the Womb World (garbha-kośa dhātu) of esoteric Buddhism, there to undertake difficult austerities.[5] For the male ascetic, the focus is upon reemergence from this womb, upon becoming "reborn" in the sense of being newly endowed with esoteric knowledge and powers. The rite of ascending into the cave at Oku no In partakes of this motif of a return to the womb, of clawing one's way into its deepest recesses to return to the original source of all life, to acquire knowledge and wisdom. The darkness and the intermittent ablutions by the secretions of the rock add a perceptual reality that tremendously heightens the visceral dimension of the experience. In the case of women participants, however, there is a self-referential quality that is alien to males.

The ritual ascent of the Oku no In cave performed by the women of the Tsuruhashi Yamanashi-kō is a much-abbreviated version of a rite which in former times would have been performed by male ascetics as part of a longer series of rites ranging over the seventy-five *nabiki* of the Ōmine-san area. In order to fully understand the significance of the ascent of the cave, it is necessary to examine the context of the rites and the ideas on which they are based. That consideration is the task of the next section.

The Nexus of Religious Ideas

This section traces the history of religious ideas associated with the rites under consideration here. Those ideas have to do most importantly with sacred mountains and the religious powers and other benefits believed to be available through spiritual training in the mountains. Studies of Japanese religions have often remarked on the importance of sacred mountains for all branches of Japanese religions: Buddhism and Shintō as well as Shugendō. It is well known that the most important motifs are (1) the mountain as the dwelling place of divinities and ancestors; (2) the mountain as the Other World; (3) the mountain as the source of agricultural fertility; (4) in Shugendō, the mountain as the geographical representation of sacred geography—as the Diamond World and the Womb World. In outlining these central ideas, this essay makes no pretense of novelty but instead seeks only to put these well-known facts before the reader as part of the ritual context.

Mountains are regarded as the abode of divinities and ancestors. That this is so may be seen in folk rites in which during the Bon festival people ascend a mountain to greet the ancestors and escort them back to their homes for a period of time, during which the ancestors are believed to return to the human world to be with their descendants. Numerous tales attest to a meeting with divinities in the mountains, and all of Japan's sacred mountains have on their slopes small shrines dedicated to numerous kami and Buddhist figures.[6]

That the mountains are regarded as the Other World in visible, geographical form is evidenced by such phenomena as the Sai no Kawara, on Osorezan in Aomori Prefecture. This naturally desolate place, a treeless expanse of gravel and stones atop a mountain, is believed to represent the riverbed where children who have died must spend their days uselessly piling up stones, only to have them swept away again. Their only consolation is the merciful Bodhisattva Jizō (Kṣitigarbha), who ministers to them out of compassion. There are numerous other examples of rites and beliefs which show that the mountains are regarded as the Other World.[7]

The *yama no kami*, often understood to be a female deity, is the best example of the way in which the mountains are regarded as the source of agricultural fertility. In the spring the mountain god is transported in some parts of Japan to the fields in the plains, there to become the *ta no kami*, or the kami of the rice fields. This coincides with spring rains, running down to the fields from the mountains with their melting snows, thus bringing life to the world of plants.[8]

Buddhist esotericism has identified specific mountains with the Womb World and the Diamond World, congruent with the maṇḍala of the same names. Direct experience of the non-difference or unity of the two is equated with a realization of emptiness. Such a realization is the key factor in attaining buddhahood in this life: *sokushin jōbutsu*. The esoteric practitioner is to enter into the world of the maṇḍala first through initiation and then progress through its separate houses. In so doing he absorbs into himself the qualities of the separate figures of the maṇḍala in their characteristic forms, various buddhas and bodhisattvas. Identifying himself perfectly with these aspects of emptiness, he progresses toward a full realization at an experiential level of this truth beyond reason.[9]

These four motifs concerning sacred mountains are part of the background of religious ideas informing the performance of ritual at Ōmine-san. It is to the history of those ideas in that more specific context that we turn next.

Cave rites of a generally Buddhist coloration are known throughout Asia. To say that they partake of the motif of rebirth is true in a general way, but it is necessary to qualify that statement considerably if we wish to articulate correctly a Buddhist interpretation of these rites.

In the case of Buddhist rites, one cannot assume that rites in caves have as their goal a simple repetition of the birth process. This is so because birth is not unambiguously a "good thing" in the Buddhist world of thought. Birth is yet another beginning of the whole round of karma, attachment, suffering, and death in endless repetitions. This being the case, in Buddhist rites we must inquire more closely as to the precise character and intent of any given ritual.

François Bizot examines Buddhist cave rites in Cambodia and shows that rites of rebirth in caves effect a symbolic reconstitution of the initiate as a New Man, who henceforth need not experience death. These rites at "la grotte de la naissance" *(raan prasut)* are performed by groups of lay Buddhists and include also a more esoteric component for monks. Similar rites of rebirth from caves are reported from several other Cambodian cave sites. They consist in symbolically making a new body by means of a return to the womb. The period of tellurian incubation aims at giving the initiate new powers.[10]

The lay pilgrimage to this Cavern of Rebirth at Phnom Sampau in Battambang begins with making offerings for the monks' rainy season retreat. On this occasion pilgrims experience collective trance. The woman of the sponsoring household kneels to receive the tutelary deity of the region, the "Lady of the Perfumed Hair," a figure central to the myth of origin of the cave which is the pilgrims' destination. Possession occurs during the trance, and with that the Lady of the Perfumed Hair is present in the body of the medium. Her main responsibility is to confer a blessing of safety upon the taxi drivers who will convey the pilgrims to the mouth of the cave. Arriving there after a colorful procession, the pilgrims are led into the cave by an old monk, a "master" *(acarya)*, who "opens the road" for them by casting water to the four directions.[11]

The cave is a labyrinth of chambers and passageways. Before a Buddha statue enshrined inside the cavern, the master admonishes the pilgrims to be mindful of the gravity of their next action: entering the "golden door" of the mother's womb. He reveals to his charges the syllables *a ra ham*, which they must chant ceaselessly. Passing through several chambers, they eventually arrive at one where a lustrous stalactite hangs above a pool of clear water. The master explains that they are now in the center of the womb, where the embryo sucks water from the mother, clasping the "umbilical cord," the stalactite. The calcineous rock in pastel colors glistening with moisture gives a sense of the body's interior as the master washes the face of each pilgrim in the pool. They light incense and recite prayers as a prelude to meditation. After silent meditation in the cave for about an hour, the pilgrims emerge. The master proclaims: "We have entered this cave and acquired great merit, because it is the womb of the August Mother *(garbh brah mata)*. The orifice is the Golden Door. Entering it to practice ascesis, we have returned to the maternal womb. Thus we have been born anew. Repent for having sullied the August Mother!"[12]

Besides pilgrims' rites, some Cambodian monks enter these caves to soak their faces in "the amniotic well" and to clasp the "umbilical cord" poised above the pool. They practice visualization meditations in which they cause an image of the Buddha seated upon the throne of illumination to appear. The meditator suppresses the breath and forces it down into his body. These practices are unrelated to the motif of the return to the womb per se. Instead, the meditator hopes to recapture the conditions of the embryo *in utero*, but without symbolically repeating the birth process. Instead, these practices refer more specifically to the process of gestation. Gestation is represented in breathing exercises, the specific moments of which are correlated with steps in the creation of the world.[13]

Creation texts speak of fashioning a personalized embodiment of Dhamma {Dharma}, on the model of the Puruṣa myth. The text begins with an invocation of Buddha. As the body's parts are enumerated, they are correlated to the creation of water, earth, fire, wind, and ether, the five elements. At the instigation of a deity called Brah Kev, the figure Buddha-gun created primal waters, land, and virtues. Concentrating on the letters *buddha ya* of Dhamma, he created a primal man, with powers of speech, sight, and hearing but lacking a conscience. Further stages in the creation of the Dhamma-Being parallel the development of the fetus. Here the candidate is transformed, first by a symbolic substitution of organs and viscera which are those of the primal being. Further, he is imbued with new qualities *(gun)* which cause him to transcend the human condition.[14]

Thus in retreating to caves for meditations upon the gestation of the human embryo, the meditator creates himself as Dhamma-Being. This autogenesis is the transformation he seeks in the Womb Cave. Far from a simple motif of rebirth, the meditator seeks the extinction of thirst for sensual objects, which can be attained only through a ritual death and reconstitution. Thus the aim is not rebirth as such but to take possession of a new body, to pass from a mortal to an immortal existence, thus breaking the chain of mundane births and deaths.[15]

The significance of Buddhist cave rites seems likely to involve something more complicated than the word "rebirth" implies. The Cambodian rites just examined illustrate the complex interplay of mythic motifs and doctrinal concerns, which precludes the unambiguous approval of yet another birth. In Shugendō, the most immediate point of reference for the ascent of the Oku no In cave, we find a similar complexity. The main focus of Shugendō ritual is the mountains themselves. To unearth their doctrinal content, it is necessary to refer to the doctrines, rites, and concepts of esoteric Buddhism, which inspire Shugendō's initiatory rites. Let us examine three components of the system: the *abhiṣeka* ceremony, the Womb World mandala, and the idea of attaining buddhahood in this existence.

We will begin with a consideration of the Womb World mandala, more properly speaking, the Mahākarunāgarbha mandala (Jpn. *Taizōkai mandara*). The word *mandala* has the meaning of a circle, that which is circular, a disk, a halo, a group, and in the Vairocanābhisaṃbodhi Sūtra (T. vol. 18, no. 848; Jpn. *Dainichikyō*), the specifically esoteric meaning of that which gives life to all Buddhas, something which causes one to be born. The Shingon school recognizes several types of mandala, which Kūkai understood as complementary representations. The purpose of utilizing mandala of elements (*mahā mandala* Jpn. *daimandara*), of attributes (*samaya mandala* Jpn. *sammaya mandara*), mandala in relief or free-standing sculpture (*karma mandala* Jpn. *katsuma mandara*), or letter symbols (*bija mandala* Jpn. *shuji mandara*) is the realization of buddhahood in this life: *sokushin jōbutsu*. It is to be understood that such a realization takes place through grades of initiation in abhiṣeka (Jpn. *kanjō*).[16]

The Womb World mandala illustrates the doctrines of the *Dainichikyō*, and its use is paired with that of the Diamond World mandala, which illustrates the doctrines of the *Sarvatathāgatatattvasaṃgraha Sūtra* (T. vol. 18, no. 865), abbreviated in Japanese as the *Kongōchōgyō*, the second great sūtra of the Shingon school. Together one speaks of the paired mandala as the *ryōbu mandara* and of the paired scriptures as the *ryōbu daikyō*. The principal doctrine of the *Dainichikyō* is that all the virtues of Dainichi (Mahāvairocana) are inherent in us and in all sentient beings. The Womb World mandala represents the perspective of the beings destined to attain buddhahood, whereas the Diamond World mandala represents the perspective of the Buddha.[17]

The meaning of the Womb World mandala is explained through a double metaphor of a lotus and the womb. The process by which meditation upon the Womb World mandala causes the aspiration for enlightenment (*bodhicitta*; Jpn. *bodaishin*) to arise is explained through comparison to a fecund womb which nurtures the aspiration. The development of this aspiration is likened to the progress of the lotus from seed to full bloom or to the gestation and eventual birth of a human embryo. The end result is the attainment of buddhahood in this life.[18]

These ideas are appropriated by Shugendō when it designates a sacred mountain as a representation of the Womb or Diamond World. In the ritual with which we are concerned here, the Oku no In cave is understood as a representation of the Womb World. Thus to practice asceticism in the mountains is to enter the Womb World with the intent of so transforming oneself as to attain buddhahood in this life.

Since the aim is to be transformed into a buddha, it is necessary to traverse the "Ten Worlds." These are explained as ten kinds of asceticism (*shugyō*). Although the full set of ten rites is rarely performed nowadays, it is appropriate to specify them in order to locate the provenance of the Oku no In rites more exactly.[19]

In Shugendō, each of the ten worlds enumerated in Buddhism on the basis of Chih-I's system is paired with a ritual propelling the initiate closer to the goal of attaining buddhahood in this life.[20] The first world is hell, *jigoku*. In this stage the initiate performs the rite called *tokozume*. He visualizes himself as Dainichi. Cutting himself in five places, he assigns one syllable of Dainichi's mantra to each cut. In the second world, that of the *preta*, or "hungry ghosts," the initiate repents *(zange)*. In full prostrations before the leader, the *sendatsu*, he confesses his sins. The third world is the world of beasts *(chikushō)*. Here, in a rite called *gobyō*, a rope is tied to the initiate's hands, and he is hoisted off the ground to weigh his sins.

In the fourth world of the *asura*, the initiate practices *mizudachi*, abstinence from drinking water or washing the head. The fifth world is the human realm *(ningen)*, and here the initiate performs a rite called *aka*. The initiate draws water and brings special wood to the *sendatsu*. The sendatsu exchanges the initiate's headgear for the yamabushi's characteristic black pillbox hat, the *tokin*, and washes the hands and face of the initiate. The sendatsu also teaches the initiate the secret letters of Dainichi. In the sixth, or heavenly realm *(ten)*, the initiates engage in *sumō* and wrestle with each other. In the seventh world of the śravaka *(shomon)*, the initiates dance with fans in either hand, in a rite called *ennen*. The eighth world is that of the pratekya buddhas *(dokkaku)*. Here the initiates undergo the rite of *kogi*, wherein each takes a black and white piece of wood in hand and places it on the altar before the sendatsu. Later these are ceremonially burned in a *goma* ceremony, and this symbolizes the funeral of the initiate, extinguishing the passions. The ninth realm is that of the bodhisattvas (*bosatsu*), and here the initiate practices abstinence from cereals for seven days in order to transform the body for the final rite.

The tenth world is that of the buddhas *(butsu)*, and the rite is *abhiṣeka, (kanjō)*. After preparatory rites of repentance, the initiates' heads are sprinkled with water, and the initiates are taught mantra and mudrā. Here they attain certain proof of their attainment of *sokushin jōbutsu*, buddhahood in this existence.[21]

Thus Shugendō appropriates to its ritual framework the idea of the Womb World maṇḍala, mapping it onto actual geographical sites, there symbolically to enact a transversing of the ten worlds, ending in the attainment of buddhahood in this life. That final attainment is ritually enacted in the *kanjō* rite. This rite has Indian origins and takes place there upon a maṇḍala specially constructed for the purpose over a period of seven days. In the *Guhyatantra* (T. no. 897) the manner of constructing that maṇḍala and of conducting the *abhiṣeka* ceremony is explained.

Both the enthronement of kings and the consecration of a disciple by a master take place before this altar set out upon the earth. On the first day the master, having asked for the protection of the earth gods, works the earth to the consistency of powder to remove stones and debris. The earth is mixed with cow dung and urine which have never before touched the earth. On the second day the site is consecrated by burying in it precious objects. On the third day twenty-four vases of flowers are arranged, and the placement of various divinities is determined. On the fourth day the site is purified by aspersion, and sandalwood powder is poured to sketch the maṇḍala of nine great Buddhas. On the fifth day the mantra of Acala is recited to rid the site of all obstacles and to bless the earth. On the sixth day the master blesses the disciple to allow him to enter the maṇḍala. Finally, on the seventh day, the master invokes all the divinities of the earth and carries out the anointing of the disciple. Following the ceremony, the maṇḍala is destroyed.[22]

Kūkai's idea of attaining buddhahood in this very existence is the culmination of his thought. Apparently Kūkai in his mid-forties reached the conclusion that such an attainment is possible, and he wrote the *Sokushin jōbutsu-gi* ("Attaining Enlightenment in This Very Existence").[23] To explain why this attainment is possible, it is necessary to review Kūkai's understanding of Mahāvairocana. His most innovative proposition equates Mahāvairocana with the dharmakāya. Kūkai reworked the traditional theory of the three bodies of buddha *(trikāya)*, adding a fourth element. Each of the four is in fact a form of the dharmakāya, and in addition to absorbing the distinctions of the traditional theory into the dharmakāya, asserts that the dharmakāya in emanation *(toru hosshin)* underlies the existence of sentient beings in subhuman realms. This being the case, dharmakāya (Mahāvairocana) pervades all existence and is not separate from any single existence.[24]

Another way of considering Mahāvairocana is as the unification of wisdom (symbolized by the *vajra*) and principle (symbolized by the lotus). The unity of wisdom and principle constitutes inherent enlightenment *(honnō hongaku)*. If Mahāvairocana pervades all existences and is also originally enlightened, then it must be that all beings share this quality. That is why it is possible for all sentient beings to attain enlightenment. They have the seed already within them. The problem is one of germinating the seed.

Kūkai explains how this is possible in his famous two stanzas that are the core of the *Sokushin jōbutsu-gi*. Of these lines the first and third are the most important.[25]

(1) *Rokudai wa muge ni shite tsune ni yuga nari.*
The six great elements are interfused and are in a state of eternal *samādhi.*

(3) *Sammitsu kaji sureba sokushitsu ni arawaru.*
When I sanctify myself by the three mysteries, the three mysteries in me are revealed.[26]

The first line consists of two propositions. First, Mahāvairocana consists of the six elements: earth, water, fire, wind, space, and consciousness. In other words, Mahāvairocana is the totality of all physical and mental elements. These elements are constantly changing and are inextricably interrelated. Second, Mahāvairocana or the six great elements are in a constant state of *yuga*, or samādhi. Thus any being desiring to unite with Mahāvairocana should practice meditation, thereby reaching harmony with the dharmakāya through samādhi.[27] The third line of Kūkai's stanza explains esoteric practice. The three mysteries are the body, speech, and mind of Mahāvairocana. When the three mysteries of Mahāvairocana are aligned with the body, speech, and mind of a being through meditation, there will be a mystic fusing of Mahāvairocana and that being through *kaji*, which Kūkai explains thus: "*[Kaji]* indicates great compassion on the part of the Tathāgata and faith *(shinjin)* on the part of sentient beings. The compassion of the Buddha pouring forth on the heart of sentient beings, like the rays of the sun on water, is called *ka* (adding), and the heart of sentient beings which keeps hold of the compassion of the Buddha, as water retains the rays of the sun, is called *ji* (retaining)."[28] The full permeating by Mahāvairocana of the being causes the three mysteries of the dharmakāya to be fully manifest in the being, a state of enlightenment in this very existence.

While this discussion has adopted the perspective of the being seeking to attain the enlightened state, other viewpoints are possible. Kūkai expresses one such in the following poem, which brings us closer again to the perspective of Shugendō:

> The Three Mysteries pervade the entire Universe,
> Adoring gloriously the maṇḍala of infinite space.
> Being painted by brushes of mountains, by ink of oceans,
> Heaven and earth are the bindings of a sūtra revealing the Truth
> Reflected in a dot are all things in the universe;
> Contained in the data of senses and mind is the sacred book.
> It is open or closed depending on how we look at it.
> Both His silence and His eloquence make incisive tongues numb.
> . . . .
> The sun and the moon shine forth in space and on the water,
> Undisturbed by gales in the atmosphere.
> Both good and evil are relative in His preaching
> The notion of I and thou will be erased and lost.
> When the sea of our mind becomes serene through samādhi and
> insight,
> He reveals Himself unconditionally as water overflows.[29]

Meanings of the Ritual

The ritual ascent of the Oku no In cave is divided into five parts: climbing the path, entering the mouth, climbing the shaft, performing offerings and sūtra recitation inside the second chamber, and the making the descent.

Climbing the path up the mountain marks a separation from the mundane world. It also constitutes an entry into the territory presided over by the yama no kami, a mountainous terrain invoking all the associations of the sacred mountain described above. The second stage, entering the mouth, can begin only after recitation of the Heart Sūtra as a preliminary purification. Entering the mouth is returning to the womb as tomb; at this stage it is the negative aspect of a symbolic death that is central. Having left the human sphere, the participant enters the maṇḍala. Climbing the shaft marks a period of liminality, a pilgrimage into the mountain's deepest recesses. This passage is purificatory and is punctuated by the repentance proclaimed in chanting "Rokkon shōjō!" In esoteric terms, this ascent of the shaft is the pilgrim's passage through the halls of the maṇḍala. To arrive finally at the second chamber is to penetrate to the core of the mountain's source of power, whether that potency be viewed as the generative powers of animal and plant fertility or, from a Shugendō perspective, as spiritual power. Seen as maṇḍala, the cave's second chamber is the center of the Womb World, occupied by Dainichi (Mahāvairocana). The descent ends in the reincorporation of the pilgrim into the human world, newly endowed with the powers whose center she has reached.

The fourth stage, the rites of the second chamber, are the heart of the pilgrimage. In Buddhist esoteric terms, to enter the second chamber is to be united with Dainichi, and this constitutes the attainment of buddhahood in this very existence. Further, because En no Gyōja, Acala, and the eight Nagas are enshrined there, the ascetic incorporates their powers as well. Recitation of the Heart Sūtra captures for the pilgrim the essence of the *prajñāparamitā:* the perfection of wisdom. From the Shugendō perspective, entering the second chamber completes the telescoped passage through the ten worlds. This is the real destination of the entire pilgrimage, and here most of all the powerful associations of the mountain are concentrated. The fire in the womb created by the pilgrims' incense and candles is not only an offering to the deities enshrined there but a furnace which forges the devotees. It steams, smokes, and bakes into them the powers they have come to acquire.

Thus the rites of the second chamber seal the pilgrimage, locking its symbolic gains into the pilgrim. From this discussion of the symbolism of this ritual, it should be clear that in psychological terms its principal motif is that of a return to the womb. The task of this section is to show why the significance of this rite differs for women and men. The meaning is different in that the ritual invokes different religious categories for women and men. This difference in turn derives from the different interaction of the symbolism of the rite with the psychology of women and men. In order to show why the rite calls into play different motifs of the history of religions, it is first necessary to take up the question of the rite's interaction with psychological structure.

One of the most important topics in current feminist scholarship concerns the differing psychic structures of women and men. The most sophisticated statement of the claim is that by Nancy Chodorow in *The Reproduction of Mothering*.[30] Chodorow shows that the social organization of gender produces "asymmetrical personality structures in daughters and sons." To recapitulate her complicated theory briefly, the mother–daughter relationship universally is characterized by continuity and complementarity. The daughter does not need to make so firm a break with her mother in order to achieve her own individuation and maturity. Her maturation will take place mostly within the world of women, and she need not renounce her mother so completely as a primary object of love as must her brothers. Boys, on the other hand, must make a clear break from the mother in order to achieve a self-identification as males through bonding with the father. They must separate from the world of women, only later to take women as their primary objects of love after achieving a basic identification as male.

One of the primary goals of forming a relation of love and affection is to recapture the complete acceptance the infant enjoys from its mother. The longing to experience acceptance entirely free of the criticism and competition characteristic of the public world is a basic aim of both women and men. The "urge to merge" has as its prototype the unity of mother and fetus *in utero*. However, this common drive is experienced differently by women and men, because of the difference of gender. For the male, the motif of a return to the womb is a coincidence of opposites *(coincidentia oppositorum)*, becoming whole by uniting with the opposite sexual principle. The self is completed by merging with something totally unlike itself, which is at the same time the source of its very existence. Thus, the time of return to the mother results in the acquisition of power fundamentally alien to the male. The matter is different in the case of women. The motif of *coincidentia oppositorum* is not operative. Instead, the motif is one of a return to the source, uniting with the source of one's own sexual principle instead of merging with the opposite. The power to be gained from such an exercise is not alien to one's own nature, but represents a recapture of its origin and fullest expression. The devotee is not the opposite of that source, but a microcosm of it.

The male's experience of *coincidentia oppositorum* differs further because of the nature of the process of his own individuation in childhood. Chodorow sums up a full exposition of the subject in this way:

> Infantile development of the self is experienced in opposition to the mother, as primary caretaker, who becomes the other.

Because boys are of opposite gender from their mothers, they especially feel a need to differentiate and yet find differentiation problematic. The boy comes to define his self more in opposition than through a sense of his wholeness or continuity. He becomes the self and experiences his mother as the other. The process also extends to his trying to dominate the mother in order to ensure his sense of self. Such domination begins with mother as the object, extends to women, and is then generalized to include the experience of all others as objects rather than subjects.[31]

Although many elements of this theory of asymmetric patterns of psychic structure in women and men are yet to be clarified, the theory as a whole promises to reveal the origins in psychic life of motifs we as historians of religions have long recognized in religious phenomena. As always, the female side of the formulation is much less clear. A break with mother must be made, but in the case of men this break must be made in order to achieve self-identification as a male. In the female case the primary bond with mother already accomplishes the gender identification. Thus the break with mother is not required in order to establish gender identification. Recently Adrienne Rich has written that the break with the world of women is required of women to satisfy what she calls "compulsory heterosexuality." This is a requirement of society, not of psychological development. While Rich's suggestion is a powerful one, it remains highly speculative.[32]

This much seems clear, however: if the male's break with the mother is crucial to his gender identification, but the female's is not, then any subsequent, symbolic return to the womb must also hold a different sort of significance for women and men. Both return to their primary and strongest love. Both aim for an uncritical, total acceptance. But whereas the adult male makes a return to the mother after a sharp break which has been the focus of his gender identification, the female's return is of a different kind. It may be that explorations of the symbolism of such rites of return to the womb as the ascent of the Oku no In cave can shed light on these psychic phenomena.

When women struggle into this womb-cave, are gripped in its vagina, and squeeze through its cervix into the crevices of a penumbral uterus, they celebrate a principle already inherent in their own sexual nature. Whereas men unite themselves with a principle opposite to their own being, women return to the power of which they themselves already represent the full flower, complete in itself. They immerse themselves in female power, absorb its atmosphere and essences, taking into themselves more of the power that is already theirs. Instead of completing their own being through unification with the opposite sexual principle, women symbolically return to the original source of all female power, from which in psychological terms they have never been separated. In this respect, the significance of the Oku no In rite differs radically for women and men.

Viewed psychologically, the principal motif operating for the female pilgrim is reunion of mother and daughter. The pilgrim is the daughter and the womb-cave is the mother. Such a reunion finds mythic embodiment in the myth of Demeter and Persephone (Kore). Jung has remarked on the differing significance for women and men of the Kore figure, and he says further: "Kore...is generally a double..., i.e., a mother and a maiden, which is to say that she appears now as the one, and now as the other."[33]

The identity of the pilgrim and the mother is the secret of the womb-cave. This is the esoteric knowledge gained from the rite on the psychological level. As Jung says:

> We could therefore say that every mother contains her daughter in herself and every daughter her mother, and that every woman extends backwards into her mother and forward into her daughter. This participation and intermingling give rise to that peculiar uncertainty as regards *time:* a woman lives earlier as a daughter, later as a mother. The conscious experience of these ties produces the feeling that her life is spread out over generations—the first step towards the immediate experience and conviction of being outside time, which brings with it a feeling of *immortality.* The individual's life is elevated into a type, indeed it becomes the archetype of woman's fate in general. This leads to a restoration or *apocatastasis* of the lives of her ancestors, who now, through the bridge of the momentary individual, pass down into the generations of the future. An experience of this kind gives the individual a place and a meaning in the life of the generations, so that all unnecessary obstacles are cleared out of the way of the life-stream that is to flow through her.[34]

The Oku no In rite refers to a reunion of mother and daughter, and to the mystical identity of the two. It is of course gender that unites them, but more specifically it is their ability to give birth, the characteristic that distinguishes them from men. It is in giving birth that the daughter becomes the mother, and hence it is highly appropriate and in keeping with the symbolic logic of the rite that it take place in a womb-cave.

Within Japanese mythology, the most relevant mythologem is Amaterasu's concealment in the Ama no Iwato, the Heavenly Rock Cave. Her concealment causes light and order to vanish from the world, and it is her reemergence that causes light and order again to rule over darkness and chaos. However, more important, Amaterasu enters the cave a Kore, a maiden, and emerges the unchallenged ruler of the High Fields of Heaven. It was in the cave that her transformation occurred. The fact that transformation in the myth and in the Oku no In cave rite takes place without male intervention is true to the motif of the female's return to the source. As Jung says of the Eleusinian Mysteries, "Demeter-Kore exists on the plane of mother-daughter experience which is alien to man and shuts him out."[35]

Conclusion

The problem examined in this chapter is one of finding a language to articulate differences in the religious experience of women and men. It is imperative to the history of religions that such a language grow out of our discipline and be fully integrated to its central aims. A language for describing women's religious experience evolved solely for the purpose of describing something about women while remaining unrelated to other issues in the study of religion would be counterproductive. We must not rest content with terms and concepts for describing women's religious experiences which simply confirm existing stereotypes about women, thereby perpetuating the sidelined, marked status we have so long "enjoyed."

What is wanted is a language that is suitable for describing the particulars of female experience but which is also linked to a discipline's methodological issues in a broader way. For example, the distinction between the public and private realms of society first articulated by feminist scholars was primarily developed in order to understand women's issues, but it has proved to hold immense utility in the study of society generally.[36] It describes a dichotomy operative in the lives of both women and men. To know and be able to apply this conceptual distinction deepens our sensitivity to a vast range of sociological and anthropological questions, whether or not the immediate focus is a "woman's issue." To be unaware of the public–private distinction is to pass over a universally important dichotomy in human society and experience. Thus it cannot be ignored or trivialized.

If our goal is to understand the meaning of religious phenomena, we cannot assume, for example, that a rite has a single, unvarying meaning. Meaning is qualified and modulated by interaction between the participants and the phenomenon's public symbolism. Without reducing the problem to a purely individual matter, when we recognize that women and men have vastly different psychic structures, we are forced to take these into account in order to reach an accurate understanding of what the phenomenon in question means to participants.

The task of articulating the meaning of a rite is not successfully completed by a recapitulation of its public symbolism. Often that recapitulation is in fact a difficult and complex task, requiring the historian of religions to trace historically the full context of a rite preserved only in fragments. Yet no matter how complete is our tracing of the nexus of ideas in which a rite or other religious phenomenon is situated, we have not yet uncovered its meaning until we consider real participants and the way that ritual achieves its transformative power through interacting with the psychic structures people bring to their participation in ritual. If in turn that psychological structure is significantly different for women and men, it becomes necessary to take account of that difference in our statements about meaning. Obviously, it would not be acceptable simply to present the meaning of a rite for males or females separately as "the" meaning. This being the case, the development of a language for talking accurately about women's religious experience is a task incumbent upon the discipline as a whole, not only upon those of us who happen to be women.

History of religions has long recognized the importance of the *coincidentia oppositorum* motif. Since Eliade's exposition of it, the idea has been usefully appropriated by many others, not only in our discipline but in other branches of study as well. The term has become standard usage for religious phenomena in which one element finds its completion by uniting with its opposite. The present investigation suggests that rites experienced by men as *coincidentia oppositorum* are not always experienced as such by women. Thus the meaning of such a rite for female participants is not *coincidentia oppositorum*, but becomes something else. At present we have no common, agreed-upon language with which to name women's return to the source.

It is, of course, true that history of religions has, again thanks to Eliade, recognized the importance in initiatory ritual of a symbolic return to the conditions of creation. This motif clearly is operative for both women and men in the rites of ascending the Oku no In cave. However, pointing to that motif is not a sufficient exposition of the rite's significance for female participants. Within the common framework of an "eternal return," men experience *coincidentia oppositorum*, and women experience a return to the source as a vehicle for completing their own being.

This essay has employed the phrase "return to the source" to describe the particular experience of women in a rite experienced differently by men. The phrase is potentially useful in pointing to a general type of religious experience, a motif perhaps as general and widespread as *coincidentia oppositorum*, and as important for men as women. In our vast inventory of rites glorifying male power and energy, we will find the same motif operative. Without attempting to list all possible candidates, two such rites that come immediately to mind are Mithraic rites of slaying the bull and male Śaivite ritual. Were this suggestion to prove useful, then the motif of a return to the source would have proved its utility in grasping the meaning of a type of religious experience had by both women and men. The facts surrounding the genesis of the term are in a sense irrelevant, just as it is relatively unimportant for us to recall Eliade's first use of the term *coincidentia oppositorum*. The more important thing is the general applicability and utility of both "return to the source" and *coincidentia oppositorum*.

Notes

Introduction

1. Writing about his own experience in the 1970s, Donald Lopez describes the changing perceptions of Tibetan Buddhism, long identified with Vajrayāna: "By that time, the Victorian representation of Tibetan Buddhism as degenerate, the farthest removed of all Buddhist traditions from the simple ethical philosophy of the founder, had reached its antipodes, being represented instead as a vast preserve of untranslated Buddhist texts." Donald S. Lopez, Jr., introduction to *Curators of the Buddha: The Study of Buddhism under Colonialism*, ed. Lopez (Chicago: University of Chicago Press, 1995), p. 17.

2. Christian K. Wedemeyer, "Tropes, Typologies, and Turnarounds: A Brief Genealogy of the Historiography of Tantric Buddhism," *History of Religions* 40, no. 3 (February 2001): 229.

3. Several very important recent works have brought this goal closer. They include Charles Orzech, *Politics and Transcendent Wisdom:* The Scripture for Humane Kings in the Creation of Chinese Buddhism (University Park: Pennsylvania State University Press, 1998); Ryūichi Abé, *The Weaving of Mantra: Kukai and the Construction of Esoteric Buddhist Discourse* (New York: Columbia University Press, 1999); George J. Tanabe, Jr., ed., *Matrices and Weavings: Expressions of Shingon Buddhism in Japanese Culture and Society*, special issue 2 of the *Bulletin of the Research Institute of Esoteric Buddhist Culture*, Kōyasan University (October 2004); Mark Unno, *Shingon Refractions: Myōe and the Mantra of Light* (Boston: Wisdom Publications, 2004); Rolf W. Giebel, tr., *Two Esoteric Sutras* (Berkeley: Numata Center for Buddhist Translation and Research, 2001); and Rolf W. Giebel and Dale A. Todaro, trs., *Shingon Texts* (Berkeley: Numata Center for Buddhist Translation and Research, 2004).

4. An important work on the Southeast Asian strain of tantric Buddhism is Max Nihom, *Studies in Indian and Indo-Indonesian Tantrism: The Kuñjarakarṇadharmakathana and the Yogatantra*, Publications of the De Nobili Research Library, vol. 21 (Vienna: Institut für Indologie der Universität Wien, 1994). See also Hudaya Kandahjaya, "A Study on the Origin and Significance of Borobudur" (Ph.D. diss., Graduate Theological Union, 2004).

5. José Ignacio Cabezón, "Two Views on the Svātantrika-Prāsaṅgika Distinction in Fourteenth-Century Tibet," in *The Svātantrika-Prāsaṅgika Distinction: What Difference Does a Difference Make?*, ed. Georges B. J. Dreyfus and Sara L. McClintock (Boston: Wisdom Publications, 2003), pp. 289–291. Cabezón's discussion is specifically directed at doxographic categories but is applicable more generally and has been adapted to our discussion here.

6. A classic example of this approach is W. Bede Kristensen, *The Meaning of Religion: Lectures in the Phenomenology of Religion*, tr. John B. Carman (The Hague: Martinus Nijhoff, 1971).

7. See Gavin Flood, *Beyond Phenomenology: Rethinking the Study of Religion* (London: Cassell, 1999).

8. See David Chidester, *Savage Systems: Colonialism and Comparative Religion in Southern Africa* (Charlottesville: University Press of Virginia, 1996).

9. In his critique of postmodernism, Richard Wolin clearly asserts a causal relation between the French anthropologist Claude Lévi-Strauss's promotion of the idea of cultural relativity (part of the intellectual background of the emic-etic distinction) and the rise of postmodernism. Richard Wolin, *The Seduction of Unreason: The Intellectual Romance with Fascism from Nietzsche to Postmodernism* (Princeton: Princeton University Press, 2004), pp. 5–7.

10. This distinction is not unproblematic. One might consider that an etic category is simply the emic category of a group of outsiders. However, the problems with these epistemological categories are even deeper. Fundamentally the distinction between the categories of insider and outsider is flawed. This latter distinction employs the metaphor of "religion as container," resulting in the idea that there are those who are inside and those who are out. There is, however, no clear or definitive way of dividing those who are inside from those who are out that could actually carry epistemic weight—despite the politicized use of this distinction. It is therefore a mistake to base an epistemological distinction like emic and etic on a bad metaphor such as "religion as container."

11. See Ronald M. Davidson, "Reframing *Sahaja:* Genre, Representation, Ritual and Lineage," *Journal of Indian Philosophy* 30, no. 1 (February 2002): 45–83.

12. Herbert V. Guenther, *The Tantric View of Life* (Berkeley: Shambhala Publications, 1972), p. 1.

13. It seems quite possible that the link between sewing and religious texts has to do with the way in which loose-leaf folios were bound together. In order to keep them in order, each was pierced with two holes. They were stacked into a pile, and a string was passed down through one hole, across the bottom, and then back up through the second hole—binding the set of teachings into a set order. The symbolism may, however, predate the use of written texts. According to J. C. Heesterman, in Vedic ritualism the "metarules" *(paribhāṣās)* distinguish between the activities providing the basic structure to rituals "the *tantra,* the 'woof' or texture, and the main part, the *pradhāna,*" which are the actions constituting the unique character of a ritual. C. J. Heesterman, *The Broken World of Sacrifice: An Essay in Ancient Indian Ritual* (Chicago: University of Chicago Press, 1993), p. 61.

14. Hugh B. Urban, "The Extreme Orient: The Construction of 'Tantrism' as a Category in the Orientalist Imagination," *Religion* 29, no. 2 (April 1999): 126; reprinted as the introduction to *Tantra: Sex, Secrecy, Politics, and Power in the Study of Religion*, by Urban (Berkeley and Los Angeles: University of California Press, 2003), p. 29.

15. Donald S. Lopez, Jr., *Elaborations on Emptiness: Uses of the* Heart Sūtra (Princeton: Princeton University Press, 1996), p. 85.

16. As André Padoux observes, "The word 'Tantrism' assuredly is a Western creation. India traditionally knows only texts called Tantras. These texts . . . fall far short of covering the entire Tantric literature; nor are only Tantric texts called Tantras" (quoted in Urban, "Extreme Orient," p. 123, citing Padoux, "A Survey of Tantrism for the Historian of Religions," *History of Religions* 20 [1981]: 350).

17. Urban, "Extreme Orient," p. 124.

18. Monier Monier-Williams, *A Sanskrit-English Dictionary* (1899; repr., Tokyo: Oxford University Press, 1982), s.v. "naya."

19. David Snellgrove, *Indo-Tibetan Buddhism: Indian Buddhists and Their Tibetan Successors* (1987; repr., Boston: Shambhala Publications, 2002), p. 118.

20. Jeffrey Hopkins, *The Tantric Distinction: A Buddhist's Reflections on Compassion and Emptiness*, rev. ed. (Boston: Wisdom Publications, 1999), p. 65.

21. *The Encyclopedia of Religion*, s.v. "Indian Buddhism," by Luis O. Gómez.

22. Vesna A. Wallace, *The Inner Kālacakratantra: A Buddhist Tantric View of the Individual* (Oxford: Oxford University Press, 2001), p. 5. See also Wallace, *The Kālacakratantra: The Chapter on the Individual together with the* Vimalaprabhā (New York: American Institute of Buddhist Studies, Columbia University, 2004), and her *The Kālacakratantra: The Chapter on the Sādhana together with the* Vimalaprabhā (New York: American Institute of Buddhist Studies, Columbia University, 2005).

23. Herbert Guenther, *The Life and Teaching of Naropa* (Oxford: Oxford University Press, 1963), p. 112–113.

24. The reader interested in the Hindu tantric theory of language is referred to the excellent works of André Padoux, particularly *Vāc: The Concept of the Word in Selected Hindu Tantras*, tr. Jacques Gontier (Albany: State University of New York, 1990).

25. On Perennialism, see Olav Hammer, *Claiming Knowledge: Strategies of Epistemology from Theosophy to the New Age*, Numen Book Series Studies in the History of Religions, vol. 90 (Leiden: E.J. Brill, 2001), pp. 170–176.

26. The issue of the subsumption of Buddhism under the universalizing—hegemonic—discourse of Perennialism is not simply a matter of conflicting interpretations, nor of conflicting claims of authority, legitimacy, or authenticity. Perennialism, also called Traditionalism, is strongly authoritarian in character and has historical connections with Fascism. The connection with the representations of tantra in the recent past is explored by Urban, who discusses, for example, Julius Evola, an outspoken Italian Fascist who manipulated tantra "in the service of right-wing violence" (Urban, *Tantra*, p. 173). Evola continued to be active in the representation of tantra in the postwar era, publishing his *Lo Yoga Della Potenza: Saggio sui Tantra* in 1968, a work which was translated into English by Guido Stucco in 1992 and remains in print under the title *The Yoga of Power: Tantra, Shakti, and the Secret Way* (Rochester, Vt.: Inner Traditions International, 1992). The emphasis on power in the title is indicative of the orientation of the author. Evola and other "Traditionalists" are discussed in Mark Sedgwick's very important *Against the Modern World: Traditionalism and the Secret Intellectual History of the Twentieth Century* (Oxford: Oxford University Press, 2004).

27. Michel Strickmann, "Homa in East Asia," in *Agni: The Vedic Ritual of the Fire Altar*, ed. Frits Staal, 2 vols. (Berkeley: Asian Humanities Press, 1983), 2:418.

28. Robert L. Brown, introduction to *The Roots of Tantra*, ed. Katherine Anne Harper and Robert L. Brown (Albany: State University of New York Press, 2002), pp. 1–2.

29. Lopez, *Elaborations on Emptiness*, p. 124.

30. Robert Sharf, *Coming to Terms with Chinese Buddhism: A Reading of the* Treasure Store Treatise, Kuroda Institute Studies in East Asian Buddhism, no. 14. (Honolulu: University of Hawai'i Press, 2002), pp. 263–264.

31. Douglas Renfrew Brooks, *The Secret of the Three Cities: An Introduction to Hindu Śākta Tantrism* (Chicago: University of Chicago Press, 1990), p. 55.

32. Ibid., pp. 55–71.

33. Stephen Hodge, tr., *The Mahā-Vairocana-Abhisaṃbodhi Tantra with Buddhaguhya's Commentary* (London: RoutledgeCurzon, 2003), p. 4.

34. Ibid., pp. 4, 5. Hodge's list is closely modeled on that of Teun Goudriaan, "Part One: Introduction, History and Philosophy," in Sanjukta Gupta, Dirk Jan Hoens, and Teun Goudriaan, *Hindu Tantrism*, Handbuch der Orientalistik, 2.4.2 (Leiden: E. J. Brill, 1979), pp. 7–9.

35. David Germano, "Architecture and Absence in the Secret Tantric History of the Great Perfection *(rdzogs chen)*," *Journal of the International Association of Buddhist Studies* 17, no. 2 (winter 1994): 205.

36. Ibid., p. 206.
37. Ibid., p. 208.
38. James H. Sanford, "The Abominable Tachikawa Skull Ritual," *Monumenta Nipponica: Studies in Japanese Culture* 46, no. 1 (spring 1991): 1–20.
39. Prapod Assavavirulhakarn, "Uṣṇīṣavijaya: A Reflection on the 'Power of Word' in Thai Tradition" (paper, triennial meeting of the International Association of Buddhist Studies, Chulalongkorn University, Bangkok, Thailand, January 2003).
40. See Randall Styers, *Making Magic: Religion, Magic and Science in the Modern World* (Oxford: Oxford University Press, 2004).
41. Miranda Shaw also asserts that Vajrayāna arose as a lay movement: "Tantric Buddhism arose outside the powerful Buddhist monasteries as a protest movement initially championed by laypeople rather than monks and nuns. Desiring to return to classical Mahāyāna universalism, the Tantric reformers protested against ecclesiastical privilege and arid scholasticism and sought to forge a religious system that was more widely accessible and socially inclusive." Miranda Shaw, *Passionate Enlightenment: Women in Tantric Buddhism* (Princeton: Princeton University Press, 1994), pp. 20–21. Here in contrast to tantra as the final decadent phase of Indian Buddhism, we find a narrative of tantra as a reform movement reacting to the corruption and aridity of mainstream Buddhist institutions. This narrative is familiar from the historiography of the Protestant Reformation, and should be just as suspect as the rhetoric of decadence.
42. If we look to the history of Mahāyāna for some ideas as to the origins of Vajrayāna, we find that the long-standing notion that Mahāyāna began with a lay devotional movement centered on stūpa worship has recently been called into question and a monastic origin suggested. See Jan Nattier, *A Few Good Men: The Bodhisattva Path according to* The Inquiry of Ugra (Ugraparipṛcchā) (Honolulu: University of Hawai'i Press, 2003).
43. See for instance, Christian Konrad Wedemeyer, "Vajrayāna and Its Doubles: A Critical Historiography, Exposition, and Translation of the Tantric Works of Āryadeva" (Ph.D. diss., Columbia University, 1999).
44. Hodge, *Mahā-Vairocana-Abhisaṃbodhi Tantra*, p. 5.
45. My thanks to Paul Copp for pointing out the importance of the difference between the Indic and East Asian ways of approaching the use of extraordinary language. As he emphasized, this is a generalization and should not be taken as an absolute distinction. For information on the use of written Sanskrit in East Asian Buddhism, see R. H. van Gulik, *Siddham: An Essay on the History of Sanskrit Studies in China and Japan*, Śata-Piṭaka Series, vol. 247 (New Delhi: Mrs. Sharada Rani, 1980); and Saroj Kumar Chaudhuri, *Siddham in China and Japan*, Sino-Platonic Papers, no. 88 (Philadelphia: Department of Asian and Middle Eastern Studies, University of Pennsylvania, 1998).
46. Padoux, *Vāc*, p. 49.
47. *Encyclopedia of Buddhism*, s.v. "paritta and rakṣā texts," by Justin McDaniel.
48. See Richard K. Payne, *Language Conducive to Awakening: Categories of Language Use in East Asian Buddhism, with Particular Attention to the Vajrayāna Tradition*, Buddhismus-Studien 2 (Düsseldorf: Hauses der Japanischen Kultur, 1998).
49. See also, Richard D. McBride, II, "Were Dhāraṇī and Spells 'Proto-Tantric' in Medieval Sinitic Buddhism?" (paper, annual meeting of the American Academy of Religion, San Antonio, Texas, November 2004).
50. Jacob Dalton, "Observations on *Dhāraṇī* Ritual Practice in the Tibetan Dunhuang Manuscripts" (paper, annual meeting of the American Academy of Religion, San Antonio, Texas, November 2004.
51. This is the "Anantamukha-nirhāra-dhāraṇī." Hisao Inagaki, *Amida Dhāraṇī Sūtra and*

Jñānagarbha's Commentary, Ryukoku Literature Series 7 (Kyoto: Ryukoku Gakkai, 1999), pp. 65–66. See also Inagaki, *The Anantamukhanirhāra-Dhāraṇī Sūtra and Jñānagarbha's Commentary: A Study and the Tibetan Text* (Kyoto: Nagata Bunshodo, 1987). For a discussion of the practice of dhāraṇī recitation in China, see Maria Dorothea Reis-Habito, *Die Dhāraṇī des Großen Erbarmens des Bodhisattva Avalokiteśvara mit tausend Händen und Augen*, Monumenta Serica Monograph Series 27 (Nettetal, Germany: Steyler Verlag, 1993).

52. Michel Strickmann, *Mantras et Mandarins: Le Bouddhisme Tantrique en Chine* (Paris: Gallimard, 1996), p. 65.

53. Nattier, *A Few Good Men*, pp. 291–292n549. The situation is perhaps not quite as clear-cut as either Strickmann or Nattier imply. Although rare, it should be noted that both *dhāraṇī* (meaning a verbal phrase used as a support for meditation) and *dhāraṇā* (meaning meditative concentration) are used in other tantric traditions. See Sanjukta Gupta, "Yoga and *Antaryāga* in Pāñcarātra" in *Ritual and Speculation in Early Tantrism*, ed. Teun Goudriaan (Albany: State University of New York Press, 1992), p. 191; André Padoux, *Vāc: The Concept of the Word in Selected Hindu Tantras*, tr. Jacques Gontier (Albany: State University of New York Press, 1990), p. 310; and Mark S. G. Dyczkowski, *The Stanzas on Vibration* (Albany: State University of New York Press, 1992), pp. 81, 119, 396n147.

54. Nattier, *A Few Good Men*, pp. 291–292n549.

55. Strickmann, *Mantras et Mandarins*, p. 67.

56. Étienne Lamotte, tr., *Le Traité de la Grande Vertu de Sagesse de Nāgārjuna (Mahāprajñāpāramitāśasatra)* (Louvain-la-Neuve: Institut Orientaliste, Université de Louvain, 1981), 1:317. What I am rendering here as "holding together" is in Lamotte's French *"tenir"* and "holding off" is *"empêcher."*

57. Glenn Wallis, *Mediating the Power of Buddhas: Ritual in the* Mañjuśrīmūlakalpa (Albany: State University of New York Press, 2002), p. 46.

58. Sakya Pandita Kunga Gyaltshen, *A Clear Differentiation of the Three Codes: Essential Distinctions among the Individual Liberation, Great Vehicle, and Tantric Systems*, tr. Jared Douglas Rhoton (Albany: State University of New York Press, 2002).

59. Yoshito S. Hakeda, tr., *Kūkai: Major Works* (New York: Columbia University Press, 1972), pp. 95–96.

60. In the process of my own initiation into the Shingon lineage all three of these vows were included. The order was tantric first, then Mahāyāna, then Nikāya.

61. Sharf, *Coming to Terms*, pp. 266–267.

62. Davidson, *Indian Esoteric Buddhism: A Social History of the Tantric Movement* (New York: Columbia University Press, 2002), p. 145.

63. See José Ignacio Cabezón, introduction to *Scholasticism: Cross-Cultural and Comparative Perspectives*, ed. Cabezón (Albany: State University of New York Press, 1998), pp. 5–6.

64. See Kenneth K. S. Chen, *Buddhism in China: A Historical Survey* (Princeton: Princeton University Press, 1964), pp. 305–311.

65. Tadeusz Skorupski, "The Canonical *Tantras* of the New Schools," in *Tibetan Literature: Studies in Genre*, ed. José Ignacio Cabezón and Roger R. Jackson (Ithaca, N.Y.: Snow Lion, 1996), pp. 100–101.

66. Snellgrove, *Indo-Tibetan Buddhism*, p. 232.

67. Ibid.

68. Although widely accepted in contemporary Japanese scholarship, the distinction between *junmitsu* and *zōmitsu* is late, dating from the mid-Tokugawa era. See, Abé, *The Weaving of Mantra*, p. 153.

69. For example, see Mircea Eliade, *Yoga: Immortality and Freedom*, tr. Willard R. Trask, 2nd ed., Bollingen Series 56 (Princeton: Princeton University Press, 1969), p. 201.

70. Reginald Ray, *Secret of the Vajra World: The Tantric Buddhism of Tibet* (Boston: Shambhala Publications, 2001), p. 4n.

71. For example, see Shinichi Tsuda, "A Critical Tantrism," *Memoirs of the Research Department of the Toyo Bunko (The Oriental Library)* 36 (1978): 167–231.

72. This is a difficult undertaking, requiring a variety of skills. For an example of how complex such considerations can be when handled responsibly, see Robert Mayer, *A Scripture of the Ancient Tantra Collection: The Phur-pa bcu-gnyis* (Oxford: Kiscadale Publications, 1996).

73. Heinrich Zimmer, *Philosophies of India*, ed. Joseph Campbell, Bollingen Series 26 (Princeton: Princeton University Press, 1951) p. 572.

74. Serinity Young, *Courtesans and Tantric Consorts: Sexualities in Buddhist Narrative, Iconography, and Ritual* (New York: Routledge, 2004), p. 135.

75. Padoux, *Vāc*, p. 48n40.

76. Robert I. Levy, *Mesocosm: Hinduism and the Organization of a Traditional Newar City in Nepal* (Berkeley and Los Angeles: University of California Press, 1990), p. 298.

77. Ibid., p. 299.

78. The importance of fantasy in relation to the projection of antisocial behavior onto others has been studied by Norman Cohn in his *Europe's Inner Demons: The Demonization of Christians in Medieval Christendom*, rev. ed. (Chicago: University of Chicago Press, 2000).

79. Levy, *Mesocosm*, pp. 336–337.

80. Urban, *Tantra*, p. 40.

81. Christopher S. George, tr., *The Caṇḍamahāroṣaṇa Tantra: A Critical Edition and English Translation, Chapters I–VIII*, American Oriental Series, vol. 56. (New Haven, Conn.: American Oriental Society, 1974), p. 75.

82. Davidson, *Indian Esoteric Buddhism*, p. 318.

83. David N. Gellner, *Monk, Householder, and Tantric Priest: Newar Buddhism and Its Hierarchy of Ritual*, Cambridge Studies in Social and Cultural Anthropology, no. 84 (Cambridge: Cambridge University Press, 1992), p. 297. See in this regard, Snellgrove, *Indo-Tibetan Buddhism*, p. 512.

84. Elizabeth English, *Vajrayoginī: Her Visualizations, Rituals, and Forms* (Boston: Wisdom Publications, 2002), p. 218, quoting Gellner, *Monk, Householder, and Tantric Priest*, p. 297.

85. Important recent works on this issue are Young, *Courtesans and Tantric Consorts;* David Gordon White, *Kiss of the Yoginī: "Tantric Sex" in Its South Asian Contexts* (Chicago: University of Chicago Press, 2003); idem, *The Alchemical Body: Siddha Traditions in Medieval India* (Chicago: University of Chicago Press, 1996); and June McDaniel, *Offering Flowers, Feeding Skulls: Popular Goddess Worship in West Bengal* (Oxford: Oxford University Press, 2004). For more general discussions of sexuality in Buddhism with attention to East Asia, see Bernard Faure, *The Red Thread: Buddhist Approaches to Sexuality* (Princeton: Princeton University Press, 1998); and idem, *The Power of Denial: Buddhism, Purity, and Gender* (Princeton: Princeton University Press, 2003).

86. Urban, *Tantra*, p. 24.

87. Ibid., p. 194.

88. Hudaya Kandahjaya, "A Study on the Origin and Significance of Borobudur" (Ph.D. diss., Graduate Theological Union, 2004), p. 23.

89. M. C. Joshi, "Historical and Iconographic Aspects of Śākta Tantrism," in Harper and Brown, *Roots of Tantra*, p. 39.

90. Keith Dowman may also hold to this view. For example he is quoted as having said that "Tantra took centuries to come out of its closet . . . but it appears that originally, in the guise of fertility cults, it belonged to the pre-Aryan tribal worshippers of the Mother Goddess." Quoted in Gill Farrer-Halls, *The Feminine Face of Buddhism* (Wheaton, Ill.: Quest Books, 2002), p. 20. As this latter does not give the specific source for the quote, I have not been able to locate the original and confirm its accuracy. It may be worth noting that the concept of the Mother Goddess as a general category is a modern invention, initiated in large part by the 1861 work by J. J. Bachofen, *Das Mutterrecht.* Rather than "the Mother Goddess," people worshipped Demeter or Durga, i.e., a specific goddess understood to be distinct from the goddesses of other peoples.

91. Eliade, *Yoga*, p. 202.

92. Shaw, *Passionate Enlightenment*, p. 21.

93. *Encyclopedia of Religion*, s.v. "Buddhism in India," by Luis O. Gómez.

94. Thomas McEvilley, "The Spinal Serpent," in Harper and Brown, *Roots of Tantra*, p. 110.

95. Jonathan Z. Smith, "In Comparison a Magic Dwells," in *A Magic Still Dwells*, ed. Kimberley C. Patton and Benjamin C. Ray (Berkeley and Los Angeles: University of California Press, 2000).

96. Urban, *Tantra*, p. 24.

97. Regarding the homa ritual, see Richard K. Payne, "Tongues of Flame: Homologies in the Tantric Homa," in Harper and Brown, *Roots of Tantra*.

98. In China, at least, that function seems to have been fulfilled by some strains of Daoist practitioners.

99. Davidson, *Indian Esoteric Buddhism*.

100. Ibid., p. 169.

101. Ibid., p. 3. See for example, Keith Dowman, *Masters of Mahamudra: Songs and Histories of the Eighty-Four Buddhist Siddhas* (Albany: State University of New York Press, 1985).

102. Davidson, *Indian Esoteric Buddhism*, p. 187.

103. Ibid., p. 121.

104. See, for example, Reginald A. Ray, *Buddhist Saints in India: A Study in Buddhist Values and Orientations* (New York: Oxford University Press, 1994), pp. 407–410. Cf. Nattier, *A Few Good Men*, pp. 93–96.

105. Davidson, *Indian Esoteric Buddhism*, p. 144.

106. This is the argument presented by Stephan Beyer, "Notes on the Vision Quest in Early Mahāyāna," in *The Prajñāpāramitā and Related Systems*, ed. Lewis Lancaster and Luis Gomez, Berkeley Buddhist Studies Series, no. 1. (Berkeley: Center for South and Southeast Asian Studies, University of California, 1977).

107. Mark Blum, "The Sangoku-Mappō Construct: Buddhism, Nationalism, and History in Medieval Japan," in *Discourse and Ideology in Medieval Japanese Buddhism*, ed. Richard K. Payne and Taigen Dan Leighton (Abingdon: RoutledgeCurzon, 2005).

108. Chen goes so far as to limit tantric Buddhism in China to the period of the three tantric masters, i.e., not including Huiguo, saying "After the death of Amoghavajra in 774 the esoteric school declined in China." Chen, *Buddhism in China*, p. 336.

109. See for example, Hakeda, *Kūkai*, pp. 31–33. Somewhat embarrassingly, this view of the history of East Asian tantric Buddhism was the basis for my own dissertation, later published as *The Tantric Ritual of Japan: Feeding the Gods, The Shingon Fire Ritual*, Sata-Piṭaka Series, vol. 365 (Delhi: International Academy of Indian Culture and Aditya Prakashan, 1991). It is my hope to correct this uncritical history in a future revision.

110. Paul Groner, "Shortening the Path: Early Tendai Interpretations of the Realization of Buddhahood with This Very Body *(Sokushin Jōbutsu)*," in *Paths to Liberation: The*

Mārga and Its Transformations in Buddhist Thought, ed. Robert E. Buswell, Jr., and Robert M. Gimello, Kuroda Institute Studies in East Asian Buddhism, no. 7 (Honolulu: University of Hawai'i Press, 1992), pp. 439–473.

111. For further information on Kakuban's views on Amida, see James H. Sanford, "Amida's Secret Life: Kakuban's *Amida hishaku*," in *Approaching the Land of Bliss: Religious Praxis in the Cult of Amitābha*, ed. Richard K. Payne and Kenneth K. Tanaka, Kuroda Institute Studies in East Asian Buddhism, no. 17 (Honolulu: University of Hawai'i Press, 2004), pp. 120–138.

112. No collection of essays, even one of broad scope and purpose, can claim to be comprehensive. More work has been published, for example, on Chinese tantra than can be included here. Of particular importance is Charles D. Orzech, "Seeing *Chen-yen* Buddhism: Traditional Scholarship and the Vajrayāna in China," *History of Religions* 29, no. 2 (1989): 87–114. Many of these studies are, however, more readily available than the selections we have presented here. Much more work needs to be done on Korean tantra, and it is reassuring to know that there some younger scholars are pursuing that topic.

The collection is heavily weighted toward Japan generally, and Shingon specifically. Despite a call to action by Stanley Weinstein many years ago, Tendai mikkyō remains woefully understudied. Similarly, the interactions between Buddhist tantra and popular religious culture included here are exclusively Japanese. Such interactions are known to have occurred in China, for example, with that great stream of religious praxis within Chinese religious culture—Daoism. However, a recent conference designed to address this very topic, "Tantra and Daoism: The Globalization of Religion and Its Experience," organized by Livia Kohn, David Eckel, and Russell Kirkland, Boston University, 19–21 April 2002, proved inconclusive. There certainly appears to be great potential for research on this topic, but so much foundational work still remains to be done on both Daoism itself and on Chinese tantra, that it is far too early to say what the interaction comprises.

113. Michael Baxandall, *Patterns of Intention: On the Historical Explanation of Pictures* (New Haven: Yale University Press, 1985), pp. 58–59. My thanks to Jan Nattier for this reference.

TANTRISM IN CHINA

1. Cf. B. Bhattacharya, *An Introduction to Buddhist Esotericism*, 2nd ed., Chowkhambha Sanskrit Studies, vol. 46 (Benares: Chowkhambha Sanskrit Series Office, 1964), pp. 32–42.
2. T. 21.404b25.
3. T. 21.400b2, 400c16, 404a24–b7. For this text also cf. S. Lévi, *T'oung Pao* 7 (1907): 118; *Indian Historical Quarterly* (IHQ) 12 (1936): 2.204–205.
4. T. 21.400a27.
5. E.g., T. vol. 14, no. 427; T. vol. 21, nos. 1851, 1356.
6. T. vol. 14, no. 428; T. vol. 21, no. 1301.
7. T. 15.141b6, 156c20.
8. T. 50.383b–387a.
9. T. 50.383b18.
10. T. 50.328a11.
11. T. 50.328a12.
12. T. 50.389b25.
13. T. 50.336a5.

14. T. 13.5.c28
15. Cf. T. 16.346a5–c6.
16. Cf. T. 55.838a28.
17. T. 21.579b1.
18. T. 21.579c2.
19. Cf. the Tzū-hsü in *Chin-lou-tzu*, 6.20b.
20. T. 21.262a6.
21. T. 21.260c20.
22. T. 21.261b8.
23. T. 21.261b12.
24. T. 50.719c20, 720a1.
25. Cf. Ōmura Seigai, *Mikkyō hattatsu shi*, 5.710–755. For Atigupta also see Appendix K of original publication.
26. *Journal Asiatique* 227.1 (1935).88.
27. Ibid., 1.88–89. For the "Octuple Maṇḍala," cf. 1.99–97; for Āṭānāṭiya and its Pali and Sanskrit versions, cf. 1.100; A. F. Rudolf Hoernle, *Manuscript Remains of Buddhist Literature Found in Eastern Turkestan*, 1.24–27.
28. E. Chavannes, *Mémoire composé à l'époque de la grande dynastie T'ang sur les religieux éminents qui allèrent chercher la loi dans les pays d'occident par I-tsing*, pp. 104–105.
29. T. 19.476b25–477b3.
30. Such as Shih-pien and Tao-lin, cf. Chavannes, *Religieux éminents*, pp. 31–32, 101–102. For the relation between Indian tantric schools and China, cf. S. Lévi, IHQ 12 (1936): 2.207–208.
31. For these masters and their translations cf. P. C. Bagchi, *Le canon bouddhique en Chine, les traducteurs et les traductions*, 2.585–610.
32. Cf. *Sung hui-yao kao*, tao shih 2.6a.
33. Cf. *Dainihon bukkyō zensho* 115.456b–457a.
34. See Tsan-ning's comment in the end of Vajrabodhi's biography and Chih-p'an's statement in the *Fo-tsu t'ung-chi* (T. 49.296a12).
35. {Chou uses the now outdated, and somewhat pejorative term "Lamaism."}
36. Neither the dynastic history nor the two huge collections of the prose and verse of the T'ang dynasty, the *Ch'üan T'ang-wên* and the *Ch'üan-T'ang-shih*, contain as much material as one would expect. A fairly large amount of material is found in the *T'ai-p'ing kuang-chi*, an indispensable collection in studying the history of this period; the *Chin-shih ts'ui-pien* and the *Pa-ch'iung-shih chin-shih pu-chêng*, two large collections of inscriptions; and the Japanese monks' itineraries contained in *Dainihon bukkyō zensho*. Above all, one must mention the texts translated by these three masters themselves and various historical works, including Tsan-ning's book, contained in the Taisho Tripiṭaka. The finds in Tun-huang have provided invaluable materials to the study of the history of the T'ang dynasty. Professor Hu Shih and Mr. Tsukamoto Zenryū have made important contributions to the history of the Ch'an and Ching-t'u sects by using these new materials. (Cf. *Hu-shih lun-hsüeh chin-chu* 1.198–319; Tsukamoto Zenryū, *Tō chūki no jōdokyō*.) Nevertheless, so far as the esoteric sect is concerned, I am not particularly benefited by any available Tun-huang manuscripts, except for a few pictures and sheets of paper on which dhāraṇīs were written. {For more recent studies on these materials, see Kenneth M. Eastman, "Mahayoga Texts at Tun-huang," *Bulletin of the Institute of Buddhist Cultural Studies* (Kyoto: Ryukoku University) 22 (1983): 42–60; and Sam van Schaik and Jacob Dalton, "Where Chan and Tantra Meet: Tibetan Syncretism in Dunhuang," in *The Silk Road: Trade, Travel, War and Faith*, ed. Susan Whitfield with Ursula Sims-Williams (Chicago: Serindia Publications, 2004), pp. 63–71.}

37. I follow Chih-p'an, who says that Tsan-ning died in 1001 at the age of eighty-two (T. 49.402b1). In his preface to Tsan-ning's work (*Hsiao-ch'u chi* SPTK ed., 21.9a), Wang Yü-ch'eng says that the master was still in sound health at the age of eighty-two. It seems that this preface was written not very long before the master died. Wang Yü-ch'eng gives the date of Tsan-ning's birth as the year chi-mao or the sixteenth year of T'ien-yu; which actually was the fifth year of Chêng-ming, of the Liang dynasty (919), because the T'ang dynasty had already fallen in 907. If Tsan-ning was born in 919 he would have been eighty-two years old in 1001. Wang also says that the sixteenth year of T'ien-yu corresponds to the seventh year of Cheng-ming, which seems to be a miscalculation. Nien-ch'ang (T. 49.659b22) gives the date of Tsan-ning's death as 996, which is evidently wrong. Wen-ying's *Hsiang-shan yeh-lu* (ts'ê 76) 3.5b says that he died at the age of eighty-four, which also contradicts the date given by Wang Yü-ch'eng and Chih-p'an.

38. *Hsiao-ch'u chi* 20.7b.

39. Ibid. Since he was only about fifteen years old at that time, the full ordination probably took place some time later, but Wang did not give a precise date.

40. Cf. T. 49.400c17.

41. For these facts cf. *Hsiao-ch'u chi* 20.8a–b.

42. Cf. *Hsiang-shan yeh-lu* 3.5b; *Liu-i shih-hua* (ts'ê 27) 2b; T. 49.397c5. For the biographies of Hsü Hsuan, Wang Yü-ch'êng, and Liu K'ai cf. *Ssū-shih-ch'i-chung Sung-tai chuan-chi tsung-ho yin-tê* 164, 59, 170.

43. *Hsiao-ch'u chi* 20.7b–9b.

44. Ibid. 7.13a, 16a, 10.6a.

45. *Hsü-kung wên-chi* (SPTK ed.) 22.3a.

46. Cf. *Kuei-t'ien lu* (ser. 17, ts'ê 9) 1.1a. It is very doubtful that the reading T'ai-tsu is correct because Tsan-ning came to the North and became the sêng-lu in T'ai-tsung's reign, when T'ai-tsu had already died. Other editions of the Kuei-t'ien lu, such as Pei-hai (ed., ts'ê 24, 1.1a), Shuo-fu (Yü ed., ts'ê 42, 1.1a), and the Han-fên-lou (1.1a) all read T'ai-tsu.

47. Cf. *Liu-i shih-hua* 2b.

48. Cf. Tsan-ning's memorial in presenting this book (T. 50.709a4) and *Fo-tsu t'ung-chi* (T. 49.400a13). *Hsiao-ch'u chi* (20.8b) and *Fo-tsu t'ung-chi* (T. 49.398c16) give 983 as the year when he received the order.

49. Cf. his preface (T. 50.710a3).

50. Cf. T. 50.709c22.

51. T. 49.400a23.

52. T. 50.709c20.

53. T. 49.400a26.

54. For a list of these books cf. Ku Huai-san, *Pu wu-tai shih i-wên chih* 12a, 18a; *Sung-shih* (all the dynastic histories used in the present work are cited from this edition), 205.10a, 22a, 25a, 206.4b, 5b.

55. T. 54, no. 2126. The number of chapters of the book as it is preserved today agrees with the number given in *Sung-shih* (205.10a). *Hsiang-shan yeh lu* (3.5a) says that T'ai-tsung wanted to know the life of the eminent monks in former times, so Tsan-ning compiled the *Sêng-shih-leh* in ten chapters to present to the emperor. Apparently he had confused the *Kao-sêng chuan* with the *Sêng-shih lüeh*, and the number given by him agrees with neither work.

56. This book is included in the *P'ai-ch'uan hsüeh-hai* (ts'ê 37).

57. *Hsiang-shan yeh-lu* 3.5b.

58. Li Hua's *Shan-wu-wei hsing-chuang* (abbreviated below as *Hsing-chuang*) gives Magadha

as the country where Shan-wu-wei's family originally lived (T. 50.290a6). Li Hua died in the early years of the Ta-li period (766–779) and was particularly known as a writer of biographies and monumental inscriptions. See his biography in *T'ang-shu* 203.1b. His biography says that he was converted to Buddhism in his later days. For his association with monks, see the biographies of Yen-chün (T. 50.798.17) and Lang-jan (T. 50.800a11) in Tsan-ning's work. According to the former he was still alive in the fourth year of Ta-li (769).

59. On Amṛtodana cf. Mochizuki Shinkō's *Bukkyo daijiten* (abbreviated below as Mochizuki), 1.476b–c, and E. J. Thomas, *The Life of Buddha*, p. 24.

60. There is no way to derive such a meaning as "good without fear" from either Śubhakara or Śubhakarasiṁha. This biography is mainly based on Li Hua's *Shan-wu-wei pei-ming ping hsü* (abbreviated below as Pei) which for the monk's name says only "[his] hao was Shan-wu-wei" (T. 50.290b16). It might imply that besides this *hao* or style he also had a *ming* or name. *Hsing-chuang* (T. 60.290a4) says: "Śubhakara's complete Sanskrit name should be Śubhakarasiṁha, of which the correct Chinese translation is Ching-shih-tzu [lit., "pure lion"]. A free translation of his name would be Shan wu-wei." Teramoto Enga in his *Zemmui sanzō no myōgi wa tohango no onyaku ka* (Shūkyō kenkyū, n.s., 8.4.93–104) suggests that Shan-wu-wei might be a Chinese transliteration of the Tibetan translation of Śubhakara: bZan Byed.

It seems to me that Shan-wu-wei is simply another name which has no relation with the Sanskrit name Śubhakara. Six stages of "fearlessness" *(abhaya)* or freedom from fear in a bodhisattva's spiritual progress are described in the *P'i-lu-che-na ching* translated by this master. The first abhaya among them is su-abhaya *(svabhaya)* (cf. T. 18.3c5 and I-hsing's commentary, T. 39.605c16). Śubhakara might have adopted this word as his Chinese name, or hao, as it is stated in the Pei. Since he is called by the hao Shan-wu-wei in this biography, I also use it in my translation.

61. It is generally agreed now that this country was located in the present Orissa. Cf. T. Watters, *On Yuan Chwang's Travels*, 2.193–196; S. Beal, *Life of Huen-tsiang*, p. 134; Hori Kentoku, *Kaisetsu seiikiki*, pp. 781–785; Mochizuki, 1.214c; R. D. Banerji, *History of Orissa* (Calcutta, 1930), 1.136–1145. The family history of the king of Oḍra is not found in Hsüan-tsang's record. But according to this pilgrim (Watters, *On Yuan Chwang's Travels*, 1.238) and Tao-Hsüan (T. 50.432a20), the king of Udyāna was said to have been an exiled Śākya. Since Udyāna was transliterated in many ways, this story of Shan-wu-wei's family could have been a confusion between identical Chinese transliterations for Oḍra and Udyāna. Pei already has this tradition. In the last quarter of the eighth century, there existed in Oḍra a dynasty of which the kings all bore the name "kara." There was even one king called Śubhakara. They were believers in Buddhism. The date of these Kara kings was worked out on the basis of the inscriptions on the copper plates discovered in Orissa and the Chinese sources (cf. S. Levi, "King Śubhakara of Orissa," *Epigraphia Indica*, 15.8.363–364; R. D. Banerji, *History of Orissa*, 1.146–160). As Shan-wu-wei was called Śubhakara and his father's name could be restored as *Buddhakara, I am inclined to suspect that they might have been the predecessors of these Kara kings.

62. The discus {Skt. *cakra*} is a kind of weapon.

63. Pei gives an alternate reading: "When I led my army [against them], it was righteousness which superseded love. Now I desire to abdicate because I should like to carry out my plan."

64. One has to obtain his parents' permission before he can be ordained.

65. A kind of meditation practiced by Mahāyānists, through which one endeavors to see Samantabhadra bodhisattva and to confess one's sins with the hope of becoming a

bodhisattva. This meditation is to be brought about by reciting the *Lotus Sūtra* for twenty-one days.

66. In describing Oḍra Hsüan-tsang (Watters, *On Yuan Chwang's Travels*, 2.193–194) says that "near the shore of the ocean in the southeast of this country was the city of Che-li-ta-lo (Charitra?), above twenty li in circuit, which was a thoroughfare and resting place for sea-going traders and strangers from distant lands."

67. Manusyayāna, deva-, śrāvaka-, pratyekabuddha-, and bodhisattva. The first two are used to denote the career of lay Buddhists who observe the five precepts, etc. The second group of two yānas refers to Hīnayāna, while the last one refers to Mahāyāna. There are three other lists of the five yānas, which differ slightly from this set and which also regard the bodhisattvayāna or buddhayāna as the highest way for salvation.

68. The three disciplines, or śikṣās, are śila, dhyāna, and prajñā.

69. Buddha's teaching is divided into three periods of which the period of the counterfeit doctrine or *pratirūpaka* is the second one. The length of each period varies in accordance with different traditions. {For the development of this theory of three different stages of the dharma, see Jan Nattier, *Once upon a Future Time: Studies in a Buddhist Prophecy of Decline* (Berkeley: Asian Humanities Press, 1991).}

70. This simile sounds rather queer. It means literally "in the daytime it is like a moon, at night it shines." It is an Indian figure of speech to compare a good person to the moon because it is bright but does not hurt the eyes, as the sun does when you look at it. This, however, still does not explain the simile very well.

71. {Or, perhaps more plausibly, he was a "Dharmaguptaka monk."}

72. It was the Indian custom to touch and kiss the feet of the man whom one reveres.

73. The word "yoga" comes from the root *yuj*, which originally means "to join" and later comes to mean "to suit." In esoteric Buddhism the term "yoga" means to concentrate one's mind in order to harmonize with the supreme doctrine and to identify oneself with the deity one worships. Hence all the rites performed by the monks of this sect, whether simple or complicated, are called yoga, because these rites are the means to identify oneself with the deity. I-hsing in his *P'i-lu-che-na ching su* (T. 3.613c14) says: "To be versed in yoga means to perform well the method of joining. It refers to one who can thoroughly understand the dhāraṇīs of the three divisions and the siddhis of the high, middle, and low grades, and know that these agree with the highest doctrine. [Then he is] regarded as able to perform yoga well." The *Chin-kang-ting yu-ch'ieh-chung lueh-ch'u nien-sung ching*, translated by Vajrabodhi, is a sūtra dealing with all kinds of rites both for individual monks to practice in daily life and for groups to perform in monasteries, and these rites are called yoga.

74. The three secrets *{triguhya}* are the secret of body *(kāyaguhya)*, of speech *(vāgguhya)*, and of mind *(manoguhya)*. In Mahāyāna Buddhism these three secrets belong to a buddha. For instance, some listener in the assembly may see Buddha's body in golden color, another one may see it in silver color, while a third one may see it in colors of various jewelry. This is a buddha's secret of body. In esoteric Buddhism a different meaning is attached to the three secrets. Amoghavajra, in his *P'u-t'i-hsin lun* (T. 32.574b13), gives a terse but clear interpretation as follows: "Among the three secrets the first one is the secret of body: the making of mudrās when inviting the saints. The second is the secret of speech: the secret of recitation of dhāraṇīs of which the words should be uttered distinctly and faultlessly. The third secret is the secret of mind: to perform the joining method [lit., to dwell in yoga] and to meditate on the bodhicitta while imagining in one's mind a white, pure, round moon." The white moon is a favorite subject for meditation.

75. In esoteric Buddhism a mudrā means a figure made with fingers. Each deity has his own particular mudrā, which is to be imitated by a worshipper. Different rites are also

to be accompanied by different mudrās. Various names are given to the two hands (such as "sun," "wisdom," etc., for the right hand, and "moon," "meditation," etc., for the left hand) and the ten fingers (such as ten "pāramitās," ten "wheels," ten "dhātus," etc.). In non-esoteric Buddhism mudrā means a gesture of Buddha's hands such as that of preaching, meditation, comforting, calling the earth to witness, etc., as we often see in Buddhist art. The number of mudrās, however, is rather limited. Hinduism made extensive use of mudrās, and they played an even more important role in esoteric Buddhism.

76. Mahākāśyapa is said to have entered into nirvāṇa on Kukkuṭapāda Mountain and preserved his body there until the descent of Maitreya, who will show his body to the śrāvakas and enlighten them. The story of Shan-wu-wei's cutting hair for Mahākāśyapa is apparently a legend; but to cut hair for the monks in prolonged samādhi in their caves was a common practice.

77. The Buddha was said to have been sixteen feet tall, twice the stature of an ordinary man. {A variant of the story probably indicates that the image is sixteen feet high and possesses all the thirty-two signs of Buddha.}

78. The ninety-six schools are frequently mentioned in Buddhist books, but it is doubtful whether all of them existed at the same time. According to I-chung, "En outre, pour ce qui est des doctrines hérétiques, il y en avait autrefois quatre-vingt-seize; maintenant il n'en subsiste plus qu'une dizaine. S'il y a des assemblées de purification et des réunions générales, chaque secte demeure dans un lieu qui lui est particulier. Les religieux et les nonnes ne contestent aucunement entre eux pour la préséance. Comme leurs lois sont différentes et que leurs doctrines ne s'accordent pas, chacun s'est accoutumé à ce qu'il adore; ils restent chez eux et ne se mêlent point les uns aux autres." Chavannes, *Les religieux éminents*, pp. 90–91.

79. {Chou uses the term "law" to render dharma, employing the term not so much in the legalistic sense, but rather as found in the now outdated idea of the laws of nature. The connotation of the term "law" has shifted since his time, however, and the term "dharma" itself has become more familiar. Hence, we have chosen to convert his uses.}

80. Hsi-chou roughly corresponds to the present Turfan in Sinkiang Province.

81. Jui-tsung reigned once in 684 and was dethroned by Empress Wu. Then he reigned again from 710 to 713.

82. The Jade Gate Pass was located in the northwestern part of Kansu Province.

83. The exact date of Shan-wu-wei's arrival in Ch'ang-an is not given in the text, but another monk's biography written by Li Hua gives the date as the fifteenth of the fifth moon.

84. T. vol. 20, no. 1145. The full title of this work is found in the text below. This sūtra contains a dhāraṇī to be recited with some rites to invoke Ākāśagarbha Bodhisattva, who would help the suppliant in gaining worldly profit.

85. *K'ai-yüan shih-chiao lu* (T. 55.572a14), in relating this event, says "On account of this, he could not translate all the sūtras." Hsuan-tsung's warm welcome to Shan-wu-wei as described in this text is very doubtful, because in his early years this Emperor was not favorable to Buddhism. The confiscation of Shan-wu-wei's books suggests that Hsüan-tsung may have so disliked this form of Buddhism as not to wish its texts to become popularly known.

86. T. vol. 18, no. 848.

87. I-hsing compiled a commentary to this sūtra (T. vol. 39, no. 1796) which is indispensable in reading the text. He, however, died before he could finish the work. A Korean monk named Pu-k'o-ssū-i wrote a commentary to the last chapter (T. vol. 39, no. 1799).

88. T. vol. 18, no. 895.

89. T. vol. 18, no. 893.

90. For Ratnacinta's biography cf. T. 50.720a15–b2. He arrived at Lo-yang from Kashmir in 693 and died in 721 Several tantric texts were translated by him. His biography says that he was learned in both vinaya and magic spells. After 705 he ceased to work on translation but stayed in a temple where he had everything made after the Indian fashion, called T'ien-chu-ssū. It is also recorded that he gave his belongings generously and held himself under strict discipline in his daily life. Nevertheless, in a sūtra translated by him, there is a siddhi to cause a dead body to steal hidden treasures, and other siddhis to sneak into a woman's room (T. 20.425b–6a). {For more on Ratnacinta, see Antonino Forte, "The Activities in China of the Tantric Master Manicintana (Pao-ssu-wei: ?–721 AD) from Kashmir and His Northern Indian Collaborators," East-West, n.s., 34, nos. 1–3 (September 1984): 301–345.}

91. {The teachings of "yin and yang," known in Japanese as Onmyōdō and discussed in Earhart's essay in this collection, are not limited to what Chou renders here in his explanatory note as "astrology." See Derk Bodde, *Chinese Thought, Society, and Science: The Intellectual and Social Background of Science and Technology in Pre-modern China* (Honolulu: University of Hawai'i Press, 1991), esp. pp. 100–103, 119–122.}

92. A story like this is found in Amoghavajra's biography. There must be a common source that later developed into two legends.

93. Emperor T'ai-tsu visited Lo-yang in 975 and went to the Kuang-hun Temple to pay his homage to Shan-wu-wei's remains. In the fourth moon of that year, the Emperor wished to offer sacrifices to heaven, but the rain did not stop. A messenger was then sent to pray to the remains.

94. It seems to be a kind of scarf used by monks, but so far I cannot find any reference to it in other books. The monks of the Ch'an sect in later days wear a kind of hood by the name of ch'an-chin, but it is not known whether these two garments are connected.

95. The toilet peas are used to wash hands.

96. This refers to Emperor T'ai-tsung, who reigned from 976 to 977.

97. It is interesting to notice that Jaina texts are specially mentioned here. Jainism had taken deep root in the southern tip of the Indian peninsula and attracted many followers. It also received the patronage of the royal families.

98. Eighteen is the traditional number of the schools of Nikaya Buddhism.

99. According to Lü, Vajrabodhi and the Persian merchants encountered a storm just twenty days before they reached China. All the rest of the thirty-odd ships were lost, but the monk's ship was safe because of his recitation of the Mahāpratisarādhāraṇī. It took three years for the monk to reach China. According to Amoghavajra's record of Vajrabodhi's own description, each of the thirty-odd ships accommodated five or six hundred people. When the ships were about to sink, the shipmaster had everything on board thrown into the sea. Vajrabodhi in his confusion forgot to save the complete text of the *Chin-kang-ting ching*, of which only the abridged version was preserved. This is the text which he translated later.

100. The Sanskrit identity of this bodhisattva is not firmly identified.

101. Here we have an instance in which a mantra—in this case one for longevity—is treated as a bodhisattva.

102. It is said that Vajrabodhi studied this sūtra under Nagajñāna, a disciple of Nāgārjuna, and it was originally composed of one hundred thousand slokas. {According to legend} this text was obtained from an iron stūpa in South India.

103. The chief deity of this text is Mañjuśrī bodhisattva, who is represented in the form of a child with a sword in his right hand and the text of *Mahāprajñāpāramitā Sūtra* in his left hand. A disciple has to receive abhiṣeka before he can be instructed in the dhāraṇīs in this text (T. 20.710a20). It is stated that Mañjuśrī will appear after one recites this

text for one month. Dhāraṇīs and accompanying mudrās are taught which summon the bodhisattva into the reciter's own body and send him away.

104. This date is wrong.

105. The stele inscription by Hun-lun-wêng says that he died when he was sitting, and told his disciples that in accordance with the Indian way one should die lying on the right side.

106. The maṇḍala of five divisions refers to the maṇḍala taught in the *Chin-kang-ting ching*. The five divisions or groups of deities are buddha, padma, vajra, ratna, and karma. The division of padma, or lotus, symbolizes the theory that within human beings there exists a certain incorruptible purity, like a lotus flower, which can never be polluted even though it grows out of the mud. The division of vajra symbolizes the wisdom which is everlasting and can destroy all mental confusion. The division of buddha symbolizes the synthesis of the two mentioned above. The division of ratna {jewel} symbolizes buddha's prosperity, while the division of karma symbolizes a buddha's work in delivering others. Each division has a head with a particular seat and a dominant color: division of buddha, Vairocana, lion seat, white; division of padma, Amitābha, peacock seat, red; division of vajra, Akṣobhya, elephant seat, blue; division of ratna, Ratnabhava, horse seat, gold; division of karma, Amoghasiddhi, garuda seat, miscellaneous color.

107. {Siddham is a Sanskrit script predating the more familiar Devanagari, but which is still used in East Asian tantric Buddhism for such things as inscribing bīja mantra on funerary monuments. This practice is also found in Japanese Zen. See R. H. van Gulik, *Siddham: An Essay on the History of Sanskrit Studies in China and Japan*, Śata-Piṭaka Series, vol. 247 (New Delhi: Mrs. Sharada Rani, 1980).}

108. {It should be noted that in the context of Indian religious culture grammar is not a secular undertaking, as it is in the West, but rather forms an integral part of the religious sciences related to the proper performance of ritual.}

109. This involves a ritual in which the disciple recites several gāthās, in which he confesses his sins, seeks refuge in Buddha, makes an oath to arouse his Bodhicitta, and last of all expresses his five greatest desires: to deliver all beings, to collect all the gaṇas, to learn the profound doctrine, to serve the Buddha, and to achieve supreme Bodhi.

110. The disciple throws a garland of flowers on the maṇḍala. He is supposed to belong to that Buddha whose division the garland hits.

111. This is a collection of hymns in praise of Samantabhadra's ten great desires: to worship the Buddha, to praise the tathāgatas, to make offerings, to confess all one's sins, to be pleased with the merits of others, to pray for the turning of the Dharmacakra, to pray for buddhas to stay in the world, to follow the Buddha, to answer the call of beings at all times, to transfer his own merits to others. {Chou suggests that this is the *P'u-hsien p'u-sa hsing-yüan tsan* later translated by Amoghavajra, T. vol. 10, no. 297.}

112. Homa is the rite of worshipping different deities by throwing offerings into a fire. There are five types of homa sacrifice. The first kind is performed to remedy one's own misfortune or any public disaster. A round earthen stove is to be used. The rite should be performed at dusk, which symbolizes rest and peace. The performer should face the north and everything should be in white. The second kind is to pray for the prosperity of either an individual or a nation. It should be performed in the morning, with the performer facing the east, which is a symbol of wealth. The shape of the stove is square and the color is yellow. The third kind of homa is performed to subdue an enemy. It is to be practiced at noon with a triangular stove. The performer faces the south and the color is black. The fourth kind of homa is to summon those in the three worst *gatis*, that is, the gatis of hell, animals, and pretas. The stove is in the shape of a vajra and the color is red. There is no specification as to time and direction. The fifth kind of homa

is performed to seek for love. The stove is in the shape of lotus and the color is also red. The performer faces the west, and the rite is to be performed in the early evening. Different maṇḍalas are used for different homas.

113. This date is wrong. It should be the twenty-ninth year of K'ai-yuan (741).

114. It was a popular custom during the T'ang dynasty to worship a deceased master's portrait in a special hall.

115. This country is identified as Java. The name is probably due to an early colonization in Java of immigrants from Kaliṅga in East India.

116. The samaya in esoteric Buddhism means the weapon or instrument which is usually held by a deity and regarded as his particular sign.

117. In 689 Empress Wu first bestowed purple-colored kaṣāya robes on nine monks. This color was chosen probably because it was the official color of the ceremonial robes of the higher officers.

118. This statement is not true, since Yuan-chao says that the master's fa-hui was chih-tsang and his hao was Amoghavajra. He called himself by the name Chih-tsang in his memorials to the Emperor before Emperor Su-tsung ordered that he should be called by his hao only.

119. An officer of the third rank could use five post-horses in traveling.

120. In 690 Empress Wu ordered a Ta-yün Temple to be erected in each of the two capitals and every prefecture all over the country, but in 738 the name of all these temples was changed to K'ai-yüan Temple by Emperor Hsüan-tsung's order. Though we find the name K'ai-yüan Temple mentioned in many places, Hsüan-tsung's order was not strictly carried out in the remote provinces. The names of Ta-yün Temple and K'ai-yüan Temple are both found in written documents discovered in Tun-huang.

121. A cakravartin or universal monarch is supposed to possess seven kinds of *ratnas* {jewels}. These are *cakraratna* (wheel), *hastiratna* (elephant), *aśvaratna* (horse), *maṇiratna* (pearl), *strīratna* (wife), *gṛhapatiratna* (minister), and *pariṇāyakaratna* (general).

122. Mahāsukhasattva is the personified deity of Mahāsukha or Great Joy, which is obtained through the realization of the inseparability of prajñā and karuṇā. This Great Joy is also compared to the joy derived from sexual union. The erotic element is one of the characteristics of esoteric Buddhism in India, but it did not develop in China. This doctrine is treated in the *Adhyardhaśatikā prajñāpāramitā*, which was translated by Amoghavajra. Is it because of its content that the authors of Amoghavajra's biographies avoid mentioning the name of this sūtra? {For a study of this text in English, see Ian Astley-Kristensen, tr., *The Rishukyō: The Sino-Japanese Tantric Prajñāpāramitā in 150 Verses (Amoghavajra's Version)*, Buddhica Britannica, series continua, no. 3 (Tring, England: Institute of Buddhist Studies, 1991).}

123. Siddhi is the last stage in a bodhisattva's spiritual career according to the esoteric school.

124. This text deals with *ālayavijñāna* {the Yogācāra concept of the deep unconscious, or "subliminal consciousness"}.

125. This sūtra has a chapter called Hu-kuo-p'in (Protection of the Country), where kings are urged to recite this sūtra whenever there is any natural calamity or hostile attack. One hundred images and one hundred seats are to be prepared, and monks to an equal number are to be invited to expound and recite this sūtra. Amoghavajra presented a memorial to the Emperor recommending a new translation of this text. His chief reason was its function of protecting the country. The names of the monks who helped him in translating this sūtra are enumerated in his memorial. The biography of Wang Chin in *Chiu T'ang-shu* says that Tai-tsung often fed more than one hundred monks in the palace and ordered them to expound the *Jên-wang-ching* whenever there was any enemy invasion. According to Tsan-ning's *Sêng-shih-lüeh*, a copy of the *Jên-wang-ching*

was carried about a hundred paces ahead of the Emperor when he was on the street. It is said that this custom started during Tai-tsung's reign. {For a complete treatment of this text, see Charles Orzech, *Politics and Transcendent Wisdom: The Scripture for Humane Kings in the Creation of Chinese Buddhism* (University Park: Pennsylvania State University Press, 1988).}

126. The particular devotion to Mañjuśrī is one of the characteristics of esoteric Buddhism as promulgated by Amoghavajra.

127. {This is a translation by Amoghavajra of the *Anantamukha[sādhaka]dhāraṇī*, T. vol. 19, no. 1009. N.b.: Chou's note mistakenly gives the number as 1909.}

128. The "a" sound and the letter representing this sound are important symbols in esoteric Buddhism. {See Richard K. Payne, "*Ajikan:* Ritual and Meditation in the Shingon Tradition," in *Re-Visioning "Kamakura" Buddhism*, ed. Payne, Kuroda Institute Studies in East Asian Buddhism, no. 11 (Honolulu: University of Hawai'i Press, 1998).}

129. According to some Mahāyāna texts a bodhisattva's spiritual career can be divided into five great stages, among which the second is called stage of preparatory disciple *(prayoga)*. Four kuśalamūlas are to be cultivated in this stage. *Kṣanti* or forbearance is one of them. Other texts put kṣanti as the sixth stage. The use of the term here seems to be generalized to include the entire spiritual stage.

130. This is the informal name by which Emperor Hsüang-tsung was generally addressed in the palace.

Esoteric Buddhism in Korea

1. The proceedings of this symposium were published in *Milgyo sasang ŭi Hanguk chŏk chŏngae*, ed. Pulgyo Munhwa Yŏngu Wŏn (Seoul: Tongguk University, 1986). Most of the papers given at the symposium were later heavily revised and expanded, and published as *Hanguk milgyo sasang yŏngu* (The Study of Korean Esoteric Thought; hereafter HMSY), ed. Pulgyo Munhwa Yŏngu Wŏn (Seoul, 1986), as part of the series on the history and doctrines of the Korean Buddhist schools.

2. As contained in *Hanguk pulgyo chŏnsŏ* (hereafter HPC), vol. 6 (Seoul, 1984), 245a–369c. This is a modern critical edition which has improved on many of the errors previously encountered in the *Taishō shinshu daizōkyō* (hereafter T.) and the *Zōkuzōkyō* (see the revised ninety-volume edition from 1981–89) (hereafter ZZ) versions. The *Samguk yusa* was compiled in or around 1285.

3. T. 2065. See also the annotated translation by Peter H. Lee, *Lives of Eminent Korean Monks: The Haedong Kosŭng Chŏn*, Harvard-Yenching Institute Studies 25 (Cambridge: Harvard-Yenching Institute, 1969).

4. For a criticism of this, see my essay "Problems with Using the *Samguk yusa* as a Source on the History of Korean Buddhism," in *Cahiers d'Études Coréennes* (Paris, 1994).

5. This work was compiled around 1145 by the Confucian scholar Kim Pusik (1075–1151). It is in the form of a historical record and generally emphasizes secular matters such as the royalty, government, the noble families. A reliable version is the *Samguk sagi*, edited by Chōsen Shi Gakukai (Seoul, 1927). For a compilation of all the material on Buddhism contained in this work, see the convenient redaction by Yi Chaejang, "Samguk sagi pulgyo ch'ojŏn" (Materials on Buddhism from the *Samguk sagi*), *Pulgyo hakbo* (hereafter PH) 2 (1964): 305–322. Among this material there is no specific reference to esoteric Buddhism.

6. This is especially pronounced when reading Kim Yŏngt'ae, "Samguk sidae ŭi sinju shinang" (Faith in Mantras during the Three Kingdoms Period), HMSY, pp. 35–89, and in Ko Ikchin, "Silla milgyo ŭi sasang naeryŏng kwa chŏngae yangsang" (A Discussion

of the Contents of the Doctrines of Esoteric Buddhism in Silla), HMSY, pp. 127–221. Other articles in HMSY follow along the same lines of reasoning and are fraught with unsubstantiated claims obviously used to fill out the large historical and doctrinal lacunae.

7. For a useful discussion of the introduction of Buddhism in Korea see Tamura Encho, "Japan and the Eastward Permeation of Buddhism," *Acta Asiatica* 47 (1985): 1–12.

8. Such as the *Saddharmapuṇḍarīka Sūtra* (T. vol. 9, no. 262), the *Lankavatara Sūtra* (T. vol. 16, nos. 670, 671) and the *Suvarṇaprabhāsa Sūtra* (T. vol. 16, no. 664).

9. Including scriptures such as the *Avalokiteśvara-ekadaśamukha-dhāraṇī* (T. vol. 20, no. 1070), *Marici-dhāraṇī* (T. vol. 21, no. 1256), *Mahāmāyuri-vidyarajñī Sūtra* (T. vol. 19, no. 988), and *Uṣṇīṣaviiaya-dhāraṇī Sūtra* (T. vol. 19, no. 968).

10. Korean *Tripiṭaka* (hereafter K.) 115, 116; T. vol. 9, nos. 265, 262. The K. numbering employed here follows *The Korean Buddhist Canon: A Descriptive Catalogue*, comp. Lewis R. Lancaster (Berkeley and Los Angeles: University of California Press, 1979).

11. K. 128; T. vol. 16, no. 664.

12. K. 19; T. vol. 8, no. 245.

13. K. 177; T. vol. 14, no. 450. For a translation from the Chinese of the main canonical scriptures related to this Buddha, see Raoul Birnbaum, *The Healing Buddha* (London: Rider, 1979).

14. For an attempt at accounting for the introduction of esoteric Buddhist scriptures into Korea, see Park Taehwa, "Hanguk pulgyo ŭi milgyo kyongjon chonrae ko" (Concerning the Introduction of Esoteric Buddhist Scriptures in Korea), *Hanguk pulgyo hak* 1 (1975): 45–62. Although not entirely successful in his endeavor, the author gives a useful overview of extant materials and provides some hints as to when esoteric Buddhist scriptures were introduced on the Korean Peninsula.

15. A thorough discussion of this can be found in Chang Ch'ungsik, Silla *Sŏk t'ap yŏngu* (A Study of Stone Stūpas) (Seoul: Ilji Sa, 1987), pp. 43–55, 170–194. See also, Chong Yŏngho, *Sŏk tap* (Stone Stūpas). *Hanguk ŭi mi* (Korea's Art) vol. 9 (Seoul: Chung'ang Ilbo, 1985), pls. 3–4, 10, 11, 22–23, 32–33, 34–35, 36–37, 38–39, 40, 44–45.

16. HPC, vol. 6, chap. 2, p. 291a.

17. K. 352; T. vol. 19, no. 1024.

18. For more information, see Chŏn Hyebong, *Na Yŏ inswae sul ŭi yŏngu* (A Study of Printing during the Silla and Koryŏ) (Seoul: Kyŏngin Munhwa Sa, 1982), pp. 19–31.

19. See also the interesting article by Ch'ŏn Hye-bong, "Dharani-sutra of Early Koryŏ," *Korea Journal* (hereafter KJ) 6 (1972): 4–12.

20. This opinion has been voiced by Mun Myongdae in his otherwise excellent study *Sŏkkuram pulsang ŭi choguk yŏngu* (A Study of the Buddhist Carved Sculptures in Sŏkkuram) (Seoul: Tongguk Taehakkyŏ Taehak Won, 1987), pp. 9–11.

21. Cf. Yi Song-mi, "Problems concerning the Sŏkkul-am Cave Temple in Kyŏngju," *Seoul Journal of Korean Studies* 1 (1988): 25–47.

22. For fine photos of the sculptures in the Sŏkkuram, see Hwang Suyŏng, *Pulsang* (Buddhist Images), Hanguk ŭi mi, vol. 10 (Seoul, 1985), pls. 125–132.

23. HPC, vol. 1, p. 479a–c.

24. This work is mentioned in T. vol. 55, no. 2184, p. 1170b; and T. vol. 55, no. 2183, p. 1153b.

25. HPC, vol. 2, 181b–232a.

26. HPC, vol. 3, 409b–418b.

27. This monk is revered as the main propagator of Pŏpsang (Skt. Dharmalakṣana) teachings in Korea. He is the author of a considerable number of works and commentaries, many of which are still extant. For a study of him and his works, see Chae Inhwan,

"Silla Taehyŏn pŏpsa yŏngu" (A Study of Dharma Master Taehyŏn of the Silla), pt. 2, *Pulgyo hakbo* (hereafter PH) 21 (1984): 67–83.

28. See HMSY, pp. 636–637.

29. Esoteric practices within the Tiantai occur already in the founder Zhiyi's teachings. See, for example, his *Fangdeng sanmei xingfa* (The Method of the Constant Samādhi), T. vol. 46, no. 1940, p. 945a, a work which is based on the *Fangdeng tuoluoni jing* (Vaipulya-dhāraṇī Sūtra), T. vol. 21, no. 1339. For a list of the early Korean monks who went to China to study Tiantai Buddhism, see my "Ennin's Account of a Korean Buddhist Monastery, AD 839–840," *Acta Orientalia* 47 (1986): 141–155.

30. Information contained in the Japanese monk Ennin's diary from his pilgrimage in Tang China from 839–846, based on observations in a Korean temple on the Shandong Peninsula, makes a connection between this Korean Buddhist temple and the Tiantai community, which dominated Buddhism on Mt. Wutai at that time. Tiantai Buddhism in the ninth century was highly influenced by esoteric practices and scriptures, and hence we may indirectly infer that Tiantai esoteric practices are likely to have been known and practiced in Silla as well. See E. O. Reischauer, *Ennin's Diary* (New York: Ronald Press, 1955), pp. 131–173.

31. Cf. HPC, vol. 6, chap. 5, p. 355a–b.

32. See Ko Ikchin, "Silla milgyo ŭi sasang naeryŏng kwa chŏngae yangsang," HMSY, pp. 156–160, 221.

33. HPC, vol. 6, p. 355a.

34. T. vol. 50, no. 2061.

35. Cf. HPC, vol. 6, chap. 1, p. 711c.

36. HPC, vol. 6, chap. 5, p. 355c.

37. Ibid.

38. Ibid., p. 356c.

39. Ibid., p. 288a.

40. See Haiyun, *Liangdu Da Faxiang cheng shizi fufa ji*, T. vol. 51, no. 2081, pp. 783c–787b; and *Da Tang Qinglong Si sanzhao gongfeng Dade xingzhuang*, T. vol. 50, no. 2057, pp. 294c–296a.

41. Dharmalakṣaṇa as used here refers to the Zhenyan tradition, and not, as one would expect, to the Chinese Faxiang school.

42. T. vol. 51, no. 2081.

43. HPC, chap. 2, 786c.

44. *Nippon daizōkyō, Tendai shū kenkyū shōso*, chap. 1, 17a–19b. It was composed by Saichō (767–822), the founder of the Japanese Tendai school.

45. Ibid., chap. 1, p. 20b.

46. See *Zōzō* (Taisho Iconographical Supplement), vol. 11, pl. 56. As we find Yirim included in a Japanese Tendai lineage, it would seem logical to consider him as part of that tradition rather than the Zhenyan school. However, the existence of Zhenyan Buddhism as a distinct school prior to the influence of Amoghavajra is open to questioning, as strict sectarian demarcations during eighth-century Tang Buddhism were relatively fluctuating. From the point of view of the Tendai school, however, there can be little doubt that Yirim is considered a master in its lineage of esoteric doctrines (Jpn. *taimitsu*).

47. *Mikkyō daijiten* (Xinwen Feng reprint), vol. 4, p. 1895c.

48. HPC, vol. 3, 383a–409a.

49. Cf. ibid., chap. 1, 385b–387c.

50. Ibid., chap. 2, 399b–401a, 403c–404a, 405c, 407a–b, 408c.

51. In a note at the end of the text, he is described as a Silla monk from Yŏngmyo Temple

(ibid., chap. 2, p. 409a), most likely a temple which was located in Kyŏngju, the Silla capital. Cf. *Pulgyo Sajŏn* (Seoul: Tongguk University, 1961–84), p. 595b.

52. For a biographical sketch of Hyech'o's life, see Yang Han-sung et al., trs. and eds., *The Hye-Ch'o Diary: Memoir of the Pilgrimage to the Five Regions of India*, Religions of Asia Series 2, Unesco Collection of Representative Works (Seoul, 1984), pp. 14–20.

53. HPC, vol. 3, 381b–382b; T. 1177A, 724b–725a.

54. HPC, vol. 3, 382c. The text is dated 774, the same year Hyech'o's master Amoghavajra passed away.

55. See Yang, *Hye-Ch'o Diary*.

56. T. vol. 50, no. 2057, p. 295a. Here it is said that he returned to his native country and widely spread the teaching. He went to China in 781.

57. Ibid.

58. T. 2081, p. 784b. Kyŭnyang is mentioned as part of the transmission here.

59. Henrik H. Sørensen, "The History and Doctrines of Early Korean Sŏn" (diss., University of Copenhagen, 1988).

60. Chōsen Sōtokufu, ed., *Chōsen kinseki sōran*, vol. 1 (Seoul, 1919–85), pp. 66–72.

61. Ibid., p. 69.

62. Ibid., p. 68.

63. Several of the monks belonging to the so-called Northern school of Chan, i.e., the disciples of Shenxiu (605–706), had studied under Śubhāhrasiṃha. Most important among these Chan adepts was Yixing, who eventually became an important exponent of Zhenyan practices, and co-translator with Śubhākarasiṃha of the *Mahāvairocana Sūtra* (T. vol. 18, no. 848). For a study of Zhenyan influence on Chan, see Tanaka Ryosho, "Tōdai ni okeru zen to mikkyō to no kōshō" (Concerning the Interchange between Ch'an and Esoteric Buddhism in the Tang Period), Nippon bukkyōgakkai nenpō, vol. 40 (1975), 109–124. See also Kenneth W. Eastman, "Mahāyoga Texts at Tun-huang," *Bukkyō bunka kenkyūsho kiyō* 22 (1983): 42–60.

64. *Chōsen kinseki sōran* (hereafter CKS) (repr., Seoul: Asia munhwa sa, 1976), pp. 560–562.

65. Yixing passed away in 727, more than a hundred years before Tosŏn was even born, for which reason there could hardly have been any direct connection between them. The source making Tosŏn a disciple of Yixing is the stele inscription contained in CKS, p. 562. See also the study by Ch'oe Pyŏng-hŏn, "Tosŏn's Geomantic Theories and the Foundation of Koryŏ Dynasty," *Seoul Journal of Korean Studies* 2 (1989): 65–92.

66. Reference to the practice of *p'ungsu* is also associated with Tosŏn's disciple Kyŏngbo (868–948). Cf. CKS, pp. 189, 193. Note that the practice of *p'ungsu* was not limited to the Mt. Tongni school of Korean Sŏn, but was also employed by the followers of the Mt. Hŭiyang Sŏn school, e.g. Kŭngyang (878–956). Cf. ibid., p. 204.

67. We first encounter the use of this expression in the *Samguk yusa*.

68. In addition to the historical problem with the *Samguk yusa*, the monks in this lineage are traditionally considered as having belonged to at least three different denominations of Korean Buddhism. I think it safe to say that the Sinin school did not exist as a distinct school of Korean Buddhism during the Silla, and even in the Koryŏ it probably did not have a historical transmission comparable to those of the Hwaŏm and Sŏn denominations. In any case reliable sources are wanting until well into the Koryŏ.

69. HPC, pp. 356b–357a, where it is said that in 936 the king commanded the two monks Kwanghak (n.d.) and Taeyŏn (n.d.) to establish Hyŏnsŏng Temple as a center for the Sinin Sect.

70. It was compiled in 1451 on the basis of government records from the Koryŏ. It is available in several modern standard editions and is reprinted almost yearly. Reference here will be made only to the chapters.

71. *Koryŏ sa*, chaps. 9, 16, etc. For a relatively sound discussion of the Sinin Sect, see Sŏ Yŏn'gil, "Koryŏ Milgyo sinang ŭi chŏngae hwa ku t'ŭksŏng" (A Discussion of the Characteristics of Esoteric Buddhist Faith during the Koryŏ), PH 19 (1982): 228–230. See also his recent study, *Koryŏ milgyo sasang sa yŏngu* (A Study of the History of Esoteric Buddhist Doctrine in Koryŏ) (Seoul: Pulgwang Ch'ulp'anbu, 1993), pp. 251–297.

72. For a brief record of this temple, see Kwŏn Sangno, comp., *Hanguk sach'al chŏnsŏ* (Collected Works on Korean Temples), vol. 2. (Seoul:Tongguk Taehakyŏ Ch'ulp'anbu, 1979), p. 1104a–b.

73. Cf. Sŏ, "Koryŏ milgyo," pp. 219–239. See also Chang T'aehyŏk, "Koryŏ cho kakchong toyang ŭi milgyo chŏk sŏnggyok" (The Esoteric Nature of the Ritual Held at the Koryŏ Court), HMSY, pp. 295–342.

74. *Koryŏ sa*, chaps. 18, 22, 30, 48, etc.

75. *T'aejong sillŏk*, chap. 28 (T'aejong 14th year). See also *Sejong sillŏk*, chap. 24 (Sejong 6th year).

76. T. vol. 55, no. 2184.

77. {See the introduction regarding the polemic nature of this hierarchical system.}

78. K. 1418.

79. K. 1442.

80. For a full list of these esoteric rituals, see Chŏng T'ae-hyŏk, "Koryŏ cho kakchong tojang ŭi milgyo chŏk sŏngnyŏk," HMSY, pp. 298–299, 303.

81. *Koryŏ sa*, vol. 3, chap. 89 (Biographical Section, chap. 2), 20b–21a. See also Yi Nŭng-hwa, *Chosŏn pulgyo t'ongsa*, vol. 1, 287–288. For a study of the activities by Tibetan lamas at the Koryŏ court, see my "Lamaism in Korea during the Late Koryŏ Dynasty," KJ 33, no. 3 (1993): 67–81.

82. *Koryŏ sa*, chap. 33, p. 674a.

83. For an attempt at describing the influence of Tibetan Buddhism during the late Koryŏ, see Yi Yŏng-bŏm, "Wŏndae lama kyo ŭi Koryŏ chŏllae" (The Introduction of Lamaism to Koryŏ during the Yuan Period), *Pulgyo hakbo* 2 (1964): 161–220. Beyond a few passages in the *Koryŏ sa* there is virtually no information to be had from Korean sources.

84. For his stele inscription, cf. T. 2089 (4), 982c–985c. See also CKS, 519–524.

85. For his stele inscription, see HPC, vol. 6, 709a–711a.

86. Naong's stele inscription also mentions that Chigong gave him a *kasaya*, a fly-whisk *(pŭlja)*, and Sanskrit books, all signs of authority. Cf. HPC, vol. 6, p. 710b.

87. See T. 2013A (two texts); T. 979.

88. HPC, vol. 6, pp. 717c–718b. There exist two other short pieces by Naong on the six gati; cf. pp. 719a–720a, 720c–721a.

89. Ibid., p. 723a–b.

90. For information on this critical phase in the history of Korean Buddhism, see John I. Goulde, "Anti-Buddhist Polemic in Fourteenth and Fifteenth Century Korea: The Emergence of Confucian Exclusivism" (Ph.D. diss., Harvard University, 1985), pp. 208–232.

91. In 1660 under the oppressive regime of King Hyŏngjong (1669–74) all Buddhist monks and nuns were forbidden to enter the capital and other major cities, and Buddhist temples were destroyed within the walls of Seoul. See Takahashi Toru, *Richo Bukkyō* (Seoul, 1927), pp. 733–757.

92. For a thorough discussion of the various means with which King T'aejong tried to curtail Buddhism, see Kim Yŏng'ae, "Chosŏn T'aejong cho ŭi pulgyo hwa ibul" (The Rejection of Buddhism during the Reign of King T'aejong of the Chosŏn), *Tongyang Hak* 18 (1988): 137–168.

93. See *Yijo sillok pulgyo ch'ojon* (Compilation of Material on Buddhism from the Veritable Records of the Yi), vol. 1, chap. 2, pp. 297–304, 342.

94. Ibid., p. 312.
95. Ibid., p. 300.
96. For a list of esoteric Buddhist material from this period, see HMSY, pp. 635–646.
97. For a survey of his life and teaching, see Nukariya Kaiten, *Chosŏn sŏngyo sa* [translated into Korean by Chŏng Hogyŏng] (Seoul, 1978), pp. 466–474.
98. For biographical information, see his autobiographical letter in U Chŏng-sang, "Sŏsan Taesa chŏn yak ko" (Concerning the Life of Sŏsan Taesa), in *Chosŏn chŏngi pulgyo sasang yŏngu* (A Study of Buddhist Doctrines during the Chosŏn on the Basis of Historical Records) (Seoul, 1985), pp. 187–206. In this letter Hyŭjŏng accounts for his life from his birth in 1520 until around 1568, when he was forty-eight years old and at the peak of his spiritual career. See also his stele inscription in CKS, pp. 852–855.
99. HPC, vol. 7, 594b–599a. This work is one of the earliest Buddhist texts dealing with liturgy to use Hangul. It gained considerable popularity and continued to be reprinted during the following centuries. For a brief discussion of its historical data, see my "A Bibliographical Survey of Buddhist Ritual Texts From Korea," *Cahiers d'Extrême-Asie* 6 (1991–92): 159–200.
100. HPC, vol. 7, pp. 737b–743b.
101. Ibid., pp. 743–752.
102. Ibid., pp. 634c–647b.
103. Ibid., p. 640a–b.
104. See Hsu Sung-peng, *A Buddhist Leader in Ming China: The Life and Thought of Han-shan Te-ch'ing, 1546–1623* (University Park: Pennsylvania State University Press, 1978), pp. 139–140.
105. See Henrik H. Sørensen, "On Esoteric Practices in Korean Sŏn Buddhism during the Chosŏn Period," in this volume.
106. For a list of the main esoteric scriptures of this period in regard to ceremonial practices, see Sørensen, "Bibliographical Survey."
107. K. (Supplement), 55.
108. In fact there several different manuals under this title.
109. Only available in the original wood block print. For a copy, cf. Seoul National University Library (Kyujang Kak), no. 1750-3.
110. HPC, vol. 10, pp. 552b–609b.
111. For a study of this important mantra in the Chosŏn period, see Kim Musŏng, "Yukcha chinon shinang ŭi sachŏk chŏngae hwa kŭ t'ŭkchil" (A Discussion of the Characteristics of the History of Faith in the Six-Character Mantra), HMSY, pp. 551–608.
112. Ed. An Chinho (Seoul: Pŏmryŏn Sa, 1931–83). This is the most comprehensive and important of the modern ritual manuals. It is bilingual Hanja/Hangul, but large sections of the litany and liturgy have been written mostly in Hangul with only occasional Hanja. It is largely based on the *Pŏmŭm chip* and the *Chakbŏp kwigam* mentioned above, but also contains material from other manuals and ritual texts. One of its merits is that it contains many sections with commentary on the rituals, making it an invaluable source for the study of the Chosŏn dynasty rituals and related practices such as the "empowerment" of Buddhist paintings and statues. In recent years the *Sŏngmun ŭibŏm* has gradually declined in popularity, especially within the Chogye Order, and is now being superseded by the simplified ritual manuals and texts published by individual "temple families" and their organizations. This reflects the clear tendency toward more individualized sectarian rituals in contemporary Korean Buddhism.
113. Seoul: Hŏngbŏp Wŏn, 1970–81. This is a modern bilingual ritual manual based in large part on the *Chakbŏp kwigam* and the *Sŏngmun ŭibŏm*. It also includes a short section on mudrās with illustrations from the *Suryuk much'a p'yŏngje ŭi ch'waryo*. As

a modern compilation, the *Pulgyo pŏpgyo kwigam* reflects the waning interest in rituals among the members of the Buddhist community; many of the old rituals are presented in abbreviated forms and new, simpler ceremonies are introduced.

114. Seoul: Pulhaeng ch'ŏ tosŏ ch'ulgwan, 1990. This is another modern ritual manual in bilingual Hangul and Hanja. Despite its title it is a relatively short work containing the texts of the most essential rituals only. Among these are the *Sasipku chae* (The Ceremony of the Forty-Nine [Days]), *Pulsang chŏman* (Painting the Pupils of the Buddha Image), and *Pangsaeng* (Releasing the Living).

115. The T'aego school was established in 1970 by the descendants of the pro-Japanese faction of the Korean sangha after a prolonged power struggle with the anti-Japanese faction in the late 1950s. The T'aego school is often referred to as the "married-monks sect." Although the followers of the T'aego school are considered to represent a reformed and secularized type of Buddhism, they in fact transmit the most ancient practices and rituals in Korean Buddhism today. Hence, one should probably seek for sectarian, doctrinal, and perhaps political differences rather than the question of orthodoxy, in attempting to understand the T'aego school's problematic relationship with the larger Chogye school.

116. For an impressive volume with photos of the rituals as practiced by the T'aego priests in Pongwon Temple in Seoul, see *Yŏngsan chae* (The Yongsan Ritual), with photos by Ven. Sonam (Seoul, 1989).

117. It was registered under its present name in 1953.

118. Basic information on the new esoteric schools in Korea can be found in Yi Chae-ch'ang, "Milgyo sasang ŭi hyŏndae chŏk ŭiyi wa chŏngae," in HMSY, pp. 609–633. Some information can also be had from Mok Chong-bae, "Korean Buddhist Sects and Temple Operations," *Korea Journal* 9 (1983): 19–27. See also Kukche pulgyo tohyŏp ŭihoe, ed. *Hanguk ŭi myŏngsan taech'al* (Famous Mountains and Great Temples in Korea), Hanguk sach'al charyo ch'ŏngsŏ 1 (Seoul, 1982), pp. 55–56, 63–64.

ON ESOTERIC PRACTICES IN KOREAN SŎN BUDDHISM DURING THE CHOSŎN PERIOD

1. See the anonymous *Yŭ sŏk ch'ilwi non* (Treatise on the Clarification of Doubts on Confucianism and Buddhism) and Hyŭjŏng's *Samge Kugam* (The Magic Mirror of the Three Families), in *Hanguk pulgyŏ chŏnsŏ* (hereafter HPC) (Seoul: Tongguk Taehakkyŏ ch'ŭlp'an sa, 1981–90), vol. 7, pp. 252b–279a, and 616a–634b. See also Han Chŏngman, *Pulgyo hwa yŭgyo ŭi hyŏnsil kwan* (Iri: Wŏngwang Taehakkyŏ ch'ŭlp'an kŭk, 1981), pp. 78–124.

2. For a major compilation of recent papers by Korean scholars on the esoteric Buddhist tradition in Korea, the reader is referred to *Hanguk milgyo sasang yŏngu* (hereafter HMSY), ed. Pulgyo Munhwa (Seoul: Yŏngu Wŏn, 1986). For an introduction to esoteric Buddhism in Korea, see my "Esoteric Buddhism in Korea," in this volume.

3. See Sŏ Yungil, "Chosŏn cho milgyo sasang yŏngu," *Pulgyo hakbo* (hereafter PH) 20 (1983): 109–141. For a list and basic description of the majority of the extant Buddhist ritual texts from the Chosŏn, see Henrik H. Sørensen, "A Bibliographical Survey of Buddhist Ritual Texts from Korea," *Cahiers d'Extrême-Asie* 6 (1991–92), pp. 159–200.

4. For a relatively sound discussion of the Sinin Sect, see Sŏ Yŏngil, "Koryŏ Milgyo sinang ŭi chŏngae wa t'ŭksŏng," PH 19 (1982): 228–230.

5. HPC, vol. 6, pp. 245a–369c; cf. ibid., chap. 5, pp. 288a, 355a, 356b–357a, etc.

6. For a study of these esoteric Buddhist schools under the Koryŏ, see Pak T'aehwa, "Sinin chong kwa Ch'ŏngji ching ŭi kaejong mitpaldal kwajŏng ko," HMSY, pp. 253–294.

Pak's survey suffers from several drawbacks as it abounds in unsubstantiated assertions and lacks proper annotation, but, most important, it reveals the dearth of reliable source materials on the Buddhist schools in question. Unfortunately the majority of Korean scholars who deal with the Sinin and Ch'ŏngji schools resort to the *Samguk yusa*, a compilation of anecdotes dated to ca. 1285, and treat it as an authority on the origin of the two schools. Even Hŏ Hŭngsik in his monumental *Koryŏ pulgyo sa yŏngu* (A Study of the History of Koryŏ Buddhism) (Seoul, 1986), which is one of the best available studies on the history of Buddhism during the Koryŏ, has almost nothing to say about the two denominations in question; see pp. 526–535.

7. As far as I am aware, there is not a single extant scripture of Korean origin that can be related to any of these schools.

8. I am here referring to the late translations of esoteric Buddhist scriptures made by Dharmapāla (963–1058), Danapala (n.d.), and Dharmaraksa (Ch. Hufa) (n.d.), which became available in Korea in the late tenth century. Among the important esoteric scriptures in question were such works as the *Guhyasamājatantrarāja* (Korean *Tripiṭaka* [hereafter K.] 1418, T. vol. 18, no. 885) and *Srivajramaṇḍālaṃkāramahā-tantrarāja* (K. 1442, T. no. 886). Numbering according to Lewis Lancaster, comp., *The Korean Buddhist Canon: A Descriptive Catalogue* (Berkeley and Los Angeles: University of California Press, 1979).

9. *Koryŏ sa* (hereafter KS), chaps. 9, 16, etc. See also Chŏng T'aehyŏk, "Koryŏ cho kak-chong toryang ŭi milgyo chŏk sŏnggyŏk," HMSY, pp. 295–342.

10. As an indication of the dearth of sources we have no extant stele inscriptions over important monks from either school, nor do we have any temple histories to which sufficient historical credibility can be given. Had any of these schools been important enough, it is unlikely that they would not have yielded at least a few National Masters *(kuksa)* or Royal Preceptors *(wangsa)* such as we find with the Sŏn, Yogācāra, Hwaŏm and Ch'ŏnt'ae schools. However, such is not the case.

11. For his stele inscription, see HPC, vol. 6, pp. 709a–711a.

12. For a study of this phase in the history of Korean Sŏn Buddhism, cf. Sŏ Yungil, "Koryŏ mal Imje sŏ ŭi sŭyong," in *Hanguk sŏn sasang yŏngu*, ed. Pulgyo munhwa yŏ ngu wŏn (Seoul: Tongguk taehakkyŏ ch'ŭlp'an pŭ, 1984), pp. 201–244. See also Han Kidu, "Hanguk sŏn sasang yŏngu" (Seoul: Ilje sa, 1991), pp. 434–504.

13. For his biography, cf. *Chōsen kinseki sōran* (hereafter CKS) (repr., Seoul: Asia munhwa sa, 1976) vol. 2:1283–89. See also T. vol. 51, no. 2089 (4).

14. Also known as Qianyan Yuanzhang. He was the primary disciple of Zhongfeng Ming-ben (1263–1323) in the Mian branch of the Linjin school. Biography in *Wudeng qhuan-shu* (Collected Books of the Five Lamps), chap. 58. *Dainihon zōkuzōkyō*, 90 vols., rev. ed. (1981–89), vols. 81–82, no. 1571, pp. 221a–222c.

15. HPC, vol. 6, p. 710c.

16. Ibid., p. 709b. Naong's stele inscription also mentions that Dhyānabhadra gave him a *kasaya*, a fly-whisk *(pulcha)* and Sanskrit books, all signs of authority (p. 710b). Here it is important to note that Naong and his followers on their part made the Indian master into a Sŏn patriarch, by proclaiming him the 108th patriarch in direct line from Mahākaśyapa; T. 1089 (4), p. 982c. This is also stated in the HPC, vol. 6, p. 710b. While this postulate is, of course, historically absurd, it nevertheless shows the great importance and ensuing authority attached to the question of lineage and transmission in late Koryŏ Sŏn. It is interesting to note that Dhyānabhadra's legacy has remained intact in Korean Buddhism right up to the present century.

17. CKS, vol. 2, pp. 1283–1289; T. vol. 51, no. 2089 (4), pp. 982c–985c.

18. T. vol. 51, no. 2089 (4), pp. 983a–984b.

19. Ibid., p. 983b.
20. T. 1113a, including the appendix. It is interesting to note that none of these texts were included in the Korean *Tripiṭka*, although they probably were circulated among Dhyānabhadra's followers in the late Koryŏ.
21. HPC, vol. 6, pp. 717c–718b. There exist two other short pieces by Naong on the six gati, ibid., pp. 719a–720a, 720c–721a.
22. Ibid., p. 723a–b.
23. "Hanguk inmyŏng tae sajŏn," p. 793b.
24. In the traditional accounts Muhak is described as a master of *p'ungsu*, which in Korean Buddhism is associated with esoteric practices; see Nukaria Kaiten, *Chosŏn sŏngyo sa*, tr. Chŏng Hŏgyŏng (Seoul: Poryŏn Kak, 1978), pp. 407–409.
25. For a discussion of Dhyānabhadra's impact on Korean Sŏn Buddhism, see Nukaria Kaiten, *Hanguk sŏngyo sa*, pp. 333–346.
26. For a very useful study of the relationship between Buddhism and the state during the early Chosŏn see Kim Yŏngt'ae, "Chosŏn T'aejong cho ŭi pulsa hwa ch'ŏkpul," *Tomgyang Hak* 18 (1989): 137–168.
27. For a discussion of this aspect of early Chosŏn Sŏn, see Ko Ikchin "Hanguk pulsŏ ŭi yŏngu" (Seoul: Minjŏk Sa, 1987), pp. 201–205.
28. By the early Chosŏn this school had declined greatly since its heyday under Uich'on (1055–1101), and later Yose (1163–1245) during the middle of the Koryŏ dynasty.
29. A subsect of the Ch'ŏnt'ae school which arose during the second half of the Koryŏ dynasty.
30. Also a Ch'ŏnt'ae subsect.
31. Since the Unified Silla this tradition had remained the major doctrinal creed in Korean Buddhism and had exercised considerable influence on Sŏn during the Koryŏ.
32. This school existed very briefly as an independent tradition. It was a subsect of the Hwaŏm school.
33. This school was based on the *Mādhyamika* philosophy.
34. The teachings of this school were based on *Yogācāra* philosophy.
35. This minor school taught *abhidharma* as its principle doctrines. It is considered a Hīnayāna school.
36. This is the school which focused on the *vinaya*.
37. For a discussion of the historical background for this merger, see John I. Goulde, "Anti-Buddhist Polemic in Fourteenth and Fifteenth Century Korea: The Emergence of Confucian Exclusivism" (Ph.D. diss., Harvard University, 1985), pp. 208–232.
38. This was the name given to the combined school of the old Sinin and Chungdo schools.
39. This was the name given to the new school combining the old Namsan and Ch'ongji schools.
40. *Taejong sillŏk*, chap. 14, p. 47.
41. Cf. *Sejong sillŏk*, chap. 24. For a discussion of the relationship between the Chosŏn state and Buddhism under King Sejŏng, see Goulde, "Anti-Buddhist Polemic," pp. 233–244.
42. See Robert E. Buswell, *The Korean Approach to Zen: The Collected Works of Chinul* (Honolulu: University of Hawai'i Press, 1983).
43. There is virtually no evidence of Ch'ŏnt'ae practice in Korean Sŏn from the fifteenth century onward. However, it is known that individual monks within the school of Sŏn continued to study the major works of that tradition. The continued importance in Chosŏn Buddhism of the *Saddharmapuṇḍarīka Sūtra* should probably be seen in this light.
44. The Sinin school together with the Chugdo school, which was a minor denomination, is stated to have controlled thirty temples by the time of the merger. The Ch'ongji school together with the Chogye school, which was a major tradition, is said to have

controlled as many as seventy temples. See *"Taejong sillŏk,"* chap. 14, p. 47. See also Hŏ Hŭngsik, *Koryŏ pulgyo sa yŏngu,* pp. 522–535.

45. For a survey of his life and teaching, see Nukaria Kaiten, *Chosŏn sŏngyo sa,* pp. 466–474.

46. Pou's merits as a Buddhist master became known to the queen dowager in 1548, and shortly thereafter they met. Pou mentions this in a poem found in *Hŏung tang chip;* cf. HPC, vol. 7, p. 548a.

47. Pou refers to this, both explicitly and implicitly, in a number of poems in the *Hŏung tang chip,* chap. 2, HPC, vol. 7, pp. 548c, 549b, 551a.

48. A brief survey of his extant works reveals a comprehensive understanding of the teachings and literature of both denominations. The high esteem in which he held the *Avataṃsaka Sūtra* can be seen in his *Hwaŏm kyŏng hubal* (Postface of the *Avataṃsaka Sūtra*). See also *Nanam chapchŏ* (The Miscellaneous Writings of Nanam), HPC, vol. 7, pp. 579b–580a.

49. The Buddhist examination was reinstated in 1552. Hyūjŏng (1520–1604), and his disciple Samyŏng (1544–1610) were among those who passed these state-authorized examinations.

50. Pou was installed here as abbot in 1551. Cf. *Yip sillŏk pulgyo ch'ojon* (Seoul: Poryon Kak, 1976), vol. 5, chap. 14, pp. 350–351.

51. HPC, vol. 7, pp. 529a–575c.

52. Ibid., pp. 576a–594a.

53. Ibid., pp. 609b–615.

54. Ibid., pp. 594b–599a. This work, one of the earliest Buddhist texts dealing with liturgy to use Hangul, gained considerable popularity and continued to be reprinted during the following centuries. For a brief discussion of the historical data surrounding it, see Sørensen, "Bibliographical Survey," *Cahiers d'Extrême-Asie* 19, 159–200 (entry no. 56).

55. Pou was also the author of the ritual text used at these occasions. See HPC, vol. 7, pp. 599a–609a.

56. For a contents list of the relevant texts in the *"wŏnyŏm yorok,"* see HPC, vol. 7, p. 576a–b.

57. This would seem to refer to the highest nondual insight as gained by adepts of Sŏn. It may also refer to the *yuandun zhiguan* (complete and sudden ceasing and contemplation) which was developed in the Tiantai school.

58. HPC, vol. 7, p. 595a.

59. Ibid., p. 596c.

60. This dhāraṇī is taught by Śākyamuni Buddha to Ananda in the important *Foshuo jiwba yankou egui tuoluoni jing.* See, T. vol. 21, no. 1313, p. 464c.

61. Ibid., pp. 598a–599b.

62. For one of the first papers of significance devoted to this aspect of Hyūjŏng's teachings, see Sin Chŏngo, "Shisan Kyŏjŏ zenji no shingon kan ni tsuite," *Indogaku bukkyāgaku kenkyu* 32, no. 2 (1984): 744–746.

63. HPC, vol. 7, pp. 634c–647b. For a brief introduction to this work, cf. my "On the *Sŏnga Kugam* by Sosan Taesa," *Proceedings of the Ninth Annual Conference,* Association for Korean Studies in Europe, 10–15 April (Chantilly, France, 1985), pp. 273–286.

64. HPC, vol. 7, p. 640a–b.

65. K. 426; T. vol. 19, no. 945.

66. K. 426, p. 106c.

67. I have employed the Korean phonetic transcription as given in the *Sŏnga kugam* for all the mantras.

68. HPC, vol. 7, pp. 642c–643a.

69. The practice of leaving out this passage appears to have begun with Yi Nŭnghwa, who did not include it in the edition of the *Sŏnga kugam.* See his *Chosŏn pulgyp t'ŏngsa* (hereafter CPT), vol. 2 (Seoul: Pohyŏn Kak, 1976), pp. 337–377, esp. p. 359.

70. See *Shōbōgenzō* (The Eye and Storehouse of the True Law), chap. 50. For a translation

of this chapter, see *Shōbōgenzō*, vol. 2, tr. Kōsen Nishiyama and John Stevens (Tokyo: Nakayama shobo, 1977), pp. 87–93.

71. T. vol. 48, no. 2023, pp. 1091c–1092b.

72. T. vol. 48, no. 2023. It was compiled into the present large ten chapter version by the Linji monk Rujin (b. 1425). The preface is dated to the sixth year of the Chenghua reign period, i.e., 1470.

73. HPC, vol. 7, pp. 737b–743b. That version of the text includes an appendix not dealt with here.

74. Ibid., pp. 743–752. This version also includes an appendix which is not discussed here.

75. The earliest account of this incident is contained in the second chapter of the *Song Chan* text *Tiansheng guangdeng hu* from 1036. See *Zengaku gyōshō*, vol. 5, ed. Yanagida Seizan (Kyoto, 1983), pp. 365b–366a.

76. As far as I am aware none of these rituals are practiced by Korean Buddhists today. Nobody I asked was able to provide me with any information on how they were practiced, beyond what the texts say themselves.

77. For a study of Great Dipper worship in Korean Buddhism, see Henrik H. Sørensen, "The Worship of the Seven Stars of the Great Dipper in Korean Buddhism," in *Religions in Traditional Korea*, ed. Henrik H. Sørensen (Copenhagen, 1993).

78. The worship of the Seven Stars of the Great Dipper is based on the esoteric and apocryphal scripture *Beidou qixing yanming jing* (The Sūtra of the Seven Stars of the Northern Dipper Extending Life), T. vol. 21, no. 1307, a scripture with roots in late Tang esoteric Buddhism. Hyūjŏng's text in question is the Ch'ilsŏng chŏngmun (Text for the Invocation of the Seven Stars), which is contained as an appendix to the *Unsu tan*. See HPC, vol. 7, p. 751a–c. At the end of the invocation it is stated that "[after] the offerings and other meritorious activities, [such as] chanting the scriptures, they are followed by prayers, and [the recitation of] the *Yanming jing* (i.e., the Seven Stars Sūtra)." Ibid., p. 751c. The ceremonial scenario of Hyūjŏng's ritual text matches closely the structure of the *Pukdu ch'ilsŏng chŏng ŭimun* (Ritual Text Inviting the Seven Stars of the Northern Dipper), as found in the *Cheban mun* (Miscellaneous [Ritual] Texts). See my "Bibliographical Survey," pp. 159–200 (entry no. 7).

79. For a full study of his life and teaching, see Kim Yŏngt-ae et al., "Hoguk taesŏng Samyŏng taesa yŏngu," *Pulgyo munhwa yŏngu* (Seoul: Tongguk taehakkyŏ, 1971).

80. HPC, vol. 8, p. 67c.

81. For his biography, see CKS, vol. 2., pp. 883–884.

82. HPC, vol. 8, p. 258a–b.

83. Ibid., p. 259a–b.

84. Hardly anything is known about his life. He was a disciple of Hyūhŏng and appears to have spent most of his time in the northern provinces of the Korean Peninsula. His collected writings, the *Kiam chip* (The Collected Works of Kiam) were published in 1648. See HPC, vol. 8, pp. 157–184.

85. Ibid., pp. 167b–c, 172b–173a.

86. Ibid., p. 170a–b. This prayer is mainly directed to the Great Dipper.

87. Ibid., p. 180a–c.

88. HPC, vol. 8, pp. 1a–23b.

89. For information on his life, see CPT, vol. 1, pp. 485–486.

90. Ibid., chap. 5, p. 19b.

91. Ibid., p. 22a–b.

92. Ibid., p. 20a.

93. A third-generation master in the line from Hyūjŏng. Biographical information is contained in the *Tongsa yŏlchŏn* (The Transmission Line of the Eastern Masters), chap. 2, HPC, vol. 10, pp. 1021c–1022a.

94. HPC, vol. 9, p. 103a–b.
95. Biographical information contained in the *Tongsa yŏlchŏn*, chap. 3, HPC, vol. 10, p. 1024a–b.
96. Cf. *Solam chapcha* (Miscellaneous Writings of Solam), chap. 3, HPC, vol. 9, p. 311a.
97. Ibid., chap. 3, p. 311b.
98. Ibid., p. 324a–b.
99. Ibid., chap. 3, p. 311b–c.
100. The stele inscription containing his biography can be found in CKS, vol. 2, pp. 1269–1271. See also the *Tongsa yŏlchŏn*, chap. 2, HPC, vol. 10, pp. 1027c–1028a.
101. CKS, vol. 2, p. 1270.
102. The original preface of the 1569 edition from Ansim Temple can be found in the CPT, vol. 3, pp. 162–163. See also Sørensen, "Bibliographical Survey," pp. 159–200 (entry no. 9).
103. Although apparently an important figure in his own time, no bibliographical traces can be found on his life in the later Buddhist literature.
104. Details on his life are wanting. From the preface to the Manyŏn Temple edition of the *Chinon chip* we are told that he lived in Manyŏn Temple in Hwasŭn-gun, South Chŏlla Province, and that he transmitted his esoteric teaching to his disciple, the Sŏn master Paekam (n.d.). *Chinon chip*, pp. 1–2.
105. Cf. the facsimile of this edition which was republished some ten years ago in Seoul. It is now extremely rare and the reader may choose to consult a modernized and revised hand-copied version with romanization of the Sanskrit, published by Poyŏn Kak (Seoul, 1987) and readily available.
106. This practice is based on the *Guan wuliang shou jing* (The Sūtra of Contemplating Amitāyus, also referred to as Amitāyus Dhyāna Sūtra), T. vol. 12, no. 365.
107. T. vol. 18, no. 876. The full title of this scripture is *Jingang ding jing yujia xiuxi pilushema sanmodi fa* (Vajra Uṣṇīṣa Sūtra's Methods of Yoga Practices [for the achievement of] Vairocana Samādhi), first chap. tr. Vajrabodhi, 731–736.
108. Ibid., p. 5b. For the original passage, see T. vol. 18, no. 876, p. 328b.
109. This is of course the celebrated Chinese Zhenyan master of the eighth century, who was a major figure in the development of esoteric Buddhism in East Asia. His dates are traditionally given as 705–774. Cf. *Song gaoseng chuan* (The Song History of Great Monks), chap. 1, T. vol. 50, no. 2061, pp. 712a–714a.
110. Ibid., p. 5b. I have been unable to identify the source of this passage.
111. There are several translations of esoteric texts on the contemplation of the character "A" attributed to Amonghavajra. Cf. T. vol. 19, nos. 953, 954(a), 955, 957.
112. The *hwadu* is the essential part of the *kongan*, upon which the Sŏn adept focuses his entire attention. For standard discourse on this practice, see Hyujŏng's *Sŏnga kugam*, HPC, vol. 7, pp. 636b–638a. {See also, Robert E. Buswell, Jr., *The Zen Monastic Experience: Buddhist Practice in Contemporary Korea* (Princeton: Princeton University Press, 1992), pp. 150–153.}
113. *Chinon chip* (Aja non), pp. 5b–6a.
114. For a description of this practice as carried out in Japanese Shingon Buddhism, see Roger Goepper, ed., *Shingon: Die Kunst des Geheimen Buddhismus in Japan* (Cologne: Museum für Osttasiatische Kunst der Stadt Köln, 1988), pp. 47–48. {Also see Richard K. Payne, "*Ajikan:* Ritual and Meditation in the Shingon Tradition," in *Re-Visioning "Kamakura" Buddhism,* ed. Richard K. Payne, Kuroda Institute Studies in East Asian Buddhism, no. 11 (Honolulu: University of Hawai'i Press, 1998).}
115. Probably the Sŏn school mentioned here indicates meditation as practiced in the

Ch'ŏnt'ae tradition. In any case I have never come across this practice in any material related to the school of Korean Sŏn.

116. *Chinon chip*, p. 6a–b.

117. For further information on this manual, and related editions, see Sørensen, "Bibliographical Survey," pp. 159–200 (entry nos. 31, 36).

118. These are both dated to 1723. See the Chŭnghŭng Temple edition published in that year, a copy of which is kept in the library of Songgwang Temple near Sunch'ŏn, in south Chŏlla province.

119. Cf. Sørensen, "Bibliographical Survey," pp. 159–200 (entry no. 51).

120. Torim Temple edition, chap. 2, pp. 25b–32a. The version of the *Sŏnmun chosa yech'amm mun hwajang sŏ* included here is an annotated but slightly abbreviated edition of that published by Puin Temple in 1660, and by Kap Temple in 1694.

121. *Pŏmun chip*, chap. 2, pp. 43b–46a.

122. Ibid., chap. 2, p. 45a.

123. Reference to the undated and slightly mutilated (early nineteenth century?) wood block copy in the Songgwang Temple library. For a brief introduction to his manual, which is quite different from that of the Torim Temple, cf. Sørensen, "Bibliographical Survey," pp. 159–200 (entry no. 31).

124. Osan edition, pp. 5b–15b. The term *komgyang* both means "to give offerings" and "to partake of offerings donated by the faithful." In common usage in present-day Korean Buddhist temples it has simply come to indicate the "communal meal."

125. Ibid., pp. 105b–106b.

126. HPC, vol. 10, pp. 552b–609b. For further information on this manual, see Sørensen, "Bibliographical Survey," pp. 159–200 (entry no. 6).

127. HPC, vol. 10, chap. 1, pp. 565c–566c.

128. Ibid., chap. 2, pp. 606b–609b.

129. For a detailed discussion of this ritual, see Yi Chigwan, "Kandang ch'akpŏp e tae han koch'al," PH 19 (1982): 49–65.

130. The standard edition is An Chinho, comp. *Sŏngmun uibŏm* (Seoul: Pomyŏn Sa, 1931–83). For a short description of this manual, see Sørensen, "Bibliographical Survey," pp. 159–200 (entry no. 49).

131. *Sŏngmun uibŭm*, vol. 2, pp. 117–118.

132. Ibid., vol. 2. pp. 278–283, 286–289, 294–295, 304–314.

KŪKAI'S "PRINCIPLE OF ATTAINING BUDDHAHOOD WITH THE PRESENT BODY"

1. For the two divisions of esotericism, see Y. Matsunaga, "Indian Esoteric Buddhism as Studied in Japan," in *Mikkyōgaku mikkyōshi rombunshō* (Kōyasan, 1965), pp. 229–230. {See the introduction for the polemic qualities of these categories.}

2. For his life, see J. M. Kitagawa, "Master and Saviour," *Mikkyōgaku mikkyōshi rombunshō* (Kōyasan, 1965): 1–26.

3. {See David Gardiner, "Kūkai's View of Exoteric Buddhism in *Benkenmitsu nikyōron*," *Mikkyō Bunka Kenkyūshō Kiyō (Bulletin of the Research Institute of Esoteric Buddhist Culture, Kōyasan University)* 5 (March 1992): 202–161 (reverse numbering).}

4. S. Katsumata, "Kōbō Daishi Kūkai no Mikkyōkan," in *Mikkyōgaku mikkyōshi rombunshū* (1965), p. 2.

5. *Mikkyō daijiten* (repr., Kyoto, 1969), p. 1404.

6. S. Katsumata, *Kōbō Daishi chosaku zenshū*, 2 vols. (Tokyo, 1968–70), 1:577–578 (hereafter Zenshū).

7. "The Writing of Kōbō Daishi: The Doctrine of Bodily-Attaining-Buddhahood," *Mikkyō-bunka Kenkyūshō Kiyō*, 29–30:31, 31:1–3.

8. T. 77, p. 391.

9. *Dainichikyō-kaidai* (concerning "Hokkaijōshin"), T. 77.2.

10. T. 77, p. 391. See "Writing of Kōbō Daishi," 31:3–5.

11. *Mikkyō daijiten*, p. 1403.

12. See ibid., pp. 1404–1405; *Zenshū*, 1:578–579; H. Nakamura et al., eds., *Shin Bukkyō kaidaijiten* (Tokyo, 1966), p. 252.

13. Their commentaries are published in the *Shingonshū zensho* (Kōyasan, 1933), 4:9–77, 79–171, 173–308, 309–464 (hereafter Zensho).

14. "Asaṃkhya" (lit., "incalculable") is a unit of number given in the *Abhidharmakośa* as the fifty-second unit of decimal numeration. One asaṃkhya kalpa is ordinarily required for a bodhisattva to attain the stage of joy, and three asaṃkhya kalpas for him to attain buddhahood.

15. Collection of esoteric scriptures.

16. Here refers to T. 19, p. 320. Kūkai interprets "genshō" as "realize with the present body," or "realize in the present life," though it is obvious that "genshō" represents "abhisaṃ budh," which means "realize completely."

17. A golden cakravartin is the noblest and most powerful of all the four kinds of cakravartins, or ideal kings, in India, and is said to reign in the four continents. The other three are silver, copper, and iron cakravartins.

18. T. 18, p. 331.

19. Early morning, midday, evening, and midnight.

20. Refers to Mahāvairocana, who is the eternally abiding dharmakāya embodied as a self-enjoyment body.

21. In the Shingon sect the ten stages *(bhūmi)* of bodhisattvas are considered to be embraced in buddhahood, whereas in other teachings they are the stages leading to buddhahood. The first bhūmi in the Shingon sect corresponds to the eighth bhūmi in the exoteric teachings (Zensho, p. 322).

22. This refers to the chapter on "Dwelling Mind" in the *Mahāvairocana Sūtra* (see Zensho, p. 92) and also to the *Fumbetsushōikyō* (full title: *Ryakujutsakongōyuga fumbetsushōishushōhōmon*, T. 18, p. 870), and Zensho, pp. 323–324.

23. A Shingon practitioner gradually acquires the merit of practices represented by the sixteen bodhisattvas and finally attains buddhahood in the present life. The sixteen bodhisattvas are four groups of four bodhisattvas attending the four buddhas in the four directions as depicted in the vajradhātu maṇḍala.

East	Akṣobhya Buddha	Vajrasattva, Vajrarāja, Vajrarāga, Vajrasādhu
South	Ratnasaṃbhava	Vajraratna, Vajrateja, Vajraketu, Vajrahāsa
West	Amitāyus	Vajradharma, Vajratīkṣṇa, Vajrahetu, Vajrabhāṣa
North	Amoghasiddhi	Vajrakarma, Vajrarakṣa, Vajrayakṣa, Vajrasaṃdhi

See Toganoo, *Mandara no kenkyū* (Kōyasan, 1932), pp. 513–514. As for the relationship between the ten bhūmis and the sixteen bodhisattvas, see Zensho, pp. 324–328.

24. T. 19, p. 594.

25. T. 18, p. 329.

26. "Vajra" implies wisdom, and "dhātu" means body (Zensho, p. 331).

27. T. 18, p. 21. See the Tibetan translation, D. T. Suzuki, ed., *Tibetan Tripiṭaka* (Tokyo, 1954–59), V, 254, v. 8 [Peking: Rgyud (tha) 115b–225b.] (hereafter Tib. T.).

28. One of the supernatural powers attributed to buddhas and other sages: power of transforming the objective world at will or that of going anywhere at will; *"ṛddhividhijñāna"*

in Sanskrit (*Mahāvyutpati*, no. 208). The Tibetan text suggests "*ṛddhipāda*" (= *rdzu ḥphrul rkaṅ*).

29. The *Mahāvairocana Sūtra*, T. 18, p. 45.

30. In the fifty-two-stage division of Bodhisattvahood, the stage of equal bodhi is the fifty-first stage and the tenth bhūmi is the fiftieth.

31. T. 31, p. 572.

32. The Shingon teaching distinguishes four kinds of buddha's body: self-nature body, enjoyment body, transformed body, and homogeneous body. The first three correspond to dharmakāya, saṃbhogakāya, and nirmaṇakāya, respectively. Enjoyment body is further divided into two: self-enjoyment body and enjoyment body for the sake of others. All the exoteric teachings, according to the Shingon teaching, were expounded either by the enjoyment body for the sake of others or by the transformed body (i.e., Śākyamuni, the historical Buddha).

33. T. 32, p. 574.

34. Five mahābhutas, i.e., earth, water, fire, wind, and space elements.

35. T. 18, p. 9. See, Tibetan translation, Tib. T., V, 247, iii, 6–7.

36. The first five letters "*a vi ra hūṃ khaṃ*" are given in the *Mahāvairocana Sūtra* (T. 18, p. 20) as a mantra for subduing the four kings of māras (devils), liberating one from the six states of existence, and enabling one to attain all-wisdom. The sixth letter "*hūṃ*" is now added to represent the consciousness element based on the following remark: "The letter '*hūṃ*' has the meaning of cause; the meaning of cause is that bodhi-mind is the cause (of buddhahood)" (T. 19, p. 609).

37. Since the original unproducedness refers to the immutable and immovable aspect of reality, "*a*" corresponds to the earth element which represents solidity (Zensho, p. 231).

38. Dharmakāya has two aspects: tranquillity and wisdom, which are compared to clear and calm water and waves producing the sound of dharma, respectively. Hence, "*va*" of *vāda* (word) corresponds to the water element (ibid., 231).

39. *Ra* stands for *raja*s (dust, impurity). Since dharma-nature is the state in which all defilements and impurities have been burnt out, *ra* corresponds to the fire element (Zenshū, 1:47).

40. *Ha* stands for *hetu* (cause). Dharma-nature is beyond all causes and conditions and is not a result of karmas, just like wind (ibid.).

41. *Kha* means space. No dharma is to be grasped, like space (Zensho, p. 361). Also dharma-nature is unhindered and unrestricted like space (Zenshū, 1:47).

42. Causal state and resultant state refer to the unenlightened and enlightened states, respectively.

43. As regards the correspondence between the five elements and the five Buddhas, Amoghavajra and Śubhākarasiṃha had different traditions:

Five elements	Amoghavajra	Śubhākarasiṃha
Earth *(a)*	Mahāvairocana	Akṣobhya
Water *(va)*	Amoghasiddhi	Amitābha
Fire *(ra)*	Ratnasaṃbhava	Ratnasaṃbhava
Wind *(ha)*	Amitābha	Amoghasiddhi
Space *(kha)*	Akṣobhya	Mahāvairocana

See Zenshū, 1:47; Zensho, pp. 115, 368–370.

44. T. 18.331.

45. T. 18.38. Cf. Tibetan translation, Tib. T., V, 267, i, 5–7.

46. T. 5.990 says, "O Sudarśana, if the earth element is pure, the all-knowing wisdom is pure; if the all-knowing wisdom is pure, the earth element is pure. . . . If the elements

of water, fire, wind, space, and consciousness are pure, the all-knowing wisdom is pure; if the all-knowing wisdom is pure, the elements of water, fire, wind, space, and consciousness are pure." Also, T. 8.831 says, "One contemplates on one's body as composed of (the elements of) earth, water, fire, wind, space, and consciousness, each element being impure."

47. T. 24.1013 says, "That all things are like illusions means that the five skandhas, viz. form, consciousness, perception, conception, and volition, the consciousness and space elements of the six elements, and the four elements—these dharmas have neither their own characteristics nor different characteristics and are like space."

48. This refers to the four kinds of buddha's body. See note 32.

49. Skt. *"bhājana-loka,"* meaning the world as the place of living.

50. The *Mahāvairocana Sūtra,* T. 18.31. Cf. Tibetan translation, Tib. T., V, 261, v, 6–7.

51. According to I-hsing, commentator on the *Mahāvairocana Sūtra,* the producing agent is the letter "A," which is identical with the dharmakāya of equality, or dharmakāya of non-form (T. 39.726). "Zuiruigyō [or, zuiruikei]" is interpreted by him as a buddha's physical forms manifested from his dharmakāya of non-form in accordance with different natures and conditions of the beings to be saved (ibid., 726). Here it is taken as meaning "zuirui," lit., "following conditions," i.e., varying in accordance with different conditions (Zensho, p. 124).

52. The three kinds of worlds are (1) the receptacle-world, i.e., the world where the Buddha's activity of edification takes place, (2) sentient beings to be edified by the Buddha, and (3) Wisdom-Enlightenment, i.e., various bodies of the Buddha emanating from Enlightenment (T. 35.418). Also they are (1) five skandhas, (2) sentient beings, and (3) worlds they inhabit (T. 25.546, etc.). "World" is here used with the sense of categories under which existing things are classified.

53. The *Mahāvairocana Sūtra,* T. 18.31. Cf. Tibetan translation, Tib. T., V, 262, i, 2–5. According to I-hsing, T. 39.727, an ācārya should meditate on his body and think as follows before establishing a maṇḍala:

Part of the body	Shape	Element	Color
Top of the head	Gem-shaped	Space	Various
Neck	Crescent	Wind	Black
	Triangle	Fire	Red
Heart	Sphere	Water	White
Navel	Square	Earth	Yellow

See Zensho, p. 34.

As regards the correspondence between the five elements and the five letters, Kūkai shows them in the *Hizōki* as follows:

Element	Color	Letter
Space	Blue	*khaṃ*
Wind	Black	*hūṃ*
Fire	Red	*ra*
Water	White	*vi*
Earth	Yellow	*a*

See Zenshū, 2:626.

54. Refers to an ācārya.

55. The *Mahāvairocana Sūtra,* T. 18.19. The passage is originally meant to show that various transformed buddhas are produced from the Tathāgata's mind. See Tibetan translation, Tib. T., V, 254, i, 6–8.

56. According to I-hsing, visible and invisible results refer to various acts of dancing and sport (i.e., Buddha's transformed bodies with which he saves sentient beings) and nirvāṇa, respectively. Also they refer to worldly results and the fruit of bodhi, respectively (T. 39, p. 700).

57. Principle is the absolute truth or the principle of naturalness which is beyond our relative perceptions and is only realized with the indiscriminative wisdom.

58. The *Mahāvairocana Sūtra*, T. 18, p. 44, says, "O Lord of Mystery, various honored ones have three kinds of bodies, namely, letter, mudrā, and figure." See Tibetan translation, Tib. T., V, 255, v, 6–7.

59. Probably refers to such sūtras belonging to the Diamond Peak divisions: T. 18.286–287, and ibid., 898–899. Cf. *Hizōki*, Zenshū, 2:616.

60. This refers to the fivefold meditation for realizing buddhahood of the Diamond Realm: (1) attainment of the bodhi-mind, which one realizes by meditating on one's mind until one perceives it to be like a full moon, measuring the length of a forearm in diameter, which symbolizes one's original (i.e., innate) bodhi-mind; (2) practice for perfecting the bodhi-mind—this is a repeated meditation on one's bodhi-mind in which one perceives the full moon in one's mind expand infinitely and, then, contract to the original size; (3) accomplishing the adamantine bodhi-mind—here one perceives in one's mind-moon the lotus-flower, vajra, or other samaya-forms of one's Honoured One, thereby making the bodhi-mind firm and solid; (4) attainment of the Vajra Body— meditation in which one attains unity with the honored one, thereby obtaining the samaya body; and (5) perfection of the buddha's body—here one's samaya body turns into the karma body of the honored one. See T. 18, p. 284, 32, p. 574. Cf. S. Sakai, "Gosōjōshinkan ni tsuite," *Mikkyō gaku mikkyō shi rombunshū* (Kōyasan, 1965), pp. 397–409.

61. According to the *Hizōki*, Zenshū, 2:623, in Sanskrit the term may perhaps be reconstructed as *mahājñānamudrā*.

62. See E. D. Saunders, *Mudrā* (London, 1960), p. 119.

63. Refers to the four kinds of dharmakayas.

64. Refers to the original Dharmakāya Buddha Mahāvairocana; also the four kinds of buddha's bodies.

65. T. 19.322. Kūkai's third line differs from that given in the *Taishō Tripiṭaka*.

66. According to Yōkai, the three syllables *oṃ, bhūḥ*, and *khaṃ* refer to bodily, oral, and mental mysteries, respectively (Zensho, p. 277). Donjaku explains that they represent the three meanings of the syllable *"a, "*i.e., unproducedness, existence, and voidness (p. 412).

67. Refers to the mudrā called "excellent body samaya." "Excellent body" here refers to the body of a buddha (ibid., p. 412).

68. The five wisdoms represent the five Buddhas in the five directions:

Direction	Buddha	Wisdom
East	Akṣobhya	Great, Perfect Mirror Wisdom (*ādarśa-jñāna*)
South	Ratnasaśbhava	Wisdom of Equality (*samatā-jñāna*)
West	Amitābha	Wisdom of Excellent Discernment (*pratyavekṣanā-jñāna*)
North	Amoghasiddhi	Wisdom of Accomplishing Metamorphoses (*kṛtyānuṣṭhāna-jñāna*)
Centre	Mahāvairocana	Wisdom of Essential Substance of Dharma Realm (*dharmadhātusvabhāva-jñāna*)

69. T. 19, p. 602.

70. While the original reads "condition" and "aspect," Donjaku explains that these terms mean the perceiving function of mind and the object of perception, respectively

(Zensho, p. 417). Alternatively, according to Shūshin, the original references to "single condition" and "single aspect" mean the non-arising of the perceiving and the perceived, and non-aspect (ibid. p. 151).

71. In the division of bodhisattvahood into fifty-two stages, the first bhūmi is the forty-first stage, and supreme bodhi is the fifty-second.

72. This is one of the three kinds of compassion, which are (1) compassion toward sentient beings with the attached view regarding self and elements, (2) compassion without self-attachment but still contaminated with the attachment to elements which constitute one's self and beings to be saved, and (3) compassion without attachment to self or elements.

73. T. 30, p. 535.

74. Self-enlightenment, because ultimate enlightenment is to be attained through the realization of one's mind-nature.

75. Lit., "Great Samantabhadra Vajrasatta." Samantabhadra represents the compassion and virtue of benefiting sentient beings, and Vajrasattva is the head of the bodhisattvas who received the esoteric teaching directly from Mahāvairocana Buddha. In esoteric Buddhism they are considered as the same bodhisattva (Zensho, p. 153). The state of the great Samantabhadra corresponds to the stage of equal bodhi (ibid.).

76. A maṇḍala ācārya is a master who establishes a maṇḍala and leads his disciples into it.

77. "Karma," is here the act of proclaiming the precepts one has received in order to produce in one's body (or mind) a karmic force for observing them.

78. "Samaya" has four implications: (1) equality of Buddha and sentient beings, (2) vow of saving sentient beings, (3) removal of evil passions through Buddha's empowerment, and (4) awakening the minds of sentient beings. Here it refers to "one hundred and eight samādhis," according to Donjaku (Zensho, p. 421).

79. In the Consciousness-Only {Yogācāra} School two kinds of self-attachment are distinguished: (1) innate self-attachment, and (2) self-attachment arising from wrong views and thoughts. The former is more deeply rooted and difficult to eradicate than the latter and is only to be removed in the samādhi immediately preceding the attainment of buddhahood, whereas the latter is removed at the attainment of the first bhūmi (i.e., the stage of joy). In esoteric Buddhism, however, specific achievements in different stages are not always followed; one's innate self-attachment is removed (or, as it is said here, transformed) in the stage of joy.

80. This means that one has attained the first bhūmi.

81. Refers to the nature *(dhātu)* of Buddha's wisdom, which is indestructible like adamant *(vajra)*. In other words, it is one's originally pure mind represented by the syllable *"a"* (Zensho, p. 426).

82. The eighth consciousness (*ālayavijñāna*, also called "store-consciousness" and "seed-consciousness"), which is the base-consciousness of one's existence and preserves "seeds" of one's actions and phenomenal manifestations of one's objective world. The seeds of adamant-nature planted in the ālaya-consciousness have the efficacy to suppress evil tendencies of mind and lead one to buddhahood (ibid., p. 53).

83. Śrāvakayāna and pratyekabuddhayāna.

84. Three mystic practices of union with five bodhisattvas, namely, Vajrasattva and four attending bodhisattvas whose names signify Desire, Touch, Lust, and Pride. By the performance of the five mystic yogas one realizes identity of nirvāṇa and saṃsāra (ibid., pp. 54–55).

85. The five states are the realms of hell, pretas (hungry ghosts), animals, humans, and heavenly beings.

86. T. 20.539.

87. *Adhipati-pratyaya* is one of the four conditions for the emergence of a mental or material

phenomenon. The four conditions are (1) *hetu-pratyaya*, the direct cause, (2) *samanan-tara-pratyaya*, the condition that the preceding thought must perish so that the present thought takes place, (3) *ālambana-pratyaya*, the condition that an object must be present so that a mental element may arise depending on it, and (4) all other conditions which contribute to and do not hinder the emergence of a thing.

88. Dharmakāya, sambhogakāya, and nirmāṇakāya.

89. The Shingon teaching is based on the Tathāgata's transcendental powers; hence, it is also called the vehicle of transcendental powers (Zensho, p. 58ff.).

90. The five are the powers of seeing anything at any distance, hearing anything at any distance, going anywhere at will, remembering former states of existence, and knowing others' thought.

91. The *Mahāvairocana Sūtra*, T. 18, pp. 12, 14.

92. T. 18, p. 22. See Tibetan translation, Tib. T., V, 256, iv, 5–6.

93. The *Mahāvairocana Sūtra*, T. 18, p. 19. See Tibetan translation, Tib. T., V, 253, iv 8–v 2.

94. The phrase *shingon shingon sō* is interpreted by Shōshin as "the noumenal substance and the phenomenal aspect of the mantra" (Zensho, p. 165), by Yōkai as "the mantra as the relative existence and the mantra as the absolute reality" (ibid., p. 297), and by Donjaku as "the cause and the effect (i.e., the real aspect) of the mantra" (ibid., p. 140). Donjaku further explains that the cause of the mantra is the recitation of the mantra and its effect is siddhi.

95. Adapted from T. 18, p. 254.

96. All the deities surrounding Mahāvairocana Buddha are manifestations of his self-nature body *(svabhāvakāya)* (according to Raiyu, Zensho, p. 68). Donjaku explains them to be self-glorifying bodies of the Buddha (ibid., p. 451).

97. The sūtra further mentions four female deities representing the bodhisattva's four cardinal virtues and eight attending female deities.

98. {"Koṭi" is a very large number, rendered variously as ten or a hundred million.}

99. The five wisdoms and the thirty-seven wisdoms correspond to the five families *(kula)* and the thirty-seven deities of the Diamond Realm maṇḍala.

100. Skt. *citta*, which is traditionally interpreted as deriving from *ci*, meaning to heap up, accumulate.

101. "Dharma" derives from *dhṛ*, meaning to hold, support.

102. The term "all-knowing wisdom" is singular in ordinary interpretation and refers to the perfect wisdom which takes numerous things as its objects and perceives their real aspects. Here it is interpreted to be numerous wisdoms that the mantra-practitioner attains.

103. The term appears at T. 32, p. 606, in which it refers to the ninth consciousness.

The Five Mysteries of Vajrasattva: A Buddhist Tantric View of the Passions and Enlightenment

1. The other major upholders of this part of the Buddhist tradition in Japan—whence the major part of the present material is drawn—are the Tendai-shū and the folk movement Shugendō. The Shingon-shū (*shū* means sect or school) is, however, the only one which sees itself as being exclusively esoteric.

2. Hatta Yukio, *Shingon-Jiten* (Tokyo: Hirakawa Shuppansha, 1985), hereafter abbreviated as SJT, followed by the number which Hatta has given the mantra and dhāraṇī in his sources. I have reviewed this dictionary in *Temenos* 23 (1987): 131–134. I hope to publish a comparative study of all the major texts which display Five Mysteries influence, but this will have to await another day.

3. T. vol. 20, no. 1125.

4. T. 20.536a4.

5. *Sangai, triloka,* which together constitute all that in the Buddhist view is unenlightened.

6. *Sattva* may also be translated as "essence." Due to the centrality of the figure and the concept of Vajrasattva, I shall generally retain the original Sanskrit form in my text. (The spelling "Vajrasatva" is also commonly found.)

7. Sometimes translated as "contact." The point is to differentiate between the simple faculty of touch and the actual act of touching: it is the latter which is relevant here. This is borne out not only by the internal evidence of the Five Mysteries texts but also by the Tibetan version of the first chapter of the Prajñāpāramitā in One Hundred Fifty Śloka, where the difference can be seen in the two terms *reg* and *reg-pa,* which are used there to refer to the two aspects of touch referred to above.

8. Sawa Ryūken, *Mikkyō-jiten* (Kyoto: Hozokan, 1975); hereafter MJT. This small dictionary, complete in one volume, is a useful supplement to the standard work in Japanese Tantric studies, the six-volume encyclopedic dictionary of Esoteric Buddhism: Sawa Ryūken et al., eds., *Mikkyō–Daijiten,* rev. and enl. ed., 6 vols. (Kyoto: Hozokan, 1970); compact ed. (1 vol.), 1983; hereafter MDJT.

9. *Bonnō-soku-bodai,* "the passions themselves are enlightenment." This principle, of paramount importance in Tantric Buddhism, expresses the conscious transformation of one's basic, passionate nature into the stuff of enlightenment. Tantric apologists have long felt it necessary to emphasize this aspect of Tantric thought and practice as a unique and radical development in the Buddhist tradition, but it is in fact largely a mere reformulation of basic Buddhist concepts, and is more radical in its overt expression than in its handling of the tradition. See my article on *mahāsukha*—the key Tantric concept of "Great Bliss"—in the forthcoming fascicule of the *Hōbōgirin,* fasc. 7 (1989), s.v. "Dairaku/Tairaku."

10. MJT, p. 222a.

11. MDJT, 2:628c.

12. The best all-round introduction to these two central facets of Shingon doctrine is still Tajima Ryujun, *Les Deux Grands Maṇḍalas et la Doctrine de l'Esoterisme Shingon* (Tokyo: Maison Franco-Japonaise, 1959).

13. A more literal rendering might be "cause and effect are not two / beings and Buddha are one essence." The first of these two didactic principles understands the *sattva* referred to by the element *st* as Vajrasattva, the second understands it as [sentient] beings.

14. This is also the bīja of the vidyarāja Aizen (Aizen-myōō, Rāgarāja), who is the guardian deity of the Rishukyō and particularly related to the final, climactic chapter of that sūtra. One may here consult MDJT, 1:4ff. *Hōbōgirin,* fasc. 1, pp. 15b–17a; p. 16a reads: "One considers him as a 'transformation,' sometimes of Vairocana, sometimes of the Bodhisattva of Adamantine Love, Aikongō, and finally sometimes of the assembly of the four Adamantine Bodhisattvas who surround the Buddha Akṣobhya in the Eastern circle in the Diamond Realm: [Adamantine] Being [That Is Vajrasattva], King, Love, Joy." Cf. the entry on Aikongō in *Hōbōgirin,* fasc. 1, p. 14b, etc.

15. MDJT, 2:628c.

16. T. vol. 20, no. 1119, one of the major Five Mysteries texts, has a standard Kongōchōkyō configuration, that is, with deities to the East, South, West, and North respectively. The maṇḍala described by the text we shall be looking at in more detail below has the uncommon configuration of two bodhisattvas on either side of the central figure. (Here, in line with the common practice in Japanese Shingon circles, I shall use the

term Kongōchōkyō to denote those aspects of Sino-Japanese esoteric Buddhist thought and practice which are based on the ideas and structures in the *Sarva-tathāgata-tattva-saṃgraha.*)

17. Cf. MDJT, 2:629a. There is a depiction of one of the forms of the maṇḍala at 629c.

18. Unfortunately, I have not been able to elicit any signs of recognition from people who work primarily with Tibetan materials.

19. Since the corresponding chapters in T. vols. 5–7, no. 220 (10), and T. vol. 8, nos. 240, 241, 242, do not offer anything more interesting for our present purposes than different vocabulary for largely the same content, we shall ignore them here.

20. Cf. MDJT, 6:100 *(Mikkyō-kyōten Kanyaku-nenpyō).* Apart from T. vol. 20, no. 1121, these texts were translated by Amoghavajra. T. vol. 20, nos. 1119, 1120(a), 1120(b) are basically the same text, the latter being a verse summary.

21. Fukuda has in fact done most of the work in this field and has just published the product of over two decades of research on the *Rishukyō: Rishukyō no Kenkyū;* Fukuda Ryōsei, *Sono Seiritsu to Tenkai,* foreword by Nasu Seiryū (Tokyo: Kokusho Kangyō-kai, 1987). Of his earlier articles on the topic of the Śrīparamādya, the following might be mentioned: "*Śrīvajra-maṇḍalālaṃkāra-nāma-mahātantra-rāja* no kozo," *Toyogaku Kenkyū* 2 (1967): 49–56; "*Shōsho-yugakyō* to *Śrīparamādi-tantra,*" *Chizan Gakuhō* 20, no. 35 (March 1972): 17–42; "Kongōsatta-gikirui no kōsatsu," *Mikkyō-gaku Kenkyū,* no. 6 (March 1976): 1–14; "*Rishukōkyō* zōkan-hikōjō no ikkadai," *Mikkyōgaku,* no. 13/14 (1977): 77–90; "*Rishukyō* to Rishukyō-hō," *Chizan Gakuhō* 28, no. 42 (March 1979): 1–12.

22. Abbreviated here as the "Diamond Peak Yoga of the Five Mysteries Vajrasattva," T. 20.535b1–539a21.

23. There is an oft-repeated reference in this literature to the full version of the *Kongōchōkyō,* though there is a great deal of doubt as to whether it ever existed as an entire unit. The basic primary text dealing with the phenomenon is Amoghavajra's description of the eighteen assemblies, *Kongōchōyugakyō-juhachi-e-shiki* (T. 18.869); cf. also Matsunaga Yūkei, *Mikkyō-Kyōten Seiritsushiki-ron* (Kyoto: Hōzōkan, 1983), pp. 187–191, 250–254; Tajima, *Deux Grands Maṇḍalas,* p. 21f.

24. T. 20.535b10f.

25. That is, śrāvaka- and pratyekabuddha. This is a clear indication that the esoteric tradition sees itself as an integral part of the Mahāyāna—even though it regards itself as the most exalted part of the latter.

26. That is, the two aspects of the Bodhisattva's practice, self-benefit and benefiting others (*jiri-rita, ātma-para-hita;* cf. Nakamura Hajime, *Bukkyō go daijiten* [hereafter, N], p. 559d; MDJT, 3:1238a). To accomplish this task the Bodhisattva manifests himself in a myriad of forms: "He divides his body into billions and sports in the destinies [Skt. *gata*], perfecting sentient beings *(bun-shin-hyaku'oku, yu-sho'shu-chū, jōju-ujō)*" (T. 20.535c15f).

27. T. 20.535c14: *nehan-shōji-fuzen-fujaku.*

28. T. 20.535c16ff.

29. T. 20.535c19. The three worlds *(sanze)* are those of past, present, and future, and might thus be more accurately translated as the three times.

30. That is, Kongō-ki-in and Kongō-ki-shingon. The mantra runs: *oṃ vajra-tiṣṭha hūṃ* (SJT, no. 1022), and refers to the thunderbolt {vajra} that arises from contemplating the buddhas while in the state of samādhi (MDJT, 2:670c).

31. SJT, no. 1735.

32. T. 20.536a9.

33. T. 20.536a9f.

34. T. 20.536a8–24.
35. SJT, no. 1672.
36. T. 20.536a29.
37. T. 20.536a29–b22. This series is SJT, nos. 1430, 1146, 1147, 1466, 1186. The mantra *suratastvam*—noted elsewhere—also generally occurs in more or less close connection with this sequence. T. vol. 20, no. 1121, is the one major exception, since it does not contain this sequence at all. T. vol. 20, no. 1122, which has the series in a corrupt form and also contains a great deal of material quite unconnected with the other texts in the group, is another exception.
38. SJT, no. 1430.
39. Illustration in SJT, no. 1430.
40. Cf. MDJT, 3:669c. MJT, p. 92a lists twelve types of añjali. On the idea of the beginning of the final section of the Bodhisattva path as being the first fusion of wisdom and skillful means, see Ian, "Dairaku/Tairaku," sec. 4.1; Per Kvaerne, "On the Concept of Sahaja in Indian Buddhist Tantric Literature," *Temenos* 11 (1975): 88–135; Joseph Needham, *Science and Civilisation in China*, vol. 5 (Cambridge: Cambridge University Press, 1983), pp. 257–288.
41. SJT, no. 1146.
42. *Shin-gachirin.* Hatta's explanation of the mantra: "Vajra-bandha indicates the lunar disc of the pure mind of enlightenment *(jōbodai-shin)* and shows the source whence the Buddhas emanate" (SJT, no. 1146, *kaisetsu*).
43. MDJT, 2:718a, describes them as being extremely important among what it calls "seal-mothers" *(in-bo)*, that is, basic elements of a ritual process, elements whence the various phases of the ritual proper spring.
44. That is, one sense of samaya.
45. MDJT, 2:718a, has detailed information on these aspects.
46. T. 20.536b8. One should remember here that in the corresponding section in T. vol. 20, no. 1119, one opens the heart with the appropriate mudrā, emulating the spiritual opening by physically striking oneself on the chest (509b6; SJT, no. 1147). The opening of the heart creates an experience of the adamantine nature of one's body, speech, and mind and stresses the attainment of *jizai*, lit., "naturally/spontaneously existing," abiding without any kind of hindrance or barrier between oneself and the enjoyment of reality. (Hence jizai also has connotations of sovereignty.) The heart having been opened, one draws the Holy Assembly of the Buddhas, Bodhisattvas, and other Divinities into oneself.
47. SJT, no. 1147.
48. Ibid.
49. *Jisshu-bonnō* (T. 20.536b11). The number is probably not significant.
50. T. 20.536b13f.
51. Hakeda described the four types as extension, intention, communication, and action respectively. Yoshito S. Hakeda, *Kūkai: Major Works* (New York: Columbia University Press, 1974), p. 90f.
52. SJT, no. 1466; *āveśa*, joining oneself, having one's faculties absorbed in an object, etc.; from *ā* root *viś*, enter or approach (cf. MW, p. 155c).
53. *Nyorai no muro-jakujō-chi* (SJT, no. 1466, the source for the rest of this account).
54. T. 20.536b17f.
55. SJT, no. 1186. The character *ban* can also be read *vaṃ*, which is in fact more common in the Shingon tradition, being associated inter alia with Mahāvairocana in his Vajradhātu aspect. However, Hatta's reading is correct, since the mention of Vajramuṣṭi entails the reading *baṃ*, this being one of the bīja associated with that

Bodhisattva (cf. MJT, app., p. 17, s.v. "baṃ"; also MDJT, 4:1826a).

56. T. 20.536b22.
57. SJT, no. 1601.
58. T. 20.536b22f.
59. T. 20.536b24–26.
60. The Thunderbolt is pertinent here because this mantra is only found in Kongōchōkyō texts.
61. SJT, no. 1605.
62. *Nara* and *narī* in Sanskrit. The word is one of several used for "person, human being" in the sense of unenlightened person. The two terms together—meaning man and woman—are taken to indicate the error of intercourse in a state of ignorance. See N, p. 1029a, where the etymology *na* root *ram* ("not-pleasure," *fu-etsu*) is suggested.
63. See Astley, "Dairaku/Tairaku," sec 5.1ff.
64. T. 19.608b29–c2
65. T. 20.536c5f.
66. This mudrā is called Vajrasattva's Great Wisdom Seal (*Kongōsatta-dai-chi-in*, 536c6). I translate *ken/muṣṭi* by "fist" here, notwithstanding the correctness of Snellgrove's observation that *muṣṭi* means "the hand, palm and fingers, as manipulated in the making of hand-gestures *(mudrā)*" (D. L. Snellgrove, introduction to *Sarva-Tathāgata-tattva-saṅgraha*, by L. Chandra and D. L. Snellgrove, Śata-Piṭaka Series, no. 269 [New Delhi: Sharada Rani, 1981], p. 30). In this case, the hands are clearly clenched in the manner of what we would call a fist.
67. SJT, no. 1353.
68. Essential functions of body, speech, and mind.
69. T. 20.536c11–14.
70. T. 20.536c15–18. *Oppō*, or *oppō-zai*, is one of the cardinal sins for a Shingon practitioner: transgressing one's Vow *(samaya)* to attain enlightenment and work for the benefit of sentient beings (cf. MDJT, 1:185c).
71. T. 20.536c19ff.
72. SJT, no. 1320.
73. The translation of this line (537a1), *kongō-satta tō abisha gen-gen*, is rather problematical. *Abisha* means "penetrate" in the sense seen above in connection with mantra (6), that is, "entering everywhere" (*hen'nyū/amaneku hairu;* cf. MDJT, 1:32c, s.v. "abisha-hō"). *Gen-gen* is one of the various terms used to indicate the manifestation of a particular deity. The meaning would appear to be that Vajrasattva now manifests himself throughout the yogin's body, there being no difference between the two after the realization of this stage. There is perhaps a connection between this and the *bīja aḥ*, which means the attainment of enlightenment (a) and entering nirvāṇa (ḥ). Cf. MJT, app., p. 17; N, 167c, s.v. "kaihanji."
74. SJT, no. 1329.
75. See the explanations of these mantra in SJT. Hatta translates *dṛśya* as *chi-ken* ("wisdom-seeing").
76. T. 20.537a4.
77. SJT, no. 234.
78. The saṃgraha deities are those of the Hook *(kō)*, Rope *(saku)*, Chain *(sa)* and Bell *(rei)*. Their respective functions may be regarded as arresting (movement, habit), pulling in (toward the Path of the Buddha), bringing to rest (and binding firmly to the practice of the Path), and finally, the production of joy in the teaching one has been brought to.
79. See previous note.
80. T. 20.537a7f.

81. SJT, no. 1776; Hatta translates *surata* here as *dairaku*, "Great Bliss."
82. *Hon'i*, that is, presumably, the relative positions they occupy in the larger Vajradhātu maṇḍala.
83. T. 20.537a12f.
84. SJT, no. 1776.
85. The first of these groups occur in the various versions as follows:
    T. vol. 20, nos. 1119, 1120a–b, 1123: group 1430–1146–1466–1186 + 1776.
    T. vol. 20, no. 1121: has only part of the first group, but there is no intervening material before the second sub-ritual.
    T. vol. 20, no. 1122: displays rather different patterns.
    T. vol. 20, no. 1124: group 1430–1146–1466–1186 + unique intervening group + 1776.
    T. vol. 20, no. 1125: group 1430–1146–1466–1186 + unique intervening group + 1776.
86. T. 20.537a14–22. Cf. MDJT, 3:621c.
87. T. 20.537a21.
88. SJT, no. 1179.
89. T. 20.537a26.
90. SJT, no. 78S. The Taishō text actually reads: "jaḥ-hūṃ-vaṃ-hoḥ, vaṃ-hoḥ, suratast-vam," but Hatta—logically in the context—gives the seventeen-syllable dhāraṇī normally assigned to the Five Mysteries, in consonance with the alternative in the Taishō edition, 20.537n24.
91. T. 20.537b3–9.
92. T. 20.537b10–23.
93. There is some doubt about the reading of the mantra here, but it would appear to have something to do with *sarva-durga-sukha-?*, "all blisses difficult to attain." Hatta offers no solution, unfortunately.
94. SJT, no. 1582. Hatta refers this to touching *(soku)* and to mutual embrace *(kōhō)*.
95. The precise form of this mantra may be in doubt, but the meaning is clear enough: the practitioner sees everything as (or in the light of) Great Bliss. As for the staff, it should be noted that the reference is to that of the *makara*, a hideous marine monster which not even the waters of the four oceans can satisfy. In this vein, a Bodhisattva's love for sentient beings is said to be insatiable. Another explanation is that a Bodhisattva should have just as little regard for his own predilections as one who would contemplate such a leviathan. Cf. *Hōbōgirin*, fasc. 1, p. 14b; MW, p. 771b, where *makara* inter alia is given as an emblem of Kāma-deva.
96. This means that in the various representations of the Five Mysteries Deities, this Bodhisattva is depicted looking away from the Assembly. The precise form of the mantra is doubtful, but the presence of the term *siddha/siddhya* (?) indicates the theme of sovereignty through perfection and the accomplishment of "that which is to be done"—always an integral part of the Bodhisattva's task, especially in this fourth and final position of the immediate entourage *(kenzoku)*. (It will be remembered that it is the Tathāgata Amoghasiddhi who governs this position in the Five Tathāgata maṇḍalas.)
97. T. 20.537b24–538a5.
98. "Marks" as in the thirty-two major and eighty minor marks of a Buddha (cf. N, 866b, s.v. "sōgō").
99. T. 20.537b28f.
100. T. 20.537c5.
101. T. 20.537c9f.
102. T. 20.537c15.
103. T. 20.538a4f.
104. SJT, no. 1338.

105. The character *aku* is ambiguous as it stands in the text (S38a16). It could be either *aḥ* or *āḥ*. Hatta (SJT, no. 1338) reads it as the latter, which accords well with the basic interpretation given in MJT, app, p. 17a, where it is described as encompassing the five discs/transformations of the letter A (*aji-gorinten:* arousing the bodhicitta/practice/enlightenment/entering nirvāṇa/the furthest extent, skillful means). Further, it is one of the bīja of Vajrasattva and of Mahāvairocana, both in the latter's Vajradhātu and Garbhakośa manifestations.

106. T. 20.538a6.

107. T. 20.538a17–19.

108. T. 20.538a20.

109. *Soshi* is generally used to designate the historical founding master of a particular sect. There is often, however, no clear dividing line between what we would call history and myth, and most sects easily go from a historical lineage to tracing their origin back to the form of Buddha particular to their own teachings. The eight patriarchs in the Shingon-shū's transmission is perhaps the most pertinent example here: cf., e.g., Alicia and Daigan Matsunaga, *Foundation of Japanese Buddhism*, 2 vols. (Tokyo: Buddhist Books International, 1974), 1:177–180; MDJT, vol. 6, *Mikkyō-hōryū-keifu*, gives a complete set of tables.

110. T. 20.528a24–b1.

111. T. 20.538b2–539a19.

112. T. 20.538b2–10.

113. T. 20.538b10–19.

114. Cf. N, 553b, 895d, 525a.

115. T. 20.538b19–29.

116. T. 20.538b29.

117. T. 20.538b29–c2.

118. T. 20.538c2–16.

119. For the Sanskrit names of these bodhisattvas, see Snellgrove, Introduction to the Chandra, *Sarvā-Tathāgata-tattva-saṅgraha*, esp. p. 17ff. (Snellgrove's groups do not correspond exactly with the ones here.)

120. T. 20.538c16–23.

121. T. 20.538c16–17.

122. T. 20.538c23–27.

123. That is, the five deities as a whole, the Vajra Family.

124. That is, the same as this maṇḍala as it appears in the main Vajradhātu system.

125. *Issai-gi-jōju (sarvārtha-siddhi)* refers to the Karma Family.

126. T. 20.538c27–539a19.

127. T. 20.539a4–19.

An Annotated Translation of the
Pañcābhisaṃbodhi Practice of the Tattvasaṃgraha

1. See *Mikkyō Daijiten* (Kyoto: Hōzōkan, 1983), p. 613. The Chinese translation can be found in T. 18.284c, 1.20ff. and elsewhere.

2. The full title in Sanskrit is *Sarva-tathāgata-tattva-saṃgraha-nāma-mahāyāna-sūtra*. The Japanese name of this text, the *Kongōchōkyō*, is based on Amoghavajra's three-chüan translation of part 1, chapter 1, of the full text (T. vol. 18, no. 865, pp. 207–223). Of course, Kūkai never saw the Sanskrit text and instead introduced Amoghavajra's translation. Nevertheless, Amoghavajra's translation is very faithful to the Sanskrit text directly translated here. The *vidhi* (Jpn. *shidai*) which incorporated the

pañcābhisambodhi practice, in turn, are based on T. vol. 18, no. 873, also translated by Amoghavajra. The *Tattvasamgraha* is also considered the fundamental text of the Yoga Tantras in Tibet. It was translated by Śraddhakaravarman and Rin chen bzaṅ po (958–1055) in the early tenth century: *De bshin gŚegs pa thams cad kyi de kho na ñid bsdus pa shes bya ba theg pa chen poḥi mdo;* Peking edition, *Bkaḥ ṅgyur Mdo Ña* (IX), 1a1–162b2: Tibetan Tripiṭaka, no. 112, vol. 4, pp. 217–283.

3. See Yoshito S. Hakeda, tr., *Kūkai: Major Works* (New York: Columbia University Press, 1972), pp. 217–222.

4. *Shoe Kongōchōkyō Bonpon Sarva-tathāgata-tattva-samgraham nāma mahāyāna-sūtram,* 2 vols. (Kōyasan: Kōyasan Daigaku Mikkyō Bunka Kenkyujo, 1983), 1:15ff.; this corresponds to T. vol. 18, no. 865, p. 207ff.

5. *Tattvāloka,* Tohoku Catalogue, no. 2510.

6. *Kosalālamkara,* Tohoku Catalogue, no. 2503.

7. *Kongōchō daikyō ō kyō shiki,* T. vol. 61, no. 2225.

8. This translation and commentary were based in part on Dale Todaro, "An Annotated Translation of the *Tattvasamgraha* (Part 1) with an Explanation of the Role of the *Tattvasamgraha* Lineage in the Teachings of Kūkai" (Ph.D. diss., Columbia University, 1986). {See also, Rolf W. Giebel, tr., *Two Esoteric Sutras: The Adamantine Pinnacle Sutra, The Susiddhikara Sutra* (Berkeley: Numata Center for Buddhist Translation and Research, 2001).}

9. For the following section see also Shiro Sakai, "Gosōjōshinkan ni tsuite," *Studies of Esoteric Buddhism and Tantrism* (Mikkyōgaku Mikkyōshi Ronbunshu) (Kōyasan, 1965), pp. 397–409.

10. See F. D. Lessing and A. Wayman, *Introduction to the Buddhist Tantric Systems translated from Mkhas Grub Rje's Rgyud sde spyihi rnam par gzag pa rgyas par brjod with original text and annotation* (Delhi: Motilal Banarsidass, 1978), pp. 29–35.

11. The division of the five stages of religious practice by Donjaku are indicated. Ānandagarbha and Śākyamitra agree with Donjaku.

12. {Samantabhadra, Jpn. Fugen, is "the all-good one." He is often represented as holding a wish-fulfilling jewel (Skt. *cintāmaṇi,* Jpn. *nyoi shu, nyoi hōju*) in one hand and a lotus or book of dharma in the other, while riding on a white six-tusked elephant. Frequently paired with Mañjuśrī, the bodhisattva of wisdom, in a triad with Śākyamuni, Samantabhadra stands for the practice of one-pointed concentration (Skt. *samādhi,* Jpn. *sammai*). See Bernard Frank, *Le panthéon bouddhique au Japon—Collections d'Emile Guimet* (Paris: Musée National des Arts Asiatiques Guimet, 1991), pp. 125–127, and Marie-Thèrése de Mallman, *Introduction a l'iconographie du tântrisme bouddhique* (Paris: Librairie d'Amérique et d'Orient, Adrien Maisonneuve, 1986), pp. 331–335.}

13. T. vol. 77, no. 2426, p. 374a.

14. *Kōbō Daishi Zenshū,* 2:199–242 (hereafter KBZ).

15. KBZ, 4:497–531; or *Nihon Daizōkyō,* 51 vols. (Tokyo: Nihon Daizokyo Hensankai, 1914–21), 47:574–587 (hereafter NDK).

16. KBZ, 4:466–496.

17. NDK, 47:335–369.

18. *Kokuyaku Mikkyō, Jisō,* 16 vols. (Tokyo: Kokuyaku Mikkyō Kankakai, 1920–25), 4:13–48 (hereafter KM).

19. Available in Kozen's commentary, *Kongōkaisho, Shingonshū Zensho,* 24:63–204 (hereafter SZ).

20. SZ, 24:387–487.

21. NDK, vol. 36, *Mikkyōbu Shōso,* pp. 509–534; T. vol. 61, no. 2231.

22. T. vol. 78, no. 2504, pp. 895–909.

23. T. vol. 78, no. 2467, pp. 37–39.
24. KM, *Jisō*, 2:25–92.
25. T. vol. 78, no. 2474, p. 115.
26. T. vol. 18, no. 873. See note 2 above.
27. Donjaku, *Kongōkai shidai shiki*, SZ, 24:205a.
28. Raiyu, *Konkaihotsueshō*, T. vol. 79, no. 2533, p. 27b, 1.15.
29. Ibid., p. 98b.
30. In regards to this mudrā, the little, ring, and middle fingers of each hand folded together and facing upward express the six destinies of living beings. The two index fingers and thumbs with their tips touching express the fourfold dharmakāya which living beings must realize. Ibid., p. 98b, and T. 18.301c, 1.14.
31. *Buddhist Hybrid Sanskrit Grammar and Dictionary*, 2 vols., 3rd ed. (Delhi: Motilal Banarsidass, 1977), 2:111.
32. Cf. E. Sakano, *Kongōchōkyō ni Kansuru Kenkyū* (Tokyo: Kokusho Kankōkai, 1976), p. 112.
33. T. vol. 18, no. 882.
34. Lessing and Wayman, *Introduction to the Buddhist Tantric Systems*, p. 27. Cf. *Mahāvyutpatti, Bonzōkanwa shiyakutaikō honyaku myōgitaishū*, ed. Ryozoro Sakaki, 2 vols., 3rd ed. (Tokyo: Kokusho Kankōkai, 1981), 2:114, entry 1487; Unrai Wogiwara, comp., *Kanyakutaishō Bonwadaijiten* (Tokyo: Suzuki Research Foundation, 1979), p. 220; see esp. Kenryu Gachirin, "Āspharanaka ni tsuite," *Ryūkoku Daigaku Ronsō*, no. 302 (1932): 212–236.
35. T. vol. 61, no. 2223, p. 34a, 1.28ff.
36. On the background of Ennin's interpretation see Ryōshū Misaki, "Jikaku Daishi no Kongōchōkyōshō no ichimondai; toku ni āspharanaka samādhi to zengakudaijo ni tsuite," *Tendai Gakuhō*, no. 23 (1981): 31–36.
37. T. vol. 39, no. 1798, p. 812c, 1.18ff.
38. T. vol. 61, no. 2225, p. 199c, 1.13ff.
39. Ibid., p. 200a, 1.8ff.
40. Ibid., p. 198b, 1.14ff.
41. Ibid., p. 199a, 1.3.
42. Ibid., p. 199b, 1.1ff.
43. Saisen, T. vol. 78, no. 2474, pp. 106–107, 111b. For the outcome of the canonization of Shingon doctrines and attainments vis-à-vis the older Mahāyāna tradition, see Kiyota Minoru, *Shingon Buddhism: Theory and Practice* (Los Angeles: Buddhist Books International, 1978).
44. Ennin does not give any names. The *Bodaishinron* which Donjaku quotes gives the following: Tsūdatsushin, Bodaishin, Kongōshin (vajra heart), Kongōshin (vajra body), Shōmujōbodai. See T. vol. 32, no. 1665, p. 574b, 1.17ff.
45. T. vol. 32, no. 1665, p. 574b, 1.22; and 573c, 1.14ff.
46. T. vol. 61, no. 2225, p. 201a, 1.15–204b, 1.1.
47. T. vol. 32, no. 1665, p. 574b, 1.9ff.
48. {Jpn. *kangiji*, the first of the ten bodhisattva stages (Skt. *bhūmi*), called "the joyful," in which the bodhisattva perfects giving (Skt. *dāna pāramitā*, Jpn. *fuse haramitsu*), and draws others to the dharma.}
49. T. vol. 61, no. 2225, p. 204b, 1.2–205a, 1.9.
50. T. vol. 61, no. 2225, p. 205a, 1.10–205c, 1.17.
51. T. vol. 61, no. 2225, p. 205c, 1.18–207b, 1.21.
52. T. vol. 61, no. 2225, p. 207b, 1.22–208c, 1.1. Cf. KBZ, vol. 2, pp. 208–209. The terms for the *pañcābhisambodhi* given by Donjaku follow Kūkai's terminology.

53. The following information is taken from Taido Kitamura, "Tantrārthāvatāra o chūshin to shita Kongōchōkyō no Kenkyū (IV)," *Mikkyōgaku*, no. 10 (1973): 26–43. Many of the preliminary exercises Buddhaguhya describes, but which will not be discussed here, are also found in the *Vajradhātu* recitation manuals in Japan, i.e., the visualization of the letters *ma* and *ṭa* in the eyes, etc.

54. T. vol. 78, no. 2474.108c; NDK, vol. 36, p. 518

55. T. vol. 77, no. 2427, p. 374a.

56. T. vol. 78, no. 2474, p. 106bff.

57. NDK, vol. 47, pp. 570–573; pp. 370–381; T. vol. 78, no. 2467, pp. 37–39; NDK, vol. 47, pp. 568–569.

THE TWELVE-ARMED DEITY DAISHŌ KONGŌ AND HIS SCRIPTURAL SOURCES

1. The author would like to thank Mr. George Sipos of the University of Bucharest for his invitation to include this essay in the first issue of the *Romanian Journal of Japanese Studies*.

    The iconography of this deity was already the subject of a paper delivered by the present author to the Eighth Conference of the International Association of Buddhist Studies, Berkeley, August 1987. In the present study, however, the author will focus on the basic texts which describe the iconography and ritual of this deity. See also Robert Duquenne's essay, "Daishō Kongō," in *Hōbōgirin, Dictionnaire encyclopédique du bouddhisme d'après les sources chinoises et japonaises*, ed. Sylvain Lévi, Takakusu Junjirō, and Paul Demiéville (Paris: Librairie d'Amérique et d'Orient, Adrien-Maisonneuve: Maison Franco-Japonaise, 1929, ongoing) (hereafter Hōbōgirin). I wish to express my gratitude to Duquenne for providing me a copy of his manuscript prior to publication. Daishō Kongō is treated in the following Japanese lexica: Ryūken Sawa et al., eds., *Mikkyō jiten* (hereafter MJ), p. 465, s.v. "Daishō Kongō"; Mikkyō Jiten Hensankai, ed., *Mikkyō daijiten* (hereafter MD), pp. 885–886, s.v. "Daishō Kongō" (with an illustration of the deity and his maṇḍala); Shinkō Mochizuki, ed., *Bukkyō daijiten* (hereafter BDJ), 4:3265–3267, s.v. "Daishō Kongō" (with an illustration of the deity and his maṇḍala).

2. Drawings of Daishō Kongō are found in the iconographic and ritual handbooks contained in the iconographic section (Zuzō-bu) of the *Taishō Shinshū Daizōkyō* (hereafter TZ). Namely: Zuzōshō, TZ, vol. 3, no. 3006, fig. 36; Shinkaku (1117–80), *Bessonzakki*, TZ, vol. 3, no. 3007, figs. 124–127; Kakuzen (1143–1218), *Kakuzenshō*, TZ, vol. 4, no. 3022, fig. 59. Paintings of Daishō Kongō are very rare. See, for example, the painting of the red-colored Daishō Kongō stored in the Sanpōin (Kōyasan, Nanbokuchō period). For an illustration, see Kōyasan Reihōkan, ed., *Daijūyonkai Kōyasan daihōzōten: Kōyasan no Myōō-zō* (English title: *Special Exhibition: The Fourteenth Exhibition of the Treasury of Kōyasan. The Figures of Myōō (Vidyārājas) at Kōyasan*) (Kōyasan: Kōyasan Reihōkan, 1993), p. 84, pl. 53; p. 108.

3. The abbreviated Japanese title of *Vairocanābhisambodhi* is *Dainichikyō;* see T. vol. 18, no. 848. The *Tattvasaṃgraha* is usually called *Kongōchōkyō* in Japanese; three Chinese versions are T. vol. 18, nos. 865, 866, 882.

4. For an introduction to Shingon Buddhism, see Taikō Yamasaki, *Shingon: Japanese Esoteric Buddhism,* tr. Richard and Cynthia Peterson (Boston: Shambhala Publications, 1988).

5. Chikyō Yamamoto, *Introduction to the Maṇḍala* (Kōyasan, Japan: Dōhōsha, 1980), p. 45.

6. See Marie-Thérèse De Mallmann, *Introduction à l'iconographie du tantrisme boud-dhique* (Paris: Librairie Adrien-Maisonneuve, 1975), p. 438; see also Tadeusz Skorup-ski, tr., *The Sarvadurgatipariśodhana Tantra: Elimination of All Evil Destinies* (Delhi: Motilal Banarsidass, 1983), p. 89.

7. See De Mallmann, *Iconographie*, p. 438.

8. See below, note 47.

9. Daishō Kongō is treated in the following medieval Japanese iconographic and ritual texts:

Jichiun (1105–60), Shoson'yōshō, T. vol. 78, no. 2484, p. 300a–c.

Jichiun (1105–60), Hizōkonpōshō, T. vol. 78, no. 2485, pp. 363c–364a.

Shōken (1138–96), Hishō, T. vol. 78, no. 2489, pp. 542b–543a.

Seigen (1162–1231), Usuzōshi, T. vol. 78, no. 2495, p. 656a–b.

Raiyu (1226–1304), Hishōmondō, T. vol. 78, no. 2536, pp. 458b–460a.

Zuzōshō, TZ, vol. 3, no. 3006, pp. 18c–19b.

Shinkaku (1117–80), Bessonzakki, TZ, vol. 3, no. 3007, pp. 352c–360a.

Kōzen (1120–1203), Mandarashū, T. vol. 4, no. 3018, p. 163a.

Kakuzen (1143–1218), Kakuzenshō, TZ, vol. 4, no. 3022, pp. 561b–576c.

Ryōson (c. 1287), Byakuhōkushō, TZ, vol. 6, no. 3119, pp. 816a–822a.

Chōen (1218–?), Byakuhōshō, TZ, vol. 10, no. 3191, pp. 638a–647a.

See also the Japanese commentaries on the *Yugikyō* contained in Zoku Shingon-shū zensho kankōkai, ed., *Shigon-shu zensho* (hereafter SZ), vol. 5; and idem, *Zoku Shin-gon-shū zensho* (hereafter ZSZ), vol. 7. The *Kōbō Daishi zenshū* (The Complete Works of Kōbō Daishi, hereafter KDZ) contains two texts on the ritual of Daishō Kongō ascribed to Kūkai (774–835): *Issai Nyorai Daishō Kongōchō saishō shinjitsu sanmaya-bon shidai kannen*, KDZ, 2:587–604; and *Issai Nyorai Daishō Kongō shidai kannen*, KDZ, 2:605–610. These texts may possibly be fabrications with a spurious attribution to Kūkai. See Roger Goepper, *Aizen-Myōō: The Esoteric King of Lust: An Iconological Study*, Artibus Asiae Supplementum 39 (Zürich: Artibus Asiae, 1993), pp. 88–89. On these texts, see Tōru Shinbo, *Besson mandara* (Tokyo: Mainichi Shinbunsha, 1984), pp. 437–442; MD, p. 2206, s.v. "Yugikyō gyōbōki."

10. See BDJ, 4:3266, s.v. "Daishō Kongō." See also the entry on Jūnihi Dainichi in MD, pp. 885, s.v. "Jūnihi Dainichi."

11. See BDJ, 4:3266, s.v. "Daishō Kongō."

12. These deities, also called Butchōson, can appear in three, five, eight, nine, or ten groups. See MJ, pp. 605–607, s.v. "Butchōson"; MD, p. 1939, s.v. "Butchō"; Hōbōgirin, 2:148–150, s.v. "Bucchō"; De Mallmann, *Iconographie*, pp. 386–387; Adrian Snodgrass, *The Matrix and Diamond World Mandalas in Shingon Buddhism*, 2 vols., Sata-Pitakka Series, vol. 354 (Delhi: Aditya Prakashan, 1988), 1:344–355.

13. See MJ, p. 465, s.v. "Daishō Kongō." Aizen Myōō is an important deity in the Japan-ese Shingon school. The iconography and the ritual of this deity are also based on the *Yugikyō*, chap. 5. Since there is no Indian or Tibetan parallel of Aizen Myōō, the San-skrit term Rāgarāja is conjectural. This deity has been studied in great detail by Goep-per, *Aizen-Myōō*.

14. See MJ, p. 465, s.v. "Daishō Kongō."

15. See Hishō, T. vol. 78, no. 2489, p. 542b.

16. See Kakuzenshō, TZ, vol. 14, no. 3022, p. 561b.

17. See Bessonzakki, TZ, vol. 3, no. 3007.

18. See MD, p. 1472b, s.v. "Daisho Kongō."

19. The *Yugikyō* is treated in more detail in Pol Vanden Broucke, "On the Title and the Translator of the *Yugikyō* (T. XVIII no. 867)," *Kōyasan Daigaku Mikkyō Bunka*

Kenkyūjo kiyō (Bulletin of the Research Institute of Esoteric Buddhist Culture) 7 (1994): 184–212. The author has been working on an annotated English translation of the *Yugikyō*, which he hopes to publish in the near future.

20. See MJ, pp. 225–226, s.v. "Gobu no hikyō"; Vanden Broucke, "Title and Translator," pp. 211–212.

21. See MJ, p. 244, s.v. "Kongōbuji"; MD, p. 720, s.v. "Kongōbuji"; Seckel 1985, pp. 83, 185, 258.

22. This interpretation of the *Yugikyō* is treated in Ihara, 1984.

23. See MJ, p. 690, s.v. "Yugitō"; MD, pp. 2209–2210, s.v. "Yugitō"; BDJ, 5:4925, s.v. "Yugitō" (and illustration). See Pol Vanden Broucke, "The Yugitō," *Oriens Extremus* 42 (2000/2001): 105–167.

24. For the "Non-duality of the Two Sections" and the two maṇḍalas, see Snodgrass, *Matrix and Diamond*, 1:124–130; Yamasaki, *Shingon*, pp. 128–140; Minoru Kiyota, *Shingon Buddhism: Theory and Practice* (Los Angeles: Buddhist Books International, 1978), pp. 83–104; Yoshito S. Hakeda, *Kūkai: Major Works* (New York: Columbia University Press, 1972), pp. 85–86.

25. See note 20 above.

26. See MD, p. 1558, s.v. "Tachikawa-ryū."

27. The question of the authorship of the *Yugikyō* is treated thoroughly in Vanden Broucke, "Title and Translator," pp. 200–208. See also Goepper, *Aizen Myōō*, pp. 10, 87; Hirohiko Katsuzaki et al., eds., *Daijō kyōten kaisetsu jiten* (hereafter DKKJ), pp. 393–394.

28. See *Taishō shinshū daizōkyō hōbō sōmoluroku*, vol. 2, no. 25, p. 212b27–28; for this catalogue, see Kōgen Mizuno, *Buddhist Sutras: Origin, Development, Transmission* (Tokyo: Kōsei Publishing, 1982), pp. 175–176, 189.

29. The standard commentaries on the *Yugikyō* can be found in SZ, vol. 5; and ZSZ, vol. 7. See also the commentaries mentioned in the entry on the *Yugikyō* in MD, p. 723, s.v. "Kongōbu rōkaku issai yugayugi kyō."

30. See chapter 5 of the *Yugikyō*.

31. This manuscript is stored in the library (Sanmitsuzō) of the Hōbodaiin (Tōji) in Kyōto. The printed text of this manuscript is included in T. vol. 19, no. 980. For Shinson (n.d.), see MD, pp. 1292–1293, s.v. "Shinson."

32. I have not yet found any reference to this text in the Japanese iconographic and ritual sources mentioned above, note 9.

33. David Snellgrove, tr., *The Hevajra Tantra: A Critical Study*, 2 vols., London Oriental Series, vol. 6 (1959; repr., London: Oxford University Press, 1971), 1:137–138, explains the Sanskrit term *samaya* (Jpn. *sanmaya*) as follows: "The basic meaning is that of 'coming together' in the literal sense of 'concurrence.' In tantric practice it refers to the 'concurrence' of absolute being and phenomenal forms, by means of which the practiser may experience that which by its very nature would otherwise have no means of experiencing. The maṇḍala and the different forms of the divinities are means of just such a kind. In this sense we may translate samaya as 'conventional form,' observing that 'convention' has also the literal meaning of 'coming together.'" See also David Snellgrove, *Indo-Tibetan Buddhism: Indian Buddhists and Their Tibetan Successors* (London: Serindia, 1987; Boston: Shambhala Publications, 2002), pp. 165–166. For the Sino-Japanese interpretations of samaya, see Ian Astley-Kristensen, *The Rishukyō: The Sino-Japanese Tantric Prajñāpāramitā in 150 Verses* (Amoghavajra's Version), Buddhica Britannica Series Continua 3 (Tring, England: Institute of Buddhist Studies, 1991), pp. 47–48.

34. This chapter opens with the manifestation of Daishō Kongō by Vairocana.

35. Also known as Vajrasattva. The first in the series of the sixteen great bodhisattvas (Jpn. *jūrokudaibosatsu*). These sixteen deities comprise the five buddhas of the Kongōkai, the "shi haramitsu bosatsu" (the four pāramitā bodhisattvas), the "hachi kuyō bosatsu" (the eight pūjā bodhisattvas), and the "shishō bosatsu" (the four saṃgraha bodhisattvas), the so-called thirty-seven deities (Jpn. *sanjūshichison*) of the central assembly of the Kongōkai mandara. See Snodgrass, *Matrix and Diamond,* 2:590–633.

36. Vairocana manifests the twelve-armed deity Daishō Kongō.

37. Jpn. Chiken-in, the mudrā of Vairocana in the Vajra Realm. On this hand-gesture, see E. Dale Saunders, *Mudrā: A Study of Symbolic Gestures in Japanese Buddhist Sculpture,* Bollingen Series 58 (1960; repr., Princeton: Princeton University Press, 1985), pp. 102–107; 102, fig. 31.

38. For this attribute, see ibid., pp. 184–191.

39. An attribute formed by crossing two vajra. Ibid., pp. 187–188.

40. The bell and the vajra are the two attributes of Vajrasattva. Also Aizen Myōō is equipped with these emblems. Concerning the connection between Daishō Kongō, Aizen Myōō, and Vajrasattva mentioned above, see note 14.

41. Symbolizes the victory of Knowledge. See Saunders, *Mudrā,* pp. 182–183.

42. Skt. *dharmacakra,* Jpn. *hōrin.*

43. The Sino-Japanese term *in* refers not only to the symbolic gestures of the hands (Skt. *mudrā*) but also to the attributes carried by divinities. See Saunders, *Mudrā,* p. 9. The number twelve stands for the two hands which form the knowledge fist, and the remaining ten hands which hold the five-pronged vajra, the lotus, etc. The Japanese commentaries correlate ten of the twelve hands with the thirty-seven deities of the Kongōkai mandara. The sword is explained as the symbol of Mañjuśrī. The wheel is seen as the symbol of Maitreya. Mañjuśrī and Maitreya are furthermore correlated with respectively the Kongōkai and the Taizō. According to the commentators, the presence of the sword and the wheel also symbolizes the idea of the "Nonduality of the Two Sections." For the esoteric meaning of the hands of Daishō Kongō see, for example, Yūgi, *Yugikyō hidenshō* (hereafter YHD), in ZSZ, pp. 208b–209a. According to another interpretation the twelve hands correspond with the twelve chapters of the *Yugikyō,* see above note 16.

44. Skt. *pañcacudaka.* The hair tied in five topknots: in the front, back, left, right, and center of the head. Compare with the hairstyle of Gokei Monju, Mañjuśrī with the Five Chignons.

45. The four cardinal points, the four intermediate directions, and the nadir and zenith.

46. "Oṃ, O Great Vajra Crown, hūṃ traḥ (= trāḥ?) hrīḥ aḥ hūṃ." This is the formula of Daishō Kongō. Hūṃ, traḥ (= trāḥ?), hrīḥ, aḥ, and hūṃ correspond with the seed-syllables *(bīja,* Jpn. *shuji)* of respectively Akṣobhya, Ratnasambhava, Amitāyus, and Amoghasiddhi, the four buddhas surrounding Vairocana in the central assembly of the Kongōkai mandara. The Japanese commentaries translate Mahāvajroṣṇīṣa as Daishō Kongōchō, "Great Victorious Vajra Crown"; see, for example, Yūgi, YHD (in ZSZ, 7:209). In Japan the deity described in this text is known as Daishō Kongō. However, judging from the title of this chapter ("Great Victorious Vajra Crown") and the appellation of this formula ("the formula of the great samaya of the highest truth of the Great Victorious Vajra Crown"), it seems that Daishō Kongō is an abbreviation. In the next text we will see that the twelve-armed deity is referred to as Daishō Kongō Butchō ("Great Victorious Adamantine Buddha Crown"; see T. vol. 19, no. 980, p. 410b22) and Daishō Butchō ("Great Victorious Buddha Crown"; see p. 410c1). It is highly probable that Daishō Kongō's name in full is Daishō Kongōchō or Daishō Kongō Butchō. According to the Byakuhōkushō (T. vol. 6, no. 3119, p. 816a) compiled by Ryōson (c.

1287), the Sino-Japanese name is Daishō Kongōchō and the Sanskrit appellation Mahājayavajroṣnīṣa ("Great Victorious Vajra Crown"). It is interesting to note that Ryōson writes the Indian version of this name in siddham syllables.

47. Jpn. *myō*, Skt. *vidyā*. An alternative term for mantra, formula.

48. "Verses." In the first six verses the effect of reciting this formula is explained.

49. The buddha-fields (Jpn. *bukkokudo*, Skt. *buddhakṣetra*) in the ten directions. See Yūgi, YHD (in ZSZ, 7:209).

50. Past, present, and future.

51. The three realms in the world of transmigration: Skt. *kāmadhātu, rūpadhātu,* and *ārūpyadhātu*; Jpn. *yokkai, shikikai,* and *mushikikai.*

52. I.e., he surpasses all buddhoṣnīṣas.

53. Avalokiteśvara and Vajrapāni, see Yūgi, YHD (in ZSZ, p. 210).

54. The body hard and indestructible like a diamond. See MD, p. 700, s.v. "kongōshin."

55. Vairocana.

56. In the next seven verses the mudrā of Daishō Kongō and the merits of this hand-gesture are explained.

57. The ten pāramitās, one of the symbolic appellations used for the ten fingers. For the symbolism and the terminology of the hands and fingers in Sino-Japanese esoteric Buddhism, see Saunders, *Mudrā,* pp. 30–34; Robert H. Van Gulik, *Hayagrīva: The Mantrayānic Aspect of Horse Cult in China and Japan* (Leiden: E. J. Brill, 1935), pp. 51–52.

58. I.e., clasping the hands, palm to palm, with the ten fingers joined with the tips on the inside. See Saunders, *Mudrā,* p. 40.

59. Jpn. *chō* means "top of the head," "crown," "summit." The patience and the vow are special appellations for respectively the left and right middle finger. For this system of symbolic names for the fingers, see Saunders, *Mudrā,* pp. 30–34.

60. Shōshin, *Yugi hiyōketsu* (hereafter YHK), in SZ, 5:276, explains shin as shin'yō, "essence, core, kernel."

61. For a figure of this mudrā, see MD, app., p. 45, no. 103. The two middle fingers are considered to symbolize the knowledge sword. The other eight fingers are said to represent the eight spokes of the wheel of the dharma. The sword and the wheel are associated with respectively Mañjuśrī and Maitreya. Mañjuśrī and Maitreya are furthermore correlated with Knowledge (chi) and Principle (ri). Hence this mudrā is considered to symbolize the Shingon concept of the nonduality of knowledge and principle *(richi funi).* See MD, p. 753, s.v. "Saishōtenrin-in"; Shōshin YHK (in SZ, 5:277).

62. I.e., vajrakula.

63. I.e., padmakula.

64. I.e., ratnakula.

65. I.e., karmakula.

66. According to the commentaries vajra and the below-mentioned beam of light, lotus, karma, and the Universally Shining One are considered to represent respectively the vajra-, ratna-, padma-, karma-, and buddhakula, the five sections of the vajra realm. See for example Dōhan, *Yugikyō kuketsu* (hereafter YKK), in SZ, vol. 83.

67. Jpn. *rishu,* Skt. *naya.*

68. Raiyu interprets this passage as follows: "If one relies on the power of the mudrā and the formula, then that which is touched (= unclean) will become a pure abode." See Raiyu, *Yugikyō shūkoshō* (hereafter YKSK), in Suzuki Gakujutsu Zaidan, ed., *Nihon daizōkyō* (hereafter ND), 33:47.

69. Here follow four formulae correlated with the four buddhas surrounding Vairocana in the Kongōkai mandara.

70. "Oṃ, O Vajrasattva-Storehouse, hūṃ." Hūṃ is the seed-syllable of Akṣobhya. In the Chinese text -sattva is written -satva.

71. "Oṃ, O Vajra-Jewel-Storehouse, trah (= trāḥ?)." Trāḥ is the seed-syllable of Ratna-sambhava.

72. "Oṃ, O Vajra-Dharma-Storehouse, hrīḥ." Hrīḥ is the seed-syllable of Amitāyus.

73. "Oṃ, O Vajra-Action-Storehouse, aḥ." Aḥ is the seed-syllable of Amoghasiddhi.

74. The next four formulae clearly represent the four samgraha bodhisattvas. Each formula is concluded by one of the four seed-syllables which represent these four bodhisattvas.

75. "Oṃ, O Vajrasattva-Hook, jjaḥ."

76. "Oṃ, O Vajra-Jewel-Rope, hūṃ."

77. "Oṃ, O Vajra-Lotus-Chain, vaṃ." sphota = -sphut?

78. "Oṃ, O Vajra-Action-Bell, hoḥ." –gaṃt = -ghaṇṭa? The bodhisattva Vajraghaṇṭa is also known as Vajrāveśa.

79. The eight preceding formulae.

80. According to Yūgi, YHD (in ZSZ, 7:213), the karma assembly of the vajra realm.

81. "Oṃ, O Vajrasattva-Sharpness, hūṃ."

82. Jpn. Myōkichijō katsusanmaya. The monju-in, the mudrā of Mañjuśrī, according to Yūgi, YHD (in ZSZ, p. 213b) and other commentators. See MD, app., p. 63, fig. 347.

83. Vajracakra, "vajra-wheel," is according to Yūgi, YHD (in ZSZ, p. 214), a secret name for Tenbōrin. See also MD, p. 732, s.v. "Kongōrinjikongō bosatsu." This is the mantra of Mandara Bosatsu (Skt. Mahācakra). This deity is sometimes identified with Ten-bōrinbosatsu. Tenbōrinbosatsu is also said to equate with the bodhisattva Maitreya. See MD, p. 762, s.v. "Zaihosshintenbōrinbosatsu"; p. 2097, s.v. "Mandarabosatsu"; Snodgrass, Matrix and Diamond, 1:443–444.

84. I.e., two hands.

85. The mother sign of the karma-mudrā explained in the Kongōchōkyō. See Saunders, Mudrā, pp. 38–39; 39, fig. 2; MD, p. 677, s.v. "kongōken."

86. According to Yūgi, YHD (in ZSZ, 7:214), the shōkongōrin-in, "small vajra-wheel-mudrā." For a figure, see MD, app., p. 63, fig. 358. On this mudrā, see MD, p. 1147, s.v. "shōkongōrin." According to MD, p. 2097, s.v. "Mandara bosatsu," the mudrā of Mandara bosatsu (Skt. Mahācakra).

87. The body will become a living maṇḍala, see Raiyu, YKSK (in ND, 33:49); Yūgi, YHD (in ZSZ, p. 214).

88. Compare above, note 75.

89. "Oṃ, O All Tathāgata-Hook, hūṃ jjaḥ."

90. "Oṃ, O All Tathāgata-Rope, hūṃ hūṃ."

91. "Oṃ, O All Tathāgata-Chain, hūṃ vaṃ."

92. "Oṃ, O All Tathāgata-Entering, hūṃ hoḥ."

93. The realization of the Kongōkai mandara in one's own body?

94. The formula of Daishō Kongō.

95. "Oṃ, O All Offerings, jaḥ hūṃ vaṃ hoḥ."

96. Compare with the five buddhas of the vajra realm. The Daishō Kongō mandara is set forth here. On this maṇḍala, see MD, p. 1473, s.v. "Daishō Kongō mandara" (and figure); BDJ, 4:3265–3267, s.v. "Daisho Kongo"; Shinbo, 1985, figs. 52–57. See also the entry on Daishō Kongō by Robert Duquenne in Hōbōgirin. According to MD this maṇḍala is used for visualization, not for initiation (Skt. abhiṣeka, Jpn. kanjō).

97. Daishō Kongō in the center of the maṇḍala. According to Dōhan, YKK (in SZ, 5:59), Daishō Kongō is called Universally Shining Lord because he is Vairocana of the vajra realm.

98. I.e., the body of the practitioner is equal to the central deity. According to Annen, *Kongōbu rōkaku issai yugayugi kyō shugyōhō* (T. vol. 61, no. 2228, p. 491c9), the own body is the maṇḍala in which the thirty-seven deities are created.

99. Jpn. Shōkongōhō. The Japanese commentaries correlate this and the next three deities with the four Buddhas surrounding Vairocana in the central assembly of the Kongōkai mandara. See, for example, Shōshin, YHK (in SZ, pp. 290–291). We have not yet found any Indian counterpart for the deities described in the maṇḍala of Daishō Kongō. Maybe we have to consider them as creations that grew out of speculation and inspired by teachings of the texts belonging to the Tattvasaṃgraha lineage.

100. Jpn. Kongōrengekō.

101. Jpn. Kongōhōdaiko.

102. Jpn. Kongōdaizenren.

103. SS and SD omit myō, "wondrous."

104. I.e., formulae. Cf. Skt. *vidyā*.

105. Most probably the mudrā of Daishō Kongō. Cf. above, stanza 14, line 1.

106. "Incense" and "flower" are the pūjā bodhisattvas Vajradhūpā and Vajrapuṣpā. According to the Japanese commentaries one only needs the above eight formulae to realize perfection, and it is not necessary to make use of the summoning hand-gestures or formulae of the pūjā bodhisattvas. See, for example, Shōshin, YHK (in SZ, 5:291); Raiyu, YKSK (in ND, 33:50).

107. Compare Skt. *vajradhara*. According to Snellgrove, *Hevajra Tantra*, 1:140, this is also the title of supreme buddhahood. According to MD, p. 922, s.v. "Jikongō," the Sino-Japanese translations of Vajradhara are Jikongō and Shūkongō. According to this lexicon this term is also used to designate all the deities of the "sanbu" ("three families") and the "gobu" ("five families"), respectively the Taizō and Kongōkai.

108. Jpn. Daishō Kongō Butchō. Cf. supra, note 47.

109. According to Nakamura Hajime, ed., *Bukkyōgo daijiten* (hereafter BD), p. 363a, s.v. "goshikikō": blue, yellow, red, white, and black.

110. Jpn. *myōō*, Skt. *vidyārāja*. Another term for formula. See MD, p. 2112, s.v. "myōō." Myōō also refers to a group of deities who are the embodiment of esoteric Buddhist formulae.

111. Kongōshi. According to BD, p. 419, s.v. "kongōshi," the abbreviation of kongōbusshi "adamantine Buddha-son." According to this lexicon the term is applied to a person who has received abhiṣeka; see p. 421, s.v. "kongōbusshi." According to MD, p. 690, s.v. "kongōshi," it refers to a disciple who has entered into the Kongōkai mandara and who has received abhiṣeka.

112. The terms Kongō and Taizō refer to the Kongōkai mandara and the Taizō mandara. These two maṇḍalas are based on the teachings of the Dainichikyō and the Kongōchōkyō. These two basic canonical sources of Shingon came into existence in India at different times and in different regions. (For the origin of these two texts, see Hakeda, *Kūkai*, pp. 19–24.) We have seen that the doctrines of these two scriptures are integrated in the Japanese Shingon school (see above, "Ryōbu Funi"). We do not know for certain whether the teachings of these two texts were already combined in India. It remains also unclear whether the notion of the nonduality of the two sections originated in China or whether it is to be attributed to Kūkai. The fact that the terms Kongō and Taizō appear side by side may be an important indication that this text may have been composed directly in Chinese, perhaps after the model of the *Yugikyō*. As a matter of fact, the *Yugikyō* also contains elements which may be associated with the Dainichikyō and the Kongōchōkyō. See Vanden Broucke, "Title and the Translator," pp. 198–199n6.

113. The maṇḍala described here is different from the one explained in chapter 8 of the *Yugikyō*. As far as we know there is no painting or drawing of this maṇḍala in China or Japan.

114. Corresponding roughly to the zodiacal sign of Scorpio.

115. Daishō Myōō. Daishō Kongō is called here a vidyārāja. Daishō Kongō does, however, not belong to the series of *mikkyō* deities called Myōō.

116. A crown carrying the five buddhas. This attribute is worn by Vairocana, Vajrasattva, Maitreya, and others. See MD, pp. 621–622, s.v. "gochihōkan."

117. Jpn. Fudō Kongō, that is, Fudō Myōō.

118. Jpn. Batō Kongō, that is, Batō Kannon.

119. Jpn. Rokusoku Kongō, that is, Daiitoku Myōō. Skt. Yamāntaka.

120. Jpn. Yasha Kongō, that is, Kongōyasha. Skt. Vajrayaksa.

121. Jpn. Happō Tennō. A series of eight celestial kings who guard the eight directions. See MD, p. 1816, s.v. "Happōten."

122. See MD, p. 1815, s.v. "Hachibutchō"; Snodgrass, *Matrix and Diamond*, 1:344–355.

123. Jpn. Kongōdōji, Skt. Vajrakumāra.

124. The buddha, the dharma, and the sangha.

125. The six migratory realms, i.e., hell, the worlds of hungry spirits, animals, asuras, men, and heavenly beings.

126. Enlightenment.

127. Jpn. Ususama Kongō, that is, Ususama Myōō.

128. Jpn. *gosho kaji*. Empowering (Jpn. *kaji*, Skt. *adhisthāna*) five places on the body by touching with the mudrā. Usually the brow, the right and left shoulder, the heart, and the throat. See MD, pp. 608–609, s.v. "goshokaji."

129. "Oṃ, O the Wrathful, hūṃ jaḥ." The seed-syllables hūṃ and jaḥ correspond with the seed-syllables of Ususama Myōō. See MJ, p. 40, s.v. "Ususama Myōō." For this formula, see Yukio Hatta, *Shingon jiten* (Tokyo: Heika Shuppansha, 1985), p. 31, no. 159.

130. See above, note 32.

131. TZ, vol. 4, p. 569a28–b6.

132. No entry on this monk in MD.

133. In the Kakuzenshō this passage is preceded by a short description of the ritual of Daishō Kongō.

134. Fujiwara Tadamichi (1097–1164) became kanpaku in 1121 and yielded the title in 1158. See Mitsunaga Takayanagi, ed., *Nihonshi jiten*, p. 1027.

135. I.e., daijō daijin.

136. See ZSZ, 7.121b.

137. During the reign of Emperor Juntoku (r. 1210–21).

138. The empress. Another example of the ritual of Daishō Kongō performed for the easy childbirth of the chūgū is mentioned in the Byakuhōshō, TZ, vol. 10, no. 3191, p. 638a2. This ritual was performed in Kenkyū 6 (1195).

139. See ZSZ, 7:120b.

140. See SZ, 33:207b.

141. See MD, p. 1664, s.v. "Dōchō."

142. See MD, p. 132, s.v. "Unjo."

143. See MD, pp. 1137–1138, s.v. "Shōken."

144. Kazuaki, p. 27.

145. We have not yet been able to examine this in more detail.

146. Kengyō Tsukamoto, ed., *Kokuyaku mikkyō: Jisō-bu* (Tokyo: Kokusho Kankōkai, 1976), 2:335n2. The Usuzōshi is mentioned above, note 6.

BREATH OF LIFE: THE ESOTERIC NEMBUTSU

1. Kushida Ryōkō, *Shingon mikkyō seiritsu katei no kenkyū* (Tokyo: Sankibo, 1965), p. 229. I have drawn on Kushida for a number of the quotations herein, as well as incorporating a considerable part of his historical analysis.

   Makashikan is the Japanese reading for *Mo-ho chih-kuan*, a text by Chih-i, founder of T'ien T'ai (Tendai) Buddhism, but here Hōnen intends the term as a synonym for the whole of the Tendai tradition. The *Ōjō yōshū* by Genshin (942–1017) is an early text of Japanese Pure Land Buddhism. Shan Tao was the last, and most important, of the major Pure Land thinkers in China. His writings provided a point of departure for the views of Hōnen, the "founder" of Japanese Pure Land thought.

2. I use the Japanese form, "Amida" (Skt. Amitābha/Amitāyus), since the Pure Land tradition was largely limited to China and Japan. Other divinity names are usually given in their Sanskrit versions.

3. Recitation of the *nembutsu* is the core practice of the Japanese Pure Land tradition (some schools make it the sole practice). The most usual version of the *nembutsu* is "Namu Amida Butsu" (Hail the Buddha Amida), and its most general interpretation is as a call on the Buddha Amida's name (*nen-*, "call"; *-butsu*, "Buddha") in hope of attaining rebirth in his Pure Land. In the earliest Pure Land texts, *nembutsu* usually meant "to remember the Buddha," the sense of *nen* as "to call aloud" only developing later. In tantric contexts *nen* often means to visualize or to make real ("evoke" in a fundamentally magical sense), and the compound *nem-butsu*, since it does not explicitly refer to Amida, can be taken to mean the realization of any Buddha. The word *nen* can also translate the Sanskrit term *kṣaṇa*, "an instant." In some Buddhist contexts this meaning suggests the transformative moment of enlightenment.

4. *Himitsu nembutsu* literally means "secret *nembutsu*." The tradition is also called Shingon *nembutsu*. Ordinarily this is taken to mean *nembutsu* of the Shingon school, but it can also be construed as something like *"dhāraṇī nembutsu,"* since *shingon* (lit., "real word") translates *dhāraṇī* and *mantra*.

5. The term "normative Pure Land" is a somewhat artificial construct. By it I mean to signify a generalized version of the received understanding of Japanese Pure Land. It is close to but not identical with the teachings of the Shinshū School. Kakuban actually predated many of its developments; Dōhan (1178–1252) and later *himitsu nembutsu* proponents reacted against it. Some Japanese Pure Land groups such as the Seizan-ha and the Ji-shū held views that were fairly close to the *himitsu nembutsu* position.

6. It should also be understood as a place where one undergoes purification.

7. The term *ōjō* consists of *ō-*, "to go," and *-jō*, "to be born." It is the standard technical term for rebirth in the Pure Land. Often it seems to act as a substitute for the conventional term for the attainment of Buddhahood, *jōbutsu*. To indicate its sectarian and technical character, I have left *ōjō* untranslated.

8. *Bodhicitta* (Jpn. *bodai-shin*) is the innate essence within mortal beings which allows them to attain (or manifest) enlightenment.

9. Meditation on the syllable "A" goes back to the roots of Shingon. The reasons for this syllable's special power are slightly complex. As the first letter of the Sanskrit syllabary, "A" symbolizes all beginnings. Since a- is also a privative prefix in Sanskrit, "A" also symbolizes all endings. That which coalesces all beginnings and endings also coheres all medial process as well. "A" is thus the Alpha, the Omega, and all in between. Additionally, *A-ji* (lit., "the character A") is, for phonetic reasons peculiar to the Japanese language, used as a transliteration of *adi-*, "primordial." finally, in its full *bīja* form, "Am," "A" is the germ of the Garbhadhātu *maṇḍala*. For a series of Shingon texts on

A-ji kan, see Taikō Yamasaki, *Shingon: Japanese Esoteric Buddhism* (Boston: Shambhala Publications, 1988), pp. 190–215.

10. Shingon's assertion of its superiority over exoteric Buddhism *(kengyō)* is based in no small part on its claim to bring salvation in a single lifetime. The most important formulation of this central tenet of Shingon is *sokushin jōbutsu,* or "buddhahood in this very body," with "body" construed to mean lifetime. The major source for this doctrine is Kūkai's *Sokushin jōbutsu gi.* There are several variants of this text. In some of them *sokushin jōbutsu* is divided into three subvarieties: *rigu sokushin jōbutsu,* as an innate quality of all beings; *kaji sokushin jōbutsu,* a rather dualistic, acquisitional form; and *kentoku sokushin jōbutsu,* a rapidly manifested form of bodily enlightenment. For more on the three kinds of *sokushin jōbutsu,* see James H. Sanford, "Wind, Waters, Stūpas, Maṇḍalas: Fetal Buddhahood in Shingon," *Japanese Journal of Religious Studies* 24, nos. 1–2 (spring 1997): 11–12.

11. *Mikkyō* (lit., "secret teachings") is the standard Japanese term for esoteric Buddhism. It usually includes all of Shingon and the esoteric wing of Tendai (called by itself Taimitsu), but one can also speak of mikkyō-ized aspects of other sects and movements.

12. Sawa Ryuken, ed., *Mikkyō jiten* (Kyoto: Hōzōkan, 1975), p. 199.

13. The *Kan muryōju kyō* is one of the three constitutive texts of the Japanese Pure Land tradition. Its title is often abbreviated to *Kan gyō.*

14. For Kakukai see Robert E. Morrell, *Early Kamakura Buddhism: A Minority Report* (Berkeley: Asian Humanities Press, 1987), pp. 89–102.

15. Miyasaka Yūshō, "Heian jidai kara Edo jidai made," in *Mikkyō no rekishi,* ed. Miyasaka Yūshō et al. (Tokyo: Shunjusha, 1977), 2:205. Miyasaka is quoting Myōhen's *Nembutsu hōgo.*

16. The twin *maṇḍalas* of Shingon represent an apparent duality that is, in fact, a unity (or better, a nonduality). The Vajradhātu *maṇḍala* (Kongō-kai) represents Vairocana's mind and the noumenal aspect of *nirvāṇa.* The Garbhadhātu *maṇḍala* (Taizō-kai) represents Vairocana's body, the phenomenal universe. Thus the physical universe infused with *nirvāṇic* awareness is an organism which, like other living organisms, consists of an inseparably fused mind and body. The sexual symbolism of *vajra* (phallus) and *garbha* (womb) signals this same unity of opposites in a more typically tantric fashion.

17. Omori Shōjō, ed., *Kōgyō Daishi zenshū* (Tokyo: Kaji Sekkai Shisha, 1909), p. 61.

18. Ibid., p. 158.

19. Ibid., p. 58.

20. The three secrets are central to Shingon's ritual procedure for eliciting noumenal reality in the apparently phenomenal world. They consist of secrets of body, *mudrās;* secrets of speech, mantric invocations; and secrets of mind, meditation, visualization, and the like.

21. *Ichimitsu jōbutsu* has some resonance with Jitsuhan's phrase *Butsugō soku shingon,* "the Buddha-name is, indeed, a *shingon* [i.e., dhāraṇī or mantra]."

22. "A-hūṃ" is vocalized "a-un" in Japanese. Tachikawa-ryū texts commonly use this double mantra to support their contention that Buddhist enlightenment and sexual ecstasy are of one substance, "a" and "un" being understood as the innate cries of lovemaking. Other of Kakuban's texts posit not "a-hūṃ" for in-breath and out-breath, but "A-A."

23. The development of a consubstantial identity between adept and divinity is called *nyūga ga'nyū,* "the Buddha entering the self; the self entering the Buddha." It is a central aspect of the Shingon procedure of self-realization.

24. Omori, *Kōgyō Daishi zenshū,* p. 538. Three texts called *A-ji kan* are attributed to Kakuban. The other two are a poetic version and a prose text, both written in classical Chinese.

25. Kushida, *Shingon mikkyō,* p. 204, cites this passage as being from the *Aji-kan shaku,* but I have been unable to find it in any of Kakuban's standard *A ji* texts.

26. I am not certain how the Sanskrit *namas* came to be translated by the characters *ki-* ("return") and *-myō* ("life"). *Namas* is sometimes transliterated with the characters *nan-* ("south") and *-mu* ("not"). This too allows for an immanental construal of the Pure Land, since the *nembutsu*, Namu Amida Butsu, itself thus states that "the Buddha Amida is not in the West," inasmuch as each cardinal direction includes every point of the compass.

27. The term *naishō* literally means "inner proof." Though not limited to Shingon, it is a very characteristic usage. The physical connotations of "inner" are in close harmony with the embodied character of "bodily buddhahood."

28. Mahāyāna Buddhism has several versions of the *trikāya* or three bodies of the buddha doctrine. Generally, *nirmāṇakāya* refers to a historical buddha in human form, the *dharmakāya* to the buddha as absolute reality, and the *samboghakāya* to a medial composite that manifests form but is noumenal in essence.

29. Omori, *Kōgyō Daishi zenshū*, p. 227.

30. As Shingon and Pure Land are "desyncretized" by Dōhan and later Shingon figures, so too were Zen and esotericism, after a period of easy accommodation, desyncretized. See, for example, Gobō's (1306–62) *Kaishin shō*, which opens with a denial of "the Mikkyō nature" of Bodhidharma.

31. The authenticity of the *Ihon* variant of the *Sokushin jōbutsu gi* is doubted by modern scholarship. But if it is a forgery, it is one of such early date that its importance to the development of Shingon thought cannot be ignored. For the three forms of *sokushin jōbutsu* see note 10, above.

32. Cited in Kushida, *Shingon mikkyō*, pp. 217–218.

33. Mibu Taishun and Miyasaki Yūshō, eds., *Tendai Shingon* (Tokyo: Shunjūsha, 1971), pp. 249–250.

34. See Allan G. Grapard, "*Keiranshūyōshū:* A Different Perspective on Mt. Hiei in the Medieval Period" in *Re-Visioning "Kamakura" Buddhism*, ed. Richard K. Payne, Kuroda Institute Studies in East Asian Buddhism, no. 11 (Honolulu: University of Hawai'i Press, 1998), pp. 55–69.

35. Kushida, *Shingon mikkyō*, p. 220.

36. Dōhan either fails to recognize or deliberately ignores the phallic symbolism that underlies the "*vajra* as root of life" usage.

37. Kushida, *Shingon mikkyō*, pp. 220–221.

38. Ibid., p. 221.

39. The common Anuttara yoga tantra usage of "bodhicitta" as a cover-term for semen should perhaps be kept in mind in this context.

40. James H. Sanford, *Zen-Man Ikkyū* (Chico, Calif.: Scholars Press, 1981), pp. 216–229.

41. Ibid., p. 220.

42. Ibid., p. 221.

43. Ibid., p. 227.

44. Philip B. Yampolsky, *The Zen Master Hakuin* (New York: Columbia University Press, 1971), pp. 128–129.

45. Kushida, *Shingon mikkyō*, pp. 222–223.

46. Furuta Shōkin, "Jōdo Shinshū ni okeru Hiji Hōmon no mondai," in *Studies of Esoteric Buddhism and Tantrism*, ed. Nakano Gishō (Kōyasan: Kōyasan University, 1965), p. 162. For further aspects of Pure Land "heresies" in the medieval period, see James C. Dobbins, *Jōdo Shinsū: Shin Buddhism in Medieval Japan*, 1989 (Honolulu: University of Hawai'i Press, 2002).

47. In tantric contexts the red and the white ordinarily stand for female blood and male semen. The place of their union is the womb. This entire passage could be read as an encoded treatment of sexual yoga.

48. Terms like "in a single thought" are found in Tachikawa texts to refer to the nondual unity of male and female orgasm.
49. *Kon* and *haku* in Japanese. Later Chinese thought held that the *p'o* faded away at death while the *hun* might survive as a sort of afterlife carrier of the personality.
50. I think the unity of sun and moon here reflects a Hiji Hōmon theory in which Vairocana is the sun and Amida the moon. In esoteric theories of gestation, sun and moon can also encode early stages of fetal development. See Sanford, "Wind, Waters, Stūpas, Maṇḍalas," pp. 14–15.
51. Furuta Shōkin, *Furuta Shōkin chosaku shū* (Tokyo: Kōdansha, 1981), 1:107–108.
52. Furuta, "Jōdo shinshū ni okeru Hiji Hōmon no mondai," p. 165.
53. Ibid., pp. 167–168. The co-option of Rennyo here may seem ironic, but from the Hiji Hōmon point of view, institutionalized Pure Land had simply lied about Rennyo's true views and suppressed his secret teachings.
54. Furuta, *Furuta Shōkin chosaku shū*, 1:111.
55. Ibid., 1:120.
56. The term "Gonaishō" consists of *naishō*, "inner enlightenment," to which an honorific prefix has been attached. This adoption of this Shingon technical term by a Pure Land "heresy" tells us much all by itself. Nonetheless, it is not unparalleled in other Pure Land "heresies." The so-called Kakushi or Kakure Nembutsu ("Hidden Nembutsu") groups of the Tokugawa period sometimes used the term Gonaihō ("Inner Dharma") as a self-description. Aizawa Shiro, *Ura no bunka* (Tokyo: Jiji Tsushinsha, 1976), p. 100. Though not simply its lineal descendant, these underground Kakure Nembutsu groups did owe a considerable debt to the *himitsu nembutsu* tradition. Other interesting names of these groups include Kuro Nembutsu (Black Nembutsu), Dozō Hiji (Warehouse Secrets), Gozō Nembutsu (Storehouse Nembutsu), and Zaike Nembutsu (Layman's Nembutsu). Like the Kakure Kirishitan (Hidden Christians), these groups were considered socially and politically dangerous. For more on the Hidden Nembutsu, see Chiba Jōryu, "Orthodoxy and Heterodoxy in Early Modern Shinshū: Kakushi Nembutsu and Kakure Nembutsu," in *The Pure Land Tradition: History and Development*, ed. James Foard, Michael Solomon, and Richard K. Payne (Berkeley: Berkeley Buddhist Studies Series, 1996), pp. 463–496.
57. Kikuchi Takeshi, "Echigo yamabushi to Gonaishō," *Shūkyō kenkyū* 51, no. 2 (September 1977): 143–144, 160.
58. Ibid., p. 147.
59. W. H. Gardner, ed., *Gerard Manley Hopkins: A Selection of His Poems and Prose* (Harmondsworth, England: Penguin, 1953), p. 54.

SHUGENDŌ, THE TRADITIONS OF EN NO GYŌJA, AND MIKKYŌ INFLUENCE

1. The characters used to write his name have several alternative readings, such as En no Shōkaku, but for consistency the reading En no Ozunu will be used throughout this essay.
2. The large problem of the relationship of sangaku shinkō and Shugendō, including some of the abundant Japanese research on sangaku shinkō, has been treated in H. Byron Earhart, "A Religious Study of the Mount Haguro Sect of Shugendō" (Ph.D. diss., University of Chicago, 1965); see part 2, chaps. 5–13. The reader is referred to this dissertation (hereafter cited as "Haguro Shugendō") for documentation of this brief sketch of Shugendō. {Dissertation published as H. Byron Earhart, *A Religious Study of the Mount Haguro Sect of Shugendō* (Tokyo: Sophia University Press, 1970).}

3. See ibid., chap. 18, "Taoism, Onmyō-dō, and Shugendō."
4. One of the difficult problems in the origins of Shugendō is whether or not there were indigenous religious practices on mountain peaks as well as at the foot of the mountains before the arrival of "continental" traditions. Most scholars feel that both the ascetic purpose of entering the mountains and also the actual climbing of the mountain are the direct result of Buddhist influence. See ibid., chap. 12, "Sangaku Shinkō and Sangaku Bukkyō ('Mountain Buddhism')."
5. See ibid., chaps. 15–17.
6. This took place between 1868 and 1872. Some Shugendō sects have been revived since World War II.
7. See ibid., chaps. 19–21. From this point full documentation will be given for the treatment of En no Gyōja and mikkyō influence upon Shugendō.
8. By mikkyō is meant here the organized traditions of esoteric Buddhism which entered Japan at the beginning of the Heian period, in contrast to the fragmentary esoteric traditions which preceded and then coexisted with mikkyō. The writer is not qualified to treat mikkyō proper, but will focus on the Shugendō acceptance of mikkyō elements. It is to be expected that the "pure" or orthodox mikkyō elements became somewhat transformed in the process of borrowing.
9. See ibid., chaps. 26–29; also H. Byron Earhart, "Four Ritual Periods of Haguro Shugendō in Northeastern Japan," *History of Religions* 5, no. 1 (summer 1965): 93–113.
10. Ryūjin Tajima, *Étude sur le Mahāvairocana-sūtra (Dainichikyō)* (Paris: Adrien Maisonneuve, 1936); and idem, *Les deux grands maṇḍalas et la doctrine de l'esoterisme Shingon* (Tokyo: Maison Franco-Japonaise, 1959).
11. Toshio Murakami holds that the doctrine of Shugendō is practically identical to that of Shingon Mikkyō. See his *Shugendō no Hattatsu* (The Development of Shugendō) (Tokyo: Unebi Shobo, 1943), esp. pp. 181–264. He gives a comprehensive analysis of Shugendō doctrine as Shingon Mikkyō, in terms of scriptures, cosmology, Buddhology *(jōbutsu-ron)*, view of man, and criticism.
12. Ibid., pp. 219–221. For an interesting treatment of Shugendō thought on becoming a buddha in the mountains, see Hitoshi Miyake, "Gendai Shugen Kyodan Josetsu— Shisō, Girei, Sōshiki" (An Introduction to the Contemporary Shugen Religious Order—Its Thought, Rites, Organization), *Shūkyōgaku Zasshi*, no. 1 (June 1962): 18–26. Taro Wakamori also recognizes the importance of soku-shin-jōbutsu, but thinks that the esoteric doctrine of jiri-funi is crucial for Shugendō. See Wakamori, *Shugendōshi no Kenkyū* (A Historical Study of Shugendō) (Tokyo: Kawade Shobō, 1943), pp. 157ff., 165–166. For a treatment of these doctrines see Tajima, *Deux grands maṇḍalas.* For example, on p. 248, "Le pointe importante de la doctrine de la secte Shingon fondée par Kūkai se résume dans ces quatre caractères [soku shin jōbutsu] 'dès ce corps obtenir [l'état de] buddha'."
13. See Wakamori, *Shugendōshi no Kenkyū*, pp. 241–243, where he treats the different characters that were used to write *"saitō goma"* and the ancient Japanese fire rites, which may have provided the precedent for adapting the Buddhist rite of goma (Skt. *homa*). He also mentions the "esoteric transformation" of such rites.
14. The various branches of Shugendō borrowed from different streams of esoteric Buddhism, and further complicated matters by forming their own modifications and sect lines. Therefore, although the esoteric influence on Shugendō is manifest, the channels of influence are difficult to retrace.
15. For an excellent treatment of the early literature making mention of En no Ozunu, see Torao Satō, "En no Ozunu Den" (Biography of En no Ozunu), *Tenri Daigaku Gakuhō* 8 (August 1956): 33–55.

16. This is one of the many possible renderings of his name. As noted, we have adopted the general reading of En no Ozunu.

17. J. B. Snellen, tr., "Shoku Nihongi. Chronicles of Japan, continued, from 697–791 AD," *Transactions of the Asiatic Society*, 2nd ser., 11 (1934): 151–239; see pp. 178–179.

18. This is the opinion of Wakamori, *Shugendōshi no Kenkyū*, pp. 24–50. Ichiro Hori has made a similar conclusion in "On the Concept of Hijiri (Holy-Man)," *Numen* 5 (1958): 2:128–160; 3:199–232; see p. 141. This point concerning En no Ozunu as "shaman" and as employing "magic" will be treated again after the introduction of the *Nihon Ryōiki*.

19. Murakami, *Shugendō no Hattatsu*, pp. 48–49.

20. Satō, "En no Ozunu Den," pp. 36–40.

21. A German translation of the *Nihon Ryōiki* was not available for comparison at the time of writing. See Hermann Bohner, tr., "Legenden aus der Frühzeit des Japanischen Buddhismus. *Nipponkoku-gembō-zenaku-ryō-i-ki,*" *Mitteilungen der Deutschen Gesellschaft für die Natur und Völkerkunde Ostasiens* 27 (1934).

22. Although the Western world heard about En no Gyōja long ago, little is known about him except that he is considered the founder of Shugendō. The early Jesuit missionaries to Japan learned of En no Gyōja through their encounters with yamabushi. See Georg Schurhammer, "Die Yamabushis; nach gedruckten und ungedruckten Berichten des 16. und 17. Jahrhunderts," *Zeitschrift für Missionswissenschaft une Religionswissenschaft* 12 (1922): 206–228; also Arimichi Ebizawa, "Yaso-kaishi to Shugendō to no Kōshō" (The Relations between the Jesuits and Shugendō), in *Kirishitan no Kenkyū* (Tōkyō: Unebe Shobō, 1942), pp. 85–127. Whereas Schurhammer and Ebizawa interpret the reports of the Jesuit missionaries, Engelbert Kaempfer gained information about En no Gyōja and Shugendō through a yamabushi informer. See Kaempfer, *The History of Japan, together with a Description of the Kingdom of Siam 1690–92*, tr. J. G. Scheuzer, 3 vols. (1727; repr., Glasgow: James Maclehose, 1906), 2:43–56. Except for occasional references, there seems to be no lengthy treatment of En no Ozunu or En no Gyōja in a Western language.

23. Later we will mention the six peacock sūtras still in existence, but it is unclear whether the previous phrase refers to one or any of them.

24. The language is ambiguous, but there is an obvious comparison of E (En) no Ubasoku with a male phoenix. This obscure reference takes on extraordinary significance when we remember that Buddha likened himself to the "Golden Peacock" or "Golden Goose." See L. A. Waddell, "The 'Dhāraṇī' Cult in Buddhism, Its Origin, Deified Literature and Images," *Ostasiatische Zeitschrift* 1 (1912–13): 155–195. This point will be taken up in the following discussion.

25. One edition interprets "lay down on the blade of his sword" as indicating suicide. However, if we remember this figure's magical power, especially his ability to fly, there seems to be no need to supply the interpretation of suicide.

26. Two modern editions of the *Nihon Ryōiki* have been compared in making this rough translation: *Nihon Ryōiki*, annotated by Takeda Yukichi, in the series Nihon Koten Zensho (Tokyo: Asahi Shinbun, 1950), pp. 102–104; and *Nihon Ryōiki*, commentary by Itabashi Rinkō (Tokyo: Shunyōdō, 1929), pp. 45–47.

27. Murakami, *Shugendō no Hattatsu*, pp. 35–38, lists these four points in a slightly different form. For more detailed treatment of the Japanese literature, including reference to the religious milieu surrounding Katsuragi and Hito-koto-nushi, see Earhart, "Haguro Shugendō," chap. 14, "En no Ozunu and the Traditional Origin of Shugendō."

28. This interpretation is followed by Wakamori, *Shugendōshi no Kenkyū*, pp. 24–50, and by Hori, "Concept of Hijiri," p. 141. Wakamori makes some conjectures about what

this magic might have been, including some ancient Japanese words referring to magic. On the other hand, Sokichi Tsuda, "En no Gyōja Densetsu Kō" (A Consideration of the Tradition of En no Gyōja), in *Nihon no Shintō* (Tokyo: Iwanami Shoten, 1949), pp. 358–384, emphasizes the Buddhist and Daoistic character of this tradition and doubts that any Japanese religious practice can be denoted by the term *jujutsu*. This word *jujutsu* is the concrete reference to "magic" in the texts, and seems to be of Buddhist origin. Tsuda prefers to use the English word "magic" rather than to include folk-religious practices (of China or Japan) within the term *jujutsu*.

29. Hori, "Concept of Hijiri," pp. 145–146, has a good treatment of this transformation.

30. Ibid., pp. 144–145, where Hori analyzes twenty-six applications by ubasoku of the Nara period for entry into the Buddhist priesthood. The twenty-six applicants had memorized, as part of their required training, a total of nineteen daranis, "all of which were believed to be the sources or vehicles of the magic power in the logos and were chanted by many applicants *(upāsaka)*." Indeed, such practices became so popular that they had to be controlled by government order, which prohibited monks and nuns from engaging in any exorcism or magic except "by the recitation of spells (mantra) in accordance with Buddhism." For this quotation from the *Sōni Ryō*, see Sir George B. Sansom, "Early Japanese Law and Administration," *Transactions of the Asiatic Society of Japan*, 2nd ser., 11 (1934): 128.

31. See Waddell, "'Dhāraṇī' Cult," p. 155, where he concludes that "the cult of Protective Spells, *Parittā* or *Dhāraṇī* . . . was probably introduced by Buddha himself." Chou Yi-liang, "Tantrism in China," *Harvard Journal of Asiatic Studies*, VIII (1944–45), pp. 241–332 {chap. 1 in this volume}, has made a detailed examination of the transmission of these sūtras to China (appendix N of the original publication), but (p. 324) he disagrees with Waddell on the use of dhāraṇī by the historical Buddha. M. W. de Visser has noted the transformation of the peacock from its feminine form in India to its masculine form in China and Japan in "Die Pfauenkönigin (K'ung-tsioh ming-wang, Kujaku myoo) in China und Japan," *Ostasiatische Zeitschrift* 8 (1919–20): 370–387. For the sūtras which survive in the Chinese canon, see Bunyiu Nanjio, comp., *A Catalogue of the Chinese Translation of the Buddhist Tripitaka* (Oxford: Clarendon Press, 1883), nos. 306–311. It appears that no. 308 ("Ku-jaku-ō-ju-kyō") of Nanjio's catalogue is the most important work for "primitive Mikkyō" in Japan. See *Bussho Kaisetsu Daijiten*, 12 vols. (Tokyo: Daitō, 1912), 2:326–327. Nanjio concluded that "This scripture was so abundant in the materials of early Mikkyō that it may be considered as the focus of the Mikkyō which was transmitted in the period of the Nara court prior to the transmission of pure esoteric Buddhism (Jun-mitsu)."

32. Tsuda, "En no Gyōja," p. 377ff., concludes that the use of the character *sen*, or wizard, in the Chinese translation of Buddhist sūtras betrays implicit Daoistic influence. One might add that the Peacock Sūtra utilizes this character. Noritada Kubo has recognized the same Daoistic influence upon Shugendō in "Dokyo to Shugendō" (English title provided as "Taoism and Shugendō"), *Shukyō Kenkyū*, no. 173 (December 1962): 24–48.

33. While Daoistic influence cannot be denied in these motifs of flight to heaven, Tsuda has examined only the *Chinese acceptance* of these translations in the setting of the so-called shinsen-shisō. However, it is well known that the character *sen* is a translation for the Sanskrit *ṛṣi*. See William Edward Soothill and Lewis Hodous, *A Dictionary of Chinese Buddhist Terms* (London: Kegan Paul, Trench, Trubner, 1937), p. 166. Mircea Eliade has pointed out that " magical flight" abounds in the beliefs of India, Buddhism, and Tibet; moreover there may have been independent development among these. See his additional note entitled "Alchemists, Yogins, and 'Magical flight,'" as well as the

section "Ascent to Heaven. Mystical flight," in *Yoga and Immortality*, tr. Willard R. Trask (New York: Pantheon, 1958), pp. 414–415, 326–330. At any rate, it seems that the background of the ṛṣi and such related themes should be reexamined before concluding that "flight to heaven" is necessarily a Daoistic influence.

34. Visser, "Pfauenkönigin," pp. 385–387, notes that although Kōbō Daishi included the Peacock Sūtra as one of "die Drei Grossen Methoden," nothing is mentioned of the peacock rite. There is some ambiguity as to who first practiced this rite in Japan.

35. It should be noted again that En no Ubasoku is not even described as having possessed the "Peacock Sūtra" as such, only the "magical formula of the peacock (or Peacock King)." Scholars seem to doubt En no Ozunu's connection with this sūtra for the following reasons: in the first place, nothing is mentioned of it in the record of the *Shoku Nihongi*, and the *Nihon Ryōiki* is already a traditional writing; in the second place, the sūtra probably was not transmitted to Japan that early. However, the use of daranis and magical formulas *(jumon)* appeared rather early both in China and Japan. Therefore, the dating of such daranis and jumon (or zōmitsu) must be considered separately from the problem of En no Ozunu and his connection with the Peacock Sūtras.

36. See Shinkyō Mochizuki, ed., *Bukkyō Daijiten* (Dictionary of Buddhism), 6 vols., 2nd ed. (Tokyo: Bukkyō Daijiten Hakkōjo, 1954), s.v. "Kujaku Myoo Gyo no Ho," 1:668–669, where this rite is called one of the four major rites of Mikkyō, and it is said that Shōbō of Daigo-ji was the first to perform it in Japan. Visser, "Pfauenkönigin," pp. 385–387, tentatively concludes that Shōshin (1005–85) was the first to perform the peacock rite; he doubts that Shōbō actually performed this rite.

37. Both Murakami, *Shugendō no Hattatsu*, p. 82, and Wakamori, *Shugendōshi no Kenkyū*, p. 63, conclude that the tradition of En no Gyōja's building a bridge is copied after the eighth-century saint Gyōgi (or Gyōki). They cite the *Sanbō-roku* of 984 where En no Gyōja is first praised after the manner of Gyōgi. The name En no Gyōja came into use about this time.

38. Satō, "En no Ozunu Den," p. 34.

39. Ibid., pp. 37, 34.

40. Other references to Zaō-gongen and En no Gyōja can be found in Earhart, "Haguro Shugendō," chap. 19.

41. Satō, "En no Ozunu Den," pp. 41–43.

42. The text is found in the *Nihon Daizōkyō*, 51 vols. (Tokyo, 1914–21), 38:245–256. See also *Bussho Kaisetsu Daijiten*, s.v. "En-no-gyo-ja-hon-gi," 1:265. The work is supposed to have been written about 724, but this reference dates it at late Muromachi. Even so, it is considered as one of the oldest works written about the tradition of En no Gyōja. I acknowledge here Shunsho Manabe, assistant in the Department of Indology, Tohoku University, Sendai, Japan, for help in reading this text and for other suggestions concerning this essay.

43. The characters *kujaku* mean literally "rescue from snake suffering." However, the three characters seem to be a play on the characters for *kujaku*, peacock, as seen in the *Nihon Ryōiki*. It is worth repeating that the *Nihon Ryōiki* tradition depicts En no Ubasoku as using the "magic of the peacock" for such devious ends as ordering about the kami and flying to heaven. By contrast, in the above tradition the writer seems to know that the Peacock Sūtra was originally linked with charms against snakebite (as can be seen in Waddell, "'Dhāraṇī' Cult").

44. Satō, "En no Ozunu Den," pp. 35–36, cites at least three other documents where "his mother dreams that a golden-colored vajra came in a cloud and descended to enter her mouth, after which Ozunu was born."

45. Himitsujō is an elegant name for Mikkyō, or esoteric Buddhism.

46. Jimyō is a special esoteric word for darani, and Jimyō-sen is the name of a "magician" who possesses this. See Soothill and Hodous, *Dictionary*, p. 302b.
47. This is the esoteric baptism or ordination, usually known as kanjō.
48. This is the esoteric "seal" or mudrā made by the "gesture" of the hands, and the formula (mantra, *shingon*) made with the mouth.
49. Mikkyō influence is also very important in the Haguro sect of Shugendō, with which the writer is most familiar. However, at Haguro, where there was a strong sense of independence, it is not En no Gyōja but Prince Hachiko who is regarded as the founder. Nevertheless, many esoteric elements are included in the traditions surrounding Prince Hachiko. The very criterion which sets up Prince Hachiko as prior to En no Gyōja is the tradition that Prince Hachiko was the first to learn the esoteric vehicle, including the rites of goma. According to this tradition, En no Gyōja first learned the rites of goma when he visited Haguro and received the tradition from the successors of Prince Hachiko. See Earhart, "Haguro Shugendō," chap. 22, "The Background and Religious History of Haguro Shugendō," for discussion and documentation.

The Cave and the Womb World

1. The author gratefully acknowledges funding received for this project from the Social Science Research Council and the Committee on Research in the Social Sciences and Humanities of Princeton University.
2. Hitoshi Miyake, *Shugendō*, Kyoikusha Rekishi Shinsho, Nihon shi 174 (Tokyo: Kyoikusha, 1978), pp. 80–93.
3. H. Byron Earhart, *A Religious Study of the Mount Haguro Sect of Shugendō* (Tokyo: Sophia University Press, 1970), p. 2.
4. Miyake, *Shugendō*, pp. 115–118.
5. See, for example, Paul L. Swanson, "Shugendō and the Yoshino-Kumano Pilgrimage: An Example of Mountain Pilgrimage," *Monumenta Nipponica* 36, no. 1 (1981): 515–584.
6. Ichiro Hori, *Folk Religion of Japan*, ed. J. M. Kitagawa and Alan L. Miller (Chicago: University of Chicago Press, 1968), pp. 141–179.
7. Ibid., pp. 170–174.
8. Ibid., pp. 150–151.
9. Ryūjun Tajima, *Les deux grands maṇḍalas et la doctrine de l'ésotérisme Shingon*, Bulletin de la Maison Franco-Japonaise, n.s., vol. 6 (Tokyo: Maison Franco-Japonaise; Paris: Presses Universitaires de France, 1959), p. 3.
10. François Bizot, "La grotte de la naissance: Recherches sur le Bouddhisme Khmer II," *Bulletin de l'Ecole Française d'Extrême-Orient* 67 (1980): 221–269.
11. Ibid., pp. 230–236.
12. Ibid., pp. 237–239.
13. Ibid., pp. 240–242.
14. Ibid., pp. 224–228.
15. Ibid., pp. 256–257.
16. Tajima, *Deux grands maṇḍalas*, p. 33–41.
17. Ibid., p. 47.
18. Ibid., pp. 47, 55.
19. Miyake, *Shugendō*, p. 140.
20. The order of ritual is described differently in ritual manuals, but the following description gives a basic outline of the system.
21. Miyake, *Shugendō*, p. 140.
22. Tajima, *Deux grands maṇḍalas*, pp. 45–47.

23. Yoshito S. Hakeda, tr., *Kūkai: Major Works* (New York: Columbia University Press, 1972), p. 87.
24. Ibid., pp. 82–83.
25. Ibid., pp. 85–87.
26. This translation is quite literal. For another interpretation, see ibid., p. 88. Also see Tajima, *Deux grands mandalas*, p. 248.
27. Hakeda, *Kūkai*, pp. 88–90.
28. Ibid., p. 92.
29. Ibid., p. 91.
30. Nancy Chodorow, *The Reproduction of Mothering: Psychoanalysis and the Sociology of Gender* (Berkeley: University of California Press, 1978).
31. Judith Lorber et al., "On *The Reproduction of Mothering*: A Methodological Debate," *Signs* 6, no. 3 (1981): 502–503.
32. Adrienne Rich, "Compulsory Heterosexuality and Lesbian Experience," *Signs* 5, no. 4 (1980): 631–660.
33. Carl G. Jung and Carl Kerenyi, *Essays on a Science of Mythology: The Myth of the Divine Child and the Mysteries of Eleusis*, Bollingen Series, no. 22 (Princeton: Princeton University Press, 1949), pp. 157–158.
34. Ibid., p. 162.
35. Ibid., p. 177.
36. Michelle Z. Rodaldo, "Women, Culture and Society: A Theoretical Overview," in *Women, Culture, and Society*, ed. Michelle Rodaldo and Louise Lamphere (Stanford: Stanford University Press, 1974).

Index

In the Buddha's Words
An Anthology of Discourses
from the Pali Canon
Edited and introduced by Bhikkhu Bodhi
Foreword by the Dalai Lama
512 pages, ISBN 0-86171-491-1, $18.95

Compiled and translated by the American monk Bhikkhu Bodhi, whose voluminous translations in Wisdom's Teachings of the Buddha series have won widespread acclaim, the anthology arranges the Buddha's discourses or *suttas* in a systematic pattern that brings to light the deep structures running beneath. The book draws upon the Buddha's discourses on a wide variety of topics ranging from family life and marriage to renunciation and the path of insight. Bhikkhu Bodhi prefaces each chapter with an illuminating introduction. For readers who have always wanted an accessible entry point to the Buddha's own teachings, this book provides the solid and reliable introduction they need. It also offers long-term students of Buddhism a scintillating collection that will stimulate much thought and discussion.

"Any amount of study or practice that helps to deepen wisdom and assist us to emerge from layers of delusion is precious. This book could contribute to this enterprise more than almost anything else in print. It gives us access to the very texture of the *dhamma,* the specific words and phrases, which guided and inspired the Buddha's original students. [...] A gift to the world."—Andrew Olendzki, Executive Director of the Barre Center of Buddhist Studies, in *Buddhadharma: The Practitioner's Quarterly*

Zen's Chinese Heritage
The Masters and Their Teachings
Andrew Ferguson
544 pages, ISBN 0-86171-163-7, $24.95

Capturing the austere beauty of the Zen masters' manner of teaching—their earthy style, humor, and humanity—*Zen's Chinese Heritage* is an intimate and profound human portrait of the enlightened Zen ancients, and an unprecedented look into the depths of this rich cultural heritage. Includes a fold-out lineage chart of the Zen ancestors.

"This excellent and exhaustive book reminds us of the vast, now neglected, patrimony of Buddhist spiritual knowledge that comes not from Japan but China. Ferguson's work is at once a history and an anthology of this fascinating tradition and includes many koans, anecdotes and stories, as well as a wonderfully clear wallchart. This splendid repository should give instruction and pleasure to the general reader as well as the professed Buddhist. Highly recommended."—*Library Journal*

Introduction to Tantra
The Transformation of Desire
Lama Yeshe
Edited by Jonathan Landaw
Foreword by Philip Glass
192 pages, ISBN 0-86171-162-9, $16.95

The classic introduction to the tantra of Tibetan Buddhism—now in a revised edition.

"The best introductory work on Tibetan Buddhist tantra available today."—Professor Janet Gyatso, Hershey Chair of Buddhist Studies, Harvard University

"No one has summarized the essence of tantra as well as Thubten Yeshe does here."—*Religious Studies Review*

Dōgen's Extensive Record
A Translation of the Eihei Koroku
Translated by Taigen Dan Leighton and
Shohaku Okumura
Edited and introduced by Taigen Dan
Leighton
Foreword by Tenshin Reb Andersen with
introductory essays by Steven Heine and
John Daido Loori
744 pages, cloth with ribbon,
ISBN 0-86171-305-2, $65.00

"This massive work will be a valuable asset not just for students of the Zen teacher Dōgen (1200–1253), but for all students of Zen and Buddhism in general. However celebrated his *Shobogenzo* might be, it presents only a partial Dōgen. *The Extensive Record* covers Dōgen's entire teaching career, especially the last ten years of his life, which he devoted wholeheartedly to training his successors. The text is remarkably easy to read while also remaining faithful to Dōgen's idiom. It is well annotated with footnotes, [and] lengthy indexes allow readers to find dates, names, Japanese pronunciations of Chinese names and so forth. A detailed bibliography of Chinese, Japanese and Western-language materials will assist readers who wish to consult other sources in their study of Dōgen in particular or Buddhism in general. [...] Three separate introductions provide so much supplemental information that no reader of this volume will be forced to turn elsewhere to make sense of it. It will reward careful study."—William M. Bodiford, in *Buddhadharma: The Practitioner's Quarterly*

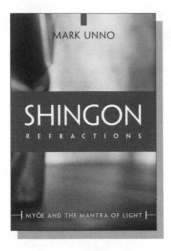

Shingon Refractions
Myōe and the Mantra of Light
Mark Unno
320 pages, ISBN 0-86171-390-7, $26.95

Shingon Buddhism arose in the eighth century and remains one of Japan's most important sects, at present numbering some twelve
million adherents. As such it is long overdue
appropriate coverage. Here, Mark Unno illuminates the tantric practice of the Mantra of
Light, the most central of Shingon practices,
complete with translations and an in-depth
exploration of the scholar-monk Myoe
Koben, the Mantra of Light's foremost proponent.

"One of the most important works in Buddhist studies to appear this year.
Its importance lies not only in the quality of its scholarship but also in the
variety of fields to which it contributes. It expands our knowledge of both
Vajrayana and Japanese Buddhism and sheds light on medieval Japanese
Buddhist conceptions of how practice is effective...an important contribu-
tion."—Richard Payne, Dean of the Institute of Buddhist Studies at the
Graduate Theological Union in Berkeley, California, in *Buddhadharma:
The Practitioner's Quarterly*

Awesome Nightfall
The Life, Times, and Poetry of Saigyo

THE LIFE, TIMES, AND POETRY OF

SAIGYŌ

WILLIAM R. LAFLEUR

Awesome Nightfall
The Life, Times, and Poetry of Saigyo
William R. LaFleur
192 pages, ISBN 0-86171-322-2, $14.95

"On anyone's list, Saigyo ranks among Japan's best poets. A master of many styles of poetry, Saigyo was [also] a pioneer in a new style, presenting a rich, darkly imagistic field with symbolic overtones. This new volume by LaFleur adds forty-three new translations to the almost two hundred previously published in his earlier *Mirror for the Moon*.... LaFleur's appealing contemporary English versions convey Saigyo's relatively informal voice and diction, and his long involvement with the poems is evident both in his translations and his commentary. This attractive new volume presents a more substantial overview of Saigyo's life and times than has been undertaken in any of the earlier English-language translations. Decades of scholarly and personal engagement with Saigyo's writings make LaFleur a reliable guide to the literary modes, techniques, and values that inform Saigyo's poetry. Many of the translations here are not only immediately appealing but reward reflection and re-reading."—*Journal of Japanese Studies*

About Wisdom

WISDOM PUBLICATIONS, a nonprofit publisher, is dedicated to making available authentic Buddhist works for the benefit of all. We publish translations of the sutras and tantras, commentaries and teachings of past and contemporary Buddhist masters, and original works by the world's leading Buddhist scholars. We publish our titles with the appreciation of Buddhism as a living philosophy and with the special commitment to preserve and transmit important works from all the major Buddhist traditions.

To learn more about Wisdom, or to browse books online, visit our website at wisdompubs.org. You may request a copy of our mail-order catalog online or by writing to this address:

Wisdom Publications
199 Elm Street
Somerville, Massachusetts 02144 USA
Telephone: (617) 776-7416
Fax: (617) 776-7841
Email: info@wisdompubs.org
www.wisdompubs.org

THE WISDOM TRUST

As a nonprofit publisher, Wisdom is dedicated to the publication of fine Dharma books for the benefit of all sentient beings and dependent upon the kindness and generosity of sponsors in order to do so. If you would like to make a donation to Wisdom, please do so through our Somerville office. If you would like to sponsor the publication of a book, please write or email us at the address above.

Thank you.

Wisdom is a nonprofit, charitable 501(c)(3) organization affiliated with the Foundation for the Preservation of the Mahayana Tradition (FPMT).